W9-BHE-185

INSIDERS' GUIDE® TO

JACKSONVILLE

THIRD EDITION

SARAH W. REISS

INSIDERS' GUIDE

GUILFORD, CONNECTICUT

AN IMPRINT OF GLOBE PEQUOT PRESS

All the information in this guidebook is subject to change. We recommend that you call ahead to obtain current information before traveling.

To buy books in quantity for corporate use or incentives, call **(800) 962–0973** or e-mail **premiums@GlobePequot.com**.

INSIDERS' GUIDE ®

Editor: Amy Lyons
Project Editor: Lynn Zelem
Layout Artist: Kevin Mak
Text design: Sheryl Kober
Maps: XNR Productions, Inc. © Morris Book Publishing, LLC

ISSN 1541-5597
ISBN 978-0-7627-5032-0

Printed in the United States of America
10 9 8 7 6 5 4 3 2 1

CONTENTS

Directory of Maps

ABOUT THE AUTHOR

Sarah Reiss is a travel, food and lifestyle writer with a reputation for fearlessness and a love of new adventures. With over 100 articles in print, and membership in The Society of American Travel Writers (SATW), Sarah makes a life on the road look like a walk in the park.

Her travel articles (which appear nationwide in publications from *Islands* magazine to OffbeatTravel.com) chronicle a life spent crisscrossing the globe with a backpack and a game-for-anything spirit. In the online world, Sarah's two blogs: City Dish with Sarah Reiss, a chronicle of her global adventures in eating, and Puddle Jumping, an homage to gutsiness and fear-facing, have made her popular with foodies and fun-seekers the world over.

Sarah holds a B.A. in journalism from Indiana University Bloomington, an MFA in writing from Naropa University, and was the chair of Creative Writing at Douglas Anderson School of the Arts in Jacksonville, FL. She has taught writing to adults at Florida State College at Jacksonville, and was the managing editor of Inside Central New Jersey magazine.

These days, Sarah lives a nomadic lifestyle, but primarily hangs out in New York City, Los Angeles, and Jacksonville, where she stays busy trying new restaurants and chasing down insider tips with her husband, Karl.

Follow Sarah on Twitter at http://twitter.com/SarahReiss, or visit her at www.sarahreiss.com where you can sign up for Sarah's RSS feeds, register for e-news, and read both of her blogs. It's the easiest way to keep up with what's happening with the busiest gal in travel writing.

ACKNOWLEDGMENTS

The current version of this book would not have been even remotely possible without the collected efforts of a number of highly connected, altruistic, and motivated individuals. I would like to send a special thank you to the following for their enthusiasm and no-questions-asked willingness to share many of their favorite locals-only hideaways.

Thanks first to Marisa Carbone and John Finotti for the extensive research that went into the creation of the original edition of this book. Thanks also to Jennifer Bryant of the Jacksonville CVB, as well as bona fide Jacksonville Insiders Jennifer Chapman, Bob White, Anna Jacobson, Andrew Dickson, Megan Mickler, Andy and Jeanne Goshen, Lauren Fincham, Jim Smith, Natalie Jones, Judella Haddad, Laura Rippell, and Walter Parks.

I owe huge debts to both Kristen Iversen, the best creative nonfiction teacher and mentor around, and Mia Bolte, whose boundless faith in my abilities has kept me writing when all I wanted was to get a desk job.

Special thanks also to the preternaturally responsive and good-humored Amy Lyons, the dedicated Julie Hill, and to Susan Finch, who works harder than anyone else I know.

This book would not have been possible without the help of Carole Wetzel who operated behind the scenes to make this project easier. I thank you; Karl thanks you; Lucy and Betty thank you.

No other was as steadfast in his dedication to this project than the unshakeable, unflappable, and ultimately hip Karl Leopold Reiss. This book, along with nearly everything else under the sun, I dedicate to him and his lifesaving sense of humor.

PREFACE

One thing's for certain: Jacksonville is no longer the sleepy Southern outpost of the 1990s. After decades of treading water, the city has finally begun to catch up with its hipper, more progressive cousins. Thanks to the influence of a coalition of newcomers and long-term movers and shakers, the city has taken an interest in contemporary art, design, and cuisine with transformational results. Now, instead of the strip-mall culture and suburban sprawl of decades past, Jacksonville has begun a love affair with Downtown living, urban lifestyles, and alternative entertainment. The result is a city that, while it may sleep, is no longer content to be at rest.

I've lived most of my life in Jacksonville. I spent my childhood here, fumbled through my teen years here, was a student in both the public and private school systems, and later came back to teach writing to high-school students at Douglas Anderson School of the Arts, one of the city's finest magnet schools, and to college students at Florida State College at Jacksonville (FSCJ). I got married here, have watched my friends raise children here, and ushered grandparents through the Community Hospice system here. In short, for better or worse, this is my town—the only city were I don't need a GPS and where I can call the executive director of the city's Cultural Council directly to find out what's happening over the weekend or where the best new restaurants are.

That's the thing about this city; as with any Southern city, its foundation is built on relationships, on knowing where to look or whom to ask. My hope is that this book becomes where *you* look when *you* have those questions, a sort of go-to guide for hip travelers.

While I take great pride in introducing all comers to the River City, I cannot guarantee that the eateries, nightclubs, or hotels will remain exactly as they were when this was published. Jacksonville is evolving daily, so be sure to call ahead to check the status of restaurants, accommodations, and attractions listed in this book. Finally, let me know about the quality of your experiences in Jacksonville so that I can make this book even better in future editions. If you have comments, suggestions, or recommendations, e-mail me at editorial@GlobePequot.com.

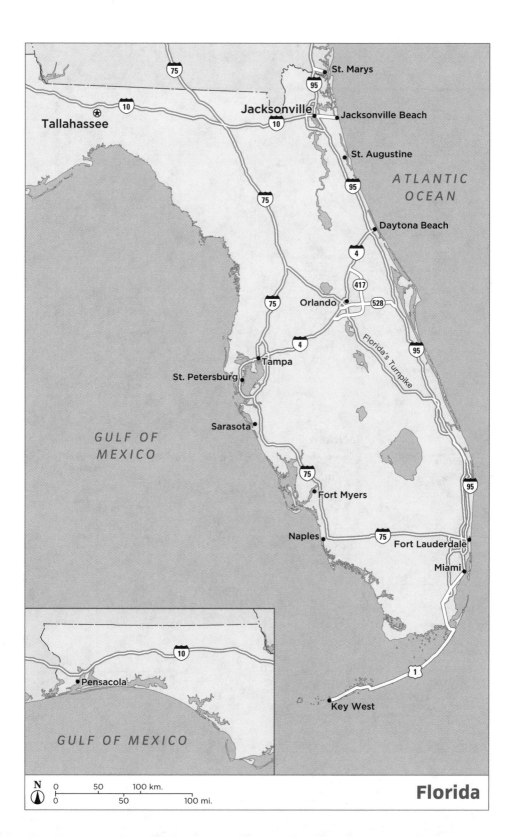

Florida

St. Marys
Jacksonville
Jacksonville Beach
Tallahassee
St. Augustine
ATLANTIC OCEAN
Daytona Beach
Orlando
Florida's Turnpike
Tampa
St. Petersburg
Sarasota
GULF OF MEXICO
Fort Myers
Naples
Fort Lauderdale
Miami
Key West
Pensacola
GULF OF MEXICO

N
0   50   100 km.
0   50   100 mi.

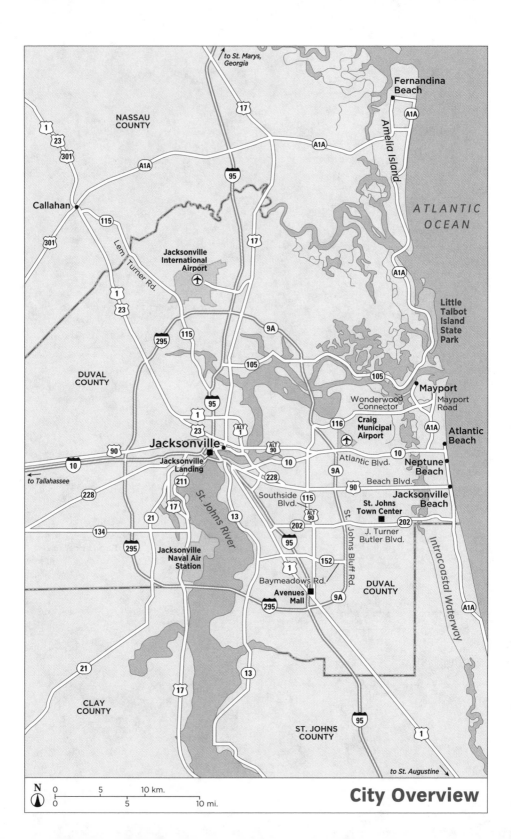

City Overview

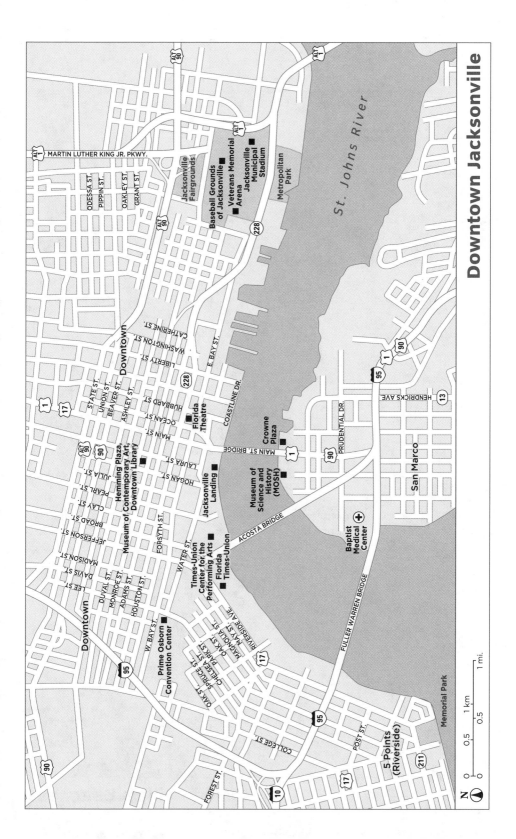

Downtown Jacksonville

St. Johns River

MARTIN LUTHER KING JR. PKWY.

Downtown

Downtown

San Marco

5 Points (Riverside)

Memorial Park

Jacksonville Fairgrounds
Baseball Grounds of Jacksonville
Veterans Memorial Arena
Jacksonville Municipal Stadium
Metropolitan Park

Florida Theatre

Hemming Plaza, Museum of Contemporary Art, Downtown Library

Jacksonville Landing

Museum of Science and History (MOSH)

Crowne Plaza

Times-Union Center for the Performing Arts
Florida Times-Union

Prime Osborn Convention Center

Baptist Medical Center

ACOSTA BRIDGE
MAIN ST. BRIDGE
FULLER WARREN BRIDGE

ODESSA ST.
PIPPIN ST.
OAKLEY ST.
GRANT ST.

CATHERINE ST.
WASHINGTON ST.
LIBERTY ST.
E. BAY ST.

STATE ST.
UNION ST.
BEAVER ST.
ASHLEY ST.
OCEAN ST.
HUBBARD ST.
COASTLINE DR.

MAIN ST.
LAURA ST.
HOGAN ST.

JULIA ST.
PEARL ST.
CLAY ST.
BROAD ST.
JEFFERSON ST.
MADISON ST.
DAVIS ST.
LEE ST.
DUVAL ST.
MONROE ST.
ADAMS ST.
HOUSTON ST.

FORSYTH ST.
WATER ST.
W. BAY ST.

RIVERSIDE AVE.
MAY ST.
MAGNOLIA ST.
OAK ST.
PARK ST.
CHELSEA ST.
SPRUCE ST.
OAK ST.
COLLEGE ST.
POST ST.
FOREST ST.

PRUDENTIAL DR.
HENDRICKS AVE.

N

0   0.5   1 km
0   0.5   1 mi.

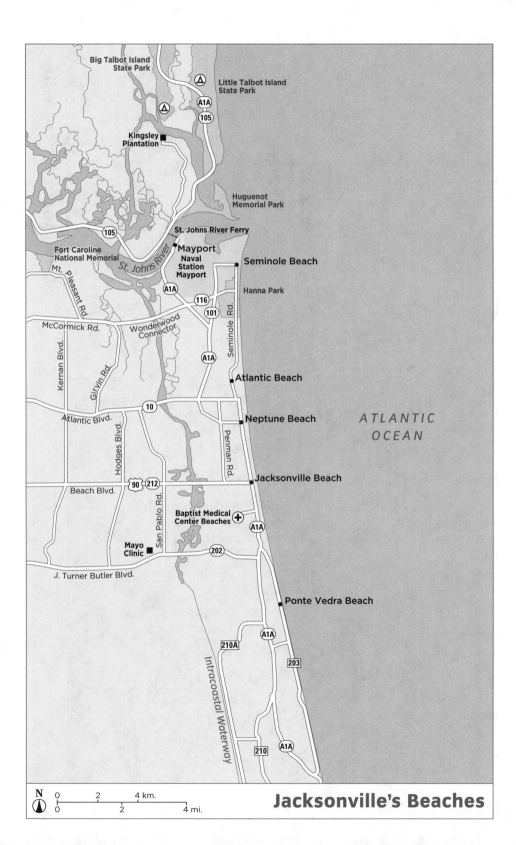

Jacksonville's Beaches

HOW TO USE THIS BOOK

Don't you hate spending good money on a guidebook only to find out that you could have figured out the same things yourself with a quick Internet search? I sure do. Even worse is the guidebook that promises the inside track but doesn't deliver anything except the well-worn path.

Relax. This is not that kind of book; this is your passport.

The *Insiders' Guide to Jacksonville* delivers what it promises: a well-edited selection of Jacksonville's highlights, gathered just for you from a coalition of the hippest, most in-the-know residents the city has produced.

Rare is the guidebook that's read cover to cover. Instead, guidebooks generally fill a need: they help you find a hotel, pick a restaurant, or ferret out something to do on a Saturday afternoon. Rest assured, the *Insiders' Guide to Jacksonville* makes it easy to do all of those things; it's packed with useful information, real-life assessments, and locals-only haunts. But there's more. Keep an eye out for the "Close-ups" and "Tips" boxes throughout the book to get the skinny on the city's signature foods, quirky secrets, little-known facts, and Insider secrets.

If you're sitting on a plane headed to Jacksonville right now, sit back, order a drink, and check out our chapter on getting around. It's full of tips on how to get from Jacksonville International Airport to anywhere you want to go. If you're still at home and using this book to plan your vacation, the Accommodations chapter is chock-full of hotel, B&B, and resort favorites that will give you a room, rate, or location to brag to your friends about.

Think of me as your local friend—constantly at your side, helping you find the best places to shop, eat, and sleep. Use the maps to get an idea of where everything is located around town, as well as the distances between neighborhoods, then set off on your own and explore, bringing this book along as you compare barbecue joints or suss out the most secluded spot for a nightcap.

Moving to Jacksonville or already live here? Be sure to check out the blue-tabbed pages at the back of the book, where you will find the **Living Here** appendix that offers sections on relocation, education, child care, health care, senior living, military, and media.

Above all, I hope this book will help you see how far the city has come and how much food, fun, and friendliness Jacksonville has to offer.

NOTE: Unless otherwise indicated, all addresses in this book are in Jacksonville proper.

JACKSONVILLE OVERVIEW

Natives, transplants, and city officials will tell you that Jacksonville is a prime place to live—cost of living is low, salaries are adequate, and amenities are increasing by the week. Jacksonville is a growing city that's managed to retain its small-town friendliness. There's still plenty of opportunity here, so Jacksonville ranks high for people who want to start a business, pay their dues in the corporate world, or live inexpensively while they pursue their art.

Spanish moss drapes the live oak trees, making the area feel more "Southern" than "Floridian." Contrary to Florida's reputation as a retirement haven, Jacksonville's young population, with a median age of 36, keeps the place hopping. The winters are mild, a fact that makes it easier to stay active year-round, but the summers are hot, humid, and can be miserable if you don't have access to the beach or a community pool.

Speaking of beaches, Jacksonville has more than 60 miles of clean, wide, sandy beaches and more than 50 golf courses in the region. The St. Johns River flows through the center of Downtown, giving locals endless opportunities for watersports while also providing a scenic backdrop for Downtown festivals and restaurants.

Did I mention that we love to eat? The city's signature foods, barbecue, fried chicken, and shrimp, turn up in myriad forms all over town. And while many Jacksonville residents are partial to old-school, family-style restaurants, the city also boasts some of the best fine-dining establishments in Florida.

After years of nursing an inferiority complex, Jacksonville has finally come into its own. The city used to be thought of as a sleepy Southern town with an odor problem. The smell of rotten eggs from Northside paper mills permeated almost every neighborhood, depending on which direction the wind was blowing. In the early nineties, city and federal officials launched an aggressive campaign to clean up the air. It worked. Some of the paper mills eventually closed; others installed high-tech equipment to eliminate the odors.

These days the air has never smelled sweeter in Jacksonville. An early boost to the city's image came in the mid-nineties when the National Football League awarded Jacksonville a football franchise, and in 2005 the arrival of the Superbowl turned Jacksonville's Downtown into a 24/7 street party. Today, the Jacksonville Jaguars play home games at Jacksonville Municipal Stadium, one of the biggest stadiums in the NFL.

Over the last decade, the economy has become even more robust with influential companies like Landstar realizing the city's advantages and relocating here. Others, like Merrill Lynch and Johnson & Johnson, made major investments in the River City. Jacksonville also serves as headquarters for the state's biggest banks. And with two bases located here, the United States Navy is one of the city's biggest employers.

All of this means that the city is growing like never before. Luxury condos have sprung up along the Northbank and Southbank of the river, and Downtown warehouses and businesses have converted to luxury condos—contributing to a new urbanism that is long overdue.

Under the 2000 Better Jacksonville Plan, new roads were built, the city began to focus on preserving parkland and green space, and locals witnessed the construction of a new, state-of-the-art Downtown library, new sports arena, new baseball field, and an updated county courthouse.

Jacksonville Vital Statistics

Mayor: Republican John Peyton

Governor: Republican Charlie Crist

Population: 1.1 million

Average winter temperatures (high/low): January: 65/40

Average summer temperatures (high/low): July: 95/71

Average annual number of sunny days: 226

Government: City and county consolidated in 1968; now one mayor and 19 city council members represent everyone, including residents of Baldwin and the communities of Atlantic Beach, Neptune Beach, and Jacksonville Beach.

Land area: 841 square miles

Residents' median age: 36

Nickname: River City

Mottos: "Jacksonville. Where Florida Begins"; "Bold New City of the South"

River: The St. Johns River flows north for 310 miles and empties into the Atlantic Ocean near Mayport.

Major universities: University of North Florida, Jacksonville University, Edward Waters College, Flagler College in St. Augustine, Florida Coastal School of Law, Florida State College at Jacksonville

Major area employers: United States Navy, Blue Cross & Blue Shield of Florida, Publix Supermarkets, Inc., Winn Dixie Stores, Inc., Baptist Health System, Mayo Clinic Average household income: $50,475

Average new home price: $155,200

Famous sons and daughters: Pat Boone, Rita Coolidge, David Duval, James Weldon Johnson, Chipper Jones, Lynyrd Skynyrd, Tim McGraw, A. Philip Randolph, Norm Thaggard, Slim Whitman, Top Models Yoanna House and Whitney Thompson, as well as Derek Trucks, Jeremy and Joshua Papelbon, Fred Funk.

Bragging rights: Jacksonville is consistently ranked as a "Top 10 Places to Live" by *Money* Magazine. Jacksonville again ranks No. 4 in Forbes.com's "America's Best Cities for the Outdoors" for 2009. Jacksonville boasts the largest urban parks system in the country, with 111,000 acres of land.

Sales tax: 7.0 percent on almost everything except for medicine and certain foods

Military bases: Naval Station Mayport, Naval Air Station (NAS) Jacksonville, Coast Guard Group Mayport

Largest industrial employer in Northeast Florida: Naval Air Station Jacksonville employs more than 19,500 people

How busy is the port? In fiscal year 2008, JAXPORT's three public marine terminals handled a total of 8.4 million tons of cargo.

Annual event with the biggest economic impact: In 2008 the Florida vs. Georgia College Football Classic generated $19.7 million for Jacksonville. A sports event mecca, Jacksonville also generated an economic impact of $16.1 million in 2008 for the Gator Bowl.

Largest daily newspaper: *Florida Times-Union*, daily circulation 185,000; Sunday circulation 250,000

Weather number: (904) 741–4311

Visit Jacksonville:

> 208 N. Laura St., Ste. 102
> Jacksonville, FL 32202
> Phone: (904) 798-9111 or (800) 733-2668
> (U.S. and Canada)
> www.visitjacksonville.com

Direct impact of travel and tourism on Northeast Florida: In 2007, 4.1 million tourists generated $2.4 billion in direct spending to the local economy, resulting in a total economic impact of $4.8 billion.

Number of lighthouses: Three: Amelia Island, Mayport, and St. Augustine

Jacksonville's favorite foods: Soul Food Bistro fried chicken, Peterbrooke chocolate-covered popcorn, Mozzarella Lubis, Tidbits' chicken salad, hand-crafted beer from Bold City Brewery, Bistro Aix's Steak Frites, and succulent oysters from Orsay

Jacksonville's active outdoor lifestyle charms visitors and residents alike. Whether your leisure pleasures tend toward golfing on world-class courses, fishing in scenic marshes, reeling in marlin from the open ocean, or just kicking up some sand at the beach, Jacksonville's got your number. And for tourists who like to pick up a little history on their vacation, Northeast Florida offers some great lessons. (Did you know that the first wine ever made in America was made right here—by Spanish priests in St. Augustine?) The area dates back to the days before Jamestown and Plymouth Plantation, when French and Spanish settlers landed on these shores and built the first fledgling communities in what would one day become the United States of America.

Regardless of when you come, how you get around, and how long you stay, this guide will help you live like a local. Enjoy!

GETTING HERE, GETTING AROUND

Jacksonville has the great advantage of being easily accessible by air, land or sea, and with over 4 million tourists coming in and out of the city every year, the city's points of entry function with remarkable efficiency.

A well-planned infrastructure of fast-moving highways makes getting around the city a breeze. In fact, the major interstate highways running through Jacksonville are so direct that they provide fast and easy access to nearly every major city in the region.

If arrival by rail raises your interest, rest assured that Amtrak services the city handily with multiple stops daily, and if seafaring stirs your blood, Jacksonville's ease of embarkation will certainly float your boat. Care to arrive by air? Thanks to a major overhaul, the city's airport is now both pleasing to the eye and user-friendly.

Give each one a try to understand Jacksonville's multi-faceted mobility first-hand.

GETTING HERE

By Air

Jacksonville International Airport (JIA) is located 12 miles, or about 15 minutes, from Downtown. After years of trying to get better air service, JIA now has something to brag about: With 22 airlines making daily arrivals and departures, direct service is available from almost all of the nation's metropolitan areas. Travelers now have more options for direct flights to cities such as Philadelphia, Washington, D.C., New York, Dallas, and Detroit.

In early 2009, the airport received a #1 ranking for customer service satisfaction by Airports Council International–North America. The facility gives arriving and departing travelers much to be happy about: Free access to the airport's Wi-Fi system makes life easier for business travelers, and a plethora of amenities from Starbucks to InMotion movie rentals ensures that travelers will have every convenience they could possibly need. While you're there, be sure to visit the Haskell Art Gallery in the main terminal. The gallery serves as a gateway to the city's arts scene with frequently changing exhibits and sculpture kiosks throughout the terminal.

Jacksonville International Airport's newest concourse, Concourse C, housing US Airways, Southwest, and American, opened in November 2008. Concourse A, which houses Delta, Continental, JetBlue, AirTran, and United, also opened in May 2008. (Concourse B has been demolished and will be rebuilt at a future date.) Concourses A and C have moving walkways, high ceilings, skylights, television screens, new retail establishments and restaurants, and additional seating.

Southwest is the leading carrier at JIA with 22 daily flights. Delta Air Lines, once the city's longtime leader, is the next busiest with 21 daily flights. US Airways, with 13 daily flights, is No. 3. Newcomer JetBlue runs three flights daily with more planned shortly.

Here are the major air carriers serving JIA, along with their toll-free reservation numbers and Web sites:

AirTran Airways, (800) 247-8726
www.airtran.com
American Airlines, (800) 433-7300
www.aa.com
Continental, (800) 523-3273
www.continental.com
Delta Air Lines, (800) 221-1212
www.delta.com
JetBlue, (800) 538-2583
www.jetblue.com

Northwest Airlines, (800) 225-2525
www.nwa.com
Southwest Airlines, (800) 435-9792
www.southwest.com
United Airlines, (800) 864-8331
www.united.com
US Airways, (800) 428-4322
www2.usairways.com

JIA's facelift added ticketing counters and badly needed baggage-handling space. It also included a newly expanded parking garage, which added 4,700 parking spaces to the airport, bringing the total number to more than 12,000. The airport also built a 200-foot moving sidewalk and two escalators to help travelers get from the garage to the ticket counter level of the terminal.

The terminal expansion also added 40,000 square feet of public courtyard space. This means more shops and eateries for airport patrons to enjoy as they wait for connecting flights or for passenger arrivals and departures.

The airport is also proud of its state-of-the-art baggage security system. JIA was the first airport in the nation to install a CTX2000, which is an X-ray device that can detect everything from bombs to chemical weapons in checked bags. Once you turn over your luggage to an airline, it takes a long and windy trip via conveyer belt to your plane. Along the way, teams of federal agents sitting in front of huge computer screens carefully assess what's inside your suitcase. If anything looks suspicious, the agents call for a luggage check and may actually open your suitcase to assess what's inside. (Here's a big tip: Do not lock your luggage. Although the agents have big key rings with all types of luggage keys on them, their first priority is to check your baggage. If they can't find the correct key, ultimately they will open the bag by any means necessary.)

City leaders believe these improvements to air travel are key components to the future of Jacksonville's economy, and perhaps the most important component if the city wants to lure international companies to do business here. For more information about JIA, call the airport's automated operator at (904) 741–4902 or check out JIA's Web site at www.jia.aero.

Regional Airports

Sometimes you just need a break from the paparazzi. Therefore, the following airports serve the corporate and private plane travelers coming to or departing from the greater Jacksonville area.

CECIL FIELD
13365 Aeronautical Circle
(904) 573-1611
www.jia.aero (click on "Cecil Field")
Drive 15 miles west of town to find Cecil Field, one of Jacksonville's three regional general aviation airports. The site is well suited for aircraft maintenance, repair, and overhaul operations. With four, 200-foot-wide runways, three of which measure 8,000 feet, Cecil Field provides a user-friendly base for corporate aircraft, general aviation, and air cargo. The fourth runway, at 12,500 feet, is one of the longest in Florida.

CRAIG AIRPORT
855–11 St. Johns Bluff Rd.
(904) 641-7666
www.jia.aero (click on "Craig")
Centrally located near Jacksonville's suburban business centers, Craig Airport is a general aviation field perfect for busy corporate executives and ideally situated for quick access to the city's beaches, Downtown business district, and Jacksonville Jaguars football games at nearby Jacksonville Municipal Stadium. In 2005 Craig reported 162,000 takeoffs and landings.

i The cheapest way to get from the airport to Downtown or the Beaches is by Express Shuttle Service. Charges are about $43 for four people to Downtown and about $63 for four people to the Beaches. Call (904) 353-8880 for information and reservations.

HERLONG AIRPORT
9300 Normandy Blvd.
(904) 783-2805
www.jia.aero (click on "Herlong")
Located on the city's west side, Herlong Airport serves as a general aviation field and prime

recreational site for small private planes, hot-air balloons, gliders, and similar craft. Herlong covers 1,434 acres of land, houses approximately 140 aircraft, and features 3,500- and 4,000-foot runways. Single- and twin-engine aircraft, gliders, helicopters, ultralights, and an increasing number of corporate jets and turboprop aircraft use this airport, which is located about 11 miles southwest of Downtown.

ST. AUGUSTINE/ST. JOHNS COUNTY MUNICIPAL AIRPORT
4794 US 1, St. Augustine
(904) 209-0090
www.staugustineairport.com
St. Augustine/St. Johns County Municipal Airport is the closest private, noncommercial airport for general aviation and corporate air travel to historic St. Augustine and the World Golf Village. This facility has three paved runways (the longest being 7,000 feet), two lighted runways, and full-service, fixed-based operations.

By Train

AMTRAK
3570 Clifford Lane
(904) 766-5110, (800) 872-7245
www.amtrak.com
Train travel is both affordable and scenic. Book a sleeper compartment and wend your way down from D.C. or speed up the coast from Miami. Amtrak offers daily service to Jacksonville's station, located on the city's Northside, about 7 miles from Downtown. Picking up and dropping off out-of-town guests at the station is super-easy, but city buses and taxis are always available to provide local transportation.

By Bus

GREYHOUND BUS LINES
10 North Pearl St.
(904) 356-9976, (800) 231-2222 (fare and
schedule information)
www.greyhound.com
For those traveling on a limited budget, Greyhound Bus is the most affordable way to get to and from Jacksonville. The bus line's main terminal is located in the heart of Downtown, where transferring to public transportation or grabbing a taxi is a snap.

By Car

Reaching Jacksonville from the Northeast or Mid-Atlantic states couldn't be easier: Hop on I-95 and head south. (I-95, the major highway running along the East Coast, cuts right through Downtown.)

As you travel south on I-95, you'll know you're getting close to Jacksonville when you cross the Georgia-Florida border. If you're headed to Downtown, Riverside, Avondale, Springfield, San Marco, or any of the other inland neighborhoods, continue on I-95 to the exit that best serves your destination. (Visitors to Riverside and Avondale may want to connect to I-10 just before crossing the river and access those neighborhoods by bypassing Downtown.)

If your destination is one of Jacksonville's beaches—Atlantic, Neptune, or Jacksonville—continue on I-95 until you see the J. Tuner Butler Boulevard (JTB) exit. Head east on JTB until you reach the beach. At that point, Jacksonville, Neptune, and Atlantic Beaches lie to the north of you (left); Ponte Vedra Beach is a quick trip to the south (right).

If you're coming from the Midwest or other parts of the South, such as Atlanta, take I-75 south to I-10 and head east. Like I-95, I-10 is a direct shot to Jacksonville. I-10 connects with I-95 within sight of Downtown, where you can head north or south on I-95. Other routes into the city include US 1 (or Philips Highway), which runs the length of the East Coast.

By Cruise

JAXPORT CRUISE TERMINAL
9810 August Dr.
www.jaxport.com
Board a four- or five-day cruise to Freeport and Nassau in the Bahamas, or treat yourself to a five-day getaway to Key West and Nassau or Half Moon Cay and Nassau on Carnival Cruise Lines,

(Q) Close-up

The St. Johns River

The St. Johns River weaves through the city like a ribbon providing a commonality between the city's disparate communities and illustrating the long and storied past of the area. The St. Johns was once a major commercial artery, but with the advent of the automobile the river became more of a headache to cross than a way to get around. Decades passed. Jacksonville started to take its river for granted and, slowly but surely, years of pollution took their toll.

Fast-forward to the 1990s when a group of motivated citizens and officials instigated a river revival and began a clean-up campaign that honored the river's value as a natural resource.

In 1998 the St. Johns River was named an **American Heritage River,** one of only 14 in the country. As such, the river became eligible for federal funding, which helped fund the building of trails along the river and the purchase of key pieces of riverfront property for preservation. A **St. Johns Riverkeeper organization** was established to advocate full-time for the river. Today's Riverkeeper, Neil Armingeon, travels up and down portions of the St. Johns almost daily, keeping abreast of the stresses and successes that affect this 310-mile waterway.

The St. Johns River starts just west of Vero Beach and ends at the Atlantic Ocean, dropping a mere 30 feet during that journey, making it one of the laziest rivers in the world. From its swampy start to its saltwater end, the river is marked by small towns, fish camps, and parks like Blue Springs State Park near DeLand. Around Palatka the St. Johns turns into a wide "river of lakes," or "Welaka," as the Timucuan Indians called it. As you head toward Jacksonville, the riverfront changes again to reveal million-dollar estates next to rambling, mid-century homesteads.

A rabid devotion to all things nautical seems to be the greatest common denominator along the entire length of the river. Every type of sea craft plies these waters—from kayaks to Cape Dories, sailboats to shrimp trawlers, pontoons to powerboats.

Naturalist William Bartram traveled the St. Johns River in a canoe in the 1700s and was one of the first to write about the river's clear water and colorful fish. Today Bill Belleville's book about the St. Johns, *River of Lakes: a Journey on Florida's St. Johns River*, discusses one of its major stressors: storm water runoff, which carries lawn chemicals and highway dirt into the river. But, says Belleville, there are still places along the St. Johns nearer its headwaters where the water is as clear as it was in Bartram's day. Belleville is optimistic that the new appreciation and awareness of the St. Johns River will only add to its health in the future.

which departs right from the JAXPORT Cruise Terminal just off Heckscher Drive. If you plan to leave a car at the terminal, prepare to spend $15 per day per passenger vehicle ($60 for a four-day cruise and $75 for a five-day cruise), and $25 per day for oversized recreational vehicles ($100 for a four-day cruise and $125 for a five-day cruise). The lot is located adjacent to the terminal building, and no reservations are required for parking.

i JAXPORT's Cruise Terminal is located about 10 minutes from the airport just off Heckscher Drive. If you're driving from the airport, take I-95 south to exit 358A State Road 105 (Zoo Parkway/Heckscher Dr.). Stay on Zoo Parkway/Heckscher Drive for about 4 miles. Turn right on August Drive into cruise terminal entrance.

GETTING AROUND

Now that you're here, it's time to explore. Grab a street map—or even better, one of the many easy-to-use Jacksonville street-map iPhone applications–and your *Insiders' Guide,* and let's go!

By Taxi or Car Service

Jacksonville International Airport is located about 12 miles north of Downtown, just off I-95. Travel into the city isn't difficult if you plan on using a rental car or car service. (Unfortunately, Jacksonville does not yet have efficient public transportation to the airport.) There are, however, reliable taxi and limo services (though the local shuttle service is cheaper).

If you want to take a taxi at the airport, you have one option: Gator City Taxi, which charges about $43 to Downtown and about $63 to the Beaches. Service is available at the entrance to JIA, or by calling them directly at the numbers below. Gator City accepts all major credit cards.

If you'd prefer a private car service, several limousine and transportation companies serve the airport. The cost will run about twice as much as a taxi. For example, Carey International charges about $100 and up to transport two passengers from the airport to Downtown.

Gator City Taxi, (904) 741-0008 or (904) 355-8294

L & L Limousine, (904) 739-8289; www.jacksonvillelimousine.net

Dana's Limousine, (904) 744-3333; www.danaslimo.com

Carey International, (904) 992-2022; www.carey.com

By Car

Jacksonville is a big city. So big, in fact (841 square miles), it ranks as the biggest city in the contiguous United States. Because of the city's size, renting a car is definitely your best bet for getting around quickly and efficiently.

Whether you're arriving by car or plan to pick up a rental at the airport, be prepared for road construction. Jacksonville is continually overhauling its roads in an effort to alleviate congestion.

Still, traffic—even at rush hours—may slow you down a little, but doesn't hold a candle to the gridlock in other cities its size.

If you're traveling to Jacksonville's beaches, you've got through routes: Atlantic Boulevard, Beach Boulevard, or J. Turner Butler (JTB) Boulevard. And since you will most likely be heading the opposite direction of any rush-hour traffic, you should have smooth sailing no matter what time of day.

In general, though, most major roads are congested during morning and evening rush hours, especially the J. Turner Butler exit off of I-95, so plan accordingly.

Car Rentals

The following car rental companies operate at Jacksonville International Airport (JIA). Call for rates and availability.

Alamo Rent A Car, (877) 222-9075; www.goalamo.com

Avis, (904) 741-2327, (800) 230-4898; www.avis.com

Budget, (800) 527-0700; www.budget.com

Dollar Rent A Car, (866) 434-2226, (800) 800–3665; www.dollarcar.com

Enterprise, (800) 261-7331; www.enterprise.com

Hertz, (904) 741-2151, (800) 654-3131; www.hertz.com

National Car Rental, (904) 240-3290, (877) 222-9058; www.nationalcar.com

Returning an airport rental car is easy. Just follow the signs from the airport property's entrance to the parking garage adjacent to the terminal building and look for your particular rental company's drop site.

Public Transportation

JACKSONVILLE TRANSPORTATION AUTHORITY (JTA)
(904) 630-3100
www.jtaonthemove.com

The Jacksonville Transportation Authority operates the city's bus system, inter-county shuttle, trolley, and the Skyway Express monorail.

The bus system serves all Duval County, from the Beaches west to Orange Park, and connects with the Skyway Express and the Downtown/Riverside trolley. Most buses also provide front-loading bike racks so that riders can transport their bikes around the city. To find bus stops, look for the tall green signs with the red and yellow JTA logo and an easy-to-read listing of route information. Beaches and Riverside Trolley stops are indicated with a colorful graphic of a trolley car. Route maps for all of the JTA transportation options are available online at www.jtaonthe-move.com, or by calling (904) 630-3100. JTA also offers free Park-n-Ride lots around Jacksonville.

THE SKYWAY
ww.jtaonthemove.com (click on "Schedules")
The Skyway, the city's elevated, electrified mono-rail transit system, services eight stations on both sides of the St. Johns River.

The Skyway operates Monday through Friday from 6 a.m. to 11 p.m., Saturday from 10 a.m. to 11 p.m., and Sunday only for special-event service, such as Jaguars football games. Stations are con-tinually monitored by closed-circuit television, and all vehicles have two-way voice communica-tions with interior video recordings. Stations and vehicles are fully accessible to the disabled.

While the Skyway has never really caught on as a commuter option, mostly because it does not reach throughout the city, it still provides a pleasant way to travel to the Prime Osborn Convention Center and Hemming Plaza (where City Hall and the Federal Courthouse are located). From Downtown, ride it across the St. Johns River to San Marco Station, where it's an easy walk to the Museum of Science and History (MOSH) and Friendship Park Riverwalk. There's also a stop near the Southbank's hotels. The final stop provides easy access to the Charthouse restaurant and Morton's, The Steakhouse.

On Jaguar game days, the Skyway is free for the three hours before kickoff and two hours after the game. The Skyway fare for non-monthly com-muters is 50 cents, and 10 cents for the elderly and disabled.

i **If you forget something on a JTA bus, call (904) 630-3189 for help locating that lost article.**

ST. JOHNS RIVER TAXI SERVICE
3189 East Old Port Circle (office)
(904) 733-7782
www.jaxwatertaxi.com
For a mode of transportation that combines fun and function, take a ride on the River Taxi, a small-craft service for short hops across the St. Johns to Jacksonville Municipal Stadium, the Jacksonville Landing, and the Southbank Riverwalk. Pick up a River Taxi from the Jacksonville Landing or from the Southbank Riverwalk near Friendship Fountain.

Give the River Taxi a try if you're staying at a hotel on the Southbank and want to get across to the Landing for drinks. Conversely, if you're staying at a hotel on the Northbank and want to cross the river to eat at Ruth's Chris or Morton's, don't drive across the Main Street Bridge. Take the River Taxi.

The taxi operates from 11 a.m. to 9 p.m. on weekdays and from 11 a.m. to 11 p.m. weekends. Tickets are available for one-way or round-trip service, and prices range from $3 for adult one-way tickets to $5 for adults going round-trip. Stadium prices vary.

Plan to wait for about 20 minutes to get on your water taxi. The trip itself takes another 20 minutes, but it's worth the extra time to experi-ence the city from the water.

HISTORY

Almost every historical account of Jacksonville and coastal Northeast Florida begins 4,000 years ago with the Timucuans, the resident Native Americans credited with the early settlement of these shores. History tells us that, like modern Floridians, the Timucuans loved their oysters, as evidenced by the discovery of huge oyster-shell mounds (or middens) in the remains of their villages in Guana State Park near St. Augustine.

EARLY EUROPEANS

Historians believe that Timucuans befriended Jacksonville's first European settlers, the French Huguenots (Protestants) who built a settlement on the St. Johns River in 1564 and named it Fort Caroline. This settlement angered the Spanish, who had claimed "La Florida" as their own in 1513 when Ponce de Leon landed near Cape Canaveral in search of the Fountain of Youth.

In 1565 the Spanish sent Pedro Menendez de Aviles to wipe out the French at Fort Caroline. Aviles also started a settlement, St. Augustine, and a Catholic mission, Nombre de Dios, firmly establishing Spanish rule in Florida, a dominion that would last some 200 years.

That dominion was not altogether peaceful and was punctuated by repeated English attacks on St. Augustine under the leadership of Sir Francis Drake and others. To protect themselves, the Spanish built a fortress, the Castillo de San Marcos, which was finished in 1695, just in time to provide shelter against attacks by the governor of South Carolina, James Moore, in 1702 and by General James Oglethorpe of Georgia in 1740. In 1763 the Spanish ceded La Florida to England.

The 20-year British reign in Florida may have been short but it was significant. During those two decades the British constructed a road from St. Augustine to Savannah called The King's Road. It crossed the St. Johns River at a narrow stretch called Cowford, a shallow crossing popular with farmers who needed to move cattle across the river. Cowford, located about where the Hyatt

Regency Riverfront stands today, is considered the humble beginnings of the settlement that later became the city of Jacksonville.

In 1783, following the American Revolution, England gave Florida back to Spain for another 37 tumultuous years. During these years "patriots," secretly sanctioned by the United States government, repeatedly attacked Florida, trying to oust the Spanish. In 1821 Spain could hold on no longer and ceded Florida to the United States.

GETTING STARTED

Once Florida became a U.S. territory, settlers quickly arrived, many via The King's Road. Cowford started to grow, and by 1822 surveyors had staked out a town on the north bank of the St. Johns River. Settlers named it Jacksonville for General Andrew Jackson, a champion of the patriots and fighter of the Seminoles. Logging and shipping were big business in those early years, in part because the St. Johns River provided an easy way to transport logs and move freight inland from the Atlantic Ocean. Florida became a state in 1845.

THE CIVIL WAR

Jacksonville's growth stopped in 1861 when Florida seceded from the United States of America and joined the Confederacy. Through the course of the war, Union troops burned down most of the city on three separate occasions. Still, Florida became the breadbasket of the Confederate

⊛ Close-up

Jacksonville Beach

Jacksonville Beach sits on a barrier island along with several other beach communities, but for centuries before these communities began, the barrier island was the wild domain of hunters, fishermen, and Native Americans who hunted and collected shellfish along the shore. By 1885 a tiny hamlet, **Ruby Beach,** had taken root. Ruby Beach wasn't much more than a post office and a few tent homes, but in short order a railroad arrived bringing tourists from Jacksonville.

With the railroad came big progress. Ruby Beach was renamed **Pablo Beach,** and a half dozen luxury resorts were built along the ocean to serve all of the tourists pouring out from Jacksonville. The first resort, Murray Hall, boasted 192 rooms, an elevator, a steam-heating system, hot and cold running water, sulfur baths, a bowling alley, and 58 fireplaces to ward off the winter chill. Sadly, no trace of Murray Hall remains in Jacksonville Beach today. Built totally of wood, it burned to the ground just four years after its 1886 opening.

As Pablo Beach grew, residents built themselves a city hall and a home for the very first American Red Cross Volunteer Life Saving Corps. Lifeguards were badly needed in Pablo Beach as tourist drownings were rising at an alarming rate. A boardwalk soon followed allowing beachgoers to promenade, enjoy restaurants and shooting galleries, and dance in pavilions at night.

By 1925 Pablo Beach residents seeking a change voted to rename their community **Jacksonville Beach** to draw upon the community's proximity to Jacksonville. During the sixties, seventies, and eighties, much of the oceanfront area in Jacksonville Beach fell into disrepair, and Jacksonville Beach ceased being the tourist draw it once had been. In the nineties, city leaders made a concerted effort to attract businesses back to the beach by building a new city hall in the heart of town and a new outdoor band shell on the block adjacent to the ocean.

Redevelopment has caught on, and Jacksonville Beach continues to enjoy a renaissance.

Army, providing the produce and cattle that fed Southern troops during the war.

The Battle of Olustee on February 20, 1864, was an unsuccessful effort by Union forces to cut off those Confederate supply lines. The South prevailed, inflicting heavy losses on hundreds of Union soldiers, many of them former slaves. The Battle of Olustee was the only major battle fought in Florida during the Civil War. Every anniversary, thousands of people watch a reenactment of the battle at the Olustee Battlefield, 90 minutes west of Jacksonville. On the Friday of the reenactment weekend, the place is teeming with school field trip groups. Saturday, being less crowded, is a better day to go. On Sunday, the reenactors present the formal scripted program, which draws big crowds, but rest assured, you can get a good feel for the reenactment by attending Saturday's dress rehearsal.

TOURISM

After the Civil War, Jacksonville started to come into its own. It became a popular tourist destination for Northerners seeking warmer winter weather. Renowned author Harriet Beecher Stowe bought an orange grove on the St. Johns River in Mandarin and wintered there for many years. She also wrote what would become the region's first guidebook, a bestseller called *Palmetto Leaves.* (See her Close-up in this chapter.)

But prosperity went up in flames on May 3, 1901, when nearly 150 blocks of Downtown Jacksonville burned to the ground in what has become known as the Great Fire. Ten thousand people were left homeless. The fire was so massive that Savannah residents reported watching it glow on the horizon. (See the Attractions and Tours chapter for more on the Great Fire.) But Jacksonville's pluckiness prevailed, and just three days after the biggest blaze in the South, the city started to rebuild.

By 1908 a new industry had taken hold here: motion-picture production. Since the city could offer moviemakers plenty of sunshine and a warm winter, Jacksonville was soon competing with Los Angeles for films. Oliver Hardy got his start here, George M. Cohan starred in his first movie here, and Lionel Barrymore filmed a movie in Atlantic Beach.

But, eventually, moviemaking faded to black. Many Jacksonville residents had become fed up with the business, and efforts to start a major film production center with badly needed indoor production studios collapsed. In his book *Old Hickory's Town*, James Robertson Ward explains the collapse: "The opponents became more out-raged when other producers made false fire alarms to get the fire trucks their scripts called for, filmed bank robberies during Sunday worship hours, and in one instance, placed a misleading advertisement in a newspaper to draw a crowd to avoid paying extras."

Eventually, World War I began, and Jacksonville found new prosperity.

i For the centennial of the Great Fire in Jacksonville, the city commissioned a 48-foot stainless steel spire by artist Bruce White. The Great Fire Memorial Sculpture sits at the intersection of Market and Bay Streets, where many people jumped into the river and drowned trying to escape the flames.

Close-up

Harriet Beecher Stowe

Call **Harriet Beecher Stowe** the original Florida snowbird. Stowe, most famously the author of *Uncle Tom's Cabin,* began wintering in Jacksonville in 1867 after buying a 30-acre orange grove in Mandarin. Stowe enjoyed the freedom Florida offered and the escape from the harsh Connecticut winters. In her writings, she waxed upon her pleasure at being able to "spend your winter out of doors, even though some days be cold; to be able to sit with windows open; to hear birds daily; to eat fruit from trees; and pick flowers from hedges, all winter long."

Stowe spent up to six months a year in Mandarin with her husband and twin daughters. She shared her enthusiasm for her relaxed lifestyle on the St. Johns River in a volume of sketches called *Palmetto Leaves*. Each chapter describes the simple things Stowe so appreciated, such as a picnic on the shores of Julington Creek, which involved catching fish, cooking it in a hole lined with leaves, and eating it the moment it was done. She gives advice on how to buy land, start a farm, and grow and sell oranges. She rhapsodizes about the St. Johns River, "the great blue sheet of water [that] shimmers and glitters like so much liquid lapis lazuli." Tourism increased almost overnight in Jacksonville once *Palmetto Leaves* was published. In fact, steamboats began pulling up at the Stowe's riverfront home so that tourists could see the woman who wrote the books that shed a light on the realities of slavery and glorified our little bend in the river.

While living in Mandarin, Stowe did not abandon her political beliefs. She helped raise money to build a school for freed slave children, which was also used as a church on Sundays. When the schoolhouse mysteriously burned down one night, Stowe, undaunted, helped raise money to rebuild it.

The Stowes enjoyed 17 winters in their Mandarin home, until 1884, when Dr. Calvin Stowe, Harriet's husband, became too sick to travel. Nothing remains of the Stowe homestead on Mandarin Road except, perhaps, some majestic oak trees trimmed in Spanish moss. If those ancient trees could talk, the stories they would tell of the early days in Mandarin and the charming woman who so loved this landscape would surely be best sellers.

SHIPS AHOY

By 1940 Jacksonville's long association with the United States Navy had begun. The navy opened an aviation training facility, Naval Air Station Jacksonville. Naval Station Mayport, homeport to destroyers and aircraft carriers, soon followed. Downtown shipyards built ships for World War II.

In June 1942 four Nazi soldiers, under direct orders from Hitler himself, landed in Ponte Vedra Beach. Their assignment: blow up power plants, factories, train terminals, and department stores anywhere in the United States. Luckily, the German operatives were stymied in New York and Chicago after a German operative turned them in.

MILESTONES

In 1968 Jacksonville residents greatly simplified their local government, voting to consolidate 133 elective offices in Jacksonville, Duval County, the Beaches, and Baldwin. No longer would there be multiple tax and property appraisers; instead there would be one government encompassing the entire county, with one mayor, city council, and police force. This consolidation also meant that the city became huge in terms of area: 841 square miles. Jacksonville residents were so proud of their efforts that they gave the city a new nickname, The Bold New City of the South.

This bold new city really popped its buttons in 1995 when the Jacksonville Jaguars played their first game in the city's new NFL-worthy football stadium. Many credit the Jaguars with putting the city on the map. And in 2005, when Jacksonville was chosen to host the Superbowl, the city planners met the game-day demand by widening roads, constructing buildings, throwing Downtown block parties, and lining up cruise ships to serve as floating hotels for all the fans who flocked to town for the sports spectacular.

ACCOMMODATIONS

Like most American cities, Jacksonville offers a plethora of options when it comes to places to stay. As of this printing, the city has over 26,000 rooms for visitors to choose from, with over 15,000 of them located in inns, hotels, and B&Bs, and another 11,000 in the in-town and beach resorts.

The more interesting hotels seem to cluster around certain areas—Downtown, Riverside/Avondale, and the Beaches. That being said, finding the exact one that both suits your needs and tickles your fancy can be challenging. So, instead of giving you a useless, encyclopedic listing of all of the hotels out there, we've done exactly what we've promised and cherry-picked only the most interesting places to rest your head while giving you a good cross section of amenities, property personalities, and prices.

Jacksonville's lodging scene is evolving all of the time, and I am sure that there are some fine options that have either opened since this printing or somehow slipped past our radar. With that in mind, feel free to use these neighborhoods and suggestions as a jumping-off place to seek out new discoveries of your own. If you find that a property that interests you is booked during your dates, don't hesitate to ask the innkeeper, especially at the independently owned inns and B&Bs, for a suggestion of a similar or potentially undiscovered property.

The area near Airport Road off I-95 is seeing a fair amount of new hotel development and has thus been nicknamed Hotel Road. As the name suggests, this road leads into and out of Jacksonville International Airport. This may be where you will find the best values through chain hotels, if value and familiarity are your priority. However, be prepared to feel removed from the action.

Another hotel hub for business travelers is the Southpoint area where I-95 and J. Turner Butler Boulevard converge. While Southpoint is centrally located and makes a fairly convenient base camp for the Beaches, Downtown, and the St. Johns Town Center shopping area, it does not win us over in terms of charm or walkability. Neither these nor the airport hotels are bad hotels; they are just not what we look for when we talk about "Insider" destinations. We want your experience of Jacksonville to be memorable on many levels, starting with a room that you'll talk about for years to come.

Price Code

Based on information available at the time of publication, the price codes associated with each type of accommodation (the average charge for double occupancy rates in peak season) serves as a general guide. Please note that fluctuations in price and availability occur frequently, so take it upon yourself to check. Also, many properties offer reduced, Web-only rates and/or can be found on discount travel Web sites such as www.kayak.com or www.hotels.com, making these price ranges highly subjective. Do yourself a financial favor and check online to find the most favorable rate. If you have any questions, call the property and confirm.

INNS AND B&Bs

Let's start with the most quaint. If you're looking for a place to stay that's not a resort or a chain hotel/motel, Jacksonville has a fine selection of inns and B&Bs to please both hipsters and romantics alike. Jacksonville's most charming inns and

B&Bs are generally located in three parts of town: a national historic district called Riverside/Avondale, Historic Springfield, and Jacksonville Beach. The Springfield, Riverside, and Avondale inns are popular with business travelers because of their proximity to Downtown. The Riverside and Avondale inns are also within walking distance of shops, restaurants, the St. Johns River, and the Cummer Museum of Art. The inns in Jacksonville Beach are all within a block of the ocean and are close to the center of Jacksonville Beach, which offers loads of nightlife, restaurants, and shopping. They're also closer to the Mayo Clinic and to Naval Station Mayport. Any of the locations—Riverside/Avondale, Springfield, or Jacksonville Beach—provide a great opportunity to step into the architectural history of the city and explore the identities of both old and new Jacksonville.

We've included one other property, a former estate on the river in Orange Park, a suburban city about 10 miles south of Jacksonville. We mention this inn because it's too beautiful to leave out. It's also convenient for anyone spending time on the Westside, near Naval Air Station Jacksonville.

All of the inns accept credit cards. If you are traveling with pets and/or children, call ahead to check the hotels' policies. All of the following are nonsmoking, and all provide some sort of breakfast. Only two of the inns are wheelchair accessible. Rates can change, so it's definitely worth asking about specials, especially if you're considering an extended visit.

Price Code

The price code reflects average room cost per night based on double occupancy.

$	Less than $100
$$	$100 to $125
$$$	$126 to $150
$$$$	$151 to $175

Riverside/Avondale/Orange Park

**THE CLUB CONTINENTAL ON THE
ST. JOHNS** $–$$$$
2143 Astor St., Orange Park
(904) 264-6070, (800) 877-6070
www.clubcontinental.com

Step back in time to Old Florida in the early 1920s, when wealthy Northerners built Mediterranean-style estates with Spanish tile, shady courtyards, and gentle fountains under the live oak trees. Such is the look of the Club Continental on the St. Johns River, built in 1923 by Caleb Johnson, heir to the Palmolive Soap Company. He called his home Mira Rio, and judging by some old photographs hanging in the club's bar, it was quite the party house—complete with a signature drink still served at the bar today, the formula for which is a well-kept secret. The property, with its beautiful gardens, has stayed in Johnson's family and today is owned and operated by his heirs. They've managed to retain the Old Florida feel while turning it into a successful business. Club Continental is a private dining and tennis club, plus a 22-room bed-and-breakfast inn. Seven of the rooms are in Mira Rio, the old house, and most of these have river views. The remaining 15 are suites, which are housed in a separate building. These rooms are by far more popular. All have balconies overlooking the St. Johns River, free wireless Internet, microwaves, and refrigerators. Several of the rooms have a Jacuzzi and a gas fireplace. Guests in Mira Rio can enjoy a free continental breakfast. Pets are allowed by request, and the inn is wheelchair accessible. There are seven tennis courts, and children will enjoy swimming in one of the property's three pools. You can even arrive by yacht and dock at the club's marina. This may well be the only inn in Florida where turtles living in an elaborate courtyard fountain come when you call them. Be sure and have the turtle food ready!

DICKERT HOUSE $$–$$$
1804 Copeland St.
(904) 387-4762
www.dickert-house.net
Betty Dickert is proud of her huge 1914 home just off the St. Johns River and wants her guests to enjoy it as much as possible, often inviting them to join her for a cup of tea in the kitchen. Choose from one of three suites in the main house. Each includes a sitting room and private bath, a full hot breakfast in the dining room, and room amenities like cable TV, VCRs, high-speed Internet, and tele-

phones. Guests can also rent the carriage house, which is wheelchair accessible. Dickert also owns an apartment building across the street, which she rents as four furnished two-bedroom suites with a sitting room and full kitchen. These are excellent for extended stays. This inn allows children of all ages as well as small pets.

i Local inns are popular spots for small weddings. Not only do guests stay at the inn, but the ceremony and reception—even the honeymoon—can be held there, too.

HOUSE ON CHERRY STREET $–$$$$
1844 Cherry St.
(904) 384-1999
www.houseoncherry.com

Writer, former English teacher and now innkeeper Victoria Freeman is known around town as a hostess and gardener extraordinaire. In the Victorian-era House on Cherry Street, she and her husband, Robert, serve as gracious, low-key hosts and exquisite conversationalists. Located on the St. Johns in Riverside, the immaculately kept inn offers a fabulous view of Downtown and is a short distance from 5 Points, the shops and restaurants of Avondale, the Florida Times-Union Performing Arts Center, the Museum of Modern Art, and the Cummer Museum of Art and Gardens. The Avondale Room offers both a queen-size four-poster bed and an antique spindle day bed. *Ziegfeld Follies'* costume designer Maude Kurtz spent 40 years creating a needlepoint chair that now rests in the room's sitting area. Combine the room with the parlor to form a large suite with a full bath. The handsome Riverside Room features a queen-size four-poster bed with an antique coverlet, a day bed, antique armoire, full bath, sitting area, and small refrigerator. Be sure to look out the window in the evenings to watch the resident snowy egrets return to their roosts. The inn is only open January through March and October through December and requires a two-night stay on weekends. Plan accordingly so as not to miss this gem. No pets or young children please.

THE INN AT OAK STREET $$–$$$
2114 Oak St.
(904) 379-5525
www.innatoakstreet.com

Tina Musico may well be the youngest innkeeper in Jacksonville. She says a little naïveté worked to her advantage several years ago when she and her husband, Robert Eagle, bought their 1902, 10,000-square-foot, wood-frame home in the heart of Riverside. When they first saw the three-story house, Tina says, it was stripped down to its studs inside, but she and Robert fell in love with it anyway. They liked the grand feel of the place and were eager to renovate. Little did they know it would take two years of their lives to put the house back together again. The inn has six bedrooms, each with a flat-screen TV and a DVD player hidden away in an antique armoire, a wine refrigerator, wireless Internet connection, hair dryer, telephone, and private bath. All the rooms are nonsmoking, and three of them on the second floor also have private balconies. The decor leans more toward minimalism than clutter, while still making use of antique furniture and rugs. Tina says she had great luck finding antiques on eBay and calls the 8-foot-wide, 1854 French Art Deco armoire in one of the bedrooms her most fabulous find. Guests enjoy a full gourmet breakfast in the formal dining room, which can include homemade sunrise frittatas and sausage roll, homemade bread and granola, and some sort of fresh fruit compote. Tina also offers a wine hour daily at 6 p.m., complete with munchies and something sweet. The formal dining room also serves as a meeting room for corporate clients, which Tina says the inn is seeing more and more of lately. The Inn at Oak Street is 10 minutes from Downtown and a stone's throw away from Riverside Market Square shopping. Tina has managed to utilize her entire house, including the basement, where there's a spa offering massage and nail services. Stop by the gift shop to take home one of the inn's cozy monogrammed bathrobes. If you're interested in renovating old homes, be sure to ask Tina where the 24 8-foot doors came from. It's quite a tale! The Inn at Oak Street welcomes children ages 12 and older.

RIVERDALE INN $$$–$$$$
1521 Riverside Ave.
(866) 808-3400
www.riverdaleinn.com

This big blue mansion on Riverside Avenue enjoys a wonderful location on what used to be Jacksonville's Millionaire Row. Just a block off the St. Johns River, a block from the Cummer Museum of Art and Gardens and two blocks from Memorial Park on the river, the inn is within walking distance of several of the city's hippest, in-town shopping and eating districts.

It took experienced innkeepers Carolyn Whitmire and Linda Walm (sisters who cut their teeth on an inn on Amelia Island) 22 months to renovate this three-story 1901 home. They added 12 bathrooms and spent lots of money refinishing the original hardwood floors. The house was built by William Kelly, a turpentine baron, and updated by architect Henry Klutho in 1921 after the Great Fire. (See the History chapter for details on the Great Fire.) The inn has eight guest rooms filled with antiques and named after streets in this historic neighborhood. Two of the rooms have working gas fireplaces, including the Park Suite, which used to be the home's master bedroom. All the rooms have DSL, HBO, private baths, hair dryers, and robes. There are also two rooms in a renovated garage in back that are fully wheelchair accessible. Whitmire and Walm serve a full breakfast, which always includes fresh fruit and something hot like omelettes or French toast with apples, in the inn's two dining rooms daily. But what makes the Riverdale most unique is the Gum Bunch Pub and The Row restaurant on the first floor. The Gum Bunch serves beer, wine, and cocktails and The Row serves dinner seven days a week and brunch on Sunday. Both are open to the public.

i Jacksonville's Ronald McDonald House is available for families with a child age 18 or younger who's being treated at a local medical facility. The 30-room facility allows families to stay for free with a referral from a doctor, nurse, or hospital social service worker. Visit www.rmhjax.org for more information.

ST. JOHNS HOUSE $–$$
1718 Osceola St.
(904) 384-3724
www.stjohnshouse.com

Choose from one of the three rooms for rent in this traditional bed-and-breakfast located in a 1914 private home just one block from the St. Johns River in Riverside. Two of the rooms, each with a queen-size bed, are in the big house. The Barnett Room has a view of the river and a private bath. The Governor's Room lacks a view and has a standing shower, but makes up for any deficiencies with a four-poster mahogany bed, reading chair, and DVD player. The Cohen Room, located in the carriage house, offers a double bed and claw-foot tub in its own bathroom and has a view that makes it feel like a tree house. All rooms have cable TV, telephones, coffeemakers, and hair dryers. Children of all ages are allowed in this bed-and-breakfast, but not pets (although the innkeepers have a friendly golden retriever named Kingsley). A full hot breakfast is served every morning on the sun porch where guests enjoy views of the river along with their meal. The inn is open November through May; but is closed in March.

Jacksonville Beach

FIG TREE INN $$–$$$
185 Fourth Ave. South
Jacksonville Beach
(904) 246-8855, (877) 217-9830
www.figtreeinn.com

Pick ripe figs from the stately fig tree in the backyard. The tree is just a short stroll from any of the six themed bedrooms in this beach home built in 1915. Every room has a private bath, queen or king bed, wireless Internet access, cable TV and VCR, iron/board, and hair dryer. One room includes a kitchenette. The Garden Room has a canopied bed and Jacuzzi tub (which makes it a popular pick for newlyweds). The Fig Tree Inn's owners/innkeepers do not live on the premises. Instead, they decided to live nearby so they could rent the entire house, which guests choose to do for family reunions, weddings, and bridal and baby showers. On weekends the innkeepers cook up the Fig Tree

Special, a cross between French toast and a waffle, in the inn's renovated kitchen, which features two ovens and a six-burner stove. The rest of the week the proprietors serve a continental breakfast, often including fresh figs, in the breakfast room. Children ages 10 and older are welcome here, depending on occupancy. The Fig Tree is beautifully decorated and extremely clean, and the innkeepers say guests enjoy sitting on its front porch, which a local magazine once dubbed one of the most engaging front porches in the city.

i Some B&Bs have a resident dog or cat. Be sure to ask about pets if you're allergic.

PELICAN PATH B&B BY THE SEA $$–$$$$
11 North 19th Ave.
Jacksonville Beach
(904) 249-1177, (888) 749-1177
www.pelicanpath.com

Joan Hubbard, a marriage and family therapist, and her civil-engineer husband, Tom, always wanted to own a bed-and-breakfast. So they sold their large home in Downtown Jacksonville, bought a piece of oceanfront property in Jacksonville Beach, and built the inn of their dreams. They now live above the store, so to speak, on the third floor. The two floors below them are dedicated to the inn. The great room on the ground floor doubles as a breakfast room, has an expansive view of the ocean, the beach, sand dunes, and sea oats, and is the heart of the inn. Joan chats away with the guests every morning as she cooks them a full, hot breakfast featuring eggs and fruit. The inn has four rooms, all on the second floor. Two are oceanfront with private balconies; all have ocean views and access to the downstairs patio. All have king-size beds, private baths with oversized spa tubs, TVs with cable and VCR/DVD players, refrigerators, coffeemakers, hair dryers, wireless Internet, and telephones. The rooms are named for the various seabirds dotting the shores outside the inn. Use the B&B's binoculars and birding books to help you identify local wildlife, or hop on a beach bike, provided free by the inn, and ride to nearby shops, restaurants,

and bars. Pelican Path is open March, April, May, July, August, and October.

HOTELS

The price code reflects average room cost per night based on double occupancy and is based on information available at the time of publication (average charge for double occupancy in peak season). Please note that fluctuations in price occur frequently.

Unless otherwise stated, all of the hotels listed have smoking and nonsmoking rooms, all have wheelchair-accessible rooms, and all take major credit cards.

$..................... under $70
$$ .... $70 to $99
$$$ .... $100 to $120
$$$$ .... $121 and up

Downtown

CROWNE PLAZA JACKSONVILLE
RIVERFRONT HOTEL $–$$$$
1201 Riverplace Blvd.
(904) 398-8800, (800) 227-6963
www.cpjacksonville.com

If you want to be close to Downtown and prefer the consistency of a larger chain, look into the Crowne Plaza Jacksonville Riverfront Hotel, located on the continually evolving Southbank and very close to the historic and eternally popular San Marco Historic District, beloved for its boutiques, variety of restaurants, and nightlife. For dinner, make a reservation at the on-site Ruth's Chris Steak House, walk across the street to Morton's, The Steakhouse, or take the River Taxi across the river to explore Jacksonville's Downtown restaurants. The hotel has 292 rooms, all with balconies, and is located just off I-95, only 15 miles south of the Jacksonville International Airport. Amenities include a business center, fitness center, heated outdoor pool, valet parking and valet laundry service, free wireless Internet, ergonomically designed workstations, cable TV, irons/boards, granite countertops, and king rooms with Tempur-Pedic Dream Spa mattresses and down pillows.

HYATT REGENCY JACKSONVILLE RIVERFRONT $$–$$$$
225 East Coastline Dr.
(904) 588-1234
www.jacksonville.hyatt.com

Located on the St. Johns River's Northbank, adjacent to the Jacksonville Landing and within walking distance to London Bridge English Pub and Downtown nightlife, the Hyatt is a newly renovated 966-room property with a heated rooftop swimming pool and fantastic views of Downtown and the river. Rooms feature Hyatt Grand Beds, iHome Stereos with iPod docks, deluxe bathrooms with Portico bath products, and wireless Internet. The hotel also offers valet parking, a 24-hour StayFit gym and sauna, and boasts proximity to 47 world-class golf courses, the Jacksonville Landing, Jacksonville Symphony Orchestra at the Times-Union Center for the Performing Arts, the Jacksonville Municipal Stadium, and the Baseball Grounds of Jacksonville.

THE OMNI JACKSONVILLE HOTEL $$–$$$$
245 West Water St.
(904) 355-6664, (800) 843-6664
www.omnihotels.com

Long a mainstay in Downtown, the Omni enjoys a great location across the street from the St. Johns River, the Landing, and the Times-Union Center for the Performing Arts. It's also a short walk away from the Skyway Express, Jacksonville's people mover, which will take you across the river to museums and fine dining, all within walking distance of the Riverplace stop. This 16-story hotel features a wood-and-marble grand staircase and 354 rooms with river views. Kids are also welcome here; the Omni Sensational Kids program caters to the Omni's youngest guests at check-in by providing them with a goodie bag containing an flashlight, a flip drum, Twizzlers, a disk launcher, a canteen, and a scented plant-able bookmark. Kids also receive a special delivery of milk and cookies to their guest room on the first night and can borrow a rolling backpack full of toys, books, and games. All rooms feature coffeemakers, hair dryers, irons/boards, minibars, terry-cloth bathrobes, free newspapers, high-speed wireless Internet, two direct-dial telephones with dataports, voice mail, 25-inch TV, and LodgeNet system featuring on-demand hit movies. Additionally, the Omni's year-round fourth-floor/rooftop heated swimming pool and sundeck overlook the St. Johns River and Downtown. Pets are welcome with prior approval. The award-winning restaurant, Juliette's Bistro, is located in the hotel lobby.

> **i** Looking for a hotel near a movie theater? The Hilton Garden Inn in Deerwood Park is located about 100 yards from the 14-screen megaplex, Tinseltown. Call (904) 997-6600 for reservations.

The Beaches

CASA MARINA HOTEL $$$–$$$$
691 North First St., Jacksonville Beach
(904) 270-0025
www.casamarinahotel.com

There's history in the halls of this oceanfront hotel, the name of which means "house by the sea" in Spanish. Built in 1925, the Casa Marina still sports a rare, original pecky-cypress ceiling in what is now the hotel's dining room. (Pecky cypress is wood pecked full of holes by birds trying to get at bugs.) The recently renovated hotel has 23 oceanfront, ocean-view, and street-side rooms, 16 of them suites with sitting rooms and sofa beds. All are extremely clean and functional, and pets are allowed in certain rooms. Guests can enjoy a continental breakfast at the mahogany bar or in the oceanfront courtyard, then head to the beach and soak up the sun. The hotel's great location in downtown Jacksonville Beach is within six blocks of many popular bars and restaurants and the beachfront band shell. But why go elsewhere when you can enjoy tapas and martinis in Casa Marina's Penthouse Lounge? Special rates are available for longer stays.

COURTYARD BY MARRIOTT JACKSONVILLE BEACH OCEANFRONT $$–$$$$
1617 North First St., Jacksonville Beach
(904) 249-9071, (888) 236-2427
www.marriott.com/jaxjv

Business travelers and families alike will enjoy this oceanfront hotel. Of the hotel's 150 rooms, 12 are spacious suites. All of the rooms have balconies; 100 are oceanfront; 50 are off-ocean. All rooms have a refrigerator, microwave, coffeemaker, free Wi-Fi, hair dryer, and an iron/board. The free business center and wireless are very popular with guests, and the hotel offers an exercise room and large oceanfront pool, where free kids activities are often held in summer. Grab a bite to eat at the marketessen, a cross between a market and a deli, in the lobby. The hotel's restaurant is open for breakfast, but not for dinner. The Courtyard Lounge offers a full bar. AAA gives this hotel a three-diamond rating.

THE PALMS RETRO $$–$$$
28 Sherry Dr., Atlantic Beach
(904) 241-7776
www.palmsretro.com
Palms Retro is a revamped kitschy beach motel featuring retro-themed rooms. Formerly The Palms a Courtyard Inn Atlantic Beach, this 1940s gem has 10 re-imagined rooms as well as a new owner, vision, and name. Stay in the "Diva Room" with a giant photo of Marilyn Monroe, "The Bad Boy's Room," papered with pictures of James Dean and Steve McQueen, or choose from one of the many quirky others.

SEA HORSE OCEANFRONT INN $$–$$$$
120 Atlantic Blvd., Neptune Beach
(904) 246-2175, (800) 881-2330
www.seahorseoceanfrontinn.com
From the street this inn looks like an old mom-and-pop Florida motel from the fifties. But walk through a breezeway to the back courtyard and you'll find a beautiful patio and oceanfront pool, perfectly framed with sand dunes and sea oats. All 38 rooms here face the ocean, but if you're on the first floor, you'll see more of the dunes than the Atlantic. This independent operation is constantly being upgraded and maintained by its diligent owners. At present, all of the rooms include coffeemakers, mini refrigerators, and HBO. The rooms are large, and so are the tiled bathrooms.

For the best views of the beach, book a night in the inn's penthouse, which has its own kitchenette. Otherwise, you'll have to go out to get breakfast, but that's not a problem. The Sea Horse is located in the heart of Town Center, a popular Beaches restaurant and shopping district.

ONE OCEAN RESORT $$$$
One Ocean Blvd., Atlantic Beach
(904) 249-7402
www.oneoceanresort.com
This luxury, eight-story, oceanfront hotel was completely renovated in 2008 and gets high marks from locals because during earlier renovations the management took extra pains to install "turtle windows," specially tinted windows that prevent light from the rooms from shining on the beach and luring hatching sea turtles away from the water. All of the 193 rooms have ocean views, and the oceanfront rooms have balconies. For extra space and comfort, book one of the three living room–bedroom executive suites. The hotel has a lovely oceanfront pool and enjoys a great location in the heart of Town Center, within steps of some of the Beaches' most popular restaurants, nightspots, and shops. Be sure to save time for dinner at Azuréa, a destination restaurant showcasing contemporary coastal cuisine with a tip of the hat to the flavors of Europe, the Caribbean, and the Americas. Azuréa's on-site sommelier brings years of experience in the fine art of wine selection and tasting.

Southpoint

INN AT MAYO CLINIC $$–$$$$
4420 Mary Brigh Dr.
(904) 992-9992, (800) 228-9290
www.marriott.com/jaxmy
If you need to come to Jacksonville to visit the Mayo Clinic, this hotel is the most convenient place to stay. It's actually connected to the Mayo Clinic, so patients or their families don't have far to go. Be careful when booking your stay, however, because there is a second hotel, the Courtyard by Marriott at Mayo Clinic, that's about

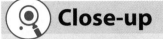

Close-up

A Seat in the Kitchen

Banking on the adage that all parties somehow end up in the kitchen, **Salt** at the Ritz-Carlton skips the middleman and starts the party there by offering 10-course dinners practically at the chef's elbow.

A seat in the dining room and a seat in the kitchen are two different experiences. The first is serene and romantic; the second is cinema verité, culinary theater at its finest. In the dining room, waiters talk sotto voce against the backdrop of ocean and sky, but step through the kitchen door and you're in another world altogether—one of clanging pots and flashing knives.

In Salt's kitchen dining experience, groups of no more than five foodies enjoy 10 courses of private dining, complete with different wines for each course, and with the added bonus of being able to observe both Chef de Cuisine Richard Gras' technique and each dish's preparation.

Kitchen guests are seated in a former storage room with a large picture window and a view, directly in front of them, of the seven chefs on the cooking line. The little half-moon table seats up to five, but the room itself gives diners a measure of privacy. Autograph seekers don't bother you in the kitchen; they don't even know you're there, which is most likely why John Travolta ate in the kitchen twice while he was in Jacksonville filming the movie *Basic*.

Sitting behind the glass wall also keeps diners safely out of the way as waiters run in to pick up their orders, as chefs dash across to retrieve something out of a refrigerator, and as dishwashers race by with a stack of freshly washed gold-trimmed plates.

The Ritz does not need to broadly advertise its seat in the kitchen. There's no need—it's an Insiders-only, word-of-mouth affair. The result: the kitchen table is usually booked every night of the month.

A 10-course **"Seat in the Kitchen" dinner** runs $175 per person without wine, $275 with wine. Reservations are required. Call (904) 491-6746 to reserve, or visit www.ritzcarlton.com/ameliaisland for more information.

---

150 yards away from the clinic itself, so the two are often confused. The Inn at Mayo Clinic's 78 suites are perfect for an extended stay. Each room has a fully equipped kitchen, cable, and all the amenities you would normally find in a well-equipped hotel room. Complimentary services include grocery shopping, continental breakfast, a hospital-campus shuttle, and free Internet. Best of all, the Inn at Mayo Clinic is located just 5 miles from the beach, so guests can drive out to walk on the beach or dine at Beaches restaurants.

WINGATE BY WYNDHAM
JACKSONVILLE $$–$$$$
4681 Lenoir Ave. South
(904) 281-2600, (800) 228-1000
www.wingateinns.com (search for
"Jacksonville")

Business guests abound here, but families will enjoy all the amenities including a complimentary hot breakfast buffet daily, and the manager's receptions Monday through Thursday evenings. The Wingate has 102 comfortable, oversized guest rooms, each with its own separate work area, free high speed Internet access, free local calls, free faxes, copies, and printing in the 24-hour business center, newspaper, Moen revolution showerheads, upgraded towels, top-of-the-line mattresses and linens, coffeemaker, iron/board, and safe.

RESORTS

Jacksonville is proud of its world-class resorts, many of which have recently undergone multi-million-dollar renovations. These are the places

So, You Want to Be an Insider...

Thankfully, Insider status is not restricted only to those who were born here. It's an acquired mantle, earned through a love of sunshine, great down-home food, and the arts. But if you really want to earn the title, there are certain rites of passage you have to scratch off your list first to even be considered. What follows is a no-holds-barred list collected from a cadre of seriously in-touch Insiders. (Look to the index to find out where to turn for more on each of these rites.) Tackle them in any order you see fit. You'll be living like a local in no time.

- ❏ Tubing the Ichetucknee
- ❏ Coming face to snout with an Okefenokee alligator
- ❏ Eating at a fish camp
- ❏ Seeing gators at the Alligator Farm, then eating one at St. Augustine Beach (our pal Andrew prefers them fried with tartar sauce)
- ❏ Watching the Space Shuttle launch from a dock on the river
- ❏ Evacuating for a hurricane
- ❏ Not evacuating for a hurricane
- ❏ Kayaking with the manatees
- ❏ Getting stranded by the Skyway while attempting to take advantage of public transit
- ❏ Attending a drag show at the Metro
- ❏ Watching Summer Classics Movies on Sundays at the Florida Theatre
- ❏ Attending the Florida-Georgia tailgate party
- ❏ Driving to Amelia Island via Heckscher Drive
- ❏ Watching a cruise ship just clear the Dames Point Bridge
- ❏ Being at a Jacksonville Suns game on a Friday night when they set off the fireworks.
- ❏ Picking up a to-go order at a drive-thru liquor store

to book if golf and tennis are your prerequisites for relaxation. Every resort listed has both in good measure, but you may have to give the edge to the Amelia Island Plantation for tennis. For years it was the locale for the Bausch & Lomb tennis tournament. The tournament has moved on to Sawgrass, but the world-class facilities remain. Four of the resorts are oceanfront; two, at this writing, have major day spas, and one has a AAA five-diamond restaurant.

E.M. Forster wasn't the only one who knew the effect that a room with a view could have on the quality of one's getaway, and all these resorts have rooms with spectacular ocean vistas or views of the golf course—or in some cases both. All have sizable banquet and meeting facilities, day programs for children, and health and fitness centers.

They're all great places to stay, and picking just one won't be easy. So come back year after year, and stay at them all.

Price Code

Based on information available at the time of publication, we offer the following price code (average charge for double occupancy in peak season) as a general guide. Please note that fluctuations in price occur frequently.

$$ .... $99 to $150
$$$ .... $151 to $250
$$$$ .... $251 to $350
$$$$$ .... $351 to $450

The Beaches

AMELIA ISLAND PLANTATION $$-$$$$$
6800 First Coast Hwy., Amelia Island
(904) 261-6161, (888) 261-6161
www.aipfl.com
All Florida developers should be required to visit this resort before they're allowed to build anything in this state. Note the thick tree canopy that's been left largely intact despite large-scale resort development. Because the early developers decided to leave the trees several decades ago, they now have a world-class resort nestled beneath a dense canopy of live oak, cypress, and palm trees. The Plantation is located on the southern half of Amelia Island about 45 minutes from Jacksonville and 25 minutes from Downtown Fernandina Beach. Amelia Island Plantation is a sprawling resort made intimate by the densely wooded terrain. This is the resort to come to if you want to rent a one-, two-, or three-bedroom villa for a week. There are over 400 to choose from. Many sit oceanfront, and all are owned by out-of-towners who allow the Plantation to rent their digs out in their absence. If you don't want a villa, the 249-room Amelia Inn and Beach Club will do nicely. All the rooms at the inn are oceanfront with balconies, and if you stay on an upper floor, you'll be able to enjoy an additional great view to the west over the tree canopy to the marsh.

Amelia Island Plantation offers 72 holes of golf and a golf school that's the envy of other resorts. Tennis enthusiasts will stagger at the 23 tennis courts and the bounty of tennis clinics that as much as guarantee they'll go home a better tennis player than when they arrived. Make a date to visit the Nature Center, located behind the reception center in the village shops, where visitors of all ages can learn about the indigenous plants and wildlife. The Nature Center also offers a plethora of tours and activities, from birding to kayaking. If a ramble isn't your thing, head for the Spa at Amelia Island Plantation, which offers Watsu, an in-water massage treatment that followers swear by for relaxation and muscle loosening. Afterward, sign up for a Segway tour around the marshes and nature areas. The Plantation provides a stunning variety of activities for all ages and interests, as well as some half-dozen restaurants for guests.

PONTE VEDRA INN & CLUB $$-$$$$$
200 Ponte Vedra Blvd.
Ponte Vedra Beach
(904) 285-1111, (800) 234-7842
www.pvresorts.com
This is it, the epicenter, the cornerstone upon which Ponte Vedra earned its reputation for luxury. The Ponte Vedra Inn & Club started more

---

It's a Dog's Life

Traveling to Jacksonville with man's best friend needn't put you in a bind. Jacksonville has a wealth of visitor-friendly dog parks to help Spot get his daily dose of social time.

- Dog Wood Park, 7407 Salisbury Rd.; www.jaxdogs.com. Day pass: $11.

- Jacksonville Humane Society Community Pooch Park, 8464 Beach Blvd.; www.jaxhumane.org. Free.

- Poochies Swim and Play Park, 985 Oak Lane, Orange Park.; www .poochiespark.com. Day pass: $10.

- Julington Creek Animal Walk, 12075 San Jose Blvd.; www.juling toncreekanimalwalk.com. Day pass $12

than seven decades ago when the National Lead Company carved a small resort for well-to-do vacationers out of a desolate tract of wind-swept oceanfront property. Since then, an entire community of expensive homes and shops has sprung up around this 300-acre, 250-room campus-style resort. And the vacationers still come as they have, in some cases, for generations. Why do so many return so often? No doubt it's for the miles of beachfront right outside their bedroom door—and the 36 holes of championship golf, the 15 Har-Tru tennis courts, and the four sparkling oceanfront pools. The inn's award-winning day spa pampers Mom (and Dad) from head to toe while the kids are well entertained in the Kids Club. No other local resort offers an oceanfront health and fitness center where you can work out while you look out over the Atlantic Ocean.

All of the accommodations feature award-winning interior design themes, a separate lighted vanity area with makeup mirror, king or queen beds with triple sheet comfort, luxury bath products, a coffeemaker with complimentary coffee and tea, plush terry robes, voice mail, and nightly turndown service with chocolate mints. Each room has its own private terrace or patio, and guests receive a complimentary morning newspaper. Regulars love the people who run this resort. The employees, some of whom have worked here for a quarter of a century, know the value of friendly, full-service attention. Guests are treated with great respect by everyone from parking valets to the general manager.

For the best deals, be sure to ask about seasonal resort packages. For instance, the Inn's bed-and-breakfast packages can really save you money on your room rate, especially if you choose to eat dinner off property at the myriad Beaches restaurants nearby. Oh, and the resort has a no-tipping policy. Instead, a nightly gratuity is charged to your account.

**THE PONTE VEDRA
LODGE & CLUB** $$$–$$$$$
607 Ponte Vedra Blvd.
Ponte Vedra Beach
(904) 273-9500, (800) 243-4304
www.pvresorts.com

With just 66 rooms, the Lodge is the smallest of Jacksonville's resorts. In essence, it is a boutique resort, which is why guests love it. The Lodge is located a mile and a half south of the Ponte Vedra Inn & Club, the Lodge's sister property, on Ponte Vedra Boulevard. Built in 1989, all the rooms here are oceanfront with either a terrace or balcony. Relax over dinner in the circular oceanfront dining room, which is intimate, like the resort itself, and features a fireplace for cozy meals in cooler months. The Lodge's three swimming pools accommodate adults and kids separately, and include a six-lane lap pool. The fitness center, where the lap pool is located, is a beehive of activity where you can take an Aquacize class, run on the treads, or detox in the sauna. Since the Lodge is owned by the same company that owns the Ponte Vedra Inn & Club, Lodge guests often "head north" to take advantage of all of the Inn's amenities such as excellent golf and tennis instruction, a day spa, two championship golf courses, shops, and restaurants. A nice touch: the Lodge (and the Inn, for that matter) publishes a nightly newssheet that's brought to your room when the maid comes to turn down your bed. The newssheet lists all the activities for the day ahead, including tidal charts and sunrise and sunset times. In 2003 the Lodge completed a $4.5 million renovation that gave each room a complete makeover. The larger rooms have fireplaces and even small kitchens with microwaves and refrigerators. All rooms have Internet access, coffeemakers, large bathrooms, irons/boards, in-room safes, fluffy bathrobes, triple sheets, and complimentary newspapers.

**THE RITZ-CARLTON,
AMELIA ISLAND** $$$–$$$$$
4750 Amelia Island Parkway, Amelia Island
(904) 277-1100, (800) 241-3333
www.ritzcarlton.com
It's hard to figure out just why this resort has such a good aura. Maybe it's the complimentary chocolate chip and oatmeal-raisin cookies waiting for guests at check in. Or maybe it's the wood-paneled lobby lounge overlooking the ocean, where guests naturally gravitate to chat, sip coffee, read the newspaper, or have a drink.

Whatever the reason, this 444-room property is pure AAA Five Diamond magic. The grounds have played host to presidents, vice presidents, and first ladies. It's the spot Jacksonville's elite choose for the occasional weekend getaway.

The Ritz is located about 30 minutes from Jacksonville International Airport and about 20 minutes from the quaint fishing village of Fernandina Beach. All rooms have ocean or coastal views, meaning that your room faces the ocean either directly or from an angle. (The coastal views are fine, and the rooms a bit less costly.) All rooms have private balconies. The large bathrooms are done in gray marble. Room amenities include luxurious 400-thread count, Egyptian cotton linens, iPod docking stations, plush robes, coffee and tea chests, European bath essentials, 37-inch flat screen TVs, Guest-Tek wireless service, twice-daily maid service, and, of course, 24-hour in-room dining.

Play golf and tennis, bob around in either the heated outdoor pool or the heated atrium pool, work out in the health and fitness center with a personal trainer, or indulge in a spa service. Kiddies need not be bored (or a buzz-kill), the children's pool and playground, nanny service, and the Ritz Kids day camp provide plenty of diversions to keep them occupied. The resort staff also has lots of fun putting together themed weekends and holiday activities. For instance, during the winter holidays the pastry chef creates a huge gingerbread house, big enough to walk into, for the hotel lobby, and the resort offers sleigh rides on Florida snow (a.k.a. the white sandy beach) complete with a bonfire and hot chocolate at the end of your sleigh ride. Don't miss the weekly Sunday brunch, which has been named "Best Brunch on the First Coast" by *Water's Edge* magazine.

i **If you didn't get a meal on your flight to Jacksonville, don't go hungry on your flight home. The Ritz-Carlton Amelia Island will provide a box lunch for you to take on-board with you.**

SAWGRASS MARRIOTT
RESORT & BEACH CLUB $$–$$$$$
1000 PGA Tour Blvd., Ponte Vedra Beach
(904) 285-7777, (800) 228-9290
www.marriotthotels.com/jaxsw

Just try to walk in the front door of the Sawgrass Marriott Resort and not feel bowled over by the lobby's sweeping view of the Players Championship Stadium Course. From the lagoon and a waterfall to the beach club, Sawgrass is one impressive property. The Sawgrass Marriott offers 508 rooms, including 24 suites and 80 two-bedroom villas. The resort is located in Ponte Vedra, just a five-minute drive away from both the Sawgrass Shopping Center's boutiques and restaurants and the Cabana Club, the resort's oceanfront, beach club oasis.

Golf opportunities abound here, thanks to the resort's cooperative marketing agreement with five area golf courses, including the Stadium Course. (The Marriott likes to boast that guests can play 99 holes of golf.) The resort also offers 11 tennis courts on four different surfaces; three outdoor pools, two heated; and two whirlpools. Active types will love the complimentary bicycles and the 24-hour access fitness center. (Don't be surprised when you get your bill; a resort fee is tacked on to every room to pay for these amenities, including the shuttle service to and from the Cabana Club and golf courses.)

On property, the Spa at Sawgrass offers a Zen atmosphere along with facials, massages, and hydrotherapy, which Mom can partake of while the kids are otherwise occupied in the year-round day camp for children called the Grasshopper Gang. Children ages 3 to 12 enjoy treasure hunts, beach and pool activities, arts and crafts, you name it, while Mom and Dad are off enjoying some free time. Don't miss the Sunday Jazz Brunch at the Cafe on the Green or dinner at the Augustine Grille. There's also a popular outdoor grille called the 100th Hole—the only place left to go after you've played all 99 holes of golf.

RESTAURANTS

You'd think that with its proximity to the ocean and river, Jacksonville would be a one-note-Johnny when it comes to restaurants, focusing only on seafood to the exclusion of international or contemporary cuisine. Well, think again! While that might have once been the case, the city's palates have collectively refined, and local restaurateurs have taken leaps to launch new intimate and experimental eateries resulting in happy local restaurant-goers and options galore.

Of course, locals remain spoiled when it comes to fresh seafood. With menu items ranging from boiled shrimp to sushi, Jacksonville's seafood menus brim with briny goodness. Whether you're headed to a backwater fish camp (a real Insider treat) or dining seaside, the area aims to please with fresh, plentiful offerings from the sea.

Plan your trip to coincide with one of the area's many seafood festivals and special events. The Isle of Eight Flags Shrimp Festival draws thousands to Fernandina Beach each spring, and the annual Kingfish Tournament, dedicated to attracting big-game anglers, is the largest of its kind in the country (see the Annual Events chapter to learn more about both).

If you prefer your dinner to come from the turf (rather than the surf), local barbecue restaurants like Mojo and Fred Cotten's serve up the slow-cooked variations of beef, pork, and chicken that made the South famous.

In short, you will not leave Jacksonville hungry.

This chapter offers not just some, but all of my Insider team's personal faves for any meal of the day. More necessarily than in any other chapter, the restaurant listings are organized by neighborhood so that you can eat close to where your activities take you, or plan your day based on maintaining proximity to a certain dish. Jacksonville is a city of neighborhoods, which you will quickly learn as you travel around town hunting down these foodie favorites.

If you're interested in really digging-in and eating like a lifetime local, see the Close-up later in this chapter and read what the locals claim as the city's quintessential food. Trust us; what you learn there may not be pretty, but it may be as close as you can get to the divine for under $7.

The skinny on reservations is simple: they're generally not necessary, unless the price point or size of the eatery would give you reason to think so. So, use your common sense and, when in doubt, call and check.

Best of all, dress is hip-casual at almost every Jacksonville restaurant, but, again, use common sense and call ahead of you have any questions.

If one of our favorite restaurants has multiple locations, you will find it listed under the location that we feel is the most visit-worthy, with the other locations listed under it.

Unless otherwise noted, all restaurants accept major credit cards. Most restaurants in Jacksonville are closed on Thanksgiving, Christmas, and New Year's Day, so if you want to dine out, call ahead and check. Sundays and Mondays tend to be a dead zone, especially with the smaller local eateries, so definitely check by phone before you head out.

Note: If a restaurant is open during the general lunch and dinner hours of 11 a.m. through 10 p.m., we simply state that the establishment is "open for lunch and dinner." However, if the restaurant keeps unusual hours, we will spell it out for you.

Price Code (per entree)

$ . . . . .Less than $6
$$ . . . .$7 to $12
$$$ . . . . $13 to $18
$$$$ . . . .$19 and over

RIVERSIDE/AVONDALE/ WESTSIDE

13 GYPSIES   **$-$$$**
887 Stockton St.
(904) 389-0330
www.13gypsies.com

Every time I even think about 13 Gypsies, I have to restrain myself from jumping in the car and racing over to sample whatever they've whipped up that morning. It's just that good. Every bit of the bread, sausage, cheese, pasta, cured meats, mayonnaise, and crème fraiche at this Spanish-inspired eatery is made fresh, every morning, by hand. Chef Howard's menu, ever-changing in its offerings, documents the migratory trail that the gypsies followed from India through Central Europe and into Northern Africa. Expect no fusion, no fuss—just good, clean, traditional flavors. Devotees know better than to show up unannounced—the restaurant only seats 14 inside and four outside, so the spots are heartily sought after, and the savory fare on the tapas menu ensures that tables are hard to come by. Items do run out, so an early-evening reservation is best to ensure that you have your choice from the full menu. Call by Tuesday morning if you want a weekend reservation. Open Tuesday through Thursday from 11 a.m. to 2 p.m. for lunch, and from 5 to 9 p.m. for dinner. Open Friday and Saturday from 11 a.m. to 2 p.m. for lunch, and from 5 to 10 p.m. for dinner. Sunday brunch is served from 11 a.m. to 2 p.m.

BISCOTTI'S   **$$$**
3556 St. Johns Ave.
(904) 387-2060
www.biscottis.net

Famous around town for their bruschetta, a thick log of crusty bread sliced and stuffed with mozzarella and topped with seasoned tomatoes and

Love Note to a Fish Camp

Dear Whitey's,

It's been too long since we've seen each other, but I can still taste your catfish and smell the brackish-tinged air rolling off the river.

I remember the day we met in 1963, when you were just a tackle shop with nine bar stools and a toaster oven. Then in 1969, when you turned that old storage room into a dining room and remodeled the bait-tank room into a kitchen, we Insiders thought we'd died and gone to fish-camp heaven. But it wasn't until 1988, when you built your new deck and restaurant that I realized that we would be together forever.

So, when that fire gutted you (no pun intended) in 2002 destroying everything but your deck, I wept...we all did...and vowed to wait for your return. It was a long year, but we stayed faithful. And while we may have dated other fish camps while you were gone, you were always on our minds.

So, thanks for coming back and for sticking around for 47 years. I'm one lucky local!

Love,
An Anonymous Insider

Whitey's Fish Camp is located on Doctor's Lake, 2032 County Rd. 220, Orange Park. (904) 269-4198. Visit www.whiteysfishcamp.com to start a love affair of your own.

🔍 Close-up

Official Food: The Lubi

Key West has its Key lime pie. Boston has its baked beans. Even tiny Brunswick, Georgia, has its Brunswick stew. So what's the official food of Jacksonville?

After much thought and debate, most locals agree that the quintessential Jacksonville food is the **Mozzarella Lubi**—an open-faced, fast food sandwich that's been sold only in Jacksonville by the extended family of founders Lu and Bill (combined to form the name Lubi) for the last 40 years.

"It's a steaming sandwich of ground sirloin, mustard, mayonnaise, sour cream, pepper sauce, and cheese that's so gooey you have to eat it with a knife and fork," says Dan Macdonald, longtime food editor for the *Florida Times–Union*.

It's fair to say that some Jacksonville residents can't imagine a life without these sloppy sandwiches. "Sometimes I just get this craving for one," said Linda Stout, an Atlantic Beach resident and Lubi lover who always orders her Lubi with one of the store's popular Cherry Limeades.

Anyone who's every ordered the combo knows that **Lubi's Cherry Limeade** deserves its own paragraph. Hardly limeade in the traditional sense—in fact, the only nod to the lime in the whole cup may be the red-stained lime quarter hovering toward the bottom—the magical interaction of this sugary-sweet cherry drink with the sandwich's tomato sauce and cheesy blanket verges on a perfect marriage.

The Lubi (along with many variations on the theme) is made right in front of you and sold counter-style, a process which is best experienced at the original Lubi's location housed in a scrappy stand-alone building on University Boulevard West.

Here's how the Mozzarella Lubi is constructed (and this is not for the calorie-conscious or taste-timid): a heaping spoonful of seasoned, fresh-ground sirloin (which is never frozen—the first key to a successful Lubi) is layered, along with tomato sauce, mayonnaise, mustard, mozzarella cheese, and a variety of spicy toppings, including the restaurant's own homemade pepper sauce, on top of an open-faced hotdog-style bun, then wrapped in foil and thrown into a microwave just long enough to melt the cheese. (Don't bother asking how they are able to put metal in a microwave; all you'll get in return is an eye roll from the counter help. Locals accept this as a necessary mystery and know not to ask.)

A Lubi comes in several varieties: the Original Famous Lubi, the Mozzarella Lubi, the Chili Lubi, the Stroganoff Lubi, the Mean Machine, and the Fiesta Lubi, which have all kept Lubi lovers returning since the late 1960s.

(In the interest of disclosure, the author must admit a long-standing addiction to the Mozzarella Lubi, a concoction that has gotten her through many a long day or trying ordeal, with her personal favorite storefront being the original location at the intersection of University Boulevard West and Old St. Augustine Road. It's not pretty or fancy, and the ladies room is often on the blink, but the staff makes one gut-busting sandwich.)

pine nuts, this exposed-brick bistro is as perfect for a Tuesday evening hang with friends as it is for a Saturday night first date. The epitome of laid-back cool, Biscotti's sits smack in the middle of Avondale's shopping district but draws fans from all over town. Biscotti's pasta, beef, and fish specials hit culinary heights thanks to fresh spices and generous portions, but don't overlook the humble, yet not-to-be-missed day-to-day fare like their famous meatloaf sandwich and eclectic salads. At the end of your meal, prepare to be overwhelmed by the dozens of desserts on display by the front door. Biscotti's is perfect for large parties, but call ahead to give the hostess the heads-up. Open for lunch and dinner Monday through Friday. On Saturday Biscotti's is open from 8 a.m. to midnight; Sunday 8 a.m. to 9 p.m. Brunch is served until 3 p.m. on Saturday and Sunday.

BOLD CITY BREWERY AND
TAP ROOM $–$$$$
2670-7 Rosselle St.
(904) 379-6551
www.boldcitybrewery.com
Presently open three days a week and closed for brewing the other four, Bold City Brewery and Tap Room is making a splash in the Jacksonville microbrewing scene. For now, Bold City is making only ales, IPAs and English ales to be precise, and their plan is to brew 12 different beers—from hoppy to malty—throughout the year. Because it licensed as a micro-brewery, Bold City cannot serve food, but has worked out a catering agreement so that visitors to the Tap Room can have something to nosh on while they drink. Tours of the brewhouse run on the hour, Saturday from 2 to 5 p.m. The Tap Room is open Thursday and Friday from 3 p.m. to close, and Saturday from 1 p.m. to close.

THE BRICK $$–$$$$
3585 St. Johns Ave.
(904) 387-0606
www.thebrickrestaurant.com
The Brick's casual-chic demeanor, street-side outdoor seating, exposed brick, and impressive pieces by local artists fit well with general mien of the Shops of Historic Avondale. Come on a night when this corner restaurant brings in live music, but don't expect to be able to talk over it, even if the bands play at normal levels the exposed brick renders the restaurant quite noisy. Still, the solid menu (think Portobello mushroom sandwich and crab cakes), solid wine list, and skilled bartenders have made The Brick a Jacksonville staple among those in the know. Come for Sunday brunch when the bar serves up spicy Bloody Marys. Open for lunch and dinner seven days a week. The Brick accepts reservations, which are a good idea, especially on weekends.

CASBAH CAFE $$–$$$
3628 St. Johns Ave.
(904) 981-9966
www.thecasbahcafe.com
Casbah Cafe serves Middle Eastern and Mediterranean cuisine. Customers enjoy the falafel, the lamb kabobs, and the Casbah pizzas, not to mention the selection of desserts and pastries. Dine indoors or outdoors on the garden patio. Ask to sit on the floor poufs (think ottoman or bean bag) and eat at the low tables in the hookah lounge. The cafe serves African coffees and has a global beer and wine selection. Belly dancers perform Thursday through Saturday nights. For something different, try the hookah pipes—3-foot ornate Middle Eastern water pipes meant for smoking flavored tobacco. For even more on the restaurant's offerings, look for Casbah in the Nightlife chapter. Children's choices are available. Open every day from 11 a.m. to 2 a.m.

COZY TEA ROOM $$–$$$
1029 Park St.
(904) 329-3964
www.cozytea.wordpress.com
I learned about the Cozy Tea Room after my most trusted Insider pals has gone there for one of the tea room's monthly, multi-course, Indian dinners. The dinners coincide with 5 Points' First Fridays (first Friday of every month) and are so popular that they are booked solid months in advance. Day to day, the 10-table teahouse has an afternoon tea menu, a chocolate truffle menu, and proper English scones. Based on the idea of a proper English tea room, the kind that owner Shika Patel has missed ever since leaving the England of her youth, the shop is cozy, intimate, and perfect for a date, girlfriend gathering, or afternoon unwind.

THE DERBY HOUSE $$–$$$
1068 Park St.
(904) 356-0227
Insiders know that The Derby House (technically Georgi's Derby House) is the best place in 5 Points to nurse a hangover. Open since 1944, this is the greasy spoon your parents warned you

about: it's cheap, salty, and delightfully off the radar, even though it sits in the heart of 5 Points. Now this corner joint has started hosting music on Friday nights, and we hear there's beer.

DREAMETTE $
3646 Post St.
(904) 388-2558
There's a reason why the Dreamette has over 5,000 Facebook fans. The die-hard local devotion that nearly every Insider feels to this ice-cream shack knows no bounds. Located in Murray Hill, Dreamette has been serving the same soft-serve menu from their front window since 1948. The main draw is the soft serve ice cream, which you order at the walk-up window. Dreamette staff will also make you a sundae, milkshake, banana split, or float. Plop down at one of the picnic benches around the side and lick away. The general rule seems to be that they close at sunset, year-round.

EUROPEAN STREET RESTAURANT $$-$$$
2753 Park St.
(904) 384-9999
1704 San Marco Blvd.
(904) 398-9500
922 Beach Blvd.
(904) 249-3001
5500 Beach Blvd. (near University Boulevard)
(904) 398-1717
www.europeanstcafe.com
The San Marco location and the Riverside locationboth draw happy bands of locals with their massive selection of brews on tap and in bottles—20 drafts and more than 130 bottles, to be exact. European Street features a daily happy hour from 2 to 7 p.m. with two-for-one specials on all beer and wine. The term "happy hour" fits well, because when the place is packed and the beer is flowing, it's hard to spot a frowner in the house. The Listening Room in the San Marco location draws local and regional bands to its tiny stage every Thursday. All locations are open daily from 10 a.m. to 10 p.m., except for the 5500 Beach Blvd. location, which closes at 9 p.m.

FOX RESTAURANT $-$$
3580 Saint Johns Ave.
(904) 387-2669
Locals know this as the hole-in-the-wall that gives greasy spoons a good name. From the horse-and-hound-themed hodge-podge gallery on the walls to the vinyl booths, The Fox certainly isn't wasting money on decor, but instead is turning its attention toward keeping locals happy with breakfast staples. Don't feel deterred by the line out the door on weekend mornings, tables tend to turn quickly as folks pack up and head for the city's various farmers' markets and art fairs. This is almost every Insider's go-to place because it's as good for celebrating a new romance as it is for soothing a hangover.

LET THEM EAT CAKE $-$$
3604 St. Johns Ave.
(904) 389-2122
www.asweetbakery.com
This tiny storefront hits a high note in Jacksonville's boutique bakery scene. The small case is filled with macaroons, peanut-butter sandwich cookies, and artfully frosted cupcakes with real buttercream icing. In perfect indie form, the owner also runs a Let Them Eat Cupcakes Truck, the first sweets truck in Jacksonville, which shows up Downtown on Wednesdays and sells the bakery's cupcakes, cookies, brownies, and cold drinks street-style.

MOON RIVER PIZZA $-$$$$
1176 Edgewood Ave. South # 2
(904) 389-4442
www.moonriverpizza.net
Hand-tossed, yummy pies and a very hip staff make this Murray Hill pizza joint one for the books. This slightly alternative pizza joint wins high praise for their specialty pizzas, like the Maui "WOW"ee and the meaty, cheesy T-Rex, and for the kitchen's ability to turn out consistently good pies with mounds of fresh ingredients. Open Monday through Saturday from 11 a.m. to 10 p.m. Closed Sunday.

MOSSFIRE GRILL $$-$$$
1537 Margaret St.
(904) 355-4434
www.mossfire.com

The Mossfire Grill serves made-to-order South-western cuisine in a friendly, casual atmosphere. Hearty selections from the munchies list include spinach con queso, chicken tortilla soup, and a fresh veggie quesadilla. The large burritos, tacos, and salads top our list of faves. Dinner entrees include tuna and other fresh fish, grilled salmon, pork loin, homemade crab cakes, and nightly specials. For dessert try the peanut butter pie, Key lime pie, or another homemade dessert. Beer and wine are served, and there's a daily happy hour. Open for lunch and dinner seven days a week. Children's menu is available.

ORSAY $$-$$$$
3630 Park St.
(904) 381-0909
www.restaurantorsay.com

If it's possible to fall in love with a mixed drink, Orsay's pear-jalapeño margarita is poised to do the seducing. Whether served on the lounging couches off the bar area, alongside items from the house-made charcuterie, or as an accompaniment to the Plateaux Grand from the Raw Bar, the drink wins Orsay's mixologists serious points for creativity. Try Orsay for an intimate birthday gathering, a chic happy hour with friends, or a first date. The restaurant is best suited to adult couples and friends, not so much for children. Open 4 p.m. to 11 p.m. Tuesday through Thursday. Friday and Saturday the restaurant stays open until midnight. Sunday brunch is served from 11 a.m. to 4 p.m. Orsay is closed on Monday.

PASTICHE $$$-$$$$
4260 Herschel St.
(904) 387-6213
www.mypastiche.com

For "Southern comfort with a French flair," Pastiche tips its hat to French and Mediterranean cuisine with seasonal menus and high-quality ingredients. The selections on the wine list hail from America, France, Italy, South America, Australia, and New Zealand. Think sweet potato fries, pickled beet and goat-cheese salad, and tandoori-style salmon. Open for lunch Tuesday through Saturday and dinner Wednesday through Saturday.

THE PIG BBQ $-$$
5456 Normandy Blvd.
(904) 783-1606

It ain't pretty, but The Pig makes some of the best damn BBQ in the city. Insiders tout it as the best hole-in-the-wall you'll ever find, and a few locals even claim to know The Pig's secret sauce recipe. If they're right, it's made from white vinegar, salt, mustard (the wet yellow kind), chili powder, thyme, and black pepper in equal proportions. Or just come in and try it for yourself. The BBQ is so good that locals are willing to forgive the less-than-tony location.

POTTER'S HOUSE SOUL
FOOD BISTRO $-$$
5310 Lenox Ave.
(904) 394-0860

There is not enough hyperbole that can be tossed around about The Soul Food Bistro. This cafeteria-style restaurant, which serves up fried chicken, collards, and oxtail (yes, oxtail) cafeteria-style, tops any real Insider's list of go-to places. Tucked just inside the revamped Normandy Village Shopping Center, the bistro suffers a bit from a scrappy neighborhood, but the food is so gobsmackingly good that you won't care. Better yet, Potter's honors anyone over 55 with a 30 percent discount all day, every day. The bistro, along with everything in the complex, which includes a gym, bowling alley, and jazz series, is owned by The Potter's House Church. As a result, what was once a run-down shell of an old mall has been reborn with candied yams, real macaroni and cheese, and a serious commitment to doing it right. Open 10:30 a.m. to 8 p.m. Tuesday through Thursday; 10:30 a.m. to 6 p.m. Friday, Saturday, and Sunday. Closed Monday.

WHITEY'S FISH CAMP $$-$$$$
2032 County Rd. 220, Orange Park
(904) 269-4198
www.whiteysfishcamp.com

(Q) Close-up

Sweet Ride

Keep an eye peeled Downtown on Wednesdays for the turquoise **Let Them Eat Cupcakes Truck.** Usually parked in front of the Bank of America building, this bakery-on-wheels carries a full load of buttercream-iced cupcakes, brownies, and peanut-butter sandwich cookies.

The truck, most recognizable by the giant cupcake bolted to its roof, is the love child of **Anita Adams,** long-time owner of **Let Them Eat Cake** in Avondale. Inspired by traveling sweets trucks, like the crazy-popular Treats Truck in New York City, Adams' Let Them Eat Cupcakes truck is on its way to developing a rabid Jacksonville following. In addition to its Wednesday sweets-fests, the truck parks and vends at every Wednesday Art Walk Downtown and in Five Points during First Fridays celebrations—a good thing for those of us who don't work Downtown.

People love the truck, says Adams, especially parents who say that it reminds them of their childhoods.

Unfortunately, the road to mobile retail hasn't been as smooth as Adams had hoped. Her original plan to park the vehicle in metered street parking during lunch hour was nixed thanks to a restrictive city code, so, at the time of publication, Adams was on the hunt for a friendly Downtown business willing to let the Let Them Eat Cupcakes Truck ply from its parking lot.

I can't imagine it's too hard of a sell. I mean, come on...consider the perks!

To find out where the truck is parked this week, visit the truck's Facebook page "Let Them Eat Cupcakes! . . .It's the cupcake truck!" at www.tinyurl.com/JaxCupcakeTruck or call (904) 389-2122. Let Them Eat Cake's bakery and storefront is located at 3604 St. Johns Ave. in The Shops of Avondale.

In the words of my favorite raised-at-the-beach Insider, "Whether you drive up to Whitey's or paddle up to Whitey's, prepare for overflowing plates and fulsome local hospitality at this fish camp. Their riverfront dining room and covered outside tables offer a great way to take a break from the sun or to wait out an afternoon storm before you get back on the water." Thanks, Anna! I couldn't have said it better myself. See the Love Letter to a Fish Camp sidebar in this section to understand the full extent of our devotion.

DOWNTOWN/SPRINGFIELD

BILLY C'S FRED COTTEN BAR-B-Q $$
2623 North Main St.
(904) 356-8274
www.fredcottenbbq.com
For some of the best barbecue in Jacksonville, Billy C's Fred Cotton Bar-B-Q is worth the trip. Located in a small, smoky storefront on Main Street, just north of Downtown proper, Fred Cotten's has

been serving the city's decision makers and construction workers alike for more than 60 years. It's not unusual to see a mayor or former mayor munching on a pork rib sandwich, while a crew of utility workers sits at the next table. Open Monday through Thursday 10 a.m. to 3:30 p.m.; Friday and Saturday from 10 a.m. to 8:30 p.m. Closed Sunday.

BURRITO GALLERY $–$$
21 East Adams St.
(904) 598-2922
www.burritogallery.com
"Local artwork and burritos. How can you go wrong?" says Jacksonville community affairs Insider Jennifer Chapman who frequents this Mexican hole-in-the-wall when business takes her across the Main Street Bridge. Busy-busy-busy at traditional lunchtimes, this Mexican eatery caters to the Downtown business crowd but is a fairly easy destination for folks coming from the Southbank, Riverside, or Avondale. Take advantage of the patio out back and spend some time checking out the

Close-up

The Westside's One-Two Comfort-Food Punch

By this point you've probably figured out that we Insiders love to eat. We know food the way a duck knows down. It's a part of us, even if it's not visible to the naked eye. So trust us when we say that when it comes to comfort food, the kind that grabs you, grounds you, and puts your heart at peace, there's no more winning combo than **The Potter's House Soul Food Bistro** followed by a trip to **Dreamette.**

The Soul Food Bistro is everything a soul-food joint should be. Owned by The Potter's House Church, the bistro's food is murderously good. The Southern-style collards, candied yams, and fried cabbage are obsession-worthy on their own, but it's the fried chicken that draws the big crowds. This fried chicken is the absolute, hands-down, no-reservations, best all-around fried chicken in Jacksonville. The pieces are meaty and the seasoning's spiciness sneaks up on you from the back end and hangs around for a while.

But the bistro pulls out the big guns with a macaroni and cheese that's so full of love and warmth that each bite makes you feel like you've been hugged by a large woman with a really big bosom. Imagine fat macaroni noodles baked in white cheese with a full layer of slightly browned cheese on top. (I have a fantasy about what's going on behind the kitchen doors, and it involves a 60-year-old lady of the church, a mountain of Muenster, and a secret

art while you're in line, but don't get too distracted as the line moves fast. The restaurant is open from 11 a.m. to 3 p.m. on Monday, and from 11 a.m. to 10 p.m. every other day. Closed Sunday.

CAFE NOLA $$–$$$$
33 North Laura St.
(904) 366-6911, ext.231
www.mocajacksonville.org/cafe
Word has it from the crowd of local politicos and up-and-comers crowding the café that the *haricot verts* is the best appetizer on the menu. This eatery, located in the lobby of the Museum of Contemporary Art on Hemming Plaza, draws a who's-who of Downtown movers and shakers with homemade soups, salads, and sandwiches. It's the ideal place to schedule a lunch with clients or get a bite after viewing the museum's excellent collection of contemporary art. Open Monday through Friday from 11 a.m. to 2:30 p.m. for lunch and on Thursday from 5 to 9 p.m. for dinner. Café Nola also opens for dinner during First Wednesday Art Walks. Reservations suggested.

CHEW $$–$$$$
117 W Adams St.
(904) 355-3793
www.chewrestaurant.com
Stop by Chew for a little bit of hipness on Adams Street. Often recommended as a great first-date spot, the restaurant makes good on their claim to offer attentive service, thoughtful surroundings, and great food at reasonable prices. Ingredients, when possible, are made in-house or sourced locally. For a real taste treat, try the Black Mission Prosciutto salad or the Short Rib Sliders. Open for lunch weekdays from 10 a.m. to 3 p.m. and for dinner Thursday and Friday from 5:30 to 9:30 p.m. Closed Saturday and Sunday.

DE REAL TING CAFE $$
128 West Adams St.
(904) 633-9738
6850 Arlington Expressway
(904) 466-9777
This super-Insider Caribbean restaurant serves island specialties like jerk or curried chicken, jerk

recipe.) The fact that the ladies on the line serve it using an ice-cream scoop makes me love it all the more.

Punch number-two comes from just down the street at a tiny neighborhood ice-cream shack called Dreamette, which has held the same spot in the Murray Hill section of Westside since 1948. Just one soft serve from this unassuming, blue-and-white, walk-up stand will make you a fan for life (for proof, just check out the numbers on their Facebook page).

Here's the drill: park, walk up to the window, order (we suggest the dipped cones or the butterscotch sundae made with real, caramelized butterscotch), then take it over to the picnic tables and dig in. There is nothing fancy, refined, or foodie about Dreamette, and that's why we love it so.

One of their fans said it best: "I have been going to the Dreamette since I was a very young girl. My grandmother and I would go there every weekend. She would get herself a banana split, and I would get a chocolate dipped ice cream cone. Not only do they have the best ice cream on the planet (especially on a hot Florida day) but they also create memories to last a lifetime! Thanks, Dreamette."

Thanks, indeed!

Addresses and hours for both The Soul Food Bistro and Dreamette are located in this chapter.

shrimp, conch fritters, Jamaican patties, steamed red snapper, and roasted fish. For something different, try the yummy curried goat. The menu also lists oxtail, but I have yet to find someone who has given it a try. The Arlington Expressway location serves a daily lunch special and several vegetarian dishes, as well as beer and wine, and is open Tuesday through Thursday from 11 a.m. to 7 p.m.; on Friday from 11 a.m. to 11 p.m.; and on Saturday from noon to 8 p.m. The West Adams Street location has a full bar but is only open Thursday through Saturday from 9 p.m. to 2 a.m. when rumor has it the owner sometimes brings in live jazz. Both locations are closed Sunday and Monday.

LA CENA $$$–$$$$
212 North Laura St.
(904) 633-9255

La Cena's Italian fine dining has attracted some of the city's heavy hitters for over 26 years. Owner Jerry Moran, a native of Long Island, New York, who worked in a number of New York City restaurants before heading south, specializes in homemade egg pasta. Joining him in the kitchen is Wilfried Hausey (former chef and owner of 24 Miramar). Between them, these two chefs have over 80 years of experience. For better or worse, the shellfish used to make the linguine alla vongale is shipped in from the upper East Coast. The wine list includes around 140 different choices with an exceptional assortment of excellent Italian wines. La Cena's dining room only seats about 80, so reservations are a must. Most of the tables turn over just once each night. "We take solid reservations," Moran says. "A table will be waiting for you when you arrive, and it's yours for the night." Dinner is served Tuesday through Saturday from 5 p.m. until late. The restaurant is available for private events seven days a week.

THE LONDON BRIDGE ENGLISH
PUB AND EATERY $$
100 East Adams St.
(904) 359-0001
www.londonbridgepubjax.com

The London Bridge is a welcome addition to the Downtown dining and drinking scene. Opened in 2002 in the heart of Jacksonville's business district, the London Bridge pub is a favorite after-work haunt of the city's young professionals. The restaurant serves classic British pub food such as bangers and mash, fish-and-chips, cottage pie, and Scottish eggs, and the beer list includes over 50 varieties. London Bridge serves lunch and dinner daily and hosts live music every Monday, Friday, and Saturday. Every second and fourth Wednesday nights are karaoke nights; Thursday is Open Mic night. Open Monday through Saturday at 10 a.m. Lunch is served until 2 p.m. Dinner service starts at 5 p.m. The bar closes when the crowd thins, usually sometime between 9 p.m. and 2 a.m. London Bridge is only open on Sunday when the Jags are playing a home game.

UPTOWN MARKET – SPRINGFIELD $$
1303 North Main St. (at 3rd Street)
(904) 355-0734
www.uptownmarket.tumblr.com
Historic Springfield just got even more hip with the Uptown Market, a delicious destination for breakfast. Think poached eggs with Applewood smoked bacon, spinach and artichoke frittatas, and thick slabs of French toast dipped in their own vanilla batter. Need I say more? Open every day for breakfast and lunch.

SAN MARCO/LAKEWOOD/ SOUTHBANK

BB's $$$
1019 Hendricks Ave.
(904) 306-0100
www.bbsrestaurant.com
Local favorite bb's offers chic dining and exceptional food—especially the popular bruschetta, a length of baguette sliced and stuffed with mozzarella, baked in olive oil and garlic, and smothered in tomatoes and pine nuts. (*NOTE:* No, you're not having déjà vu; this bruschetta is the same as the one at Biscotti's. Both restaurants are operated by the same owners.) Other Insider favorites include the rock shrimp salad, the polenta sticks,

and the artisan cheese plate served with Medjool dates, dried apricots and bananas, candied walnuts, fresh honeycomb, and slices of toasted baguette. Finish with one of their gobsmacking desserts and a frothy cappuccino. The small, full bar is a popular spot for a quick bite or after-work socializing. A separate counter handles take-out orders. Open for lunch and dinner Monday through Saturday. Closed Sunday.

BEACH ROAD CHICKEN DINNERS $$–$$$
4132 Atlantic Blvd.
(904) 398-7980
www.beachroadchickendinners.com
Since 1939, this converted clapboard house on a scrappy length of Atlantic Boulevard has earned multi-generational devotion from both the after-church set and staunch foodies. Think family-style bowls of creamed peas and heaping platters of Southern-fried chicken accompanied by two-handed glasses of sweet tea, slaw, and biscuits. Come see why *Southern Living* named this the "Best Fried Chicken in the South" in 1999 and why they made the 2009 Florida Dining Hall of Fame in the September 2009 issue of *Jacksonville Magazine*. Nothing's changed before or since—and that's a really good thing. Open for takeout from 11 a.m. The dining room opens at 4 p.m. Tuesday through Saturday, and at 11 a.m. on Sunday. Closing times vary, but generally hover around 8 p.m. or until the dining room empties. Closed on Monday.

BISTRO AIX $$$–$$$$
1440 San Marco Blvd.
(904) 398-1949
www.bistrox.com
Modeled after a French bistro, Bistro Aix is dark and cozy. The food contains mostly Provençal and Mediterranean dishes like artisan breads, hummus, grilled pizzas, risottos, and roasted chicken with garlic. Try the roasted tomato soup, the grilled lamb sirloin on a chickpea puree, or the grilled tuna over whipped potatoes with baby spinach, lemon-garlic butter, and chive oil. Bistro Aix's wood-fired oven produces tasty, inventive pizzas.

Stop by Aix's Onyx Bar for L'Heure du Cocktail happy hour weekdays from 4 to 7 p.m. The bar-

What makes Sweet Tea so different?

Northerners be advised: **Sweet Tea** is not the same as sweetened iced-tea (and many is the Southerner who vacations north or west only to be sadly disappointed by iced tea that arrives at the table with sugar settled at the bottom).

Sweet Tea, so sweet that it is almost an acquired taste, can be made in a number of ways. The easiest way is to place 6-8 teabags in a gallon jar or pitcher with 1-2 cups of sugar. Pour 4 cups of boiling water over the sugar and tea bags and stir until the sugar dissolves. Let the brew steep to your desired strength (some say 6 minutes, some say 20, some say an hour), then fish out the tea bags (without squeezing them) and add another 4 cups of cold water and ice. (Tip: Many Southern gals also use a pinch of baking soda as a secret ingredient to cut any bitterness in the tea.)

Recipes vary, but as any Southerner will tell you (and Jacksonville, although technically in Florida, has deep Southern roots and traditions) no grainy impostor will ever take its place.

And of that, we are proud.

tenders produce a good martini and offer selections from an international wine list (250 selections available by the bottle and 50 by the glass), tap beers, and bottled microbrews. The dining room features original 1940s brickwork, a curved marble-and-copper "chef's bar," and an exhibition kitchen. Outdoors, the garden patio dining can be pleasant when weather permits. The Aixpress Market offers desserts and specialty drinks, and the restaurant has adjacent private dining and conference facilities. Be advised that the best parking is behind the restaurant on Philips Street. Open for lunch and dinner Monday through Thursday and for dinner only on Saturday and Sunday.

THE FRENCH PANTRY $$
6301 Powers Ave.
(904) 730-8696
Bucking the notion that location has anything to do with popularity, The French Pantry is so sought after for lunch that devotees are known to plan their afternoons to avoid the peak. Plunked down in the center of an industrial area, the eatery specializes in crusty bread and sandwiches made from dreamy combinations of international cheeses and gourmet meats. Widely touted as "the best lunch in Jacksonville," the shop is only open on weekdays, and only from 8:30 a.m. to 2:30 p.m., so plan your visit wisely. Community seating is the rule, so expect to wait your turn and share a table. Do yourself a favor and make sure there's and extra notch on your belt as the sandwiches are huge.

HALA CAFÉ & BAKERY
4323 University Blvd. South
(904) 733-1855
9735 Old Saint Augustine Rd.
(904) 288-8890
www.halafoods.com
The go-to place for all things Middle Eastern, Hala Café and the adjacent store on University Boulevard South serve up hummus, tabouli, and lamb shank to die for. The lunch buffet provides great value with a steaming array of hot items and a fresh complement of cold salads, all made fresh daily. What the locations lack in ambience they more than make up for in taste and authenticity. Call ahead or drop in for take-out orders. Open for lunch and dinner. The retail store, which stocks not only foods but also other regional items like hookahs and Middle-Eastern drums, is worth a visit just for the experience. Both restaurants are open Monday through Saturday from 10 a.m. to 9 p.m.; the adjacent retail store (University Boulevard only) is open seven days a week from 9 a.m. to 9 p.m.

HAVANA-JAX AND CUBA LIBRE BAR $$
2578 Atlantic Blvd.
(904) 399-0609
www.havanajax.com

If you find yourself hankering for a Cuban sandwich or arroz con pollo, this try this Latin-influenced restaurant at the intersection of Beach and Atlantic Boulevards. Owner Silvia Pulido serves up authentic Cuban dishes such as a signature paella that inspires a hearty word-of-mouth following. The menu also includes chicken, steak, roast pork, and seafood dishes served with rice, black beans, and plantains. This is the place to come for Cuban pastries and Café Cubano. Beer, wine, and spirits are served along with tropical milkshakes. Lunch orders can be phoned or faxed in. Fine cigars are available for purchase, but must be enjoyed after you leave the restaurant. Havana-Jax is open for lunch and dinner Monday through Saturday. The adjoining Cuba Libre Bar offers Latin music, a dance floor, a large-screen projection television, leather couches, and exotic drinks native to the Caribbean. The club stays open late on weekends.

LA NOPALERA MEXICANO RESTAURANT $$
1629 Hendricks Ave.
(904) 399-1768

The food and service are consistently good at this family-owned-and-operated Mexican restaurant. The no-nonsense waitstaff keeps the chips and salsa coming and the portions are large and satisfyingly sloppy. Think traditional Mexican dishes such as tamales, fajitas, and pork tacos, or combos like La Favorite, as well as daily specials. For dessert order up some flan or share an order of sopapillas. Try a house margarita. Or just stick with beer or soda. There are other locations around town, but the Hendricks Avenue location is the hands-down favorite. Open for lunch and dinner seven days a week.

THE LOOP PIZZA GRILL $$
2014 San Marco Blvd.
(904) 399-5667
www.looppizzagrill.com

It goes against our policy to list a large chain (there are 26 locations to date), but if you're craving a burger, the original Loop, located on the San Marco Square since 1981, is the one to go to. Combining the convenience of a fast-food restaurant with the individual attention and quality of a restaurant, The Loop provides a hassle-free good time. The Loop remains consistent in serving quality food at reasonable prices. Try the charbroiled Loop burger, the original Chicago-style pizza, or the thin-crust pizza with one of the Loop's soups or salads. Leave room for a hand-scooped milk shake or brownie sundae. Beer and wine are served. Noisy and amenable to kids, The Loop is open for lunch and dinner daily.

LUBI'S $-$$
2940 University Blvd.
(904) 733-3734
3930 Sunbeam Rd.
(904) 260-6100
11633 Beach Blvd.
(904) 642-3800
500 N 3rd St. (A1A)
Jacksonville Beach
(904) 270-1007
www.lubis.com

As we noted in the earlier Close-up, the Mozzarella Lubi is a dearly loved Jacksonville specialty that defies categorization. Part Sloppy Joe, part who-knows-what, the Lubi is an aluminum-foil wrapped mish-mash of seasoned ground beef, tomato sauce, condiments, and cheese that inspires widespread devotion and crosses boundaries of race and class. Best eaten with a fork and knife, the Lubi is a true Insider winner. Sure, there are other options on the menu, but why bother when the namesake is this good? All four are open for lunch and dinner, but with slightly different hours. The Sunbeam location is the only one open on Sunday.

MATTHEW'S RESTAURANT $$$$
2107 Hendricks Ave.
(904) 396-9922
www.matthewsrestaurant.com

A long-standing four-diamond, four-star restaurant winner, Matthew's, headed up by chef/owner Matthew Medure, continues to collect accolades. The restaurant consistently garners top ranking from publications like *Florida Trend* and *Folio Weekly*. Consider ordering the chef's tasting menu, which pairs each course with an appropriate wine. Matthew's extensive wine list contains more than 2,000 bottles housed in the newly designed wine cellar. This is a higher-end establishment, so be sure to dress smartly in no less than business-casual attire. Open for dinner Monday through Saturday. Reservations are recommended.

METRO DINER
3302 Hendricks Ave.
(904) 398-3701
www.metrodinerjax.com

The line out the door says more than any review ever could. The Metro Diner is a Jacksonville staple with a stick-to-your ribs menu and a come-as-you-are atmosphere. While it can be a little pricey for eggs, the parking leaves a lot to be desired, and the coffee is just plain coffee, the ambiance and food make up for the inadequacies. You'll probably have to wait a bit to get a seat, but the people-watching is part of the fun. Use the time to peruse the menu—we suggest the creamed chipped beef on toast or the omelette of the day. Neither option ever disappoints. The Metro is super-noisy, so it's popular with families, and the kids love heading to the back patio to check out the face carved into the tree. Open for breakfast and lunch seven days a week from 7:30 a.m. to 2:30 p.m.

MOJO BAR-B-QUE–
A SOUTHERN BLUES KITCHEN $$–$$$
1607 University Blvd. West
(904) 732-7200
www.mojobbq.com

Possessing, quite possibly, the highest taste-per-bite ratio of all of the city's barbecue establishments, the Lakewood-based Mojo Bar-B-Que infuses every plate of ribs, brisket, and chicken with an eye-rolling Mojo spin that has to be tasted to be appreciated. Think Southern classic cooking with blues themes resulting in gobsmacking specialties served in a laid back, down-home, one-of-a-kind atmosphere. From the folk art paying homage to blues legends on the walls to the fast, friendly service, Mojo caters to the local obsession with barbecue in a way that keeps the place packed at peak mealtimes. Come a little early or be prepared for a modest wait. The staff wins extra points for friendliness, so don't be bashful about asking for a to-go cup for your drink (preferably sweet tea). Why? Because when you do so, the server doesn't just return with just a cup; the server returns with a full cup of whatever it is you were drinking. Good old Southern hospitality! Be sure to read about Mojo Kitchen BBQ Pit and Blues Bar in the Beaches restaurant section. That location has all the same food, plus a full bar and live music.

MORTON'S, THE STEAKHOUSE $$$$
1510 Riverplace Blvd.
(904) 399-3933
www.mortons.com/jacksonville

While pricey, and part of a national chain, Morton's remains a great choice for expertly prepared classics as filet mignon, rib lamb chops, and whole baked Maine lobster. The vegetables are fresh, and the portions are generous, so come hungry. The extensive wine list complements the selection of beef and seafood dishes that have made Morton's famous. For dessert, don't miss the Godiva Hot Chocolate Cake—chocolate cake topped with fresh raspberries and vanilla ice cream. Open seven days a week after 5 p.m.

PIZZA PALACE $–$$$
1959 San Marco Blvd.
(904) 399-8815
www.pizzapalacejax.com

Looking for a low-budget treat? Try an evening at the sidewalk tables of this San Marco landmark. Order a pitcher of beer and watch the world go by. The sidewalk tables are a popular dinner destination for locals with pets, so expect to see a furry friend or two under the next table. Start with a Greek salad and follow with a hand-tossed pie or calzone. The place is supremely family-friendly, which can also lead to the inside being noisy. But

Slow cooked staples

Hands-down, barbecue is the people's choice when it comes to eating in Jacksonville. The plethora of barbecue chains in town (**Mojo, Woody's,** and **Bono's**) and the staying power of old-school joints like **Billy C's Fred Cotten Bar-B-Q** pay tribute to the local obsession. The spices and sauces may change, but the method stays the same: slow cook over a low fire for hours on end. The result is meat that falls off the bone.

Sauces range from sweet to spicy to smokin' hot, but a true Jacksonville staple is the yellow, mustard-based sauce gracing the table of every barbecue joint in town. Concocted from mustard, honey, and some form of hot pepper, the recipes are highly guarded, but take-out bottles are usually for sale at the register.

Each barbecue joint has its own personality, but there is one thing you can be sure of: the presence of **sweet tea,** and lots of it in 64-ounce (or bigger) cups that often require two-handed drinking and are refilled as soon as you put them down. Most barbecue restaurants will send you out the door with a full-sized take-out cup of tea to go, so be sure to mention if you do not want this. (Be prepared for bemused looks if you say no.) And be prepared for any number of endearments from sugar to honey to darlin'. It may be a cliché, but barbecue joints are one of the last great holdouts of Southern niceties like this. Enjoy them while you can.

the pizzas delivered to your table on elevated trays are good enough to make you overlook any noise issues. Open seven days a week for lunch and dinner. On Friday and Saturday they stay open until 11 p.m.

RUTH'S CHRIS STEAK HOUSE $$$$
1201 Riverplace Blvd. (inside the Crowne Plaza Hotel)
(904) 396-6200
www.ruthschris.com
The perfect place to take your honey for a romantic dinner or to treat out-of-town guests, Ruth's Chris is the "home of serious steaks." A Best of Jax winner for Best Restaurant and Best Steaks in Jacksonville, Ruth's Chris serves Midwestern, custom-aged, U.S. prime beef, cooked in 1,800-degree ovens specifically designed and built for Ruth's Chris. The secret? Butter melted on top of the flash cooked steaks. (It's best not to think of your arteries at this point.) In addition to steak, the menu includes some fresh seafood, live Maine lobster from the tank, and several choices of a la carte side dishes. Order from the full bar which features an extensive selection of wines. Open daily for dinner. Reservations and smart dress suggested.

TAKE AWAY GOURMET $$–$$$$
2103 San Marco Blvd.
(904) 398-6676
www.marketandcatering.com
This little take-out business on the point in San Marco has been many things over the years, but this is one of the best. TAG items are prepared in-house by a team of chefs throughout the day. The menu changes daily and seasonally, so visit the Web site to see what's on today's menu. Food is sold for $8.50 a pound, or all-you-can-eat with a drink for $12.50. At dinnertime, pick up a dinner with two sides for $19.95. The TAG Gourmet Grab Menu is released on Thursday for the following week, but must be ordered one day in advance.

TASTE OF THAI $–$$$
4317 University Blvd. South
(904) 737-9009
www.tasteofthaijax.com

A mom-and-pop Thai restaurant located in the same plaza as Hala (a shopping center sometimes referred to by locals as the International Plaza for its confluence of world cuisines), Taste of Thai serves unpretentious Thai cooking in a cozy space that's packed most of the time, especially on weekends. The location reads "strip mall," but the quality—as well as the chef's willingness to adjust the heat of any dish down to neutral or up to blazing—overrides any external aesthetic failings. Open for lunch Monday through Friday from 11 a.m. to 3 p.m. and on Saturday from noon to 3 p.m. The restaurant closes at 3 p.m. every day and re-opens at 5 p.m. for dinner. Closed Sunday.

TAVERNA $$-$$$$
1986 San Marco Blvd.
(904) 398-3005
www.tavernasanmarco.com
Very new on the local scene, Taverna is turning heads among San Marco and Downtown Insiders. Serving both tapas and regular entrees, Taverna pleases with roasted garlic hummus, goat cheese ravioli, and the cheese and charcuterie plates. The place has a tendency to be loud (some say boisterous), which is just the ticket if that's what you're in the mood for. Hip locals are turned on by the modern-rustic décor, the "great, but not-too-big" wine list, and the street-side patio seating. Open for lunch and dinner Tuesday through Saturday.

TIDBITS RESTAURANT $-$$
1076 Hendricks Ave.
(904) 396-0528
www.tidbitsfood.com
Open for lunch only, this old-school Jacksonville standby has served the Southbank and San Marco business crowd for 25 years. It's neither fancy nor especially chic, but it's about as Insider as you can get. Long lines of devoted lunch-breakers flock to this no-frills eatery for the chicken salad served in pita or domed on an iceberg salad plate. Follow it up with a slice of iced pound cake and you can practically call yourself a local. Open weekdays from 11 a.m. to 2:30 p.m.

THE WINE CELLAR $$$$
1314 Prudential Dr.
(904) 398-8989
www.winecellarjax.com
A Jacksonville rite of passage? Maybe. It seems like everyone was taken to The Wine Cellar at some point over the last 35 years. Located on the Southbank, The Wine Cellar, while being totally respectable, has remained seriously under the radar, which is too bad as their wine list wins the *Wine Spectator* Award of Excellence year after year, and their fine dining is really memorable. Give them a try for half-priced martinis, cocktails, and house wines at happy hour, and then transition on to dinner. If you find yourself on a dull date, the "mingle" menu alone will give you something to talk about.

BAYMEADOWS/MANDARIN

CLARK'S FISH CAMP
SEAFOOD RESTAURANT $$-$$$
12903 Hood Landing Rd.
(904) 268-3474
www.clarksfishcamp.com
Tucked away on Julington Creek at the foot of Hood Landing Road, this fish camp restaurant has been serving up watery wonders for decades. In the early days it was a ramshackle wooden shanty that sold bait and tackle next to a boat ramp. Nowadays it's a ramshackle wooden shanty that sells seafood and prime rib next to a boat ramp. These days, though, the screened porch has been glassed in and air-conditioned, but you can still eat outside on the deck overlooking Julington Creek. Just bring some bug spray and make sure there's a breeze, or the mosquitoes will eat you alive.

This is a favorite restaurant for boaters, who often pull up, tie up to the dock, and eat inside. If you're adventurous, try the Florida gator tail (tastes like chicken) or the fried catfish (tastes like catfish). The fried shrimp dinner is as delicious as you'd expect here, and it comes with fried hush puppies and two sides, like coleslaw and a baked potato or french fries. Landlubbers can order chicken or red meat, including prime rib.

Clark's has a large, loyal following, so try to get here as early as possible. There's a good chance you'll have a wait on the weekends, and the restaurant only accepts reservations for parties of eight or more. The old fish camp–style of this restaurant, plus its location on the creek, makes it a great choice for anyone who'd enjoy seeing what rustic Florida was once all about. Open for lunch Saturday and Sunday and for dinner daily.

DON JUAN'S $$–$$$
12373 San Jose Blvd.
(904) 268-8722
www.donjuansjax.com
Don Juan's Restaurant is many of the things we Insiders like: it's locally owned, it's authentic, and there's a mariachi band. The burritos, enchiladas, chimichangas, and tacos are super-fresh and made 100 percent from scratch. Sit on the patio and order one of Don Juan's top-shelf margaritas, Primaritas, made with Patrón Silver topped with Grand Marnier. They cast everything in a golden glow, even the mariachi music.

GUBBIO'S $–$$
5111 Baymeadows Rd.
(904) 731-9900
Overlook the red-checked tablecloths and the strip-mall location; it's the food that has made Gubbio's a true Mandarin favorite. Named after a small town in Italy, Gubbio's offers pizzas, calzones, pastas, and subs. For dinner, order one of the daily specials or try Gubbio's signature dish, Chicken Milano, served with a white cream sauce and topped with melted mozzarella. The seafood, veal, lasagna, fettuccine Alfredo, and shrimp primavera are popular, too. Bread is made fresh daily. Finish your meal with a frothy cappuccino. Beer and wine are served. Open for lunch Monday through Friday and dinner daily.

INDIA'S RESTAURANT $–$$
9802 Baymeadows Rd.
(904) 620-0777
www.indiajax.com
Vegetarians especially love this popular Indian restaurant, named by *Folio Weekly* in its Best of Jax for 2008 issue. Start your lunch or dinner with samosa—crispy fried triangles of dough stuffed with delicately spiced potatoes, peas, and, if it's your pleasure, meat. The vegetable curry and chicken tandoori entrees, specialties of the house, will wow your taste buds. Be sure to order some naan—a light, flat Indian bread baked in a clay oven. A cold Indian beer, such as King Fishers, balances out the heat and complements the meal. For a sweet treat, try a mango lassi, a mango-flavored yogurt drink. Kids eat for half price from the buffet, and a children's menu is available. Be sure to check out the dinner specials for some real off-the-menu treats. For dessert, order kulfi (Indian ice cream) or rice pudding. Beer and wine are served. Open for lunch Monday through Saturday and dinner daily.

i Even though the Jacksonville Farmers' Market at 1810 West Beaver St. is a great place to buy everything from honey to honeydew melons, you're not likely to find it written up as a tourist attraction. Open since 1938, the Jacksonville's Farmers' Market, Florida's oldest farmers' market, hosts over 200 farmers and vendors year-round and is located in an industrial part of town. This real working-farmers' market offers some of the best fresh produce around and was the winner of *Folio Weekly's* Best Farmer's Market designation for 2009. The market is open 365 days a year from pre-dawn to dusk. The Web site is www.jaxfarmersmarket.com.

MEDITERRANIA RESTAURANT $$–$$$
3877 Baymeadows Rd.
(904) 731-2898
www.greek-restaurant.com
Old-world atmosphere and good service make this family-owned-and-operated Greek and Italian restaurant an area favorite. Yummy house specialties like fresh seafood, veal chops, and rack of lamb and traditional Greek desserts have won Meditterania a loyal following. Beer and wine, especially a large selection of Greek wines, are offered. Open for lunch Monday through Friday and dinner Monday through Saturday.

OUTBACK CRAB SHACK $$-$$$
8155 County Rd. 13 North, St. Augustine
(904) 522-0500
www.outbackcrabshack.com

The last time I went to Outback Crab Shack, my husband and I heard a thud next to the table and looked down to see a four-foot water moccasin that had dropped out of the rafters and landed on the floor a few feet away from our feet. Within seconds a couple men from the kitchen ambled out and captured the snake using a method involving a broom and a bucket. Within minutes, lunch proceeded as if nothing ever happened. That's what you get when you have dinner in a shack on a river in the middle if the woods far away from the things of man.

Technically in St. Augustine, but feeling more like outer-Mandarin, Outback Crab Shack, along with a scant handful of old-school fish camps along the inland waterways, represents the best of the old-Florida lifestyle. Nestled among overhanging water oaks, Outback serves up heaping portions of fish, shrimp, and other seafood, but locals come for the kettle-boiled platter—a combination of crawfish, garlic crabs, clams, blue crabs or shrimp with corn, sausage, and potatoes delivered to the table on a huge metal platter. It's meant to be shared, so come with a group and be ready to get messy. Dine indoors or out on the deck, depending on the weather. On the weekend, Outback often books live music during the day, but the deck gets packed quickly, so come early if you don't fancy waiting. After lunch, take a walk along the dock—a great vantage point for alligator and turtle viewing. Open seven days a week for lunch and dinner.

THE TREE STEAK HOUSE $$-$$$$
11362 San Jose Blvd.
(904) 262-0006
www.thetreesteakhousejax.com

Man and woman can't live by seafood alone. The old-school Tree Steak House offers the ideal alternative, especially if you don't want to have to take out a second mortgage to pay for dinner. The specialty of this good-old-boy standby is rib-eye steak that your waiter will measure off and cut at your table, if you so desire. If you want seafood, try the cashew grouper. Dinners are served with a baked potato and salad. Tree Steak House offers a full bar and lounge and serves dinner daily.

VILLAGE BREAD CAFÉ $-$$
5215 Phillips Hwy.
(904) 732-2261

The location leaves a lot to be desired, but the yumminess of the food makes up for the iffy address in spades. The Café, an outgrowth of the wholesale bakery next door, serves fresh breads, muffins, cupcakes, and pastries supplemented by ciabatta breakfast sandwiches, French toast, eggs, and some of the best darn bagels around. After breakfast, pick up a few loaves or something from the bakery case to take home. Open 7 a.m. to 3 p.m., Monday through Saturday. The Café has also recently opened a satellite location in The Jacksonville Landing and has plans to open a Mandarin location.

VITO'S $$-$$$$
3825 Baymeadows Rd.
(904) 737-9236
www.vitosjax.com

If you want real Italian food go to Vito's, a family restaurant that smacks of the Italian restaurants in New York and New Jersey. The staff is overtly friendly and has earned a serious neighborhood following. The walls are covered with photos, paintings, and drawings of the longtime staff and patrons, a tip of the hat to the value Vito's places on community and family. Open for lunch and dinner Monday through Friday and for dinner only on Saturday and Sunday.

TINSELTOWN/SOUTHSIDE

BASHA'S MEDITERRANEAN CUISINE $-$$$
13799 Beach Blvd.
(904) 821-4747

The combination of Basha's Lebanese kebabs, roasted meats, and their killer secret garlic sauce recipe thrusts this small and unassuming cafe toward the top of our Insider charts. Recently re-opened in a new location by the daughter of its late founder, the new location retains all of the hush-hush magnetism of the original with grape leaves, falafel, lamb, and gyro wraps. Locals have called this neighborhood a "culinary wasteland," which makes the opening of Basha's a food-lover's neighborhood oasis. Try the labneh (traditional mélange of sour cream and yogurt mixed with mint and garlic) with the gyro meat and wash it down with a Lebanese beer. You'll love it all; trust me.

BLUE BAMBOO $-$$$$
3820 Southside Blvd.
(904) 646-1478
www.bluebamboojacksonville.com
Try not to be dissuaded by the so-so location along Southside Boulevard. Blue Bamboo is an example of a great restaurant with a not-so-great address. The restaurant offers excellent Asian/American fusion, especially with their "Street Eats"—small plates of Asian-style street-vendor food that promise to eradicate culinary boredom. (Executive Chef Dennis is also the author of the book *Hip Asian Comfort Food*.) Stop here for a decent meal before or after a movie at Tinseltown. The salads and lighter fare please with fresh ingredients, and the entrees sing with fresh twists on traditional Asian flavors. Blue Bamboo also offers cooking classes one Saturday per month. Classes run $38 per person and include lunch and a glass of wine or cocktail. Open for lunch Monday through Friday from 11 a.m. to 2 p.m.; for dinner Monday through Saturday 5 to 10 p.m.; and dinner on Sunday from 5 to 9 p.m.

CANTINA LAREDO $$-$$$$
10282 Bistro Dr.
(904) 997-6110
www.cantinalaredo.com
Even though this is part of a larger chain, this is a pleasant addition to the Jacksonville dining scene and has become a destination in itself. Cantina Laredo serves contemporary Mexican cuisine supplemented by excellent tableside guacamole and well-mixed margaritas. Try the enchiladas Veracruz or the exceptionally good fajitas. The

Sunday brunch draws big crowds, but since this is the only Mexican brunch menu in town, it's worth the wait. Open for lunch and dinner daily and brunch on Sunday.

MADRID $-$$$
11233 Beach Blvd.
(904) 642-3741
If you love food with Latin zip and smoldering heat, Madrid is your place. Located in an unassuming strip center on the Southside, this festive restaurant bursts with personality. The Venezuelan owners serve up popular dishes from a variety of Latino countries. The traditional Cuban sandwich of ham and roast pork is popular with the lunch crowd, as is their version of the Cuban shredded beef specialty *ropa vieja*. *Sopas*, or soups, are considered a specialty of the house and can accompany an entree if you wish. They make just three: black bean, chile verde, and caldo gallego—a white bean soup with Spanish sausage and potatoes. Locals love the chile verde, a *sopa* of roasted, peeled, and diced green chilies that are slow cooked with a light chicken broth. It goes down smooth but can pack quite a punch. The owners also make the popular Venezuelan dish, arepas, corn cakes filled with *ropa vieja*, picadillo, roast pork, and cheese. Finish it all off with tres leches—pound cake dipped in a mix of three different types of milk. Open for lunch and dinner Monday through Saturday. Closed Sunday.

PATTAYA THAI GRILLE $$$
9551-1 Baymeadows Rd.
(904) 646-9506
www.ptgrille.com
Pattaya Thai was among Jacksonville's first Thai restaurants, and it's still a favorite. Located centrally enough to draw from most of the city, Pattaya Thai provides a quiet oasis of good food. In fact, the readers of *Folio Weekly* voted Pattaya Thai the best Thai restaurant in Jacksonville for seven years in a row. The portions are large, the food is fresh, and the chefs do not use MSG. Be sure to order the spring rolls—they're memorable, as is the Pad Thai. All of the soups are homemade (the coconut soup is especially

Catch of the day

Fried local shrimp is many Insiders' personal pick for the last meal they want to eat before they die. That's because local shrimpers working out of Mayport, a tiny fishing village near the mouth of the St. Johns, net-fish the waters off Northeast Florida every day of shrimping season, hauling in the fattest and finest shrimp around.

A typical Jacksonville fried shrimp dinner includes lightly batter-fried shrimp, hush puppies, coleslaw, and corn or collard greens. The lunch counter inside **Safe Harbour Seafood Market** next to the Mayport Ferry makes some of the best lightly batter-fried shrimp in the area (see their listing later in this section).

Travel along Heckscher Drive on the Northside and you'll likely see fishermen in tiny boats hoisting the day's catch onto the docks. To make like a real Insider, wait at the docks and buy your shrimp directly from the fishermen, then invite your pals over for a shrimp boil and a cold beer.

Atomic's fabulous made-to-order fish tacos are the stuff of seaside-taco-shop dreams. In the realm of cheap eats, this place earns the crown. Abiding by the motto: "Food that's out of this world at down-to-earth prices," Atomic's owner has a rep for being earnest and friendly. By all means, order the Super Grouper and Marvelous Mahi, and don't pass on the black beans (with the topping). You've never had anything like them!

BEACH HUT CAFE $$
1281 Third St. South
Jacksonville Beach
(904) 249-3516
Open since 1988, Beach Hut is the place to go for breakfast in Jacksonville Beach. The portions are generous, and the service is friendly. While Beach Hut serves both breakfast and lunch, the restaurant is best known for its breakfast. The place serves about 1,000 eggs a day (no kidding) and serves them at picnic tables and at the counter. The restaurant is open seven days a week from 6 a.m. to 2:30 p.m. Seating is first-come, first-served, so allow plenty of time, especially on the weekends.

BUKKETS $$-$$$
222 North Oceanfront Dr.
Jacksonville Beach
(904) 246-7701
www.bukketsbaha.com
Located just off Jacksonville Beach's boardwalk, Bukkets specializes in oysters, wings, seafood, salads, and sandwiches. Proudly unrefined and often rowdy, Bukkets draws people in with its boardwalk tables and cheap beer. Thanks to the full bar and live entertainment, Bukkets is frequented by a young-ish crowd of locals. Lunch and dinner are served daily. Happy hour is Monday through Friday from 5 to 8 p.m. Open seven days a week for lunch and dinner.

good). And all of the dishes can be ordered from mild to smokin' hot. Open for lunch Monday through Friday from 11 a.m. to 2:30 p.m. Dinner is served Monday through Saturday from 5 to 9:30 p.m. Closed Sunday.

THE BEACHES

ATOMIC FLYING FISH SEAFOOD
TACO GRILL $-$$$
120 Third St. South, Neptune Beach
(904) 444-8862

CARIBBEE KEY ISLAND
GRILLE & CRUZAN RUM BAR $$-$$$$
100 First St., Neptune Beach
(904) 270-8940
www.caribbeekey.com

Catch a little of the island flavor at Caribbee Key where specialties include conch fritters, Cruz Bay mussels, and seafood platters galore. For dessert try the Key lime pie. The upstairs bar is open until 12:30 a.m. daily, but the kitchen closes at 10 p.m. Lunch and dinner are served every day. Come out for live music and dancing on the weekends. Call ahead for dinner reservations.

CHINA CORAL $$
830-12 Hwy. A1A North, Ponte Vedra Beach
(904) 273-8776
If you're in the mood for seafood but want it a little spicier, China Coral provides a zippy option through the use of Shanghai, Mandarin, and Szechwan spices. In addition to the regular menu, China Coral serves daily lunch combination dishes and dinner specials. Favorites include fresh fish and seafood entrees, crispy fish and crispy duck, and a stir-fried string bean dish. Beer and wine are served. Open daily for lunch and dinner.

DAVINCI'S PIZZA $$-$$$
469 Atlantic Blvd., Atlantic Beach
(904) 241-2001
www.myspace.com/call2412001
Go here for a blissfully limited menu of New York-style pizza made in traditional brick ovens with fresh, high-quality ingredients. Independently owned and operated, DaVinci's chooses to make their dough and sauce from scratch. As serious about having a good time as they are about making good food, DaVinci's fully embraces the beach lifestyle and has even been rumored by locals to trade "items of interest" for pizza—although the details on that are fuzzy and no one's going on the record. When the DaVinci's folks aren't stoking the ovens, they're "dreaming up new recipes…hittin' the beach, enjoying live music, playing sports, or spending a lazy Sunday-Funday with our friends and family." If there exists a more fitting tribute to the beach lifestyle, I don't know what it is. Open Tuesday through Saturday for lunch and dinner. Closed Sunday.

DWIGHT'S BISTRO $$$$
1527 Penman Rd., Jacksonville Beach
(904) 241-4496
www.dwightsbistro.com
After two hurricanes, two restaurants, and two kids in St. Thomas, Virgin Islands, wisecracking chef Dwight Delude said "too much" and moved to Jacksonville Beach. Local diners are indeed grateful.

Don't be fooled by the rough exterior. Opened in 1996, Dwight's Bistro is a cozy 40-seat place that has gained a strong following among area connoisseurs looking for consistently great meals and an extensive wine list. The Mediterranean-style bistro serves fresh ravioli and pasta, awesome crab cakes, grilled quail, veal, and lamb. Dinner is served Tuesday through Saturday, with beer and wine. As the restaurant has only eight tables, reservations are a must.

ELLEN'S KITCHEN $
1824 South Third St., Jacksonville Beach
(904) 246-1572
Ellen's has been serving breakfast and lunch at the Beaches for more than 40 years. A full breakfast menu is served all day. Known for homemade sausage gravy and hash browns, Ellen's is also famous for Pat's special (two eggs on top of hash browns with melted cheese) and its crab cake Benedict. Come in before 9 a.m. for the early-bird specials. For lunch, choose from sandwiches, burgers, pork barbecue, BLTs, patty melts, and salads, as well as daily specials. Open seven days a week from 7 a.m. to 2 p.m.

GIOVANNI'S $$$$
1161 Beach Blvd., Jacksonville Beach
(904) 249-7787
www.giovannirestaurant.com
A Beaches tradition for more than 30 years, Giovanni's offers seafood dishes and innovative continental cuisine with an Italian flair. After dinner, head upstairs to the piano bar for live tunes Tuesday through Saturday. Opens at 5:30 p.m. for dinner Monday through Saturday. Closed Sunday.

HOMESTEAD RESTAURANT $$–$$$
1712 Beach Blvd., Jacksonville Beach
(904) 247-6820
www.homesteadrestaurant.us

Enjoy family-style dining in a cozy log cabin at Homestead Restaurant, where home-cooked family-style meals have been the norm since 1947. The Homestead building is as famous for being haunted by the ghost of Mrs. Alpha O. Paynter as the restaurant is for its fried chicken. The Homestead also serves seafood, chicken and dumplings, and country fried steak with heaping portions of collard greens, biscuits, and creamy grits. For dessert try a slice of Southern apple pie with ice cream or mango Key lime pie. The Homestead runs early bird specials on Monday and Tuesday from 4 to 6 p.m. and is open for dinner daily. Brunch on Sunday features gospel singers, mimosas, and Bloody Marys. (NOTE: The Homestead has come under new ownership and no longer serves family-style chicken and sides. While not life-or-death, this change does come as a bummer to those of us who grew up loving that particular Homestead tradition.)

LULU'S WATERFRONT GRILLE $$
301 North Roscoe Blvd., Palm Valley
(904) 285-0139
www.luluswaterfrontgrille.com

Located on the Intracoastal Waterway in Palm Valley, LuLu's can be reached by car or by boat. The menu offers seafood, steaks, chicken, pasta, and salads. Lulu's has a full bar and a weekday happy hour from 4 to 7 p.m. Tee off on Lulu's Tee-Box mini, dockside putting green and try to land your ball in the white bucket across the Intracoastal Waterway. Dine indoors or outdoors on the screened waterfront deck. Open daily for lunch and dinner, and Sunday brunch.

LYNCH'S IRISH PUB $$
514 North First St., Jacksonville Beach
(904) 249-5181
www.lynchsirishpub.com

Sure, the Guinness is creamy, but Lynch's, an authentic Northern Irish pub, also serves Irish stew, corned beef and cabbage, shepherd's pie, bangers and mash, fish-and-chips, steaks, and pasta. Take your pick from a full range of appetizers, sandwiches, and daily specials. The full-service bar has 50 imported beers on tap, and the pub offers live entertainment almost every evening (see the Nightlife chapter). Open for lunch Saturday and Sunday, and dinner daily.

MEZZA LUNA $$$
110 North First St., Neptune Beach
(904) 249-5573
www.mezzalunaneptunebeach.com

Located in the heart of Neptune and Atlantic Beaches' restaurant row, Mezza Luna embodies casual relaxation. Owner Gianni Recupito is an old hand at running popular restaurants in the Jacksonville area. The chicken and veal specialties are popular choices, as are the seafood specials and wood-burning oven pizzas. For dessert, try the tiramisu-tini or the bread pudding with Irish whiskey sauce. There's a full-service bar with a weekday happy hour and an extensive wine list. Open Monday through Saturday for dinner.

MOJO KITCHEN BBQ PIT & BLUES BAR
1500 Beach Blvd.
(904) 247-6636
www.mojobbq.com

Beloved for their flagship in-town location listed earlier in this section, Mojo's Beaches outpost not only serves up their signature gobsmacking barbecue, but also hosts live music. Imagine downing a platter of Mojo's signature brisket then letting it all digest to the live sounds of blues legends like John Lee Hooker Jr. (The author must admit, again, that like Lubi's, she has absolutely no objectivity whatsoever when it comes to Mojo's barbecue; it's just that good. You'll just have to trust her on this one.)

OCEAN 60 RESTAURANT
WINE & MARTINI BAR $$$$
60 Ocean Blvd., Atlantic Beach
(904) 247-0060
www.ocean60.com

Ocean 60 has it all: great food and an impressive wine list in an intimate setting. This 50-seat restaurant benefits from an extensive, inventive menu cooked up by chef Daniel Groshell, a graduate of the Culinary Institute of America in Hyde Park. His wife, Rachel, is the general manager and has made certain that the attentive servers can answer all of your menu questions. The Groshells like to say their food is "rustic," as opposed to artful—meaning that it hasn't been overworked or overtouched in the kitchen.

This chef espouses fine dining with a Mediterranean or New World flair and a fondness for fresh seafood. The classic French onion soup with cheese rusks earns raves from most diners. And you just can't go wrong ordering fresh shrimp this close to Mayport.

Things really get interesting when it comes to choosing an entree. Try the porcini-seared salmon, or the Brazilian-style churrasco and bacon-wrapped shrimp. More adventurous fish lovers may want to try the two-pound snapper, imported from Costa Rica, which Groshell fries whole, complete with head, tail, and eyes. It arrives stretched across your plate and scored so that you can easily eat one side, then flip the fish and eat the other. Ocean 60 also offers wine tastings from 6 to 8 p.m. every Monday evening and is one of the only restaurants in town where you can order a two-ounce "taster" of wine from the extensive wine list to see if you like the selection enough to order a glass or even a bottle. It makes for some fun sampling. Ocean 60 is open for lunch and dinner Monday through Saturday and can also be booked for private parties.

PARSON'S SEAFOOD RESTAURANT $$$$
904 Sixth Ave., Jacksonville Beach
(904) 249-0608
www.parsonsseafoodrestaurant.com
The Parson family is well known for their seafood restaurants, which originated in Mayport. This old-school, family-style restaurant has a separate bar and an extensive menu of seafood as well as steaks and chicken. Try a shrimp sandwich for lunch or the popular Super Combo Seafood Platter for dinner. Children have their own menu selections. There are three separate dining rooms and an outdoor patio. The private dining room

seats 50. The full bar offers daily happy-hour specials. Open for lunch and dinner daily.

PUSSER'S CARIBBEAN BAR
AND GRILLE $$–$$$$
816 A1A North, Ponte Vedra Beach
(904) 280-7766
www.pussersusa.com
Pusser's Bar and Grille serves Caribbean cuisine alongside regional faves. Ask to sit on the upper deck where you can suck down tropical rum drinks, including the infamous Pusser's Painkiller, and watch the sun go down. Pusser's has live entertainment on the upper deck Wednesday through Saturday, as well as occasional cooking classes and fun promotions.

RAGTIME TAVERN AND
SEAFOOD GRILLE $$$
207 Atlantic Blvd., Atlantic Beach
(904) 241-7877
www.ragtimetavern.com
Long considered one of the Jacksonville area's most popular restaurants, Ragtime specializes in fresh seafood, with several daily specials and pasta dishes to choose from. Ragtime doesn't take reservations, but the food is worth any wait. Popular menu items include the grouper picatta, sesame tuna, and the grouper Oscar. Order a Dolphin's Breath Lager from the taproom where the beer list is extensive enough to satisfy all comers. There is a full-service bar with happy hour Monday through Friday and live entertainment Thursday through Sunday. Open for lunch and dinner daily and for Sunday brunch.

RESTAURANT MEDURE $$$$
818 North Hwy. A1A, Ponte Vedra Beach
(904) 543-3797
Jacksonville restaurateur Matthew Medure (Matthew's in San Marco) has done it again with another top-notch eatery. Selected by *Florida Trend* magazine as one of the state's top restaurants, Restaurant Medure offers a sophisticated dining experience and private dining rooms. The menu is haute cuisine with an emphasis on a wide variety of local and imported fish and

seafood, cooked with Southern, Mediterranean, Asian, and Middle Eastern influences. The lounge is open from 4 p.m. to 1 a.m., offers a full bar, and sometimes has live entertainment. Open Tuesday through Saturday from 5:30 to 10:30 p.m. Reservations suggested.

RITE SPOT $$–$$$
1534 North Third St.
Jacksonville Beach
(904) 247-0699
www.ritespotrestaurant.com

If it's home-style cooking you want at reasonable prices, this is the spot. A casual eatery located in the North Beach Plaza, Ritespot's daily specials and menu feature fresh seafood, Mayport shrimp, fresh fish, chicken-fried steak, pork chops, and pot roast. Supplement with mashed potatoes and gravy, fried okra, pickled beets, and hush puppies. Corn muffins and biscuits come with the meal. Save room for a homemade milk shake or something from the bar. Dine in or take out. Open for breakfast, lunch, and dinner daily but closed from 2 to 5 p.m.

SAFE HARBOR SEAFOOD MARKET
(AT THE MAYPORT FERRY) $–$$$
4378 Ocean St., Atlantic Beach
(904) 246-4911
www.safeharborseafood.com

The first time I went to Safe Harbor, we were invited there by friends who were out in Mayport on business and didn't have time to come into town. GPS engaged, we drove out through the Beaches, turned north on Mayport Road, and drove until we reached a wide spot in the road near the ferry. Before we went inside, our friends prepped us, saying that while Safe Harbour wasn't fancy, it was good, adding that, unlike some of the grocery stores in the area, it didn't smell fishy. Boy, were they right. Safe Harbor is an immaculately kept, long-counter seafood market teeming with in-the-know locals who drive out from town with their coolers to pick up fresh-off-the-boat seafood. The market is equally popular with the weekend lunch crowd who order fish and shrimp baskets with fries and slaw

and devour them on the deck overlooking the river and the surrounding marshes. The setting is pure Jacksonville—the one most of us remember from our youth—and the nostalgia, combined with the freshness of the morning's catch, made for a near-perfect meal. Open Monday through Saturday from 10 a.m. to 5:30 p.m.; closed Sunday

SINGLETON'S SEAFOOD SHACK $$
4728 Ocean St., Mayport
(904) 246-4442

Located just a block before the ferry, this restaurant has been serving seafood since the 1960s. Local favorites include the fried shrimp dinner and the blackened or grilled fish. Order from daily lunch and dinner specials or the fresh catch of the day. Dine inside or on the enclosed porch overlooking the St. Johns River. Adjacent to the dining room, Captain Ray's Model Boat Museum features more than 200 models. Open for lunch and dinner daily.

SLIDERS OYSTER BAR
AND SEAFOOD GRILLE $$–$$$$
218 First St., Neptune Beach
(904) 246-0881

Insiders love the casual, friendly atmosphere of this restaurant located a block off the ocean. I must admit to having spent a good part of my youth here, ordering platters of steamed oysters with my best friend, shucking them into a bucket and drinking beer until the wee hours. Sliders is known not only for its oysters (hence the name), but also for its specialties, which range from simple grilled fish tacos to more elaborate entrees like Butter Nut Grouper. The menu also features plenty of non-seafood choices like pastas, salads, and chicken-cheese-spinach quesadillas. By the way, if you want a great local souvenir, buy a Sliders T-shirt, which features the restaurant's pink flamingo logo. Eat inside or out on the patio at this kid-friendly restaurant. (See our Kidstuff chapter.) And think of me while you're shucking. Open for dinner only.

SUN DOG DINER $$$
207 Atlantic Blvd., Neptune Beach
(904) 241-8221
www.sundogjax.com

Proud of their "no one is a stranger" policy, this Art Deco restaurant has 1950s counter stools and cozy booths separated by glass and chrome. The emphasis is on steak, seafood, and pasta dishes. Entrees include ahi tuna sashimi alongside grilled meatloaf and crab cake sandwiches, Caesar salad, and Southwestern Mahi salad. The grill tempts carnivores with half-pound hamburgers, and don't pass on the bleu chips!

For dessert try the upside-down apple crisp and Oreo cheesecake. The weekend brunch offers steak and eggs, plus huevos rancheros, and seafood frittata. There's entertainment—from live music to trivia—nightly. Open for lunch and dinner daily with brunch on Sunday.

TACOLU BAJA MEXICANA
1183 Beach Blvd., Jacksonville Beach
(904) 249-TACO
www.tacolu.com
Serious locals love this newbie at Jacksonville Beach. Located just a few blocks from the sand, TacoLu makes every scrap of the food they serve right there, by hand, no exceptions—especially the guacamole, which is the key to any good taco shop's success. TacoLu shines in the fish tacos and margarita departments, but, who are we kidding, everything on the menu rocks. In their own words, "If you want a Taco Bell taco, then go to Taco Bell… At TacoLu, we make everything as fresh as we can, and try to be better than anywhere else. We don't want to change your mind about Mexican food, just open it up a bit." Well said. Open Tuesday through Sunday for lunch and dinner (with brunch on Saturday on Sunday). Closed on Monday.

TENTO CHURRASCARIA $$$$
528 North First St., Jacksonville Beach
(904) 246-1580
www.tentochurrascaria.com
At $39 a head, this upscale house of meat, governed by the more is better principle, provides a solid argument for fasting both before and after your visit. Voted Best New Restaurant and Best Service in 2008 by the readers of *Jackson-ville Magazine,* Tento's meat-lovers milieu is a local favorite. If you've never been to a churrascaria before, let us explain: the restaurant uses churrasco, the open-flame cooking style developed by cowboys (or gauchos) on the southern plains of Brazil, to spit-roast all manner of meat which they then parade table to table, slicing off slabs to anyone displaying a green chip. Flip to the red chip for a breather.

THAI ROOM $$$
1286 South Third St., Jacksonville Beach
(904) 249-8444
www.thai-room.com
Thai Room is spacious but cozy. Dine at a table near the fountain or in one of four large booths outfitted with Thai pillows. Chef Thong Thine's specialties are crispy duck, snapper Lad Na, noodles of the drunk, and green curry. The extensive menu includes several vegetarian and spicy dishes, along with satay (chicken or beef), a customer favorite. For dessert try the purple sweet rice topped with coconut and served warm. The restaurant serves beer and has a large wine selection. Dine in or take out. Open for lunch from 11 a.m. to 2 p.m. Monday through Friday and for dinner at 5 p.m. Monday through Saturday.

THE 3RD STREET DINER $$
223 Ninth Ave. South, Jacksonville Beach
(904) 270-0080
www.thirdstreetdiner.com
If you find yourself at the Beaches and have a hankering for breakfast—no matter what time of day or night—fear not. The 3rd Street Diner is the ticket. "We serve breakfast 24/7," says owner and operator Nick Koutroumanos. Well, almost. The diner, opened in 2003, serves breakfast (and other lunch and dinner foods) from 6 a.m. to 2 a.m. seven days a week. Specialties include fresh seafood and pasta dishes, stuffed grape leaves, seafood moussaka, Greek salads, and gyros. All of the baked goods are made at the restaurant. For dessert, indulge in the New York–style cheesecake. Like any diner worth its salt, 3rd Street Diner boasts a loaded jukebox and a full bar.

NIGHTLIFE

Going out for cocktails in Jacksonville can be a challenge since many of the most popular hangouts are far apart. This means that your designated driver could clock some significant mileage if you're bar hopping from one side of town to the other. But new clubs are opening all the time, especially in the Springfield, Riverside, Avondale, and Downtown areas, so you can bar hop within a certain neighborhood, minimize your travel and still have a good time.

As is the rule nationally, patrons must be 21 to buy alcohol in Florida, though 18- to 21-year-olds are permitted inside some clubs; they just can't consume any alcoholic drinks. Many of Jacksonville's best nightspots are also popular restaurants, so be prepared to share space with diners. We've noted cover charges when they apply and also the general type of crowd each club attracts.

In the Springfield, Riverside, Avondale, Downtown, and Southside areas, club attire is hip and fashion-forward. At many Beaches bars, flip-flops and jeans are OK, but as more and more upscale clubs open at the Beaches, that standard of dress may evolve. (Maybe not; Beaches residents do tend to operate under the "No shoes, no shirt, no problem" motto.)

Finally, some people enjoy Jacksonville's casino ships where the slot machines and blackjack tables open for business once the ships are a mile offshore.

If the hours are unusual, we have listed them. Otherwise, most clubs stay open until 2 a.m.

RIVERSIDE/AVONDALE/WESTSIDE

CASBAH CAFE
3628 St. Johns Ave.
(904) 981-9966
www.thecasbahcafe.com

Looking for something different? Check out the Casbah, a popular Middle Eastern–style cafe where you can smoke flavored tobacco (apple, banana, grape, etc.) in a hookah, a large pipe with several hoses. Single flavors are $12; blends are $15. Hookah fans say they're hooked on this smooth way to enjoy tobacco. Belly dancers keep patrons entertained Thursday through Saturday, and mouth-watering vegetarian dishes are par for the course. The Casbah also offers a large selection of global beers like a Kingfisher from India or an Almaza from Lebanon. There's usually a nice crowd here in the evenings, mostly young professionals.

FIRST FRIDAYS IN FIVE POINTS
Intersection of Park, Margaret and Lomax Streets
www.5pointsjax.com

Considered both an arts event and a nightlife event, First Fridays in 5 Points bring out Jacksonville Insiders in droves. This year-round, boozy mash-up of art, music, and food signifies the best of what's happening in the city's grassroots arts scene and provides great cause for optimism. Ignore the fact that the event starts at 5 p.m.; it doesn't really get going until around 7 p.m. or after the sun goes down. Five Points businesses put on the dog with hors d'oeuvres, wine, and arts happenings of all kinds. Be sure to check out The Underbelly (inside Anomaly), Blu salon, and Flat File Gallery at the 5 Points Theatre, all of which use the event to promote art by emerging artists.

THE METRO
2929 Plum St.
(904) 388-7192
www.metrojax.com

There's always something going on at Metro, Jacksonville's number-one gay and lesbian club. Located in Riverside, close to the intersection of College Street and Willowbranch Road, the club is popular with every aspect of the rainbow—from average Joes to well-heeled impersonators. On Thursday, female impersonator Sondra Todd hosts Sondra Todd's Star Search, popular with emerging talent of all persuasions. Metro opens at 4 p.m. Monday through Friday, 6 p.m. on Saturday, and noon on Sunday.

STEAMWORKS
822 Lomax St.
(904) 329-4724

Think of Steamworks as a dance spot-cum-British pub, inspired by Jacksonville's indie clubs of yesterday (The Milk Bar and Art Bar), where artists can meet, network, and perform. Food is available, but the club finds its greatest identity as a place for the 18 and over crowd to dance, hear music, and hook up with friends. The club's most popular dance nights, Thursday and Friday, feature an indie rock DJ. Stop by on Wednesday, Saturday, and Sunday for an eclectic musical selection. Tuesdays are pure rockabilly. The club is open 11 a.m. to 2 a.m. daily, with a $3 cover after 9 p.m. on Thursday and Friday. Wednesday through Friday Steamworks hosts a happy hour from 5 to 7 p.m.

WALKERS
2692 Post St.
(904) 894-7465
www.walkersbar.com

Jacksonville needed the dose of urban design brought to town by Walkers Bar.

Drawing inspiration from the chic urban landscapes of New York and Boston, Walkers breathed new life into a 1929 gas station, updating the space to accommodate wine lovers from all neighborhoods. Think exposed brick and visible ceiling beams. At this printing, the owner plans to feature a 100+ bottle selection with new wines coming into the rotation all the time. Wines by the glass start at a reasonable $5, and bottles of champagne can be found for around $20. Look for a tapas menu and live music on the weekends. For a real kick try the pear saketini. Open 4:30 p.m. to 2 a.m. Tuesday through Saturday.

DOWNTOWN/SPRINGFIELD

CLUB TSI DISCOTHEQUE
333 East Bay St.
(904) 424-3531
www.clubtsi.com

Looking for an underground club in the Downtown area where the music is fresh and the crowd is cool? Head over to club TSI for karaoke with Ugly Ed every Tuesday night, and Dance Party with DJ Nick Fresh every Friday. Located just off the St. Johns River, TSI attracts local, national, and international shows every week of the year and hosts their own eclectic lineup of indie club nights throughout the rest of the week. It is, without a doubt, the place in Jacksonville for the newest in music.

THE IVY ULTRA BAR
113 East Bay St.
(904) 356-9200
www.theivyjacksonville.com

One of the nicer night spots in Jax, The Ivy runs on par to Mark's in terms of hipness, but has the dubious advantage of being bigger. The Ivy offers complimentary valet, which is nice, and does not charge a cover. The combination of location and chic-ness draws an under-40 crowd. Happy hour is from 4 to 8 p.m., with different drink specials every day of the week.

THE LONDON BRIDGE ENGLISH PUB AND EATERY
100 East Adams St.
(904) 359-0001
www.londonbridgepubjax.com

London Bridge has long been a favorite after-work and weekend hangout for the city's young professionals and Downtown urbanites. The beer selection is over 50-long and the kitchen serves classic British bangers and mash, fish-and-chips, cottage pie, and Scottish eggs. London Bridge serves lunch and dinner daily, and there's live music every Monday, Friday, and Saturday. Stop by every second and fourth Wednesday for karaoke, or on Thursday for Open Mic night.

MARK'S
315 E. Bay St.
(904) 355-5099
www.marksjax.com

A notable newcomer to the upscale Downtown club and lounge scene, Mark's caters to a hip and fabulous 30-something clientele with Indie Lounge Tuesdays, Acoustic Wednesdays, and weekday happy hour from 4 to 7:30 p.m. And for Pete's sake, please dress appropriately. The attire is chic, so leave the sports T-shirts and baseball hats at home. Mark's opens at 4 p.m. Tuesday through Friday and at 8 p.m. on Saturday.

THE PEARL
1101 North Main St.
(904) 791-4499
www.myspace.com/thepearlofspringfield

The Pearl draws an edgy young crowd to Springfield with its DJs, dance floor, drink specials, great staff, outdoor patios, and über-hip location. Be warned that this is for hipsters, not oldsters, who would probably feel out of place. On Saturdays at The Pearl, DJs spin everything from new wave to synth pop. Wednesday night is both Ladies Night and karaoke time. Expect a modest cover charge.

SHANTYTOWN PUB
22 West 6th St.
(904) 798-8222
www.myspace.com/shantytownpub

Not your parents' pub, Shantytown brings it with Metal Mondays, Random Control Tuesdays (with trivia), Vinyl Wednesdays (records, not clothes), Thursday night Shenanigans, live music on Friday and Saturday, a soul/funk cookout every Sunday (bring your own meat and/or veggies), and serious drink specials every night. The Springfield location keeps it edgy, the Insider vibe keeps it real.

THE SINCLAIR
521 W. Forsyth St.
www.thesinclairjax.com

A new Downtown hot spot, The Sinclair puts a chic spin on what some have referred to as Sherlock Holmes–style decor. With artwork by Jacksonville artist Ryan Strasser and music played low enough so that you can flirt without having to yell, the Sinclair adds much-needed depth to Jacksonville's on-the-town offerings.

THREE LAYERS
1602 Walnut St.
(904) 355-9791
www.threelayersacoffeehouse.com

The Downtown/Springfield in-the-know crowd loves Three Layers, named by the owners for its three separate identities, all housed under one roof. First, the coffeehouse serves up memorable desserts and coffee—think red velvet or orangesicle cake in a loft-like space complete with Wi-Fi. Second, the Cellar wine bar draws oenophiles with its laid-back neighborhood charm, and the outdoor Zen garden is magically landscaped and provides the perfect spot to unwind in the later evening. The crowd tends toward 30- and 40-somethings who appreciate the extraordinary desserts and local artwork. Come by on Sunday for soup and salad and watch the movies playing all day long on the big screen in the coffeehouse.

i For the very latest on what bands are playing where, pick up a copy of *Folio Weekly,* Jacksonville's free alternative magazine.

SAN MARCO/LAKEWOOD

CUBA LIBRÉ
2578 Atlantic Blvd.
(904) 399-2262
www.cubalibrebar.com

Many argue that Cuba Libré is Jacksonville's only authentic Cuban hot spot.

Established in 1994 as just a small bar in Havana-Jax Café, the city went crazy for the authentic taste and evocative rhythms of Cuba that the bar and restaurant offered. Over the years, Cuba Libré Bar has grown into the city's first upscale Latin club and now occupies its own distinct space on Atlantic Boulevard. Cuba Libré offers dance classes, Latin music, a dance floor, a large-screen projection television, plush leather couches, and exotic drinks native to the Caribbean. Order a mojito, the drink that was first mixed in Cuba and made famous worldwide by author Ernest Hemingway. Of course, the drink that made the club famous, a Cuba Libré, is always in style. Come experience one of Jacksonville's best-kept secrets. Open until 2 a.m. most nights. Closed on Sunday.

ENDO EXO
1224 Kings Ave.
(904) 396-7733
www.myspace.com/theendoexoclub
Endo Exo describes itself as "more South Beach than San Marco." The club has three areas: the main bar, where most people hang out; the outside patio, where smokers gather; and a dance floor sporting big couches and a bed. Come here for Open Mic Mondays and Island Explosion Wednesdays. Endo Exo likes to think of itself as a place for the 21-to-55 crowd, not for teenyboppers, so come dressed stylishly, which the owner says means no hats, no T-shirts, and no flip-flops. Expect to pay a cover charge of around $5 to $10 depending on the night. Check out Endo's MySpace page to learn more.

THE GROTTO
2012 San Marco Blvd.
(904) 398-0726
www.grottowine.com
One of the longer-standing grown-up meeting places in San Marco, The Grotto operates as both a wine and tapas bar and a retail shop. Order wines by the glass or choose from broad selection of vintages from everyday table wines to sought-after favorites. The eclectic tapas menu features Bruschetta de Grotto and Wild Mushroom Crostini that pairs beautifully with the well-curated wine selection. The ivy-covered iron gates, outdoor courtyard, marble bar, copper-arched ceilings, and plush velvet couches cater to a mature crowd with a love of fine wine and great conversation. Perfect for a first date or a quiet evening with friends. Make a date to attend one of the Thursday wine tastings. They run from 6 to 8 p.m. and cost a modest $5 per person, with $3 refunded on your first purchase. The Grotto is open Tuesday and Wednesday 11:54 a.m. to 11:03 p.m., Thursday through Saturday 11:57 a.m. to midnight-ish, and Sunday 4 to 10 p.m. Closed Monday. Tapas menu served nightly from 5 p.m. until 30 minutes before closing.

JACK RABBITS
1528 Hendricks Ave.
(904) 398-7496
www.jackrabbitsonline.com
Located on the less-polished, more edgy side area of San Marco, Jack Rabbits is both easy and hard to miss. It's painted bright red outside and fully embodies its hole-in-the-wall reputation. Regulars love the grungy interior and outstanding lineup of live music, from local groups to the most up-to-the-minute national touring acts. Call the club for show schedules and ticket information.

SAN MARCO THEATRE
1996 San Marco Blvd.
(904) 396-4845
www.sanmarcotheatre.com
Locals love being able to order wine and a pizza at this landmark movie theater where every third seat had been replaced by a bar table and wait-staff roam the aisles taking orders. Built in 1938 by architect Roy Benjamin (who also built the beautiful Florida Theatre), the theater still retains the Art Deco style that locals cherish. Recognized by USA Today as one of 10 best classic cinemas in the United States, the San Marco Theatre remains one of two movie theaters in town (the other being the 5 Points Theatre) where you can enjoy a frosty beer and a movie simultaneously. Check the Web site for showtimes and upcoming special events.

SQUARE ONE
1974 San Marco Blvd.
(904) 306-9004
www.squareonejax.com

Square One is a hip club located in the heart of San Marco and is popular with young professionals, who often come after work for the club's happy hour when beer, wine, and mixed drinks are all half price. Stop by Square One after a movie or dinner in San Marco for live music and spinning DJs. Prepare to pay a cover after 10 p.m., when the bands begin playing. Visit the Web site to find out the current live music lineup. Happy hour 4 to 7 p.m. Closed Sunday.

TERA NOVA LOUNGE
8206 Phillips Hwy.
(904) 733-8085
www.teranovalounge.com or www.myspace
.com/teranovalounge

Terra Nova Lounge has made a sincere run at raising the standard in Jacksonville's nightlife. The contemporary interior, top-shelf liquor selection, bottle service, and eclectic music mix has made it popular with Southside locals. Up the ante and request the VIP treatment. You must be 21 or older to enter, and stylish attire is required.

BAYMEADOWS/SOUTHSIDE/MANDARIN

THE COMEDY ZONE
I-295 and San Jose Boulevard
(904) 292-4242
www.comedyzone.com

Located inside the Ramada Inn Mandarin, the Comedy Zone offers an ever-changing lineup of stand-up comedians. Brett Butler has performed here, as has Carrot Top and, in his day, Mickey Rooney. The club doesn't get as many celebrity acts as it would like, but lesser known comedians can be very entertaining. The Ramada Inn also offers special package deals that include a room, dinner, and tickets to the show. Otherwise, show tickets range from $10 to $25, depending on the night. The club is 21-and-over with a one-drink minimum.

SEVEN BRIDGES GRILLE & BREWERY
9735 North Gate Parkway
(904) 997-1999
www.7bridgesgrille.com

Head here for drinks or dinner before or after taking in a movie at Cinemark Tinseltown, a 20-screen movie complex on the other side of the parking lot. Treat yourself to one of the brewery's six different microbrews. By far, one of the best places in town (Ragtime, Bold City Brewery, and River City Brewing Co. being the only other options) to taste local, craft-brewed beer. Seven Bridges' and its brewmaster take their 1,500-liter batches very seriously. The Sweet Magnolia Brown Ale is especially popular.

Listen to the Bubble

Keep an eye out throughout the streets of Downtown for the city's whimsical, orange-and-white, cartoon-style dialogue "Bubbles" in storefronts, in windows, and along sidewalks throughout Downtown. The bubbles reveal to visitors (and locals, too) fun facts about the city's history, culture, parks, riverfront, dining, nightlife and events. Bubbles, which are part of Downtown Jax's **"Explore the More"** campaign, alert passersby to a building's history and highlight signature products. The project's aim? To spread the good word about the Downtown renaissance.

Downtown Jax's mobile Web site, dtjax.org, makes it easy to get the names of all of the Downtown-area shops and restaurants and an up-to-the-minute calendar of events, on your phone. And if you forget the Web address, just find a parking meter; as of 2010, the dtjax.org Web address will be posted on meters throughout the city.

THE BEACHES

THE ATLANTIC
333 North First St., Jacksonville Beach
(904) 249-3338
www.myspace.com/atlanticjax
Twenty-somethings (think fresh scrubbed college grads) frequent The Atlantic, for the self-described "Best Weekend Party at the Beaches!" The inside club area is somewhat small, but there's room enough for live music and dancing to DJs and occasional live music. Open Thursday through Saturday. The Atlantic is located in the same complex as the Ocean Club, so finding a parking space can take awhile.

BO'S CORAL REEF LOUNGE
201 Fifth Ave. North, Jacksonville Beach
(904) 246-9874
www.bosclub.com
Open since 1964, Bo's Coral Reef is the only gay and lesbian nightclub at the Beaches. Offering a "mixed crowd and no drama" atmosphere, Bo's is a study in nightclub yin and yang: a totally rocking dance floor in the main bar and a quiet outdoor patio bar in the garden. Locals love the karaoke and female impersonators as well as Bo's famous frozen margaritas, which are just $3 on Tuesday nights. Bo's is located just a block off the ocean, "where the natives are restless and very friendly." Haters stay home—Bo's has a zero-discrimination policy, and they mean it. Open seven nights a week from 4 p.m. to 2 a.m.

BUKKETS BAHA
222 North Oceanfront, Jacksonville Beach
(904) 246-7701
www.bukketsbaha.com
Young men in their 20s tend to gravitate to this bar on the boardwalk in Jacksonville Beach. The outside beachfront area is popular year-round as a great place to sit with friends and enjoy beer, wings, and the Atlantic Ocean. Bukkets is located on a busy corner of Jacksonville Beach, which makes it people-watching paradise. If that doesn't do it for you, shoot a round of pool, play video games, watch TV. Bukkets often brings in live music on the weekends. Open from lunchtime and on into the wee hours.

FREEBIRD CAFE
200 North First St., Jacksonville Beach
(904) 246-2473
www.freebirdlive.com
Ronnie VanZant's famous lyric "If I leave here tomorrow, will you still remember me?" is immortalized in this venue founded by his widow, Judy, and daughter, Melody. Authentic Skynyrd memorabilia, as well as gold and platinum records, are encased on the walls of this eatery, which has a Hard Rock Café vibe. (See the Close-up in this chapter for more on Jacksonville's own Lynyrd Skynyrd band.) Freebird Cafe may be a bar and a restaurant, but at heart it's a music club where bands new—and not so new— perform. Sure it has deep Southern rock roots, but all genres are represented here and supported with first-class sound and lighting. Blues guitarists from all over the country often find their way to this stage. This gem of a club can hold 700 people and has two full bars. Keep in mind that this is a nonsmoking, general-admission, standing-room-only, music venue, and there's usually a cover charge depending on who's performing. Freebird is located in the heart of Jacksonville Beach, directly across the street from Bukkets and just a few blocks away from Ocean Club, the Atlantic, Lynch's, and the Ritz. Check the Web site for the upcoming lineup.

THE LEMON BAR
120 Atlantic Blvd., Neptune Beach (behind the Sea Horse Oceanfront Inn)
(904) 246-2175
www.seahorseoceanfrontinn.com
The Lemon Bar, tucked away behind the Sea Horse Oceanfront Inn, is as Insider as Insider can be. A popular hangout for Neptune Beach and Atlantic Beach locals who show up on bicycle, The Lemon Bar also attracts folks from all over town. Located right on the ocean, the bar is run by the motel but manages to feel hip and separate from it. Listen to the waves crash on the beach while you sip frozen drinks and flirt with local beach bums. The bar is known to close dur-

Close-up

Lynyrd Skynyrd

If you grew up on Jacksonville's Westside in the late sixties and early seventies, chances are you have a **Lynyrd Skynyrd** story to tell. For the uninitiated, Lynyrd Skynyrd, a popular Southern rock band, was named after Leonard Skinner, a gym teacher at Robert E. Lee High School in Jacksonville who suspended two of the band members for repeated dress code violations, including hair that touched their ears. Ronnie VanZant, the band's undisputed leader, organized the group in 1964. The band initially played under many names before arriving at Lynyrd Skynyrd, a "disguised dis" to the old coach. (Leonard Skinner, by the way, is actively involved in helping keep the band's memory alive. He often attends Skynyrd events and signs autographs.) Perhaps the group's most famous song is "**Freebird**," which, according to BMI, has been played on the radio more than two million times. On October 20, 1977, the band was riding high, en route to a gig in Baton Rouge, Louisiana, when their chartered plane ran out of gas over a Mississippi swamp. The resulting crash killed three of the seven band members, including Ronnie VanZant. These days, Lynyrd Skynyrd still exists with three original band members and Ronnie's younger brother Johnny singing vocals.

ing winter months and rainy periods, so call to make sure it's open before heading out.

LYNCH'S IRISH PUB
514 North First St., Jacksonville Beach
(904) 249-5181
On Mondays, this Irish pub hosts a fab 80s night when the club is packed with 20- to 30-year-olds amped up for a retro evening. Lynch's is known for its good music, good pub food, good drinks, and good Guinness. If you're into the Irish pub thing, go on any other night around 5 p.m., order a plate of fish-and-chips, and talk with the bartenders who hail from Northern Ireland. Lynch's serves a full menu until 1:30 a.m.

MONKEY'S UNCLE
1850 South Third St., Jacksonville Beach
(904) 246-1070
www.monkeysuncletavern.com
When you just have to belt out some karaoke, come here. The karaoke setup is located right by the front door, so if you really lay an egg, you can make a quick getaway. The drinks are cheap and strong here, and the crowd skews older. Monkey's Uncle has been a watering hole at the beach for years. It's located in a strip center near

a popular movie house and includes a poolroom, a patio bar, and entertainment nightly from live music to the aforementioned karaoke. Happy hour runs from 2 to 7 p.m., and there is a full-service liquor store on-site.

OCEAN CLUB
401 North First St., Jacksonville Beach
(904) 242-8884
www.myspace.com/ocjax
The Ocean Club is a current favorite on the Beaches club scene. Located in a renovated lounge right on the ocean, the club has a huge room for dancing, a pool room, an outside oceanfront deck, and a spacious bar to sit around, order drinks, and meet people. *NOTE:* There is a dress code here, unusual for Beaches nightspots: no flip-flops, sneakers, shorts, or jeans. Lots of would-be patrons get angry over this, but the club has no problem filling up. In fact, there's usually a long line to get in. Be warned: the club admits 18+ patrons on Thursday nights.

PETE'S BAR
117 First St., Neptune Beach
(904) 249-9158
**www.petesbar.net or www.myspace.com/
petesbar**

Author John Grisham turned Pete's Bar into a national icon when he made it a featured locale in his book *The Brethren*. Pete's was the first bar to open in Duval County after Prohibition, and it no doubt has some regulars who've been coming ever since. The crowd here is very mixed: neighborhood residents who play pool and drink longnecks and tourists who've read that no bar-hopping excursion to the Beaches is complete without a stop at Pete's. This place can get mighty crowded, which makes it difficult to find a seat. Oh, and if you value your life, try not to bump into a pool player while he or she is taking a shot. They're not very gracious about it.

RAGTIME TAVERN AND SEAFOOD GRILLE
207 Atlantic Blvd., Atlantic Beach
(904) 241-7877
www.ragtimetavern.com
Ragtime is a supremely good brewpub, bar, and tapas bar (and that means three full bars here) that sits just one block from the ocean. It's also a popular restaurant (see the Restaurants chapter). The crowd here is more mature, late 20s and up, and boasts a cadre of regulars who live within walking distance and let hardly a night go by without a visit. Be sure to try a glass of Dolphin's Breath, a popular beer brewed on the premises and named by a local contest winner. Ragtime is a good place to meet a teacher, musician, or a naval officer. Expect large crowds here on the weekends and live music in the brewpub that reverberates throughout the restaurant and tavern.

> **i** The Florida Highway Patrol often sets up late-night roadblocks on Beach and Atlantic Boulevards, the two main highways leading to the Beaches, to check for drunk drivers or anyone driving with a revoked or suspended license.

SUN DOG DINER
207 Atlantic Blvd., Neptune Beach
(904) 241-8221
www.sundogjax.com

As the name suggests, this is largely an eatery (see the Restaurants chapter), but after 9:30 p.m. it's also a club with a full bar, dance floor, and live music. Sun Dog is located a block from the ocean, across the street from the Ragtime Tavern and Seafood Grille. Locals come to hear friends play music—everything from acoustic guitar to modern jazz. The decor is part of the charm; it's a new diner built to look like an old one.

GAMBLING VENUES

THE POKER ROOM AT ORANGE PARK KENNEL CLUB
455 Park Ave., Orange Park

THE POKER ROOM AT ST. JOHNS GREYHOUND PARK
6322 Racetrack Rd.
(904) 646-0002
www.jaxkennel.com
The Orange Park Kennel Club and St. Johns Greyhound Park both offer Poker Rooms that are as much fun for accomplished players as they are for beginners. Each location boasts around 40 tables offering Texas Hold 'em; 7-card Stud; Omaha; 7-card, 8 or Better; Omaha, 8 or Better; and Crazy Pineapple, along with daily tournaments. Expect to slap down a $40 buy-in for regular games and a $100 buy-in on No Limit Texas Hold 'em games. The busiest time of the week is Saturday afternoon, when the owners say the places fill up with their two major types of customers: college students and retirees. The minimum age to play here is 18; 21 for World Series of Poker Satellite events. Be sure to tip the dealer if you win a hand.

One difference worth noting is that that the Poker Room at Orange Park Kennel Club offers Rookie Night every Wednesday night from 7 to 9 p.m. Rookie Night is free, and you have a great chance to win prizes—including $40 worth of chips. Additionally, training tables are open at both Poker Rooms from 5 to 8 p.m. weekdays and from 1 to 8 p.m. on weekends.

Expect multimedia overload as both rooms are lined with upwards of 40 big-screen TVs broadcasting live greyhound, thoroughbred, and jai alai action from across the country. Both locations also offer made-to-order sushi, a full bar, and table service. Both locations are open Sunday through Thursday from noon to midnight and Friday and Saturday from 1 p.m. to 1 a.m.

SUNCRUZ CASINO
4378 Ocean St., Mayport
(904) 249-9300
www.suncruzcasino.com
Jacksonville's casino ships are popular with gamblers and non-gamblers alike. The gamblers are drawn to the ship for obvious reasons: high stakes and big fun. Non-gamblers enjoy having the opportunity to get out on the water for a few hours. SunCruz, located in the historic fishing village of Mayport, offers four daily cruises, food, drink, big-screen TVs, and ocean gambling once the ship gets a mile off the Florida coast and into international waters. SunCruz offers Blackjack, Texas Hold 'em, Let It Ride, and 3-Card Poker as well as 300 Vegas-Style slots, Roulette, Craps (5x Odds), mini-Baccarat, and free drinks while you're playing. Ships sail twice daily from Wednesday through Sunday, once at 11 a.m. and again at 7 p.m. Cruises run between four and five-and-a-half hours, depending on the day and time. Check SunCruz's Web site for the cruising schedule.

HEALTH, FUN, AND FITNESS

Whether you're stopping in for a visit or staying for good, you'll want to take advantage of Jacksonville's indoor pursuits, and outdoor recreation. Apart from the well-subscribed leisure endeavors of running, beach sports and river sailing (see the Annual Events, Parks, and Boating and Watersports chapters for more on those), Jacksonville natives also love the free-wheeling trifecta of cycling, yoga and dancing.

Forget the hotel treadmill; think downward-facing dog with an ocean view, or the down-stroke of your bike pedal as you glide along the coast. And if you love the swirl of a skirt and the call of a tune, the city's numerous folk dancing clubs invite all comers with pre-dance lessons and an all-are-welcome attitude.

So, whether you like your fitness speedy, spinning or contemplative, Jacksonville accommodates an active lifestyle with fitness options to spare.

YOGA

Jacksonville loves its yoga studios, so travelers need not feel at a loss. New studios appear to pop up (or disappear) monthly, so the following is a listing of what we feel to be the most tried-and-true of the bunch. While we are not able to list all of the fine yoginis in the city, we feel sure that the following list will provide you with an experienced teacher and a reliable place to unroll your mat (or borrow one if need be).

BIKRAM YOGA—JACKSONVILLE
1531 Atlantic Blvd., Neptune Beach
(904) 714-5750
www.bikramyogajax.com

BLISS YOGA SHALA
1615 Thacker Ave.
(904) 514-0097
www.blissyogashala.com

DISCOVERY YOGA—TRAINING AND
CLASSES
3 Davis St., St. Augustine
(904) 824-7454
www.discoveryyoga.com

POWER YOGA—SAN MARCO SOUTH
3825 Hendricks Ave. 32207
(904) 655-4642
www.yoga-power.com

DANCES

Loosen up with Jacksonville's folk dancing community. Dances for all levels and in all styles are going on around town throughout the week. In all cases, newcomers are welcome and lessons are available in the beginning of the evening before the dance starts in earnest. Other drop-in lessons and socials in all styles, too many to list here, are available throughout the city. A quick Internet search will turn up the latest additions and some new ones we Insiders don't even know about yet.

DANCEFLORIDA CONTRA DANCE
Riverside Presbyterian Church, Kissling Hall
849 Park St.
(904) 396-1997
www.danceflorida.com
Learn the swings and promenades of contra dance and make some new friends in the process. Popular nationwide, contra dancing seems to be particularly popular in Jacksonville where

dances draw folks of all ages and skill levels from teens to seniors. Head to Riverside Presbyterian Church every third Friday and dance from 8 to 11 p.m. Experienced locals teach dance basics at 7:45 p.m. Organizers ask for a donation of $7 for adults and $3 for those 18 and under to help pay for the live band and caller. Bring a food or beverage item to share and take a dollar off of your admission. Beginners and singles are heartily welcomed and may find their dance cards filled for the entire evening.

FIRST COAST SHAG CLUB
River City Brewing Company
835 Museum Circle
www.firstcoastshagclub.com
Come down to River City Brewing every Wednesday night for shaggin' on the St. Johns with the First Coast Shag Club. Club members teach Carolina Shag Dance and dance to beach music until 10 p.m. The club offers free beginner and intermediate dance lessons and open dances. Intermediate shag lessons run from 7 to 7:30 p.m., basic shag lessons go from 7:30 to 8 p.m. There's no cover charge and plenty of free parking and a breathtaking nighttime view of the city skyline.

ST. ANDREW'S SCOTTISH COUNTRY DANCE OF JACKSONVILLE
Mark Spivak's Dance Extension
3740 San Jose Place
(321) 302-4152
www.danceflorida.com

This group meets almost every Thursday evening at a local dance studio. Classes start promptly at 7 p.m. and continue until 9. Participants are asked to chip in $3 to pay for the hall. You do not need a partner to attend, and everyone is welcome. Organizers suggest that you wear soft-soled shoes such as leather dance shoes (ghillies) or ballet shoes. No street shoes are allowed in the dance room.

CYCLING CLUBS

OPEN ROAD BICYCLES WEEKLY RIDES
4460 Hendricks Ave. (Miramar Center)
(904) 636-7772
www.openroadbicycles.com
Jacksonville's friendliest local bike shop, Open Road offers group rides every evening except Sunday. Rides are organized by ability level, so just choose the level that's right for your level of fitness and show up. In fact, come a little early to check out the store and meet some new friends.

Weekly Road Ride Schedule:
Monday: 6:15 p.m., 25 miles, 20-22 mph
Tuesday: 6 p.m., 45 miles, 30+ mph
Tuesday: 6:30 p.m., 20 miles, 18-20 mph, no drop (road bikes, please)
Wednesday: 6:15 p.m., 25 miles, 20-22 mph
Thursday: 6:15 p.m., 25 miles, 20-22 mph, bridge workout
Saturday: 7:30 a.m., 25-40 miles, speed varies
The use of helmets and lights, as needed, is mandatory on all rides.

SHOPPING

Jacksonville, once a shopping desert, has transformed into a shoppers' delight. This has much to do with the development of St. Johns Town Center, a modern outdoor plaza offering luxury brands like Louis Vuitton and restaurants like Cantina Laredo that are both new to the area and surprisingly good. Shopping also got more hometown-fun with the arrival of the Riverside Arts Market under the Fuller Warren Bridge every Saturday where folks from all walks of life come on Saturday mornings to meet and mingle over apples, meat pies, and local artwork.

What follows should give shoppers, spontaneous or otherwise, a starting point. The shopping center listings are arranged by neighborhood, including Riverside/Avondale, Southside/San Marco, and the Beaches. Downtown Jacksonville isn't a shopping mecca because, like a lot of cities, most of the stores headed to the suburbs in the 1960s. The Jacksonville Landing and a few scattered specialty stores are still Downtown draws, but have not been able to keep up with the times as much as the newer shopping plazas have.

The area also has some nearby outlet malls, which are about 40 minutes south of Jacksonville in St. Augustine. While not necessarily Insider, the outlets have recently expanded to include some luxury brands with slightly lower prices. Be aware: some designer outlets only stock merchandise that has been specifically designed for their outlet locations' lower price point and do not carry the same merchandise as their normal retail stores do. That being said, the good stuff still makes appearances at reduced prices.

After the shopping centers, the chapter is divided into areas of interest such as Women's and Men's Clothing, and Bookstores, each of which is followed by a listing of local-favorite specialty shops. (It's impossible to list all of the fine stores in Jacksonville, that would be a book unto itself, but this list hits most of the high points.)

Jacksonville's Farmers' Market and Arts Market scene has boomed in recent years. Look to that section for activities best enjoyed on a sunny afternoon with or without the kids.

In the end, there's no shortage of places to spend your money in Jacksonville. May you find plenty of fine goods and plenty of bargains!

MALLS AND SHOPPING CENTERS

Riverside/Avondale

FIVE POINTS
Intersection of Park, Margaret and Lomax Streets
www.5pointsjax.com
One of Jacksonville's oldest and most mercurial neighborhoods, Five Points sits in a little vortex in the Riverside area. The area is not only historic but also filled with contemporary character. Five

Points favorites like Edge City, Rainbows and Stars, Fans and Stoves Antique Mall, and Midnight Sun ensure that the intersection remains both grounded and edgy.

SHOPS OF HISTORIC AVONDALE
On St. Johns Avenue between Talbot and Van Wert Avenues
www.historicavondale.com
This is one of the prettiest places to shop in all of Jacksonville. St. Johns Avenue runs through Riverside and Avondale, two historic neighborhoods with majestic oak trees and elegant old homes,

some dating back to the early 1900s. Stroll along St. Johns Avenue, or detour down a shady side street toward the river to take in more beautifully renovated homes. Boutiques, restaurants, art galleries, and spas line St. Johns Avenue, which is anchored by Biscotti's, a popular neighborhood eatery with a loyal citywide following (see the Restaurants chapter). Across the street The Brick offers live music and a solid beer, wine, and liquor selection.

Southside/San Marco

AVENUES SHOPPING MALL
10300 Southside Blvd.
(904) 363-3060
www.simon.com
The Avenues is located in that amorphous area of Jacksonville called the Southside, more specifically off I-95 at Philips Highway. This indoor mall offers more than 160 stores, kiosks, and eateries, including national anchor stores Dillard's, Belk, JCPenney, and Sears. You'll also find such well-known shops as Pottery Barn, Williams-Sonoma, Jos. A. Bank, Talbot's, Banana Republic, Abercrombie & Fitch, Eddie Bauer, and more. MAC Cosmetics has a stand-alone store, which is a favorite place to buy contemporary makeup and get the help you need applying it. The mall has a busy food court, free covered parking decks, and large uncovered parking lots.

SHOPS OF SAN MARCO
San Marco Boulevard near Atlantic
Boulevard and Hendricks Avenue
San Marco Square is one of the more charming of Jacksonville's shopping areas. Some 30 shops, eateries, and art galleries make up the Square, which is located on three streets: San Marco and Atlantic Boulevards and Hendricks Avenue. The Grotto is a popular wine bar and store that hosts wine tastings every Thursday. (You get a portion of the participation fee back if you buy the featured wine. See the Nightlife section for details.) The Write Touch is a small stationery store with an impressive and elegant selection of fine stationery and desk accessories. Edward's is a

much loved tobacco shop, which also sells good "guy" gifts like walking canes, picture frames, and chess sets. Stellers Gallery is worth a stop even if you aren't looking to buy artwork. Theatre Jacksonville is one of the best places in the city to see a community theater production, and check out nearby Bistro Aix or Pizza Palace when you're ready for lunch or dinner (see the Restaurants chapter).

ST. JOHNS TOWN CENTER
4663 River City Dr. (J. Turner Butler
Boulevard, Gate Parkway exit)
(904) 998-7156
The new jewel in Jacksonville's shopping crown, the continually expanding St. Johns Town Center draws over 10 million visitors each year with the center's 1.1 million square feet of stores and restaurants, including many that you won't find anywhere else in Jacksonville. St. Johns Town Center features 11 anchor stores such as Dillard's, Target, Barnes & Noble, Dick's Sporting Goods, DSW, and 150 attractive specialty stores to the tune of Anthropologie, Apple, Banana Republic, Bare Ecsentuals, Brooks Brothers, Coach, Guess, LACOSTE, Louis Vuitton, lululemon athletica, Kate Spade, Sephora, and many others. Restaurants, many new to the area, honor a variety of nationalities and cater to most price points. Cantina Laredo offers excellent gourmet Mexican fare, while The Capital Grille, Mitchell's Fish Market, J. Alexander's, Maggiano's Little Italy, and many others draw crowds throughout the week.

The Beaches

BEACHES TOWN CENTER
200 First St., Neptune Beach
(904) 241-1026
www.beachestowncenter.com
Located across the street from the ocean at the end of Atlantic Boulevard, this charming shopping area is only about 3 blocks long and 2 blocks wide and is surrounded by beautiful beach homes. To understand the geography, it helps to realize that the north side of Atlantic Boulevard is Atlantic Beach and the south side is Neptune Beach. Town Center

encompasses both communities. The Book Mark has been consistently voted the best independent bookstore in the city by readers of *Folio Weekly*, the city's free alternative magazine. If you're lucky, you'll catch a favorite author here for a reading and book signing. Cobalt Moon is a great place for travelers to take a yoga or Tai Chi class on a walk-in basis. Town Center also boasts two of the most popular nightspots in the city: Pete's Bar and Ragtime (see the Nightlife chapter).

SAWGRASS VILLAGE
1300 Sawgrass Village Dr.
Highway A1A, south of J. Turner Butler
Boulevard, Ponte Vedra
(904) 565-2635
www.sawgrassvillagepvb.com
Sawgrass Village is located in Ponte Vedra, directly across TPC Boulevard from the Sawgrass Marriott Resort. In fact, resort guests are some of the Village's best customers. There are some 40 specialty shops and eateries here. One Hot Cookie makes one-of-a-kind, made-to-order cookies and ice cream desserts. Aqua Grill is a local favorite for its lakefront dining, patio seating, and full-service bar. Get a mani-pedi at Sawgrass Nails or have your color touched up at Albert Paul's salon. Sawgrass Village also boasts a liquor store, a Publix grocery store, and a drugstore.

ST. AUGUSTINE PREMIUM OUTLETS AND
PRIME OUTLETS
I-95, exit 95 at SR 16
(904) 825-1555, (904) 826-1311
www.premiumoutlets.com
www.primeoutlets.com
This newly revived set of outlet centers went through a tired period but has found new life with an infusion of luxury brands like Dooney & Bourke, Kate Spade, Gucci, Hugo Boss, Michael Kors, St. John, Escada and BCBGMAXAZRIA. Two huge outlet malls blanket the east and west sides of I-95 at exit 95. St. Augustine Premium Outlets is located on the west side of the interstate, with 95 factory stores representing Aeropostale, Bass, Tommy Bahama, Izod, Gap, J. Crew, Reebok, Calvin Klein, and more. Prime Outlets, located

on the east side of the interstate, is where the above-mentioned luxury brands are located, alongside upwards of 75 other factory outlet stores, including American Apparel, Fossil, Greg Norman, Guess, Juicy Couture, Kenneth Cole, Lucky Brand Jeans, Saks Fifth Avenue OFF 5th, and 2b bebe. Both outlet malls have food courts, huge parking lots, and moderate bargains. The outlet malls are a good 45-minute drive south of Jacksonville on I-95.

During the holidays, Prime Outlets hosts a "Pajama Party" Black Friday sale with special midnight access given to pajama-wearing shoppers.

i For gift-worthy chocolates, visit Three Sisters Chocolate on San Jose Boulevard in Mandarin. The candy is made in the store, and if you don't see what you want, candymakers will create it for you. Special-order chocolate-enrobed strawberries are a real taste treat.

FARMERS' MARKETS/ARTS MARKETS

HEMMING PLAZA MARKET
117 W. Duval St.
Across from City Hall in Hemming Plaza
(904) 874-9418
www.downtownjacksonville.org (search
"Hemming Plaza Market")
Locals love shopping at the Downtown market in Hemming Plaza every Friday when the square fills with baked goods, fresh-cut flowers, and produce. Vendors showcase handmade goods, seasonal crafts, and more with a backdrop of live music and Downtown's beautiful architecture. The market runs from 10 a.m. to 2 p.m. every Friday.

JACKSONVILLE FARMERS' MARKET
1810 West Beaver St. (US 90)
(904) 354-2821
www.jaxfarmersmarket.com
Established in 1938, this recently remodeled outdoor market has remained a great place to buy fresh fruits and veggies and has earned a devoted

🔍 Close-up

Clean Green Food

A little over a decade ago, young couple Aaron and Erica Gottlieb founded **Native Sun Natural Foods Market** after a shift to an organic foods and vegetarian diet helped Aaron overcome chronic fatigue. The experience, and the insight gained along the way, convinced the couple to dedicate their lives—and livelihoods—to helping others eat right. In 1997 they opened Native Sun Natural Foods on a busy spot on San Jose Boulevard and have since become one of the city's greatest entrepreneurial success stories by offering "fresh, flavorful, and nutritious all-natural and organic foods and products that are free from pesticides, growth hormones, chemicals, artificial preservatives, and genetically-modified ingredients."

In the years since, the store has practically doubled in size (as has Aaron and Erica's family; check out the family photo hanging in the entryway of the store) and has done well enough to open a second location on Baymeadows Road.

Staffed by nutrition, education, and food research specialists, both locations bank heavily on giving customers plenty of information and personalized attention. This kind of dedication has earned the company serious recognition nationwide. In 2008 they were named Retailer of the Year by *WholeFoods Magazine* and won a Top 50 Retailer award from *Better Nutrition Magazine*. In 2003 and 2009 they were picked as Jacksonville's Best Natural Foods Store by the readers of *Folio Weekly*, and they won *Folio's* Best Organic Cuisine category in 2009. Native Sun was also named one of the country's Top 100 Health Food Stores by *Health Food Business* magazine and is listed among the city's 100 Top Shops by *Jacksonville Magazine*.

These days, Native Sun continues to hold its own in the presence of national green giants like Whole Foods, which came to town and opened very nearby in early 2009. The store continues to thrive by nature of the staff's sincere dedication to knowing their customers (many by name) and caring about what they need. In response, customers have voted with their business and stayed loyal to the local-kids-that-could.

following of longtime locals. But you're not likely to find this market written up as a tourist attraction. Jacksonville's Farmers' Market is located in an industrial part of town, and it's a real working-person's market. Over 200 farmers cart in oranges by the bushel and produce fresh out of the ground. This market is a real slice of Jacksonville's rural farm life and the people who make their living from it. And the prices can't be beat. Check out the ethnic specialties, hard-to-find items, and imported foods. Open every day of the year from before dawn to just after dusk.

RIVERSIDE ARTS MARKET (EVERY SATURDAY, APRIL THROUGH DECEMBER)
Under the Fuller Warren bridge on Riverside Avenue at I-95
904-554-6865 (information only)
www.riversideartsmarket.com

Since its grand opening in April 2009, the Riverside Arts Market (RAM) has taken hold as the new hip thing to do on a Saturday morning. Modeled after the outdoor markets of the Pacific Northwest, the Jacksonville version is very popular with 20-somethings and the stroller set. The market buzzes with art, pastries, produce, barbecue, live music, and the occasional mime or fire-breather. This is one of only a few venues where a wide variety of artists can hawk their wares week-by-week. The market also serves a valuable community function of cutting out the middleman and connecting locals with the farmers who are growing the food they put on their tables.

The family-friendly benefits of having a space in Riverside where locals can buy their weekly produce at the same time as they can listen to five hours of live music against the backdrop of the St. Johns River is not lost on Jacksonville. As a result the market is happening from open to close. Kids are charmed by the jugglers, clowns, magicians, balloon artists, troubadours, and performance artists roaming the aisles, while grown-ups load up on fruit, vegetables, meat pies, pastries, fresh bread, dairy products, honey, and eggs. Look for the popular Children's Creativity Center housed in a large tent filled with artistic play and learning activities for the kids. As an added bonus, the market sits at the terminus of the River Walk, a boardwalk that connects to all sorts of activities along the river.

ANTIQUES

AVONLEA ANTIQUE MALL
8101 Philips Hwy.
(904) 636-8785
www.avonleamall.com
This place calls itself the largest antiques mall in North Florida, and though that's hard to prove, a walk inside might convince you that there's some truth to that statement. You can spend an entire day here just walking around browsing different dealers' displays of furniture, art glass, antique toys, jewelry, leaded-glass windows, clothes, books—the list goes on and on. Avonlea is located on Philips Highway across from Lowe's. It's open Monday through Saturday from 10 a.m. to 6 p.m. On Sunday they open at noon. There's also a cafe snuggled inside a corner of the mall where you can sip a cup of hot tea and enjoy something sweet.

i The beach is a great place for a summer-evening picnic after 6 p.m., when the sun's gone down a bit. Head to Turtle Island Natural Foods Market, 363 Atlantic Blvd., for homemade dips, cold salads, entrees, cold beer, and wine, then walk two blocks to the ocean and enjoy! Check out their Web site, www.turtleisland foods.com, for a listing of seasonal events designed to increase holistic awareness and support healthy lifestyles.

BOOKSTORES

THE BOOKMARK
299 Atlantic Blvd., Atlantic Beach
(904) 241-9026
Consistently voted one of the best independent bookstores in the city, The Bookmark is a great place to go if you want a good read but need some help finding it. Owner Rona Brinlee has many connections with agents and publishers and brings in popular authors several times a month for readings and book signings. If she doesn't have the book you want, she'll order it and have it to you in a matter of days. The Bookmark is just a block from the ocean, which makes it a great stop for beachgoers who need a beach read. The free gift-wrapping makes running from the store to a birthday party a breeze.

i Looking for a good used book? Head to Chamblin Book Mine on the Westside or the new Chamblin's Uptown near Hemming Plaza Downtown. With over 1,000,000 (yes, one million) books in its inventory, Chamblin is the largest used-book store in Northeast Florida and lends itself to heady afternoons spent rummaging among the stacks. Call (904) 384-1685 or visit www. chamblinbookmine.com for more info.

THE BOOK NOOK
1620 University Blvd. West
(904) 733-4586
If you're looking for a bookstore in the San Marco area, drive south on San Jose Boulevard to The Book Nook in Lakewood, a place that some locals consider independent-bookstore heaven. In the front of this large shop you'll find the mass-market books mixed in with lots of gifts. Step inside further and you'll find a large selection of science fiction paperbacks and romance novels. Better yet, there's a ginormous selection (no exaggeration) of magazines along one side of the store. The shop serves a diverse clientele, so the owner tends to carry an equally diverse selection of books and magazines. If you can't find it here, the store will order it for you, and chances are if you

need a gift, you'll find that here as well. (Author's tip: The Book Nook is located across the parking lot from a Starbucks, so grab a good read then head over and tuck in over a latte.)

CHAMBLIN BOOK MINE
4551 Roosevelt Blvd.
(904) 384-1685
www.chamblinbookmine.com
Ron Chamblin has bought, sold, and traded more "new, used, and nonexistent" books here than some public libraries. Chamblin's stacks contain over a million books, as of the last count. He also sells magazines, comic books, records, CDs, books on tape, and videos. This store is beautifully labyrinthine, but there's never any need to feel lost or overwhelmed; if there's a book you want, the staff can usually put their hands on it. (Apart from the items in the store, Chamblin keeps lots more in storage.) Chamblin also buys used books for cash or store credit.

If you're looking for something in particular, the store's Web site has a function through which you can search their entire catalog of used books before you make the drive over. This astonishing database lists the book's condition, size and price, and enables you to purchase the book online through PayPal and have it shipped directly to your home. But don't miss out on the joy of coming to the store in person, especially when you have time to browse. You won't be disappointed. Open Monday through Saturday from 10 a.m. to 6 p.m.

Be sure to visit Chamblin's Uptown at 215 N. Laura Street near Hemming Plaza. The new location boasts a cafe, Wi-Fi and the same staggering selection of titles that made the original an Insider favorite.

CHILDREN'S CLOTHING AND TOYS

AMY'S TURN
1415 North Third St., Jacksonville Beach
(904) 241-5437
Budget-conscious shoppers love browsing through the clothing and toys at Amy's Turn.

Some things are more used than others, so make sure you have time to ferret out the great bargains hidden here. Your pocketbook will be happy with the results. Amy's Turn also sells consignment clothes for teenagers and very hip adults, but it's the baby stuff, some of it brand new, that dominates the rooms. Open 9 a.m. to 5 p.m. Monday through Saturday.

THE HOBBIE HORSE OF AVONDALE
3550 St. Johns Ave.
(904) 389-7992

THE HOBBIE HORSE OF SAN MARCO
1972 San Marco Blvd.
(904) 306-0606
www.thehobbiehorse.com
The Hobbie Horse practically screams "loaded fairy godmother." With a large selection of traditional and preppy children's clothing, as well as upscale toys like Madame Alexander dolls and porcelain tea sets, The Hobbie Horse caters to a higher-end customer with a specific idea of how little ones should look. Feeling a little cheeky? Check out the selection of mother/daughter outfits.

LOLLIPOP LANE
363 Atlantic Blvd., Neptune Beach
(904) 246-0001
From clothes to toys, there are bargains galore in this tiny consignment store. The owner, Beth, is very child-friendly and doesn't mind if your kids pull out a few toys to play with while you shop. Some items are brand-new; others are gently used. It's definitely worth a stop.

THE TOY FACTORY
The Jacksonville Landing
Independent Drive
(904) 353-4874
www.thetoyfactory.net
Business travelers who've promised to bring home a surprise for their kid will appreciate the convenience of this store located in The Jacksonville Landing. The Toy Factory is packed with classic toys, from Breyer horses to yo-yos. The store also stocks up-to-the-minute toys, books, and a

good selection of inexpensive baubles that your child can buy with his or her allowance money. Open Monday through Thursday 10 a.m. to 8 p.m., Friday and Saturday 10 a.m. to 9 p.m., and Sunday from noon to 5:30 p.m.

HOME AND SPECIALTY SHOPS

ANOMALY
1021 Park St.
(904) 354-7002
www.anomalyfivepoints.com

Not your grandma's macramé. Anomaly is a haven for indie designers and crafters of all kinds. The 5 Points shop gives independent designers a chance to sell their wares by consignment at their store. Think quality handmade clothing, reconstructed vintage clothing, unique jewelry, craft kits, indie magazines, one-of-a-kind belt buckles, and more. Anomaly also encourages its fans to "practice random acts of crafting" through kitschy classes in knitting, card making, and other handmade arts.

THE BATH AND LINEN SHOPPE
2058 San Marco Blvd.
(904) 398-7147
www.thebathandlinenshoppe.com

Sheets with obscenely high thread counts are just some of the delights of The Bath and Linen Shoppe, a San Marco tradition for more than three decades. Come here to outfit your entire bed or bath with the finest Italian linens, French soaps, and Asian silk kimonos. Owners Edward George and Kelly Barnett, who are brother and sister, may sell luxury, but they know that a commitment to high-end service is what keeps them in business. They'll make handy suggestions to help you find anything, including a gift for that person who has everything.

COBALT MOON
217 First St.
(904) 246-2131
www.cobaltmooncenter.com

Step into this store and you'll instantly feel transported to Northern California where the clothes are diaphanous, drumming and chanting fill the air, and the incense is always burning. The gift shop, located inside a much larger healing center (a great place, by the way, for travelers to take a yoga or Tai Chi class), offers a solid collection of CDs and books as well as candles, incense, and clothing.

COWFORD TRADERS
3563 St. Johns Ave.
(904) 387-9288
www.cowfordtraders.blogspot.com

The name of this shop harkens back to the early days of Jacksonville when the city was called Cowford and was not much more than a riverside pit stop along the Kings Road. This shop is a lot more sophisticated than its name implies. Look here for everything from furniture to kitchen items to writing paper. Even if you're just browsing, there's a good chance you won't leave Cowford Traders empty-handed.

EDWARD'S
2018 San Marco Blvd.
(904) 396-7990
www.edwardsofsanmarco.com

Edward's, which markets itself as more than just a tobacco shop, carries a large selection of fine cigars, pipes, and tobacco. Stop here for sophisticated man-gifts such as fountain pens, walking canes, and chess sets. And because you can light up in the store (think imported cigars and English tobacco), the inside always smells, slightly or strongly, like a combination of an old gentlemen's club and Grandpa's attic.

NESTLIVING—FURNITURE + LIGHT ETC.
1020 Park St.
(866) 905-8080
www.nest-living.com

Carrying an impressive selection of interior designs by Artek, Artemide, Ferm Living, Herman Miller, Knoll, LeKlint, Vitra, and more, this 5 Points design haven is one of the city's most accessible purveyors of modern furniture, lighting, and accessories. Nest is located in 5 Points and if you find something great that won't fit in your suitcase, Nest will ship it anywhere in the mainland United States for free.

🔍 Close-up

Jacksonville Ambassadors

On hand to give directions, answer questions, provide assistance, or chivalrously walk you to your destination, the **Downtown Ambassadors** are Jacksonville's Downtown safety and hospitality team.

Established in 2001, the Ambassadors have made a tremendous impact on locals' and visitors' perceptions of the Downtown area, which was once thought a little too seedy for comfort.

Today, the Ambassadors serve as an extra set of eyes and ears on the street, working closely with the Jacksonville Sheriff's Office and the city to improve relations in the fast-growing and constantly evolving Downtown area.

Here's a short list of some of the services that Ambassadors are on-hand to help with:

Provide you with useful **directions** and **maps.**

Escort you to your destination.

Help you **locate a business.**

Call for **medical assistance.**

Direct you to the **best parking.**

Share a smile and a **watchful eye.**

Contact the police if you need help.

Easily recognizable in their bright orange shirts and pith helmets, the Ambassadors walk and bike throughout Downtown Jacksonville, day and night, ready to lend a hand. Ambassadors are on duty Monday through Thursday from 7 a.m. to 9 p.m., Friday from 7 a.m. to 11 p.m., Saturday from 10 a.m. to 11 p.m., and Sunday from 9 a.m. to 5:30 p.m. Visit www.downtown jacksonville.org to learn more.

MIDNIGHT SUN IMPORTS
1055 Park St.
(904) 358-3869
www.themidnightsun.net
Not just for hippies, Midnight Sun is the perfect example of how a couple of Deadheads with a love of the patchouli and Southeast Asia can turn a passion for travel into a thriving business. Started over a decade ago by a young couple who parlayed their love of international adventure into a thriving import business, Midnight Sun is the place to go for anything from Balinese hand-carved doors to extraordinary fabrics. The owners travel to Bali every year to purchase hand-carved goods and furniture, to India for vibrant silks, and to Nepal for one-of-a-kind jewelry.

THE WRITE TOUCH
1967 San Marco Blvd.
(904) 398-2009
www.thewritetouch.com
If you've never known the pleasure of a perfectly balanced pen gliding across high-end stationery, stop in at The Write Touch and give it a try. The store calls itself a San Marco tradition with good cause. When a local mother needs a birth announcement, she comes here. When a bride needs a wedding invitation, she comes here. When a busy executive needs personalized stationery, she comes here. The stationery is truly fine, the service is friendly, and you'll enjoy the rarefied shopping experience.

GOLF

LAUDEN GOLF OF PONTE VEDRA
330 Hwy. A1A, Ponte Vedra
(904) 543-1433
www.laudengolf.com

Serious golfers may already know about Lauden Golf, a national golf products manufacturer headquartered in Jacksonville. Owner Jim Laudenslager is often behind the counter of his Ponte Vedra store, an unassuming place where all the local PGA Tour players come to get their clubs repaired. Laudenslager owns the patent on 108 golf-related products, including a club he calls the No.1 selling golf club in Florida—the Trifecta Plus, touted as the longest and most accurate fairway wood you can buy. Stop by the Ponte Vedra shop in the spring at TPC time when the shop is buzzing and notable pro golfers have been known to drop in. Open six days a week and on Sunday by appointment.

NORTH FLORIDA GOLF BALL CO.
815 Beach Blvd., Jacksonville Beach
(904) 247-5377
www.northfloridagolfball.com

If you hit a $5 golf ball into a water hazard, chances are it will end up here. With this in mind, the owner of North Florida Golf Ball Co. periodically dons SCUBA equipment and cleans out the ponds at various golf courses. He then resells the balls, either wholesale or retail, at his Jacksonville Beach shop. Prices, depending on the quality of the ball when it's fished out of the lagoon, range anywhere from 50 to 80 percent less than if you were to buy it new.

PGA TOUR STOP
World Golf Village, St. Augustine
(904) 940-0418
www.tourstop.com

This two-story golf superstore befits a golf mecca like World Golf Village. Everything known to man and woman that has to do with golf is sold here, from furniture with a golf theme to golf togs to special bracelets said to help cure a golfer's aches and pains. Take a swing at the four sizeable hitting areas where you can try out the myriad clubs for sale.

TOURNAMENT PLAYERS CLUB
110 TPC Blvd., Ponte Vedra
(904) 273-3235
www.tpc.com/sawgrass

Although this is a semiprivate club, the golf shop is open to the public. It has a great selection of golf shirts, many with a little logo that says TPC, which stands for The Players Championship, the annual golf tournament played on the Sawgrass Stadium Course. Anything from the shop is sure to please the golfer in your life. Tell the security guard at the west gate to the Sawgrass Country Club that you want to go to the golf shop, and he or she will let you through.

JEWELRY STORES

JACOBS JEWELERS
204 Laura St.
(904) 356-1655

Travelers staying at Downtown hotels will appreciate Jacobs Jewelers' convenient location just off Hemming Plaza. This serious Insider haunt has been serving Jacksonville since 1890 and has developed a reputation for quality diamonds, fine china, and old-school service. Be sure to take a gander at the 15-foot cast-iron clock located just outside its front door. That's classic Jacksonville! Closed Sunday.

MIRIAM'S
1966 San Marco Blvd.
(904) 398-7393
104 Bartram Oaks Walk
(904) 230-7194
2400 South Third St., Jacksonville Beach
(904) 339-0309
www.miriamsjewelry.com

Located in historic San Marco, Mandarin, and Jacksonville Beach, Miriam's specializes in hip, unusual jewelry with a large selection of silver, gold, and gemstones. And if you need to consign that diamond engagement or wedding ring that reminds you too much of your ex, Miriam's is a good place to do it.

UNDERWOOD'S JEWELERS
2044 San Marco Blvd.
(904) 398-9741
3617 St. Johns Ave.
(904) 388-5406
330 Hwy. A1A North, Ponte Vedra
(904) 280-1202
www.underwoodjewelers.com
Underwood's is Jacksonville's most traditional and most popular jewelry store, as evidenced by its Best Jewelry Store of 2009 win in *Folio Weekly*. Underwood's first opened in 1928 in Palatka, selling watches and diamonds, before expanding to Jacksonville in the 1940s. Today, Underwood's carries a large selection of jewelry by Judith Ripka, Mikimoto, and David Yurman, as well as a comprehensive selection of fine china, silver, and gifts.

MEN'S CLOTHING

KARL'S CLOTHIERS
1990 San Marco Blvd.
(904) 306-1850
www.karlsclothiers.com
This is one of Jacksonville's best bets for custom clothing—think suits made from Italian wool or shirts stitched from Sea Island cotton. You'll have to wait about two and a half weeks to receive your custom clothing, but having the right fit makes it worth the wait. Stocking such lines as Canali, Ravazzolo, and many others, Karl's specializes in both contemporary and American classic designs. Don't leave without checking out their collection of leather shoes and belts.

ROSENBLUM'S
5500 San Jose Blvd.
(904) 733-8633
2400-203 South Third St., Jacksonville Beach
(904) 247-9755
www.erosenblums.com
Richard Rosenblum is well known as one of the most gregarious shop owners in the city. Famous for remembering the neck size, sleeve length, style preferences, and occupation (and often even birthdays and spouse's names) of returning customers (even those who only come in once a year), Rosen-

blum has developed a loyal following throughout town. The San Jose Boulevard store, situated on the St. Johns River, is the hub, with the Jacksonville Beach location serving the Beaches communities. Founded by brothers Richard and Bob's grandfather more than 100 years ago, Rosenblum's takes their reputation for quality, service, and hospitality very seriously. Their custom clothing, especially shirts, which can be tweaked with countless variations in fabric, cuff, and collar, lasts for years. Keep an eye out for their trunk shows and annual sales and ask about their Lifetime Alterations policy, Closet Cleaning services, and special Made to Measure Value Events.

SURF SHOPS

AQUA EAST SURF SHOP
696 Atlantic Blvd., Neptune Beach
(904) 246-2550
www.aquaeast.com
Aqua East is the Big Kahuna of local surf shops. At first glance, the large selection of itsy-bitsy bikinis, baggies, sandals, and T-shirts makes it look like a chain store, but walk upstairs, where the new and used surfboards are sold, and the talk is all surf. Aqua East also offers lessons on how to get up on that board.

i Peterbrooke's chocolate-covered popcorn, chocolate-dipped Nutter Butters, and chocolaty graham crackers top our list of Insider treats. The popcorn combines salty and sweet with eye-rolling effects, and the Nutter Butters prove that you really can improve on the world's most perfect cookie. Visit Peterbrooke's San Marco location at 2024 San Marco Blvd. and prepare to restrain yourself . . . or not.

SUNRISE SURF SHOP
834 Beach Blvd., Jacksonville Beach
(904) 241-0822
www.sunrisesurfshop.com
This is where local surfers have shopped since 1975. Sunrise has a great collection of wet suits and new and used surfboards, as well as boards to rent for an

SHOPPING

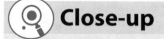 **Close-up**

Hot Sauces

Shopping for a quintessential Jacksonville souvenir? Forget flamingo-themed tchotchkes (there aren't any flamingoes in Jacksonville anyway) and head to a specialty food or grocery store to buy a bottle of locally concocted **pepper sauce**. Northeast Florida is a hotbed for the fiery stuff, with several popular brands manufactured in the Jacksonville area and sold around the nation.

The area's condiment commerce started in the early eighties when Chris Way, owner of **Barnacle Bill's**, a St. Augustine restaurant, wanted to create a fish sauce. He grabbed some datil peppers, tomatoes, and honey and started mixing. (Food historians believe that datil peppers crossed the ocean on trading vessels sailing from Cuba to La Florida in the early 1800s, then found their way into the gardens surrounding the Spanish stronghold of St. Augustine.)

Way's concoction was an instant hit, and demand quickly grew. A customer who worked at the Winn-Dixie grocery store chain promised Way that he'd get the sauce on his store's shelves if Way would start bottling it. By 1985 Way realized that he had a hot commodity on his hands and started bottling the sauce.

He formed a company—**Dat'l Do-it, Inc.**—planted 1,500 datil pepper plants on the Dat'l Do-it corporate farm, and developed new products like Hellish Relish, Hot Vinegar, and Datil Pepper Jelly. He even opened a Dat'l Do-it Hot Shop on historic St. George Street in St. Augustine. By 1993 bottles of Dat'l Do-it hot sauce graced the tables of homes and restaurants across the nation, and sales reached nearly half a million dollars.

afternoon. Teenagers love the cool T-shirts and the store's frequent two-for-one specials.

WOMEN'S CLOTHING

CRAVE
1018 Park St.
(904) 357-3654
www.cravedenim.com
Crave in 5 Points is a jackpot of indie designer brands and premium denim for men and women. With pieces from Antik Denim, James Jeans, Alice & Trixie, and Earnest Sewn, as well as Mat and Nat purses, Boheme jewelry, and blouses from Lyric Culture and Gypsy 05, Crave is a good starting place for any day of shopping. Men aren't left out; Crave's selection of English Laundry and Rock and Roll Revolution shirts were chosen for their great tailoring and fit. Bonus: book an appointment for a private fitting and you'll have the store and the owner all to yourself store for an hour or more.

EDGE CITY
1017 Park St.
(904) 353-9423
www.gunnel.com
Owned by the alternately mercurial and reticent 5 Points fixtures, Tom and Gunnel (no last names necessary), Edge City has been keeping teens and 20-somethings stylishly turned out since 1975. Fashion hounds will want to buy everything in this store, from dresses to headbands to antique mirrors. Shop for the latest lines from Betsey Johnson, Vivienne Tam, French Connection, and more. Little known fact: the store also sells discounted overstocks and end-of-the-line clearance pieces in their booth at Fans and Stoves Antique Mall down the block.

EMLY BENHAM
3635 St. Johns Ave.
(904) 387-2121
2400 South Third St., Jacksonville Beach
(904) 246-1401
http://emlybenham.wordpress.com

These days, Way and his partners say that sales are still increasing. For instance, they closed the store on St. George Street because the sauce was sold all over town anyway and a corporate store wasn't necessary. They stopped growing their own peppers because it was too time-consuming. Area farmers could grow them just as well, and they were happy for the work. But Way and his team have continued to get their pepper sauce and other products on store shelves throughout the country.

The success of Dat'l Do-it fired up other hot sauce aficionados like Tom Nuijens, who owns **Half Moon Bay Trading Company** in Atlantic Beach. Half Moon's biggest seller is a line of Iguana-brand pepper sauces, which he manufactures in a factory in the hills outside San Jose, Costa Rica. Nuijens, an avid surfer, then imports the sauces and sells them around the world, from Australia to Sweden.

Nuijens used to be the creative director at a large Jacksonville advertising agency, and it shows. All the pepper sauces are artfully labeled with an iguana on the bottle and come with names like Iguana Mean Green, Iguana Island Pepper, Iguana Triple X, Iguana Bold Gold, and Iguana Radioactive. (Can you guess which one's the hottest?)

Nuijens says his pepper sauce is so popular that restaurant owners complain to him that people steal the bottles from the tables. Still, there must be lots of people who buy it, because the company enjoys blockbuster sales year after year. Iguana pepper sauces are sold in specialty food stores at the Beaches as well as through the company's warehouse at 210 Mayport Rd. in Atlantic Beach. The warehouse is open Monday through Friday from 9:30 a.m. to 4:30 p.m., except when, as Nuijens puts it, "there's surf."

With locations in Jacksonville and Jacksonville Beach, Emly Benham carries shoes, bags, and accessories to flip over. Stocking the latest from jewelry designer Alexis Bittar as well as clothing from the hippest of the hip, including Balenciaga, One of 2, Prada Rossa Linea, and White + Warren, Emly Benham is one of the best places to find a variety of cutting-edge collections in town. The St. Johns Avenue location is open Monday through Friday 10 a.m. to 5 p.m. and Saturday 10 a.m. to 4 p.m., but the beach location is open an hour later (6 p.m.) Monday through Saturday. Both shops are closed on Sunday.

KRISTA EBERLE
2020 San Marco Blvd.
(904) 396-2711
240 A1A, Ponte Vedra
(904) 280-6944
Local gal Krista Eberle stocks designer clothing by Nicole Miller, BCBG, Michael Stars, and more in her San Marco store. The San Marco store exudes a rarefied air and has high-end appeal.

OLIVE
1988 San Marco Blvd.
(904) 346-1900
www.oliveclothes.com
Want to feel both hip and pretty? Head to Olive, one of the city's best places to snap up feminine-yet-wearable dresses and denim from Trina Turk, Milly, Tibi, Citizen, Velvet, BCBG, Rock & Republic, and more. Olive also hosts seasonal trunk shows, so be sure to check if your visit coincides with one of these wallet-friendly events.

REVE
1958 San Marco Blvd.
(904) 398-9399
Several ago I fell so in love with a lime green wallet by the cruelty-free accessories company Matt & Nat that I was willing to hand over a sizeable chunk of my then-paltry salary to the gals at Reve in exchange for it. The fact that I still carry (and adore) the wallet today is a testament to Reve's inventory's long-term appeal. Reve carries frolic-

some lines like T-bags, Hype, Sweet Pea, R Jean, Butterfly Dropout, Custo Barcelona, and more. The collections aren't easy on the wallet, but very little of value ever is.

ROSIE TRUE
1960 San Marco Blvd.
(904) 396-7463
2400-104 S. 3rd St.
(904) 247-8464
www.rosietrue.com

If you value funky, timeless pieces that turn heads and inspire envy, swing by Rosie True where noteworthy denim, cashmere, shoes, jewelry, and underpinnings reign supreme. Rosie True stocks collections by Calypso, Billy Blues, Susana Monaco, Jake's Dry Goods, AG, and Grassroots. Think feminine, positive, languid, and gorgeous.

VENUS SWIMWEAR
11711 Marco Beach Dr.
(888) 782-2224
www.venusswimwear.com

Looking for a very Florida bathing suit? Head to the Venus Swimwear store located off Beach Boulevard near the company's own swimwear factory. Tops and bottoms are sold separately, so mix and match to your heart's (and body's) content. The outlet store also has lots of sales and clearance prices on floaty dresses and cover-ups, as well as last year's swimsuit designs. If you look hot in a Venus swimsuit, try entering the annual Venus Swimwear Model Search. Find out how on the company's Web site.

VIOLET
1007 Park St.
(904) 355-4449

Violet loves the funk. Established almost a decade ago in 5 Points as a 100-percent vintage shop, this independent boutique has undergone a style evolution under its new owner, Texie. These days, Violet offers a well-edited selection of eclectic, international clothing, fragrances, handbags, jewelry, and more. Think Anthousa, Built by Wendy, Erica Weiner, and Lotta Jansdotter.

SALONS AND SPAS

Jacksonville Insiders love to look good. Thankfully, an undercurrent of hip new salons and spas has joined with some traditional favorites to add depth and edge to the city's beauty scene. The majority of the city's more hip and forward-thinking salons can be found in the Riverside, Avondale and 5-Points areas, while the Beaches are home to some time-honored standbys that serve as elegant and reliable go-tos.

Thanks to the city's plethora of options, it's generally not difficult to get an appointment at any of the city's spas and salons, even on short notice. So pick up the phone and make a date for a new do, a facial, a massage, or a mani-pedi with any of these Insider faves.

ALPHA BEAUTY CLINIC
4131 Southside Blvd.
(904) 998-9977
www.alphabeautyclinic.com
The treatments at Alpha are the stuff of spa dreams. Book a Microcurrent Facial or the newly introduced Alpha Bamboo Massage Therapy. Alpha also offers traditional body treatments here such as waxing (try the Sphinx bikini wax) and manicures/pedicures with add-ons like paraffin and thermal seaweed masks that will make your hands and feet feel like new again. The Copacabana Bronze and Glow, which involves a sea salt glow plus tanning, gives you that sun-kissed glow without hours on the beach. To make it even more convenient for international travelers, Pycckuú (Russian), Espanõl, Português, Hindi, Punjabi, Tagalog, Italian, English, and even Texan are spoken.

BLU
820 Post St.
(904) 353-4411
Eclectic and easy to get to no matter where you live, Blu's color and razor cuts are turning heads. The salon's walls stage original works by local artists and the stylists are hip and popular.

CALVIN COLE SALON AND DAY SPA
675 Atlantic Blvd., Atlantic Beach
(904) 246-6622
www.calvincolesalon.com
Calvin Cole enjoys a great location in Atlantic Beach within walking distance of the shops and hotels of the Beaches Town Center. The salon offers haircuts, color, and mani-pedis as well as a variety of massages, salt glows, and body mud masks. Call first and they'll usually squeeze you in. The salon stocks AVEDA hair, skin care, makeup, and body products, as well as the Dermalogica clinical skin care line.

CASABLANCA BEAUTY CENTER & DAY SPA
5209 St. Johns Ave.
(904) 389-5533
www.casablancabeautycentre.com
It's best to call ahead if you want an appointment. But once you're on the appointment track, you'll be treated like a king or queen whenever you're here. Casablanca is known for its makeovers, and experts are available for makeup, hair color, haircut, waxing, massage, nails—you name it. Ask about the Day of Beauty. Book one and you'll leave a better you. Closed Sunday.

DIRTY BLONDE SALON
2409 Third St. South, Jacksonville Beach
(904) 241-4247
This is a very cool little place. Count on getting a good haircut and good color here. It's also a popular stop for waxing and facials. Best of all, you won't have to wait months for an appointment. And you don't even have to be a blonde.

HAIR PEACE
815 Lomax St.
(904) 356-6856
A 5 Points institution, Hair Peace attracts a varied clientele from Downtown businessmen to hip teens. The salon's old-school décor, affable owner, and core group of long-term stylists all contribute to the salon's position as a Riverside staple.

LOCKSTAR CUT & COLOR STUDIO
869 Stockton St.
(904) 388-7270
www.lockstarstudio.com
In-the-know locals and Riverside hipsters love the modern edge and motto, "If you aren't living on the edge, you're taking up too much space." Think tattoos, a friendly attitude, and a great cut.

ROYAL ESSENCE SPA & NAILS
4866 Big Island Dr., Suite 3
(904) 565-4209
www.royalessencenailspa.com
A hidden gem disguised as a chain manicure salon, Royal Essence is a new, family-owned-and-run nail and waxing spa with amenities and friendliness to spare. Located adjacent to St. Johns Town Center, Royal Essence excels service, value, and personal relationships. Manicures and pedicures come with complimentary paraffin treatments, hot-stone arm and leg massage, and hot towels. The shop is super-clean, the staff is eager to please, and you'll leave feeling like you got way more than your money's worth.

THE SPA AT THE PONTE VEDRA INN AND CLUB
200 Ponte Vedra Blvd., Ponte Vedra
(904) 273-7700
www.pvspa.com
You don't have to be a guest at the Ponte Vedra Inn and Club to enjoy The Spa. Anyone with an appointment and some extra bucks in his or her pocket can come here and live like a blueblood, if only for a few hours. This popular day spa does it all, from haircuts to facials, nail care, body scrubs, and massages. Most customers choose to schedule more than one beauty treatment. Come early or make time in between or after treatments to sip complimentary mimosas or sparkling water and relax in the garden's hot pool. You'll leave feeling like a million bucks.

ATTRACTIONS AND TOURS

Jacksonville is an outdoor town, and visitors often find that they're way more active here than they normally are at home. In the summer, once the heat of the day begins to ease up, neighborhoods, parks, and the Beaches come alive, and the chances are very good that you'll find yourself doing something here that you'd never do at home, say riding bikes to dinner, running on the beach at sunrise, fishing from a kayak, or horseback riding in the surf.

The diversity of attractions here, coupled with Jacksonville's natural beauty, keeps visitors coming back to play tennis, golf, fish, or just lie on the beach year after year.

I've divided the activities and tours into the following categories: Activities, Museums, and Points of History so that you can more easily find what you're looking for. Some items straddle both categories, like the Museum of Science and History, which is both a museum and a great kids' spot.

Definitely schedule something historical during your time here. A great pick in that category is Kingsley Plantation, an indigo and cotton plantation from the early 1800s that is now a national park. There's the "big house" that owner Zephaniah Kingsley called home, and the remnants of many small tabby huts where his slaves lived.

We also recommend at least one tour, be it an art tour at the Cummer Museum, or a self-guided tour of Downtown. After all, who doesn't like going home a little smarter than they were when they left?

In addition to the listings in this chapter, don't hesitate to check out other chapters and combine your activities; for example, why not combine a visit to the Museum of Contemporary Art with lunch at De Real Ting or cocktails at one of the many Downtown nightspots.

We've done our best to include up-to-the-minute information about hours and admission fees, but if you're on a tight budget or tight schedule, please call ahead to check if anything has changed since this book was published.

Price Code

$ . . . . Less than $5
$$ . . . . $6 to $10
$$$ . . . . $11 to $15
$$$$ . . . . $16 and over

ACTIVITIES

AMELIA RIVER CRUISES $$$$$
(877) 264-9972
www.ameliarivercruises.com
All aboard for a two-hour ferry cruise past salt marshes and wilderness beaches on Cumberland Island's western shore. Keep an eye out for wild horses, the ruins of Dungeness, and wildlife galore. Cruises run March through February.

Adults $26, seniors $24, children under 12 years-old $20, children under three come along for free.

ATP TENNIS COURTS $$$$
201 ATP Tour Blvd., Ponte Vedra
(904) 285-6400
www.atptennis.com
The Association of Tennis Professionals is the governing body for men's professional tennis. At tour headquarters in Ponte Vedra, there are 17 tennis courts of grass, clay, and cushioned hard surface. Tennis fans of all ages can take lessons or clinics from former tour players, then shop for tennis togs in the pro shop. Call in advance for class and clinic schedules or court reservations.

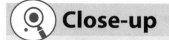

Close-up

Whip It Good

Just when you thought Jacksonville had become a one-note town in terms of sports, in roll the **Jacksonville Roller Girls** and their aptly named **New Jax City Rollers, River City Rat Pack,** and **Duval Derby Dames** roller derby teams. Notorious for re-invigorating the serious sport of roller derby in Northeast Florida, these roller chicks bring it—and bring it hard!

First the basics: the Jacksonville Roller Girls are a flat-track roller-derby league. Originally formed as the First Coast Fatales, the league consists of three skull-smacking teams. (The fact that Jacksonville has enough women interested in putting their noses on the line in championship roller derby speaks volumes.)

The New Jax City Rollers All-Star team finished fourth place in the Sunshine Skate Tournament in 2008 and adopted the battle cry "Duuuval!" as a shout-out to their home county.

Part of the **Women's Flat Track Derby Association (WFTDA),** the Roller Girls play by the rules; it just so happens that those rules include whipping team members into opposing skaters to bust up a road block, and jumping over skaters who are trying hard to trip them up.

Among their league cohorts, the Roller Girls have earned a reputation for "hitting hard, playing strong (despite the score), and then showing fine hospitality and sportsmanship by partying and celebrating with friends, fans, and the opposing team well into the night."

Their hard-living image and reputation won the Roller Girls the distinction of Best Local Cult in 2008 by the readers of *Folio Weekly.*

But the girls (Dublin Pain and Project Doomsdame included) are not without pity or at least a philanthropic spirit. They give their time, labor, and goods to a plethora of organizations including The Blood Alliance (not pun intended), Wolfson Children's Hospital, and Susan G. Komen for the Cure.

But don't let their good nature fool you. Unlike other sporting events where your mind wonders what you're missing on television as your feet wander to the snack bar, Roller Girls' matches are so rip-roaring thrilling that you'll only leave your seat to jump up and cheer.

Start practicing your Duuuval! battle cry now. The season starts in February, and you'll want to be warmed up.

Visit www.jacksonvillerollergirls.com to learn more about these daring dames.

---

i You'll never walk alone thank to www.MeetUp.com, a Web site listing hundreds of hobby-specific meet-up groups in Jacksonville for people who love everything from playing kickball to singing karaoke to strumming the ukulele. This easy-to-navigate site creates instant community and proves that there really is someone out there flying the same freak flag as you are.

JACKSONVILLE EQUESTRIAN CENTER $–$$$$
13611 Normandy Blvd.
(904) 573-4895
www.jaxevents.com/equestriancenter.php
Anyone with an interest in horseback riding will appreciate this new facility. Located on Jacksonville's Westside near the Cecil Commerce Center, the equestrian center includes a 123,000-square-foot indoor arena that seats 4,000 spectators around a show ring. There are also two outdoor rings and an outdoor practice ring, as well as

barns where owners can board their horses. This venue was built for horse shows and competitions, but it also gives horse lovers a place to ride. The center is located on 832 acres and shares some of that land with the Cecil Recreation Complex. The Cecil complex includes a large community center and a four-field fast-pitch softball complex for girls. There's also an indoor Olympic-size pool that's open to all Jacksonville residents. Admission to the pool is free.

JACKSONVILLE SUNS BASEBALL GAMES AT THE BASEBALL GROUNDS OF JACKSONVILLE $$–$$$$
301 A. Philip Randolph Blvd.
(904) 630-3900
www.jaxsuns.com

When the city's old Downtown ballpark was razed, people were skeptical about what might come in its place. But when the new stadium opened in 2003, Jacksonville thrilled at what has become one of the premier minor league ballparks in North America. The park features an old-fashioned design, brick facade and a grass seating berm, and reminds fans of the grand old days of the game. The park features great sightlines and truly comfortable seating. The concessions are plentiful, and the bathrooms are kept clean. Book one of the 12 luxury skyboxes or four skydecks. The park caters to youngsters with a playground, and groups will love the "knuckle," a unique nine-foot high mound for seating at the left field corner. The park boasts the longest distance between home plate and center field in the Southern League—420 feet. And, as I can attest from personal experience with older family members, the park is completely wheelchair accessible, including the dugouts, camera wells, and playing field.

JACKSONVILLE ZOO AND GARDENS $$–$$$
370 Zoo Parkway
(904) 757-4463
www.jacksonvillezoo.org

The Jacksonville Zoo and Gardens features over 1,500 rare and exotic animals, and its renowned botanical gardens contain over 1,000 species of plants. Special features include Play Park, Gardens of Trout River Plaza, and Giraffe Overlook. Be sure to visit the award-winning Range of the Jaguar exhibit. A brand new permanent exhibit, Asian Bamboo Garden and Komodo Dragon Exhibit that features the Moon Gate, the Lotus Pool, the Orchid Pavilion, and the Bamboo Mist Forest, opened in March 2009. The Asian Bamboo Garden currently supports 111 plant species and varieties and 29 species and varieties of bamboo. The Komodo Dragon exhibit is set in an Indonesian fishing village and features two komodo dragons, the largest lizard in the world. The zoo is open from 9 a.m. to 5 p.m. with extended hours from March 7 to September 7 and on holidays.

i S.S. *Marine Taxi* and *The St. Johns Riverkeeper* offer "My St. Johns River Boat Trips" on the second Saturday of each month. Take a guided trip along the St. Johns River to learn about the history and ecology of this valuable and timeless waterway. Trips include hands-on activities for all ages. The Water Taxi departs from Friendship Fountain Park. Reservations required; www.stjohnsriverkeeper.org.

KAYAK ADVENTURES $$$$$
(904) 249-6200
www.kayakadventuresllc.com

Kayak Adventures specializes in taking small groups on relaxing and informative eco-friendly kayaking trips around Guana Reserve and from the Timucuan Preserve to Cumberland Island. All of the guides are American Canoe Association certified instructors and are committed to making sure your kayak excursion is a safe, splashy good time. Tours of Northern Florida's waterways run every weekend of the year and offer specialty instruction, as well as photography and fishing focuses. The owners are happy to set up corporate and private tours for groups large and small. Owner Rachel Austin will show you a Florida you've never seen before. She'll take you out for a moonlight paddle or teach you how to fly fish from a kayak. Full-day and half-day beginner-friendly excursions are available.

KAYAK AMELIA $$$$$
(904) 251-0016, (888) 305-2925
www.kayakamelia.com

Learn the history of native Timucuan Indians as you paddle your kayak through inland marshes and creeks. Ray and Jody Hetchka are certified Eco-Heritage Tourism providers, which means they know a heck of a lot about both kayaking and the history and ecology of Amelia Island, a Northeast Florida barrier island. They're also really good about pointing out such local critters as herons and egrets, and if you're really lucky, you may find yourself paddling next to a dolphin. Trip times depend on the tides and currents, but whenever you go, don't forget the sunscreen and the bug spray. Kayak Amelia also offers bike and eco-tours.

LITTLE TALBOT ISLAND $-$$$$$
South of Amelia Island, North of Ft. George Island
www.floridastateparks.org/littletalbotisland

With more than 5 miles of white sandy beaches, Little Talbot Island is one of the few remaining undeveloped barrier islands in Northeast Florida. Walk through the maritime forests, desert-like dunes, and undisturbed salt marshes on the western side of the island but be sure to reserve a few hours for quiet contemplation. Be on the lookout for a diverse family of wildlife from river otters, marsh rabbits, and bobcats to a variety of native and migratory birds. Bring a rod and spend the morning fishing for bluefish, striped bass, redfish, flounder, mullet, and sheepshead in the surf and tidal streams. Then shift gears for the afternoon and surf, hike, kayak, or just stroll the shoreline and picnic (reserve a beachside picnic pavilion for a little extra shade). If you feel like pitching a tent and staying the night, the full facility campground along the eastern salt marshes of Myrtle Creek provides great recreational opportunities for campers. Be warned that sites close to the creek are known to flood during the extreme tides associated with a full moon, a new moon, or a strong storm. If you want more info about camping in the park, call the Ranger Station at (904) 251-2320 or simply reserve a site through

Reserve America at (800) 326-3521. To rent a kayak or book a guided paddle tour of the inland waters, contact Kayak Amelia at (888) 305-2925. If you prefer to get your kicks on dry land, sign up for a guided Segway tour of Little Talbot Island or Fort George Island with Ecomotion Tours (www.ecomotion.com). Reservations are required. Call (904) 251-9477.

> **i** Florida's hurricane season runs from June to November.

RAILS TO TRAILS/JACKSONVILLE-BALDWIN RAIL TRAIL
(904) 630-5400
www.traillink.com

Exercise for miles without having to worry about cars on the Jacksonville-Baldwin Trail, created from 14.5 miles of unused railroad track (formerly the Seaboard Railroad Line). The trail is paved so that bikers, hikers, and in-line skaters can all enjoy the rural landscape. There are three trailheads: the east trailhead, a third of a mile north of Commonwealth Avenue on Imeson Road; the western trailhead, a quarter mile north of Beaver Street on Brandy Branch Road; and the Baldwin trailhead, just off Center Street in the city of Baldwin. Many think that the Baldwin trailhead is the best of the three because of the restaurants and convenience stores nearby. (There are also convenience stores at some of the seven crossroads that intersect the rail trail.) Bikers must make arrangements to rent bikes in town as there are no bicycle rental stores near the rail trails. Directions to the Baldwin trailhead: from Jacksonville, take I-10 west to exit 343 (US 301). Head north on US 90. Turn left, drive west about 2 miles, then turn right on Route 121/Brandy Branch Road. The marked trailhead is on the right.

RIPPLE EFFECT KAYAK ECOTOURS
St. Augustine
(904) 347-1565
www.rippleeffectecotours.com

Chris Kelley teaches science from a kayak at this real-deal environmental outfitter. Voted Best Place to Kayak in *Folio Weekly*'s 2007-2009 Best

Close-up

Causing a Ripple Effect

Chris Kelley, the lead guide and owner of **Ripple Effect Ecotours** (www.rippleeffectecotours .com), is obsessed with far-flung outposts and vulnerable habitats. He studied off-the-grid, self-sufficient living in North America's final frontier: Baja, Mexico's La Frontera; studied marine life in the Sea of Cortez; explored the Baja Desert; and spent a decade decoding the mysteries of the natural world by both land and sea.

After two years of exploring the Florida coastline on their 34-foot sailboat, Chris and his wife fell in love with St. Augustine's untouched beauty. The two put down roots and Chris began a serious study of science, education, and conservation, which led him to his next great love: teaching ecology and conservation from inside a kayak.

In essence, Ripple Effect provides the teaching platform; North Florida supplies the curriculum.

Ripple Effect Ecotours soon partnered with Marineland and the University of Florida's Whitney Lab to further research, education, conservation, and natural interpretation via kayak, a vehicle that provides Chris and his ecotour guests with unique access to the southern boundary of the Guana Tolomato Matanzas National Estuarine Research Reserve (GTM-NERR).

Together, he and his guests paddle through the Jordon and Mellon Island Sites in Faver-Dykes State Park, the Princess Place Preserve, and the Pellicer Creek Aquatic Preserve, a biologically rich area that led to the nomination of the Matanzas River as the country's 25th National Estuarine Research Reserve.

Thanks to their alliance with Marineland, Ripple Effect's tour rates ($50 per person) include admission into the **Marineland Dolphin Conservation Center**, a guided kayak tour, and even a few photos to remember it all by.

All of Ripple Effect tours entice in different ways: our favorite is the Guana Astronomy tour, which takes lucky paddlers out into the Guana River for an evening of stargazing from the vantage point of Ripple Effect's "firefly" kayaks. The company's other tours, all led by certified Florida master naturalists (guide Joe Woodbury recently received the Kenner Award, the state's highest award for natural interpretation), explore topics such as Timucuan Indian encampments, fishing from a kayak, and the Zen of kayaking.

After hours (and we learned this completely by chance), Chris is a killer mandolin player and singer. Catch him the next time he sits in with local groups like Tammerlin, at which point you can make a date to head out on the water with him.

Maybe you can even convince him to hum a few bars beneath the stars.

of Jacksonville issues, Ripple Effect runs tours throughout the week to some of the area's most beautiful and ecologically diverse locales in Faver Dykes State Park, Guana River, Anastasia State Park, Marineland, and the Guana Tolomato Matanzas National Estuarine Research Reserve (formerly known as Guana River State Park). Join owner Chris Kelley or guide Joe Woodbury for one of Ripple Effect's Zen Kayak Tours where they teach about topics such as the connection between mindfulness and kayaking. Be sure to check the schedule on Ripple Effect's Web site for upcoming trips like the Guana Astronomy Star Gazing Kayak Tour where paddlers get to gaze at the night sky above the Guana River from one of Ripple Effects' glowing "firefly" kayaks. Check out the Close-up on Ripple Effect and Chris Kelley in this section to learn more about this gem in the waterways.

ROBERT W. LOFTIN NATURE TRAILS AT THE UNIVERSITY OF NORTH FLORIDA (UNF) CAMPUS
1 UNF Dr.
(904) 620-5951
www.unf.edu/recsports/nature
Many is the Jacksonville youngster who has fond memories of running through the nature trails and boardwalks at the University of North Florida, where 5 miles of trails weave through over 500 acres of natural habitat. The trails are open to the public 365 days a year from sunrise to sunset. Locals love the interpretive education signs along the Red Maple Boardwalk, the Blueberry Trail, and the Goldenrod Trail. The Florida Fish and Wildlife Conservation Commission long ago designated the campus a state protected Bird Sanctuary to control hunting around campus, so bring your binoculars. Today, this sanctuary designation continues to protect hundreds of acres and millions of organisms on the UNF campus. Be sure to bring strong bug spray; depending on the time of year, the mosquitoes can be fierce.

MUSEUMS

**CUMMER MUSEUM OF ART
AND GARDENS $-$$**
829 Riverside Ave.
(904) 356-6857
www.cummer.org
Upon her death in 1961, Ninah Mae Holden Cummer bequeathed her home, gardens, and collections to the Cummer Museum. Today, the Cummer remains full of quiet beauty and old-world charm. The museum's collection of Meissen porcelain is one of the three finest in the world, and the galleries house impressive collections of European and American art, as well as a significant collection of Japanese woodblocks. Perhaps best of all are the two acres of English and Italian gardens along the St. Johns River, which Mrs. Cummer managed to create, a feat in itself given Florida's sandy soil.

The museum also has an award-winning children's wing, called Art Connections, which is many

a parent's best friend on a rainy day. (See the Kid-stuff chapter for more on Art Connections.)

The Cummer is open 10 a.m. to 9 p.m. Tuesday, and from 10 a.m. to 4 p.m. Wednesday through Friday, Saturday from 10 a.m. to 5 p.m., and Sunday from noon to 5 p.m. The Cummer is closed on Monday and major holidays. A good time to visit the Cummer is on Tuesday after 4 p.m., when museum admission is free.

**MUSEUM OF CONTEMPORARY ART
JACKSONVILLE (MOCA) $-$$**
333 North Laura St.
(904) 366-6911
www.mocajacksonville.org
MOCA occupies a sleek, renovated space in a 1931 Art Deco building that used to house the Western Union Telegraph Company. The city's new Downtown library wraps around the museum, giving MOCA an added sense of place and community. The collection includes more than 700 works of art, including regional art, photography, and prints, representing artists such as Alexander Calder, Alex Katz, Robert Longo, and Helen Frankenthaler. Be sure to bring the children to the top floor, to experience the interactive family learning center called ArtExplorium Loft. The center teaches kids all about line and design, photography, and folk art. On your way out, grab a bite at Cafe Nola (short for North Laura). It's a great place to eat lunch or sip a pot of tea and enjoy something sweet. The museum is open from 10 a.m. to 4 p.m. Tuesday through Sunday; Thursday it stays open until 8 p.m. Sunday it's open from noon to 4 p.m. and is free for families. The museum is also open (and free) from 5 to 9 p.m. on the first Wednesday of the month for Art Walk. The museum is closed on Monday. Visit the Web site to confirm the current hours of operation.

**MUSEUM OF SCIENCE AND HISTORY AND
THE ALEXANDER BREST PLANETARIUM $$**
1025 Museum Circle
(904) 396-6674
www.themosh.org

(Q) Close-up

Saving Lives

Quietly standing guard on the ocean in Jacksonville Beach, sandwiched between a multimillion-dollar hotel and a high-end restaurant, sits one of Jacksonville's oldest traditions: the **American Red Cross Volunteer Life Saving Corps.** Started in 1912 as a way to teach young men how to save lives in ocean rescues, the corps now admits women, which is a good thing.

To join the Corps you have to be at least 16 years old and a strong swimmer. Would-be lifeguards must also pass a four-month training program and final exam, which includes endurance tests such as a 550-meter swim (22 laps) in 10 minutes or less and a mile run on the beach in 8 minutes or less. There is also a written test, based on textbook studies, and performance tests, where students perform standard surf rescues both with and without a buoy.

About 120 lifeguards are needed to work the 18 lifeguard towers in Jacksonville Beach. Monday through Saturday, members of the Corps wear red swimsuits, but every Sunday and holiday during summer, these same lifeguards don a navy blue swimsuit and volunteer as members of the Volunteer Life Saving Corps, thereby maintaining a tradition of volunteerism that began long before they were born.

The Volunteer Life Saving Corps is also a tradition within some families. Fathers have worked here, and so have their sons or daughters. The ranks of the Corps include more than 5,000 alumni, some of whom were lifeguards as far back as the 1930s. These days their hair may be gray, but those who can still pass the endurance tests are still allowed to "sit the towers" as volunteer lifeguards on Sundays and holidays—and many of them do.

The men and women of the Corps sit the towers Monday through Sunday from 7 a.m. to 7:30 p.m., constantly scanning the water for swimmers in trouble. It's been this way for just shy of 100 years, and if the volunteer lifeguards have their way, it will be this way for at least 100 years to come.

There are really two museums here—a science museum and a local history museum—so, as you might imagine, this is a busy place.

On the history side, an exhibition called Currents of Time gives visitors the history of Northeast Florida from the days of the Timucuans to the present, including artifacts from the *Maple Leaf*, the Union transport ship that sank in the St. Johns River during the Civil War.

Science-wise, visitors can get up close and personal with a life-size replica of a right whale, one of the rarest species of whale in the world, which calve off the coast of Jacksonville every winter. Visitors can also meet the museum's mascot, Tonka, a 403-year-old alligator snapping turtle. Tonka, or another animal of local interest, is often brought out to greet the public on weekdays at 2 p.m., when a museum naturalist hosts a show-and-tell called Featured Creature. Animal

guests have included owls, alligators, possum, and other indigenous wildlife.

The Alexander Brest Planetarium offers a variety of programs, including a variety of Cosmic Concerts. In addition, Kidspace is a popular permanent exhibit for children five and under. (Find out more in the Kidstuff chapter.) MOSH is open Monday through Friday 10 a.m. to 5 p.m., Saturday 10 a.m. to 6 p.m., and Sunday 1 to 6 p.m.

POINTS OF HISTORY

AMERICAN RED CROSS VOLUNTEER LIFE SAVING CORPS
2 North Ocean Front, Jacksonville Beach
(904) 249-9141
www.redcrosslifeguard.org
Built in 1947, this is one of the oldest buildings in Jacksonville Beach. Better yet, the Volunteer

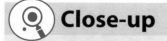 **Close-up**

Troubled Waters

A **rip current**, also called a **run out**, is a swift current traveling away from shore. Sometimes rip currents are easy to spot, but most of the time they're impossible to detect. A rip current starts in a slough, a body of water trapped between a sandbar and the beach during the changing of the tides. As the water tries to escape the slough, a hole forms in the sandbar and the water rushes out. Rip currents are especially dangerous to weak or non-swimmers, who may find themselves trapped in water that's quickly carrying them away from shore. The person panics and tries to swim back to shore, an exercise in futility for even the strongest swimmers. Lifeguards advise that the best thing to do if you are caught in a rip current is to stay calm. Then swim parallel to shore until you reach slower waters and can swim back to the beach. Better yet, lifeguards advise all beachgoers to swim in front of a lifeguard tower so that they can keep an eye on you.

Lifeguards are constantly peppered with questions about sharks, especially since the summer of 2001, when sharks in Florida waters attacked some 30 people. Tourism in the state suffered a setback when many would-be beachgoers stayed home. The reality is that many of the attacks happened in Volusia County near New Smyrna Beach; Duval County logged only three shark attacks that year, none of them fatal and none of them in the waters off Jacksonville Beach. Shark attacks are rare in our waters and fatalities are even rarer. Still, experts say, the ocean is the shark's home. It's their habitat. Sharks are a fact of life, and people take a calculated risk when they enter the water.

Life Saving Corps, which started in 1912, is the oldest lifesaving corps in the United States. Over the years, lifeguards have rescued thousands of people from drowning. If the off-duty guards are not too busy dealing with beach emergencies, they'll take you on a free tour of their building, which includes dorm rooms and a tower with a killer view up and down the coast. (See the Close-up in this section for more on the long tradition of the Volunteer Life Saving Corps.) Free.

ℹ️ For an up-to-the-minute calendar of cultural events in Jacksonville, visit www.culturalcouncil.org or www.experience jax.com.

ANNABELLE LEE AND THE LADY ST. JOHNS $$$$
1840 Perry Place
(904) 306-2200
www.jaxrivercruises.com
Some say the St. Johns River, which runs through the heart of Jacksonville, is the soul of the city. The best way to see the beauty of this 310-mile-long waterway is from the water, and the *Annabelle Lee* and *The Lady St. Johns* make it easy to do just that. Authentic paddleboats will take you up and down the St. Johns while you enjoy lunch or dinner, dancing, and great sights. Both the *Annabelle Lee* and *The Lady St. Johns* have been in operation for years, and can be booked for weddings, company picnics, even outings to St. Augustine. Prices vary depending on time of day and length of cruise, but generally a dinner and dancing cruise will cost about $40 per person. Reservations are required.

JACKSONVILLE HISTORICAL CENTER
317 A. Philip Randolph Blvd.
(904) 665-0064
www.jaxhistory.com
Even those who don't thrill at the thought of history will appreciate this historical center. Here, Jacksonville's history has been boiled down to some of its most interesting moments, including The Great Fire and the arrival of the silent-film industry. The center features wall displays full of pictures

and easy-to-read explanations about notable milestones in the history of Jacksonville. Admission is free. We recommend a quick call ahead to make sure the center is open on the day you wish to visit.

i One of the best movie theaters around is at the Jacksonville Museum of Contemporary Art where you can see documentaries and foreign films that you won't find anywhere else in town.

KARPELES MANUSCRIPT LIBRARY MUSEUM
101 West First St.
(904) 356-2992
There are 10 Karpeles museums located in historic buildings across the United States. One of the manuscript libraries in the network is in Jacksonville and sits near Downtown, a quiet jewel in this historic part of the city. Altogether, the Karpeles Libraries form the world's largest private collection of important original manuscripts and documents. The originals circulate among the 10 libraries, which means that at any given time, there are 40 original documents on display in Jacksonville in exhibitions such as Great Moments in Medical History or World War II, Beginning to End in the Pacific. Visitors can also see the original draft of the Bill of Rights, the original score of "The Wedding March," or Einstein's description of his theory of relativity. The museum also hosts exhibitions by local artists throughout the year in its beautiful old building, formerly The First Church of Christ Scientist, built in 1921. The Karpeles is open Tuesday through Friday from 10 a.m. to 3 p.m. and on Saturday from 10 a.m. to 4 p.m. Free.

KINGSLEY PLANTATION
11676 Palmetto Ave.
(904) 251-3537
www.nps.gov/timu
This is the former home of Zephaniah Kingsley, once one of the most active slave traders in America. He married a young African, Anna Madgigine Jai, whom he bought as a slave after she was sold into slavery by an opposing Senegalese

---

A Bike with a View

To see the city and surrounding areas by on two wheels, contact one of these excellent local bike rental shops.

Open Road Bicycles–San Marco, Miramar Center
4460 Hendricks Ave.
(904) 636-7772
www.openroadbicycles.com
Monday through Friday 9 a.m. to 6 p.m. and Saturday 10 a.m. to 5 p.m.

Bicycles Etc.
8036 Philips Hwy.
(904) 733-9030
10095 Beach Blvd.
(904) 997-8114
www.bicyclesetc.net
Monday through Friday 10 a.m. to 6 p.m., Saturday 9 a.m. to 5 p.m., and Sunday 11 a.m. to 5 p.m.

---

tribe when she was just 13. Anna bore Zephaniah four children and helped him run his plantations, which covered more than 32,000 acres and were worked by more than 200 slaves. Anna was freed by Kingsley in 1811 and later acquired her own land and slaves. These days Kingsley Plantation is operated by the National Park Service. The plantation house, the oldest remaining plantation house in Florida, has had many owners since Zephaniah and probably doesn't look a whole lot like it did in his day, but a number of haunting tabby (a building material made from a mix of lime, sand, and water) slave quarters stand as eerie reminders of a painful era in American history. Park Rangers give excellent daily tours, explaining in great detail what life was like at Kingsley Plantation in the early 1800s. Kingsley is open every day, except Christmas Day, from 9 a.m. to 5 p.m. Admission is free.

The Great Fire

Friday, May 3, 1901, started innocently enough with spring temperatures on the rise and a westerly wind keeping the air from feeling too still. But the day quickly turned devastating when, at 12:30 p.m., a cinder from a chimney landed on fibers drying in the sun at the **Cleaveland Fiber Factory** at Union and Davis Streets. In short order, the fibers caught fire, and so did the wooden factory building. Eighteen-mile-an-hour westerly winds fanned the flames, which quickly consumed the surrounding wooden buildings at an alarming rate.

The Jacksonville Fire Department scrambled to put out the flames. Every one of the city's 40 firefighters was called to duty, as were five horse-drawn carts, a pumper, a hook and ladder, a truck, and the fire chief. High winds carried burning embers, spreading the fire throughout the area. Eventually 2,368 buildings encompassing 146 city blocks burned to the ground. At the height of the inferno, Savannah residents more than 100 miles to the north saw a bright glow on the horizon. Legend has it that people saw the smoke from as far away as North Carolina.

After seven hours of chaos, firefighters finally got a break. The wind died down, and an hour later the fire was brought under control. Remarkably, only seven people died in what has come to be called the **biggest blaze ever** in the South, yet 10,000 Jacksonville residents were left homeless. The nation rallied to help, and within days nearly $230,000 in cash and $200,000 in goods arrived from all over the country as Jacksonville began to rebuild.

---

i You may want to consider becoming a member of the Jacksonville Zoo. The price of membership is actually less than it costs a family of four to visit the zoo twice in one year.

LAVILLA MUSEUM AND RITZ THEATRE COMPLEX $–$$
829 North Davis St.
(904) 632–5555
www.ritzlavilla.org

This museum honors LaVilla, a once-thriving African-American neighborhood in Downtown Jacksonville. Different rooms echo different aspects of African-American life at the turn of the 20th century. The museum showcases a schoolroom, a church, a living room, and a barbershop, and explores the history of African Americans in Northeast Florida, well before "La Florida" became a state in 1845. There is also an animatronic exhibit remembering two of LaVilla's most famous citizens, James Weldon Johnson and his brother, John Rosamond Johnson, who wrote the words and music to what became known as the Negro national anthem, "Lift Every Voice and Sing." The on-site art gallery displays the work of African-American artists. The museum is open Tuesday through Friday 10 a.m. to 6 p.m., Saturday 10 a.m. to 2 p.m., and Sunday 2 to 5 p.m.

i Local kids love the activities at the Museum of Science and History, like Cosmic Concerts laser shows in the Planetarium and The Slithery Slimy Sleepover, the ickiest camp-in ever. For a schedule of upcoming camps or sleepovers, visit www.themosh.org

KIDSTUFF

In the early 1990s Jacksonville found itself on *Money* magazine's list of 50 Fabulous Places to Raise a Family. The magazine reported what local residents had known for a long time: the combination of community, cost of living, weather, and especially the Atlantic Ocean made Jacksonville a good place to put down roots.

Children won't be bored in Jacksonville, thanks in large part to the weather (year-round warm temperatures and sunny skies) and the geography. The city grew up on the banks of the St. Johns River then expanded east to the Atlantic Ocean to include the beach. Think of Jacksonville's beaches as one giant public park. Here children can teach themselves how to surf year-round by practicing over and over on relatively small waves, or they can attend summer surf camp to learn the basics of balancing on a board. And, if you think surfing is just for boys, you need to head to the beach and see who's out there. Girls are learning to surf in record numbers, and by and large, the boys don't seem to mind sharing the waves.

The beach is also a great place to picnic, ride bicycles, fish, fly a kite, take a long walk, gather shells, kayak, swim, camp at Hanna Park, or simply relax year round. Ditto the St. Johns River and its tributaries, which offer countless places for children to fish.

If your children prefer dry land, just head to the closest riverbank and cast a line. But better yet, call one of several guide companies and head out in a kayak. Bonus: Children will get a firsthand lesson in environmental science as they experience an estuary system and see the animals that live in it. Children under 16 do not need a fishing license in Florida, but they will need a hat and some sunscreen, so plan accordingly. Be sure to read the Parks chapter for more ideas on things to do outdoors.

And there are other highlights: a museum of science and history designed just for kids, an art museum with an award-winning children's education wing, parks, swimming pools, water parks, and water slides.

If you want to hit the road, there are easy day trips that offer children some fabulous history lessons. Check out our Day Trips chapter for some inventive ideas.

For up-to-the-minute information on things to do, check out the weekend section of the *Florida Times-Union*. It's included in the newspaper every Friday and will give you a great lineup of the current events.

As of printing, this chapter is up to date, but it never hurts to use the phone numbers provided to call ahead and make sure nothing has changed.

Happy trails!

Price Code

$	Less than $6
$$	$6 to $10
$$$	$11 to $15
$$$$	$16 and over

TOP 10 RESOURCES FOR JACKSONVILLE MOMS

1. The beach. Buy some cheap sand toys and head to the ocean. It will keep kids of all ages occupied for hours. Parking can be hard to find, so here's a real Insider's tip: drive to Beach

Avenue at Atlantic Beach and park in designated parking places near the accesses. These places fill up fast, so go early.

2. Museum programs. Local museums know that children are some of their best patrons and cater to them. The moms' network speaks highly of the Drop-In Art program at the Cummer Museum of Art and Gardens. It's an hour-long, Tuesday-evening arts experience for kids ages 4 to 10. The program runs from 5 to 6 p.m. and costs $5 per child. But arrive early—classes fill up fast.

3. Neighborhood parks. From small pockets of green to urban playscapes, parks are an important part of Jacksonville. Don't miss South Beach Park and Sunshine Playground, the large community park in Jacksonville Beach that was the brainchild of two volunteer moms, who spent 2 years planning it, soliciting donations, and organizing volunteers to build it.

4. Storytimes. These are a great way to introduce your children to new books. The city's library system is constantly adding new readers and programs. The big chains have the space to really go all out, sometimes including snacks and crafts in their storytimes.

5. Animal adventures. Parents love the Jacksonville Zoo. The Alligator Farm in St. Augustine is also a big winner; so is BEAKS, a nonprofit sanctuary on Big Talbot Island for injured birds. And if you're looking for a fun day trip, try Marineland, south of St. Augustine.

6. St Johns River Ferry. For just $5 you can drive your car onto a ferry and cross the St. Johns River between the fishing village of Mayport and Fort George Island. It's a short trip, but kids of all ages enjoy getting on a boat, especially with the car. Departures are basically every 30 minutes, but call (904) 241-9969 for a more detailed schedule.

7. Camping and fishing. There are some beautiful and convenient camping spots within the city limits. Bring a rod and reel, because you can drop a line at most campgrounds.

8. Football. From the Florida Gators to the Florida State Seminoles to the Jacksonville Jaguars, the region's myriad teams make it easy to take in a game if you visit at the right time of year. Tailgating, as you may expect, is equally big around here.

9. Public libraries. Jacksonville has beefed up its public library system, and it shows. Most branches offer free family programs, faithfully attended by many moms and kids of all ages.

10. *First Coast Parent.* A monthly newspaper with up-to-the-minute listings of events and programs for children. It's free, and you can pick it up at the library, as well as many other locations around town. They also have an information-packed Web site listing camps, festivals, and the like; www.firstcoastparent.com.

MUSEUMS

ART CONNECTIONS AT THE CUMMER MUSEUM OF ART AND GARDENS $–$$
829 Riverside Ave.
(904) 356-6857
www.cummer.org

Art museums don't get much better than this. Your child will love learning about art, science, and imagination on the computers at Art Connections, which is an entire award-winning wing of the Cummer Museum of Art and Gardens that was designed just for kids. Children can use the computers to learn principles of shape, color, line, and texture, or they can roll up their sleeves and do a rubbing or a collage. They can also learn about Florida history through paintings in the Cummer's collection or watch a movie about Picasso. (See the Arts chapter for more on this Jacksonville gem.) Admission to Art Connections is the same as general museum admission. Best of all, museum admission is free every Tuesday evening from 4 to 9 p.m. Check out the Cummer's Web site to find out about art classes and special events.

JACKSONVILLE FIRE MUSEUM
1408 Gator Bowl Blvd.
(904) 630-0618
www.jacksonvillefiremuseum.com

Firefighting has come a long way since the 1800s when Jacksonville residents used to throw glass balls filled with water at a fire. Some of these early "fire extinguishers" are on display at the Jacksonville Fire Museum; so is an extensive exhibit on the Great Fire of 1901, which wiped out most of Jacksonville. The museum's most prized possession is a steam pumper from 1898. The contraption had to be pulled by horses, which lived in the fire station under the same roof as the firemen. The museum itself is housed in the old Catherine Street Fire Station, which was destroyed in the Great Fire and rebuilt soon after. The entire complex is adjacent to Kids Kampus, Jacksonville's children's park. Admission is free, but at this writing the museum is only open on Wednesday from 9 a.m. to 4 p.m., so call and plan ahead if you want to visit.

i Jax WaterTaxi/S.S. *Marine Taxi* provides fun rides back and forth across the river, stopping at Friendship Fountain, the Jacksonville Municipal Marina, The Jacksonville Landing, and several hotels. Adults $3; children and seniors $2. The Web site is www.jaxwatertaxi.com.

KIDSPACE AT THE MUSEUM OF SCIENCE AND HISTORY (MOSH) $$
1025 Museum Circle
(904) 396-6674
www.themosh.org
Kidspace is a hands-on area that encourages kids to learn to love science. Children just call it fun. Your climbing toddler will find herself hanging from the limbs of a huge indoor tree house; once you pull her away from that she'll love the water area, which is basically a low trough with water running through it and filled with lots of water toys. (Plastic smocks are hanging nearby to help your child stay dry. As if!) The museum has also provided a large wooden train set within easy reach for would-be conductors. Kidspace is located on the main-floor lobby, but children will be interested in the rest of the museum as well, including the Alexander Brest Planetarium—a great place to track Santa's progress in December as he leaves the North Pole and heads to Jacksonville. (See the Attractions and Tours chapter for more on this museum.) Ask at the front desk about animal programs. The museum keeps lots of native creatures (snakes, turtles, etc.), which specialists bring out for feeding and petting at various times during the day.

KIDS KAMPUS
1410 Gator Bowl Blvd.
(904) 630-5437
www.coj.net (search "Kids Kampus")
Kids Kampus is not a natural beauty (although it's beautifully located on the north bank of the St. Johns River) but is a man-made wonder that your children will adore. The best feature of Kids Kampus is the large free water park that provides a great place for families to cool off in the summer. The water park has two areas: one for toddlers and one for bigger children, plus there are benches within the water park where parents can keep an eye on their kids and still get sprinkled. A small water slide, jungle gym, and squirt guns contribute to the fun in the bigger kids' water park area.

This 10-acre park also offers an area called Safe City, where children learn how to bicycle safely on city streets by donning helmets and riding tricycles. Safe City has a working traffic light, a railroad crossing, and small plastic versions of some Jacksonville buildings. This route is built on 2 inches of rubber, so if anyone takes a spill, injuries will be minimal. Kids Kampus also offers a history of Jacksonville through innovative signage, ball fields, jogging trails, a 50-seat amphitheater, and covered pavilions for picnics or birthday parties. Free.

ANIMAL ATTRACTIONS

BEAKS
12084 Houston Ave.
(904) 251-2473
Located on Big Talbot Island en route to Fernandina Beach, this nonprofit bird sanctuary is well worth the effort to find and visit. When you pull into the parking lot, the welcome committee—a pair of peacocks—will usually stroll over to greet you. Children love walking the trails in this pristine North Florida setting and stopping at various cages housing injured birds in the process of being nursed back to health. About 2,000 injured birds are brought to the sanctuary every year. Some patients—like a bald eagle that was shot in the wing and can never live in the wild again—have become permanent residents. Admission is free, but donations are very welcome. The sanctuary is currently changing its hours of operation, so please call before visiting. Free.

ℹ️ Sleep overnight in The Jacksonville Zoo and get an exclusive behind-the-scenes look at a zookeeper's job during "Full Moon Family Sleepovers." The theme changes each month to reflect the Native American name of the full moon for the month. Sleepovers run from November through February. Visit www.jacksonville zoo.org for more information.

JACKSONVILLE ZOO AND GARDENS $$–$$$
370 Zoo Parkway
(904) 757-4463
www.jacksonvillezoo.org

What kid doesn't love the zoo? At the Jacksonville Zoo, kids can get eye-to-eye with a real giraffe at Giraffe Overlook, then reach out and feed them. The zoo's Play Park is a 2.5-acre kid's dream with a 4,000-square-foot Splash Ground play area with climbing, slides, and a goat-petting zoo. Kids of all ages will love the new Wildlife Carousel's gorgeous renditions of every kid's favorite wild animals. For additional fun, hop aboard the zoo train, which loops around the entire zoo with stops at the Kids' Shop and at Main Camp where you can disembark and explore at your own pace. The train runs an additional $4 for adults and $2 for children. Strollers are available for rent.

MARINELAND $$–$$$
9600 Ocean Shore Blvd.
(904) 460-1275
www.marineland.net

Why drive all the way to SeaWorld when your child can stand on an elevated trainer's platform, hold a fish in his or her hand, have a dolphin jump up and eat it, and still stay this close to Jacksonville? Marineland, the world's first oceanarium was built in 1938 and, thanks to a dedicated few, remains open today. There may not be a killer whale here, but there are plenty of dolphins in the Dolphin Conservation Center, a 1.3 million gallon series of dolphin habitats. An impressive complement of interactive programs—such as The Quest, The Immersion, Discover Dolphins, Dolphin Designs, Touch & Feed, Trainer for a Day, Twilight Adventure,

Trainer Camp, Summer Camps, and Kayak Tours—allows guests to experience the dolphins up-close or "glide into the dolphins' aquatic world from a sloping beach to swim with Marineland's gentle residents." Your general admission ticket enables you to view the dolphins through 6-by-10-foot acrylic windows as they swim, play, and interact with guests. Reserve your space in the programs in advance so as not to miss out. And don't forget a change of clothes. Those dolphins make a big splash when they jump for their fish. (See more about this attraction in the Day Trips chapter.) Marineland is open daily from 8:30 a.m. to 4:30 p.m.

ST. AUGUSTINE ALLIGATOR FARM ZOOLOGICAL PARK $$–$$$
999 Anastasia Blvd.
(904) 824-3337
www.alligatorfarm.com

This could well be the single best place to take your children in all of Northeast Florida. Kids are fascinated by alligators, a true Florida attraction, and this place offers wall-to-wall alligators—more than a thousand of them. Guests walk on a wooden boardwalk and peer down at the gators lying in pools below. For an added attraction, visit at feeding time; then you'll see these creatures, which appear so sedentary, move faster than you ever realized they could. Kids will also enjoy the large collection of rare birds and snakes. Naturalists offer hourly programs, which could include a chance to hold a snake or pet a baby alligator. Open seven days a week from 9 a.m. to 5 p.m. (6 p.m. in the summer). Check out their Web site for admission discounts for AAA, military, senior citizens, and larger groups.

SPORTS AND LEISURE

ADVENTURE LANDING $$$$
1944 Beach Blvd.
(904) 246-4386
4825 Blanding Blvd.
(904) 771-2804
2780 State Rd. 16, St. Augustine
(904) 827-9400
www.adventurelanding.com

🔍 Close-up

Turtle Watch

You could say that the staffers of **Beaches Sea Turtle Patrol** have hundreds of grandchildren—the four-legged kind that live in the ocean. Turtle Patrol staffers hop in a special dune buggy every morning from May 1 to October 31 to patrol Jacksonville's beaches for the female loggerhead turtles (and sometimes leatherbacks) that crawl ashore on these beaches, the same beaches where they were born, to lay their eggs. The turtles dig a hole in the sand, push out about 100 golfball-size eggs, cover the nest with sand, and then return to the sea. Even the Patrol has a tough time catching this happening, but they regularly patrol the beaches during nesting season for signs that a female has crawled ashore (turtle flippers leave a distinctive pattern in the sand). Once they locate a nest, they date it and stake it off to protect the eggs while they develop. (Children are usually curious about these little havens and fascinated to learn that there are sea turtles growing inside them.)

It takes about two months for the eggs to develop, and the sand temperature, interestingly enough, helps determine the sex of the hatchlings. Scientists have found that cooler sand tends to produce more males, while warmer sand produces more females. Nature has programmed the hatchlings to dig their way out of their nests by the light of a full moon, which guides them to the ocean. It's important that no artificial light from, say, a street lamp or a restaurant confuses the hatchlings or they will lose their way and end up smashed on the road.

Jacksonville families have been known to sit by these nests nightly, waiting for the miniature turtles to emerge so that they can watch the hatchlings scurry to the water and begin their life in the sea. Beaches Sea Turtle Patrol operates a 24-hour sea turtle hotline (904-613-6081) so that beachgoers can report problems or get nest updates. Visit www.bstp.net to learn more.

There are two Adventure Landings in Jacksonville and one in St. Augustine. Most parks have Adventure Speedway Go-Karts, Adventure Golf (two 18-hole miniature golf courses), laser tag in a multi-level arena, a video and gaming arcade, the Wacky Worm Roller Coaster, Frog Hopper, Max Flight Coaster Simulator, batting cages with varied skill levels, on-site food services, and snack bars. The whole family will enjoy the Shipwreck Island Play Village, the centerpiece attraction for kids, young and not so young. Multiple slides, water cannons, and waterfalls ensure hours of fun. There are separate prices for the water park, which is only open in summer, and for attractions like bumper cars and laser tag. Admission prices for adults and kids are based on the activities and services desired, check the Web site or call for details, for example, adults who are merely accompanying a child and do not plan to swim can purchase a less-costly ticket. Open Sunday through Thursday 10 a.m. to 10 p.m., and until midnight on Friday and Saturday.

J&S ANTIQUE CAROUSEL $
Davenport Park
180 San Marco Ave., St. Augustine
(904) 823-3388
More than 2,000 carousels were built in the United States between the 1880s and 1930s, but only around 165 are still in service. The wooden carousel in St. Augustine, built in 1927, still has the magic. Kids of all ages love to climb aboard a white charger with a wooden mane and ride around and around to the wonky strains of a calliope. The carousel operates from Sunday through Thursday from 10 a.m. to 9 p.m. and Friday and Saturday from 10 a.m. to 10 p.m.

THE FIRST TEE AT THE BRENTWOOD GOLF COURSE $$–$$$
1157 Golfair Blvd.
(904) 924-0401
www.thefirstteejacksonville.org

Sponsored by the World Golf Foundation, this nine-hole course was built to teach golf to economically disadvantaged kids, but anyone can play here. It's located on the Northside on a beautiful old golf course. The First Tee is geared to kids, and the pros are very accessible if the young ones need guidance or have questions about their stroke. The First Tee operates over 260 First Tee chapters worldwide and has served over 1,500 children, ages 7 to 17, since 2001.

SAWGRASS STABLES & 3 RIVERS ADVENTURES $$$$
4185 Corbin Rd.
(904) 940-0200
www.3riversadvfl.com
This is the stuff that memories are made of. If you want to take your child horseback riding on the beach, or kayaking on one of the many waterways in the area, these are your folks. Your adventure begins the second you pick up the phone to arrange the what, when, and where. You might call it adventure by appointment, but the end result will be fun, fun, fun.

THE UNIVERSITY OF NORTH FLORIDA AQUATIC CENTER $
4567 St. Johns Rd. South
(904) 620-2854
www.unf.edu/recsports/aquatics
Sometimes you just feel like swimming in a pool instead of in the ocean, and when that time comes, the sparkling Olympic-size pool at UNF fits the bill. It's covered for year-round swimming, but in summer the sides are open for sunshine and sunbathers. Children enjoy watching the divers at the deep end practice flips and turns off the high and low boards. Swim for the day, or take swimming lessons, diving lessons, or synchronized swimming classes. Check out the Web site for details and prices for their extensive programs and opportunities.

TUNNELZ & TUMBLEZ $$$$
5285 Shad Rd.
(904) 886-9784
www.tunnelzntumblez.com

Looking for a clean, friendly, and secure environment for your kids to burn off some energy? Tunnelz & Tumblez offers a 2,000-square-foot laser tag arena, as well as mini-golf and speedy slides. Kids love the multi-level soft play structure with its gigantic slides, swings, challenge paths, and web mountains. And the activities are all inside, which makes this attraction perfect for a hot or rainy day (or for containing wild kids). Open Sunday through Thursday from 10 a.m. to 6 p.m. On Friday and Saturday evenings the center stays open until 8 p.m.

YES YOU CANVAS $$$$$
6012 San Jose Blvd.
(904) 993-9047
www.yesyoucanvas.com
Just as much fun for kids as it is for grown-ups, Yes You Canvas promises to teach you to paint in just two hours. Using a step-by-step method that guides you through every stroke, kids will create a masterpiece suitable for framing. No skill required; smocks provided. Visit the Web site to choose from the extensive schedule of kids' (and adult) classes, some of which are only one hour. Kids must be accompanied by an adult (this isn't a drop-off service), but adults will find themselves so engaged that they'll want to paint, too.

PARKS, WATER PARKS, AND PLAYGROUNDS

KIDS KAMPUS
1410 Gator Bowl Blvd.
(904) 630-5437
www.coj.net (search "Kids Kampus")
This is the city's premier park for children with 10 wonderful acres of playground equipment and amusement located in Metropolitan Park on the St. Johns River close to Downtown. At an area called Safe City children can borrow tricycles and helmets and ride on 4 miniature blocks of Downtown, stopping at red lights and schools and stores made from Little Tykes houses. Youngsters can experience solar power or become a drop of water and discover the St. Johns River. From the brightly colored playscapes to the digging

Beach Rentals

Jacksonville is riddled with companies ready to rent you any of the equipment you could possibly need for fun in the Florida sun, but for an all-inclusive clearinghouse of rental options, visit **www.rentbeachstuff .com** where you can rent everything from beach cruisers to tandem bikes, surfboards, boogie boards, single and tandem kayaks, fishing poles, umbrellas, beach chairs, snorkel sets—even beach towels, blankets, baby playpens, and volleyball sets. Fancy some beach games? Beach Rentals stocks horseshoes, bocce ball, volleyball, Frisbee, and football sets, ready to go. Bonus: they drop off and pick up the gear for free, so no running around town necessary.

and sliding equipment, Kids Kampus offers a fun way to stimulate and motivate your little ones' imaginations.

Best of all, there's a wonderful water park here with squirt guns, sprinklers, jungle gyms, and even a small water slide. It's only open in summer, when it's a great place to cool off. Lifeguards make sure nothing gets too wild. Admission is free.

SOUTH BEACH PARK AND SUNSHINE PLAYGROUND
Corner of South Beach Parkway and Osceola Street, Jacksonville Beach
(904) 247-6100
www.jacksonvillebeach.org (search "Sunshine Playground")
This is truly a community park. It's the brainchild of two Beaches moms, who worked for 2 years raising the money, designing the park, and organizing 2,106 volunteers who built it in just five days. Kids love climbing on, crawling through,

and swinging on all of the play structures in the playground. Be sure to check out the clever touches built into the structures themselves, such as musical instruments and artistic tiles created by local kids. The park has gone through a recent renovation and now has restroom facilities, basketball courts, tennis courts, and picnic shelters, as well as the children's playground, fitness trail, all-purpose field, , gazebo, , two grills, and three volleyball courts. The park is open daily from 7 a.m. to 7 p.m. Admission is free.

TREE HILL NATURE CENTER $
7152 Lone Star Rd.
(904) 724-4646
www.treehill.org
Tree Hill is a city park, urban wilderness, and wildlife preserve located right in the middle of Arlington. The center encompasses 50 acres of hilltops, woods, wetland areas, and a freshwater stream; is riddled with wildflowers; and is chock-a-block with wildlife-viewing areas. Visit the indoor nature center, where kids can learn about the environment and the critters that live in it through the interactive exhibits, learning laboratory, wildflower gardens, and nature trails. Bottom line: This is a good place to teach your children about the wild outdoors. Open Monday through Saturday from 8 a.m. to 4:30 p.m. Closed on Sunday and on major holidays.

THE WATER PLAYGROUND AT KATHRYN ABBY HANNA PARK $
500 Wonderwood Dr.
(904) 249-4700
www.coj.net
This water park, located in the heart of Hanna Park, is open only from the middle of April through September. Children ages nine and under are welcome here, and they will love splashing around in the sprinklers and climbing on the plastic playground equipment. Lifeguards keep vigil. Admission to the water park is covered by your admission to Hanna Park itself. The park is open from 8 a.m. to 8 p.m. daily from April through October, and from 8 a.m. to 6 p.m. daily from November through March.

Among the Nations

Don't miss the **World of Nations Celebration**, North Florida's largest multicultural event, held each spring in Metropolitan Park and arguably one of the best family festivals Jacksonville offers its residents. The celebration draws well over 75,000 visitors who share a love of international food and world music, as well as a fascination with the cultures and traditions that make up our world.

Wander among the nations' tents where native speakers dish up the food specific to their homeland. Not an adventurous eater? Come anyway; the spectrum of traditional music, dance, and storytelling alone is worth the trip. Be sure to come early on Saturday morning to witness the naturalization ceremony during which as many as 50 people are sworn in as U.S. citizens. Visit www.coj.net (search "World of Nations") to learn more.

CAMPING

HUGUENOT MEMORIAL PARK $
10980 Heckscher Dr.
(904) 251-3335
www.coj.net (search "Recreation")
Anglers love Huguenot Park, which is located on a small spit of sand and silt bordered by the Atlantic Ocean on one side and the St. Johns River on the other. It's the only beach left in Duval County where you can drive your car onto the sand, which means the beach is crowded with day trippers who bring cars, grills, umbrellas, and big coolers. There are just 71 primitive campsites at Huguenot, and most of these sites have spectacular views across the St. Johns River to the ships at Mayport Naval Station. But be careful swimming here. The park is located near where the St. Johns empties into the Atlantic Ocean, so swimming can be dangerous. Even though the camping is considered "primitive," the campground does offer restrooms, showers, a dump station, public phones, a playground area, swimming, fishing, windsurfing, boating, bird watching, and a boat ramp. Pets are allowed, but they must stay on a leash.

KATHRYN ABBY HANNA PARK $–$$$$
500 Wonderwood Dr.
(904) 249-4700
www.coj.net (search "Recreation")
It's hard to imagine a camping spot that feels so away from it all but is actually well within the Jacksonville city limits. Just 25 minutes from Downtown you'll find 450 acres of pristine North Florida woodland for kids to run wild in, a mile and a half of secluded beach, trails for hiking and biking, and 60 acres of stocked freshwater fishing. The park's nearly 15 miles of bike trails offer enough ease or challenge to satisfy riders of all levels. Long Trail and Back 40 are well-suited to novices ready to test their off-road skills. More adventurous riders will love trails like Grunt, Misery, and Tornado Alley, all of which offer a wild ride through the trees. The 300 campsites fill up fast (many are occupied by RV campers who stay for a while), so call ahead for a reservation. Hanna officials have also built four one-room cabins that are air-conditioned and are a great place for families to rent. There's a two-night minimum on the cabins, which rent for a modest amount per night. Whether you come for the day or spend the night, you'll leave a happy camper.

ON STAGE

JACKSONVILLE SYMPHONY
ORCHESTRA $$$
300 West Water St.
(904) 354-5547
www.jaxsymphony.org
The Jacksonville Symphony offers a host of family-friendly concerts every season that provides a great way to introduce children to the world of

Beethoven and Bach. The series includes a Halloween-week concert called Symphonic Spooktacular (even the conductor dresses up) and a Holiday Pops Concert in December. Nearly a third of the people taking advantage of the symphony's programs are children who love the concerts, symphony schools, and Youth Orchestra. The symphony's Starry Nights concerts during spring and summer draw carloads of families. Tickets can be purchased at the box office or online.

KIDS NIGHT OUT

AL'S PIZZA $$-$$$$
303 Atlantic Blvd., Atlantic Beach
(904) 249-0002
www.alspizza.com
By the slice, or by the pie, Al's White Pizza, made with ricotta and fresh tomato, is a hands-down kid favorite. Al's creative pies, like the Spicy Caribbean Pizza, provide both the variety and the bedrock that keeps this Beaches establishment in hot demand with the stroller set. But don't limit yourselves to the pies; the house calzones, salads, BLTs, subs, and pastas are worth trying, too.

THE LOOP PIZZA GRILL $$
2014 San Marco Blvd.
(904) 399-5667
www.looppizzagrill.com
Even picky eaters are known to gobble up the Loop's chicken fingers, hamburgers, hot dogs, pizza, and fries. The Loop also serves salads and soups to please the adults in the group. Check out the menu online.

SLIDERS OYSTER BAR AND
SEAFOOD GRILLE $$-$$$
218 First St., Neptune Beach
(904) 246-0881
Try Dawson's Fish Dinner, named after the owner's daughter. It includes a nice piece of white fish, some fresh broccoli, and great mashed potatoes that even the pickiest eater will enjoy. Or order your child a burrito filled with black beans, chicken, or beef. Parents will especially enjoy it here because they can still feel as though they're eating someplace cool, even with the kids along. Dine inside or out at this popular Beaches eatery, where the food is fresh and families are welcome. Open for dinner only.

SWEETS

DREAMETTE $
3646 Post St.
(904) 388-2558
Kids love the picnic tables and the walk-up-and-order charm of Dreamette. Located in Murray Hill, Dreamette has been serving the same soft-serve menu from their front window since 1948. The main draw is the soft serve ice cream, which you order at the walk-up window. Dreamette staff will also make you a sundae, milkshake, banana split, or float. Plop down at one of the picnic benches around the side and lick away. The general rule seems to be that they close at sunset, year-round.

THE EDGEWOOD BAKERY $
1022 South Edgewood Ave
(904) 389-8054
www.edgewoodbakery.com
Since 1947, Edgewood Bakery has been crafting custom cakes and cookies that kids adore. Baked with all natural ingredients and no preservatives, the goodies are so tasty that in 1995 Edgewood Bakery was voted best bakery in the Southeast by the Southeastern Retail Bakers Association. If you go to the River City Playhouse for a children's theater performance, stop in at the bakery a few doors down and pick up some gingerbread cookies. Jax kids have been enjoying them for decades. They're legendary!

i Many argue that the best ice-cream store in town is Brusters on Atlantic Boulevard near Kernan Road. Even though this is part of a larger East Coast chain, its ice cream remains popular with the stroller set. Be sure and try the seasonal specials, including blackberry and apple-caramel ice creams. Call (904) 221-1441 for more info.

LET THEM EAT CAKE $–$$
3604 St. Johns Ave.
(904) 389-2122
www.asweetbakery.com

Both kids and adults love the specialty sweets from this tiny bakery's storefront in Avondale. The small case is filled with macaroons, peanut-butter sandwich cookies, and artfully frosted cupcakes with real buttercream icing. In perfect indie form, the owner also runs a Let Them Eat Cupcakes Truck, the first sweets truck in Jacksonville, which shows up Downtown on Wednesdays and sells the bakery's cupcakes, cookies, brownies, and cold drinks street-style.

PETERBROOKE CHOCOLATE
FACTORY $–$$$
1470 San Marco Ave.
(800) 771-0019
www.peterbrooke.com

Named after the founder's children (Peter and Brooke), Peterbrooke Chocolates have been a Jacksonville favorite since the factory's founding in 1983. Like fine artists, the elves at Peterbrooke Chocolatier mold and hand-dip a menagerie of chocolate bears, cats, dogs, and other delightful items. Think creamy fondant centers, cordial cherries, handmade truffles, and fresh-picked strawberries that are hand-dipped in chocolate daily. Kids love watching the chocolate being made into all sorts of delectables, including chocolate-covered pretzels, chocolate-covered strawberries, and chocolate-covered Oreos and graham crackers. The free samples alone are worth the trip. Peterbrooke's production center is listed above; in addition, the chocolatier has eight neighborhood shops. If you can't make it to the factory, at least stop by one of the stores to stock up on the chocolate.

RITA'S ITALIAN ICE $
393 North Third St., Jacksonville Beach
(904) 246-1762
www.ritasice.com

There's nothing sweeter after a day in the hot sun at the beach than to head to Rita's in Jackson-ville Beach for an Italian ice. While this is a large national chain, its proximity to the beach makes it, if not Insider, at least situationally relevant. You can't miss the place; it's on the main drag near the Jacksonville Beach City Hall. Rita's sells many flavors of Italian ice, including local favorites mango and passion fruit.

STORYTIMES

BARNES & NOBLE BOOKSELLERS
10280 Midtown Parkway
(904) 928-2027
11112 San Jose Blvd.
(904) 886-9904
www.bn.com

Moms in the know keep an eye on their local store's event schedule for some clever and engaging storytimes and activities. All programs are free, and there are often special events, so call the store. Hours vary by location.

BORDERS BOOKS & MUSIC
8801 Southside Blvd.
(904) 519-6500
www.borders.com

Borders refreshes its children's offerings monthly. Take your tot by to hear stories read aloud by local favorites. Call the store or visit the Web site to download the latest kids calendar. Free.

JACKSONVILLE PUBLIC LIBRARY
(MAIN BRANCH)
303 North Laura St.
(904) 630-2665
www.jpl.coj.net

Boasting a full calendar of free activities including arts and crafts, storytellers, and more, the city's new main library, which opened in 2005, is the largest public library in the state. Jacksonville also has 20 regional, community, and neighborhood branch libraries offering storytimes along with a host of other kids programs. To find out about the latest one-time and recurring events, call the library or check out the calendar on their Web site.

ANNUAL EVENTS

Jacksonville has such a calendar-busting quantity of annual events that most locals don't have enough time to attend them all. From the artistic mash-up Art After Dark to the fuzzy Humane Society fundraiser The Fur Ball, the Jacksonville social calendar will give even the most seasoned socialite a run for her money. Many of the events are such an ingrained part of the year that locals plan around them, putting off vacations or delaying dates until after one event or another has passed.

It's fair to say that most of our big events revolve around music, food, and the outdoors. Events like the four-day music festival Suwannee SpringFest, the international food and culture extravaganza World Of Nations, and the duffers' draw The Players Championship golf tournament tally record attendance year after year.

Pay special attention to April and May, which has become the city's unofficial festival season when you can attend a different Downtown or Beaches event almost every weekend.

The city of Jacksonville provides a great online event planner at www.coj.net/events that gives the exact dates (they often vary from year to year), times, and phone numbers for many events around town.

Again, there is not space enough to list every single event in these pages, and we all know by now that an encyclopedic listing is not our goal. Instead, we have spotlighted our Insider faves—many of them are time-honored traditions and some are relative newcomers on the scene. But, rest assured, all of them offer a darn good time.

Enjoy!

JANUARY

DR. MARTIN LUTHER KING JR. PARADE
101 East Union St.
(904) 807-8358
www.mlkfdn.com

Marching bands from all over Northeast Florida practice for weeks in preparation for the annual Downtown parade honoring Dr. Martin Luther King Jr. Church youth groups build floats, high school ROTC members shine their shoes, and debutantes have their hair done. This parade, which takes about two hours from start to finish, honors Dr. King's dream that, one day, man would not be known for the color of his skin.

Dr. Martin Luther King Jr. was no stranger to Northeast Florida. On June 11, 1964, he was jailed for trying to eat at an all-white restaurant at the Monson Motor Lodge in St. Augustine. A day or two later, members of King's nonviolent contingent went swimming in the Monson's all-white swimming pool to protest King's arrest. The manager became so enraged when King's followers refused to get out of the pool that he dumped muriatic acid into the water near where the protestors were swimming. It was an act heard round the world. Today, Jacksonville hosts many celebrations to honor the memory of Dr. Martin Luther King Jr. on his birthday, from a pancake breakfast to church services to this lively Downtown parade.

THE GATOR BOWL (OFFICIALLY THE KONICA MINOLTA GATOR BOWL)
Jacksonville Municipal Stadium, 1 Stadium Place
(904) 798-1700
www.gatorbowl.com

In-the-Know

Want the skinny on what's going on in Jacksonville this weekend, next month, or over the holidays? These city-obsessed Web sites and blogs will keep you in-the-know and up-to-date. For example, Make a Scene Downtown throws rooftop and riverfront Pool Splash Parties in the summer and shows movies on the side of the CSX building at the Northbank Riverfront Park—all at little or not cost to you. Also, be sure to check out Visit Jacksonville's mobile-friendly Web site, http://iJax.mobi, from your iPhone. Here are our favorite Jax-centric arts and events sites:

City of Jacksonville: www.coj.net

Cultural Council of Greater Jacksonville: www.culturalcouncil.org

Downtown Vision: www.downtownjacksonvile.org

EU Jacksonville: www.eujacksonville.com

Experience Jacksonville: www.ExperienceJax.com

I Want a Buzz: www.iwantabuzz.com

Jacksonville Events: www.JaxEvents.com

Jacksonville Scene: www.JacksonvilleScene.com

Jax Stylefile: www.jaxstylefile.wordpress.com

Jax Underbelly: www.jaxunderbelly.com

Make a Scene Downtown: www.facebook.com/makeascenedowntown

Metro Jacksonville: www.metrojacksonville.com

The Outer Box: http://theouterbox.com

The Urban Core: www.theurbancoredotcom.blogspot.com

U Don't Know Jax: www.Udontknowjax.com

Urban Jacksonville: http://UrbanJacksonville.info

Visit Jacksonville: www.VisitJacksonville.com

For over 64 years the Gator Bowl Association has been leading the charge when it comes to New Year's Eve and New Year's Day celebrations in Jacksonville. At the heart of the celebrations is The Gator Bowl, a New Year's Day college football game featuring such big-ticket teams as Florida State or Notre Dame. The festivities begin on New Year's Eve when the Gator Bowl Association sponsors a rowdy Downtown parade starring the marching bands from the two universities playing in the game. Afterward, parade watchers usually grab a bite to eat before hitting The Jacksonville Landing or Metropolitan Park for an evening of free music and midnight fireworks sponsored by the city.

FEBRUARY

BLACK HISTORY MONTH
Various locations
www.coj.net (search "events")
From the Jacksonville Zoo to the Ritz Theatre, numerous organizations make a special effort to honor Black History Month. Make plans to

visit the open house at the Clara White Mission, attend dance and music performances at the Ritz Theatre, or take part in a Black History Day Tribute at the Museum of Science and History. Check the city's Web site for this year's schedule of events.

DOUGLAS ANDERSON'S EXTRAVAGANZA
2445 San Diego Rd.
(904) 346-5620
www.da-arts.org
Jacksonville is home to Douglas Anderson School of the Arts, one of the top (and most respected) performing arts magnet schools in the country. Once a year, the top students from each of the school's eight disciplines present what they and their instructors deem to be the highest level of creative work that their department has to offer. The result is a multimedia showcase that draws packed houses year after year. Forget the average high-school talent show—the student performers at DA are mature, talented, and disciplined, and this event showcases exactly that. The performances have grown so popular in recent years that the school has had to move the event from the school's own theater to the Moran Theatre inside The Times-Union Center for Performing Arts located at 300 Water St. The Visual Arts & Cinematic Arts Galleries open at 6:30 p.m. The performance begins at 7:30 p.m. Contact the school early for ticketing details.

MUCH ADO ABOUT BOOKS
Prime Osborn Convention Center
303 West Laura St.
(904) 630-1995
www.muchadoaboutbooks.com
Sponsored by the Library Guild, this fund-raiser has generated hundreds of thousands of dollars over the years to buy books and computers and to sponsor after-school programs within the Jacksonville Public Library system. The two-day event brings nationally known authors to Jacksonville for writing seminars, readings, and signings. The celebration is also marked by a dinner gala that gives guests a chance to rub elbows with the authors.

NORTHEAST FLORIDA SCOTTISH GAMES & FESTIVAL
Clay County Fairgrounds
2497 State Rd. 16 West
www.neflgames.com
Bringing a "wee bit o' Scotland" to Northeast Florida, the Scottish Games are a rollicking good time. After the whiskey tasting (of course), make time to watch Scotophiles compete on harps, bagpipes, fiddles, and drums before moving on to Highland dancing, traditional Scottish athletics, and demonstrations featuring Scottish dogs, sheep herding, falcony, Gaelic language, and, of course, battle-axe throwing. Don't miss the pub-crawl, which departs from Seven Bridges restaurant in Tinseltown the next day. And don't blame us if the affiliated events, like the kilted golf tournament, leave you pining for the old country.

THE OLUSTEE BATTLE FESTIVAL AND OLUSTEE BATTLE REENACTMENT
US 90, 2 miles east of Olustee
(386) 755-1097
www.olusteefestival.com
Love a man in uniform? How about a man in 1860s frock coat and kepi? Every February, hundreds of Civil War re-enactors gather at the Olustee Battlefield State Historic Site about 90 miles west of Jacksonville to commemorate the largest Civil War battle ever fought in Florida. In February of 1864, a force of some 5,500 Union soldiers began marching west to try to take Florida. They chose to make their stand in a forest east of Olustee. During the battle, the Union lost 1,861 soldiers, the Confederates 946. Many of the Union casualties were former slaves who were unarmed. Re-enactors strive for accuracy when they bring the battle back to life every year, and this is one history lesson you won't want to miss. The reenactment always happens over a weekend so the dates change every year. Check the Web site for dates and times.

Double-Decker Whiz Bangs and Aerial Sizzlers

Jacksonville loves its pyrotechnics. Really. Give the city leaders any opportunity to get their hands on some fireworks and it's bombs away! And they don't cheap out; these shows are bombastic and brilliant, especially the "waterfall" fireworks cascading off the Acosta Bridge—the signature of all of the Downtown displays.

You'll get the best view of the Downtown fireworks shows from the Northbank Riverwalk, Southbank Riverwalk, the Cummer Museum, The Jacksonville Landing or Metropolitan Park.

Mark your calendar for these annual spectacles:

All Summer Long
Massive incendiary displays cap off Jacksonville Suns' Friday home games at The Baseball Grounds Downtown. Don't miss the spectacular season closer after the final game on July 3 or 4.

April
Jacksonville Jazz Festival, Metropolitan Park (Memorial Day weekend)—The Jazz Festival went for decades without fireworks, but all that changed when the fest moved from Metro Park to Downtown. Prepare to be stunned by double-decker whizzers and all that jazz.

July 4
The city launches fireworks from three barges in the St. Johns River and "waterfall" fireworks via strobes on the Acosta and Main Street bridges in a star-spangled tribute to percussive excess.

November
The Jacksonville Landing Tree Lighting, Downtown (Friday after Thanksgiving)—The Tree Lighting is an-all day affair with choral groups and the ceremonial plugging-in of the Landing's massive tree at sundown. The fireworks add the ultimate exclamation point.

Jacksonville Light Parade, Downtown (Saturday after Thanksgiving)—This is the biggest fireworks show of the year with the city's signature "waterfall" fireworks shot from two Downtown bridges in a cacophony of double-decker whiz bangs and aerial sizzlers.

December
New Year's Eve Fireworks Spectacular, Downtown (Dec. 31)—In a bombastic display, the city launches fireworks from one barge in front of The Jacksonville Landing and another barge in front of the Hyatt Regency Hotel. Soak it up; the next fireworks won't come again until baseball season.

WHALE OF A SALE (JUNIOR LEAGUE OF JACKSONVILLE)
Greater Jacksonville Agricultural Fairground
510 Fairgrounds Place
(904) 387-5497
www.jlweb.org/jacksonville
The motivated ladies of Jacksonville's Junior League organize this enormous, two-day, 1,200-family garage sale at the city's fairgrounds. The sale provides a great way to go green by giving residents a way to reduce, reuse, and recycle their cast-offs. Come shop from among the thousands of donated items. The prices are low and the value is high. The preview party (a $35 ticketed event held the night before the sale) is catered and has huge silent auction component.

i You don't have to be a professional cyclist to participate in the fall Bike MS PGA Tour Cycle to the Shore to raise money to fight multiple sclerosis. The 150-mile ride starts at the St. Johns County/ St. Augustine Airport and heads south to Daytona Beach then back again in just two days. Riders can also choose to the "One Day, One Way" option of 86 miles. All meals are provided for the cyclists throughout the weekend, which is welcome touch. Call (904) 332-6810 for more information or check out the MS Web site, http://bikefln .nationalmssociety.org.

MARCH

THE AMELIA ISLAND CONCOURS D'ELEGANCE
The Ritz-Carlton Hotel, 4750 Amelia Island Parkway, Amelia Island
(904) 636-0027
www.ameliaconcours.org
Even if you don't especially like car shows, you'll enjoy this one. Guaranteed. The Concours d'Elegance, which is French for "parade of elegance," is a vintage car show with over 1,000 of the sweetest classic cars you've ever seen. Take a trip through time with Bugattis, Packards, and even ultra-rare Pierce Arrows. The event is held at the Golf Club of Amelia Island, in the shadow of the Ritz-Carlton resort. Stroll around this beautiful course and check out the cars, or park yourself on a green and watch the cars parade by. The show is a huge draw for the area resorts and hotels, which fill up early with car enthusiasts.

ART AFTER DARK
The Florida Theatre
128 E. Forsyth St.
(904) 355-2728 (box office)
www.floridatheatre.com
One of the most in-the-know fund-raisers among Jacksonville's artistic set, Art After Dark started in 1997 to support the Friends of the Florida Theatre and has grown into one of the best ways to get a first peek at work by the city's most interesting visual artists, both established and about-to-be-discovered.

Build your art collection by purchasing pieces by artists who may very well dominate the art scene in the future. Most of the pieces showcased throughout the lobbies are for sale, and 90 percent of the proceeds go directly to the artists. Don't miss the on-stage silent auction or the music and dancing in the back alley.

BLESSING OF THE FLEET
Downtown Riverfront
(904) 630-3690
www.coj.net (search "Blessing of the Fleet")
Whether you own a yacht, a sailboat, or even a dinghy, a prominent city spiritual leader will sprinkle holy water on (or near) your vessel during a large public ceremony—a tradition that dates back to the early days of Christianity when fishermen and their boats were blessed in the name of safe seas and bountiful catches.

GATE RIVER RUN
Jacksonville Municipal Stadium
3931 Baymeadows Rd. (offices)
www.gate-riverrun.com
For over 33 years, the Gate River Run has been drawing thousands of athletes—over 14,000 runners and walkers in 2009—to Jacksonville for the nation's largest 15K race. This run showcases

Close-up

Annual Whale Sightings

Like swallows returning to Capistrano, northern right whales return from New England to the warm waters off Northeast Florida to bear their young every winter.

Two longtime scientists at Marineland of Florida, David Caldwell and Melba Caldwell, first noticed this phenomenon in the early 1960s. They'd stand atop an oceanarium at the seaside theme park, gaze at the Atlantic, and watch the whales dip and fluke in the warm, shallow waters off the Florida coast. It wasn't long before they realized that, on a very consistent basis, one whale became two. From this, they deduced that the waters off Jacksonville, Ponte Vedra, and St. Augustine were the whale's natural calving grounds.

The northern right whale is the most endangered whale species in the world. Scientists now believe only 400 northern right whales are left in the Atlantic Ocean. There are southern right whales in the waters off Australia, but they don't travel into this hemisphere.

The Caldwells shared their observations on northern right whale reproduction with scientists at the **New England Aquarium,** who were already so alarmed at the severely low numbers of this once plentiful species that they came to witness the Caldwells' theory in person.

In short order, **Marineland** became the headquarters for the **Marineland Right Whale Survey project,** which continues to this day. Volunteers from as far north as Cumberland Island, Georgia, to as far south as Flagler Beach, Florida, can call Marineland whenever a right whale is sighted offshore, especially a right whale with a calf. Sightings are most frequent in December, January, and February but have been known to continue into March and April. Marineland tries to document a sighting with photographs. At the end of calving season, the center sends its collective data to the New England Aquarium. Scientists there keep a photo ID catalogue of the whales and assign each one a number to help keep track of the population.

Sadly, right whale sightings off the Northeast Florida coast remain few and far between. These days the biggest danger to these slow-moving creatures (they move, on average, about 1 mile an hour) is getting run over by a ship. Hence the U.S. Navy, the Coast Guard, and commercial

both the city and the St. Johns River by winding through Downtown and over two of the city's seven bridges, including the rather steep Hart Bridge at the end of the race. And with more than $85,000 in prize money, as well as travel expenses for top runners, the USA Track and Field Association considers the Gate River Run one of its national championship events. And if you're not in shape to compete in the 15K, there are other runs the entire family can enjoy. At 8 a.m., an hour before the 15K, there's a noncompetitive *Florida Times-Union* 5K Run & Walk for Charity. After the 15K, you can watch the Adidas Junior River Run, a one-mile fun-run for children 13 and under, and the Diaper Dash, a "run" for 12- to 48-month-olds.

GREAT ATLANTIC SEAFOOD & MUSIC FESTIVAL
Seawalk Pavilion, Jacksonville Beach
www.jaxbeachfestivals.com
Fans of Florida, Louisiana, and Key West seafood cooked blackened, fried, boiled or Cajun-style will love this festival. Dance to the tunes of Zydeco, jazz, blues, and beach music, and stick around for the fashion show, kids rides, games, crafts market, and 5K run.

SUWANNEE SPRINGFEST (AND MAGNOLIAFEST IN THE FALL)
Spirit of the Suwannee Music Park
3076 95th Dr., Live Oak
(904) 249-7990 (administrative offices)
www.magmusic.com

ships are working together to try to prevent this. When a right whale is sighted during calving season, ships radio the Coast Guard, which broadcasts the sightings to all ships in the area, warning them to slow down and be on the lookout for the whales.

Marineland remains proactive in trying to find right whales and document them with photographs, and their scientists have received grant money to lease slow-flying planes called **Air Cams** to document the migration. (As an aside, Air Cams were originally designed for National Geographic photographers to use in wildlife studies in Africa.) Marineland scientists with telephoto lenses lean like stuntmen out of the planes to photograph the whales while pilots fly in a box pattern, a typical search-and-rescue strategy, in areas predetermined by previous sightings. The planes are also relatively quiet, so they don't scare the whales away.

Photographs are an important way of identifying right whales, which form callosities, or callous-like growths, on top of their heads at a very young age. The callosities are made from tissue similar to fingernails. Because they are light in color, they stand out clearly. To scientists, a whale's callosities are just like a fingerprint, making each whale identifiable as an individual.

In 2002 Marineland scientists experienced unbelievable whale-sighting luck. In one week they photographed three pairs of right whales from a blimp on loan from Fuji Film. Two pairs were mothers with their calves; the other pair was two adults.

Scientists believe 15 calves were born off the South Georgia and Northeast Florida coast in 2002. In a normal year 11 calves are born, so that makes 2002 an above-average birth year. "When you only have 300 individuals, you have to question how many are actually available to get pregnant in any given year," said Joy Hampp, current coordinator of the Marineland Right Whale Survey project.

Hampp says it's an absolute thrill to see a right whale. "It's really a privilege," said Hampp. "They are so rare we don't know how long we'll be able to see them off our coast. Plus, they are 45 feet long and weigh 60 tons. To see them in the water frolicking with their babies is just an experience of a lifetime for many people. It's something you never forget."

Visit www.aswh.org/whale/main.html to learn more about the project.

Magnolia Music & Events puts on the best folk music festivals in North Florida, hands-down. Enhanced by the bucolic setting of Spirit of the Suwannee Music Park, SpringFest draws the best in Americana or grassroots music, a rich blend of new and traditional folk, bluegrass, newgrass, roots rock, alternative country, singer/songwriter, rhythm and blues, Cajun, and Celtic music, plus a few indefinable hybrids.

Spirit of the Suwannee Music Park sits about an hour outside of town on 580 wooded acres on the banks of Florida's Suwannee River. Plan to camp, especially if you like to fall asleep to the sounds of jam sessions coming from neighboring campsites. The park has plenty of sites available with complete facilities for both RVs and tent campers.

Along with the camping, the park offers nearly 12 miles of trails for hiking, biking, horseback riding, and nature exploring. Bring along a fishing pole and drop your line from the dock on Rees Lake. Rent canoes and bikes at the on-site canoe outpost, and if the weather's not too chilly, nearby Suwannee Springs offers great swimming.

If camping's not your thing, the nearby town of Live Oak offers enough hotel rooms that you can hang with the music all day long and still sleep on a real bed in an air-conditioned room at night.

Visit the Web site to purchase tickets for a single-day, the full festival, or any variation in-between. Look to the October section for the listing for the sister festival, MagnoliaFest.

APRIL

BEACHES SANDCASTLE CONTEST AND PARADE

Sea Walk Pavilion, Jacksonville Beach
(904) 270-1658
www.jacksonvillebeach.org

The Beaches Sandcastle Contest kicks off the season with sandy flights of fantasy—think octopi, prehistoric fossils, and mermaids—with prizes in several categories based on difficulty of design, craftsmanship, and overall appearance. No more than three people may work on any one sculpture, except in the "Family" and "Groups" categories where up to five people can collaborate. Don't miss the parade on Sunday.

CUMMER BALL & AUCTION

829 Riverside Ave.
(904) 899-6038
www.cummer.org

Jacksonville socialites preen and make chitchat at the Cummer Ball, an annual event hosted by the Cummer Council. The black-tie event features dinner, dancing, fabulous live and silent auctions, drawings, and much more. Proceeds from the evening benefit the Cummer Museum of Art & Gardens. Call for reservations and information.

JACKSONVILLE JAZZ FESTIVAL

Locations throughout Downtown
(904) 630-3690
www.coj.net (search "Jazz festival")

The Jacksonville Jazz Festival provides a great opportunity to hear world-class jazz in the Downtown venue. Jazz greats like Grover Washington Jr., Al Jarreau, Spyro Gyra, and the Manhattan Transfer have all played in this four-day festival. The Great American Jazz Piano Competition at Florida Theatre traditionally kicks off the festival. Some call the competition the best event of the entire festival—as four or five jazz pianists compete for top honors in an intimate setting. (A bit of trivia: in 1983 Harry Connick, Jr. competed in the Great American Jazz Piano Competition and lost—in fact, he didn't even place. But, to be fair, he was only 16 at the time.)

MPS GROUP CHAMPIONSHIPS

Sawgrass Country Club
10034 Golf Club Dr., Ponte Vedra
(800) 486-8366
www.mpsgroupchamps.net

The perennially popular Bausch & Lomb Championships at Amelia Island was recently renamed the MPS Group Championships and relocated to Sawgrass. Tennis fans flock to Sawgrass to witness one of the most prestigious events on the Sony Ericsson Women's Tennis Association Tour. The match-ups, which are played on green clay, include 32 main-draw and 32 qualifying players, with a 16-team, main-draw doubles competition where players face off for $220,000 in prize money.

OPENING OF THE BEACHES FESTIVAL

Downtown Jacksonville Beach
(904) 247-6100
www.jacksonvillebeach.org

Every spring, the city of Jacksonville Beach ceremonially "opens" the Beaches for the season. This is something of a misnomer, of course, because the beaches never close, but it's a good excuse to have a festival. This one starts with a sometimes-raucous parade that can include nightmare-inducing numbers of Shriners zooming around in electrified minicars. Join the crowds to hear local and regional bands in the evening at the outdoor band shell in Jacksonville Beach. Surrounding the band shell are all the makings of a festival, including kids' rides and food booths.

RIVERSIDE AVONDALE SPRING TOUR OF HOMES

(904) 389-2449
www.riverside-avondale.com

This is the city's premier home tour, through which participants have the chance to see inside about a dozen historic homes, churches, schoolhouses, and gardens. At each stop, guides share anecdotes about the building and the communities of Riverside and Avondale. The homes have usually undergone extensive renovations and redecorating. Tour officials hand you a map of the sites when you buy your tickets. (We advise driving between the homes as the area is fairly spread out.) In the end you'll leave Riverside and Avondale with a new knowledge of the district, which is listed on the National Register of Historic Places as one of the largest historic districts in the Southeast.

SPRINGING THE BLUES FESTIVAL
Sea Walk Pavilion
6 North Oceanfront, Jacksonville Beach
(904) 249-3972
www.springingtheblues.com
This popular family event includes a crafts market, children's games, plenty of local seafood, and a 5K run. But what everyone really enjoys is the music—blues tunes from the Mississippi Delta to Chicago. Some of the acts are well known while others are just getting started, but they all play the blues like they've lived it. The music will not disappoint and neither will the setting, which is right next to the ocean in Jacksonville Beach.

WORLD OF NATIONS CELEBRATION
Metropolitan Park
(904) 630-3690
www.coj.net (search "World of Nations")
North Florida's largest multicultural event, held each spring in Metropolitan Park, is arguably one of the best family festivals Jacksonville offers. The celebration draws well over 75,000 visitors with a love of the international food, music, culture and traditions that make up our world.

Wander among the nations' tents where native speakers dish up the food specific to their homeland. Not an adventurous eater? Come anyway; the spectrum of traditional music, dance, and storytelling alone are worth the trip. Be sure to come early on Saturday morning to witness the naturalization ceremony during which upwards of 50 people are sworn in as U.S. citizens.

MAY

ISLE OF EIGHT FLAGS SHRIMP FESTIVAL
Downtown Fernandina Beach
(866) 426-3542 or (904) 261-5841
www.shrimpfestival.com
For more than 45 years, this festival—a four-day

salute to the area's famous crustacean—draws hordes of people to the tiny town of Fernandina Beach. The festival kicks off on Friday with the traditional spaghetti dinner and Shrimp Festival Pirate Parade, and ends on Sunday with the Blessing of the Shrimp Fleet. (Saturday brings The Invasion of the Pirates, so watch your booty, Matey!)

The festival also brings the Annual Shrimp Festival 5K Run/Walk and the Annual Katie Caples Memorial 1-Mile Youth Run. (For information on the run, call the YMCA at 904-261-1080 or visit Active.com.)

Between shrimp binges, wander through the 275-plus artist's booths lining Fernandina's modest downtown, or stroll along the docks and appreciate the shrimp boats that brought this North Florida delicacy to you.

JACKSONVILLE FILM FESTIVAL
128 Forsyth St., Suite 200
(904) 355-2247
http://filmfestival.jacksonville.com
Conceived in the spring of 2002, the Jacksonville Film Festival strives to connect Jacksonville to its early "Hollywood of the South" moviemaking roots, focus attention on independent film and filmmakers, and contribute to the Downtown renaissance. Insider events include an opening night VIP reception, filmmaking panels, international gala, and after-parties. Check the Web site for the lineup and venues, which usually include The Florida Theatre, 5 Points Theatre, the Museum of Contemporary Art, and The Omni hotel.

JACKSONVILLE HUMANE SOCIETY
FUR BALL GALA
(904) 725-8766
www.jaxhumane.org
Now in its 10th year, the Jacksonville Humane Society's Fur Ball Gala attracts more than 350 animal lovers (and around 150 pets) annually for an evening of fine dining, live and silent auctions, wet noses, and hilarious costumes. NOTE: This is the city's only black-tie event for people and their pets so the dress gets very . . . creative. In past years, Miss Daisy's Delights pet bakery has offered a pet-treat bar for four-legged attendees and Pet

Butlers' staffers have been on hand to walk pets or escort them to a time-out area where they can rest. Of course, like any good ball, this one crowns its own (albeit furry) king and queen.

JACKSONVILLE SPRING MUSIC FESTIVAL
Metropolitan Park
(904) 630-3690
www.coj.net (search for "Jacksonville Spring Music")

Every spring, Jacksonville sponsors a free music festival at Metropolitan Park, a beautiful riverfront venue in Downtown Jacksonville. This one-day festival usually coincides with Memorial Day and features an evening of music by well-known bands. There is no fee for admission, but you may have to pay to park your car. And don't bother with that picnic basket—the guards won't let you bring it in. Instead, buy your food and drink from the plethora of vendors who hawk their wares in the park.

> **i** The Jacksonville Film Festival is held every May and includes several film-related lectures and workshops. Go to http://filmfestival.jacksonville.com for details.

THE KUUMBA FESTIVAL
Visit the Web site for festival location and details
(904) 632-5555
www.kuumbafestivalfl.org

Kuumba, which means "creativity" in Swahili, is the perfect name for this family festival, which celebrates African-American pride, culture, and creativity. The festival kicks off with a parade of participants dressed in colorful costumes of African royalty. Think African music, dancing and cuisine. Honors are given for the achievements of local African-Americans. Kuumba is supplemented by professional workshops covering African dance, health-related issues, motivation, empowerment, and education. The Festival also features a youth tent and community rally, games, guest speakers, and entertainment by local and national acts.

THE MUG RACE
Rudder Club of Jacksonville
8533 Malaga Ave., Orange Park
(904) 264-4094
www.rudderclub.com

This annual race, held on the first Saturday in May and sponsored by the Rudder Club of Jacksonville's sailing aficionados, is billed as the longest river race for sailboats in the country. Over 200 sailboats enter the 38-mile race from Palatka to Jacksonville every year. The winner gets bragging rights for a year and "The Mug." Wind or no wind, The Rudder Club awards 100 trophies, including ones for the fastest and slowest boats (which, in 2008, logged 8 hours and 12 hours, respectively).

THE PLAYERS CHAMPIONSHIP
100 PGA TOUR Blvd., Ponte Vedra Beach
(904) 285-3700
www.pgatour.com

Watch the best professional golfers vie for the winner's cup on The Stadium Course at the Tournament Players Club at Sawgrass. Early in The Players Championship week, the galleries are small and fans can walk the perimeter of the course, following their favorite golfer at close range. By the weekend, though, the course is packed and you have to hustle to stay close. Many people try a different approach and just park themselves by a favorite hole and watch the golfers come by. This premier event comes with just one warning: the weather is sometimes as big a story as the golf, with torrential downpours, biting wind, or, if you're lucky, spring temperatures and sunny skies. See the Golf chapter for more on this popular event.

SPAR HOME AND GARDEN TOUR
1321 North Main St.
(904) 353-7727
www.sparcouncil.org

SPAR, short for the Springfield Preservation and Revitalization Council, whose purpose is to provide leadership to the residents of Historic Springfield to revitalize, preserve, and restore the community, sponsors an annual tour of the neighborhood's homes, gardens, and sites of interest. Touted as Jacksonville's first and old-

Run Pie-boy, Run!

Get ready to love this town.

One of Jacksonville's quirkiest annual events ever, the **Run for the Pies**, proves that not only will Jacksonville take any excuse to stage a run, but they've got the stones to pair it with a pie-eating contest and call it a sport.

As a part of their annual slate of runs, 1st Place Sports hosts this twilight **5k Championship** and a **5k Open Race** every June through the broad streets of Downtown. Consider the Championship Race the bookish older sister to the freewheeling fun of the Open Race. The Championship racers are in it for the time, but the open racers definitely seem to be having more fun with pie carrying, pie eating, and pie costume contests held throughout the day. Hilarity ensues as runners plod through the five-lap Downtown course both in costume (think pregnant bakers, slices of pie, and cans of whipped cream) and dreaming of the sugary incentive waiting at the finish line.

The folks at 1st Place Sports are good people, not just because they organize almost every race under the sun in this town, and not just because they give away Mizuno running shoes to the top Championship racers, but because anyone who can sell the idea of combining running and pie deserves a gold star in marketing.

It's actually not a hard sell. Just imagine, you've run 5k, you stagger across the finish line into the chute, and Blammo! A stranger thrusts not a Gatorade, not a Powerbar, but a whole pie in your hands. Now imagine this 200 times over, and you get the picture.

The idea of tucking into a pie before your heart rate even has a chance to slow down is quirky enough, but the fact that the race is also followed by a pie-eating contest that devolves into a whipped-cream free-for-all really takes the cake...I mean pie.

After the race, 1st Place Sports gives away free beer, free pizza, and thousands of dollars in sports gear and running shoes. But come on; we just want a pie...and maybe a medal. But definitely a pie.

See the listing in the June activities section for more details.

est subdivision, Springfield was established in 1869 and is currently enjoying a decade-long gentrification, with many of the condemned and downtrodden beauties undergoing restoration by hardworking urban pioneers. Visit www .sparcouncil.org to find out where to buy tickets.

WAVE MASTERS SURF CONTEST
1171 Beach Blvd., Jacksonville Beach
(904) 241-0600
www.wavemasters.org
Wave Masters Surf Contest, the largest, open, ama-

teur surfing contest in North Florida began years ago when the Wave Masters, a ever-growing group of 25-and-older doctors, insurance agents, construction workers, and computer programmers whose sole commonality was a love of longboards, staged a contest with the hope of raising the image of surfing in the community (and raising a little money for local charities). The contest was a success and has evolved into Florida's favorite, open, amateur surfing contest. This annual event draws over 300 competitors from all over the Southeast and thousands of enthusiastic spectators.

JUNE

RUN FOR THE PIES
The Jacksonville Landing (start and finish)
(904) 731-1900
www.1stplacesports.com/pies.htm
It really doesn't get any better than this. Every summer, 1st Place Sports hosts two twilight 5k races (championship and open) where every racer who beats a certain time is rewarded with a whole pie as they pass through the chute, not to mention free pizza, beer, and live music during the awards ceremony and after-party. We love that not only did someone think of this, but that they also got big corporate sponsors like OE&S to come along for the ride . . . I mean run. (Read the Run Pie-boy Run! sidebar in this chapter to learn more.)

SAIL JACKSONVILLE
North and Southbank Riverwalks
(904) 630-3690
www.coj.net (search for "Sail Jacksonville")
Sail Jacksonville, a spectacular, three-day festival of ships, has it all, including a pirate battle on the St. Johns (complete with booming cannons) and a Norway Viking Ship Race. Ship tours and seamanship demonstrations are available when the ships are dockside. Also on display is a 1960s replica of the H.M.S. *Bounty*, which was built for MGM for use in a movie. (The original was commissioned in 1787 and was destroyed after a mutiny.) The new ship has been used in several feature-length films, documentaries, TV shows, as a tourist attraction, and is now an educational venture.

Best photo opportunity: the Parade of Sail, when the ships arrive en masse in Downtown Jacksonville. Children enjoy their own special festival area that includes music, arts, crafts, and even special guests from the Jacksonville Zoo. (Be advised that Sail Jacksonville does not happen every year; check the city's Web site.)

JULY

THE AT&T GREATER JACKSONVILLE KINGFISH TOURNAMENT
Sisters Creek Marina
8203 Heckscher Dr.
(904) 251-3011
www.kingfishtournament.com
Only 1,000 boats are allowed to enter this week-long fishing tournament that draws anglers from all around. Fisherfolk compete with rod and reel to see who can bring in the biggest kingfish in Northeast Florida. Most folks return year after year to enter this tournament, which carries a hefty $400 entry fee per boat. It's usually hotter than Hades all week long, but participants don't seem to mind, in part because the prize structure is so enticing—more than $700,000 in boats, cash, and other prizes. Early in the week there's a Junior Angler Tournament, a chance for young ones to try their hand at catching an elusive kingfish.

If you're a landlubber, be not dismayed. This is a party packed with events and entertainment including a boat show, exhibitions, a food festival, a Liar's Tent, and the Boatique, the headquarters for Official Tournament Merchandise. When you hit entertainment-overload, retire to the stands and watch as anglers weigh in their daily catches.

FIRST COAST PRIDE STREET FEST & PARADE
Locations throughout Riverside and Historic 5 Points
(888) 411- 6482
www.firstcoastpride.com
After a brief falter in recent years, the First Coast Pride Festival is back in full force with an opening parade that begins in historic Avondale (at the corner of St. Johns and Van Wert Avenues), moves through the historic Riverside District, and ends at Riverside Park in 5 Points where from noon until 6 p.m., the park buzzes with live music, food vendors, and booths sponsored by local GLBT-friendly businesses and organizations.

Don't miss the rollicking First Coast Pride Block Party along the parade route or the MOSAIC High Energy Diversity Dance Party (traditionally held in the 5 Points Theatre building) that lasts until 3 a.m.

Many gay bars, popular restaurants, hotels, shops, and gay-friendly businesses sponsor special events and parties throughout Pride Week. Check local gay newspapers and Web sites, such as www.GayJax.com, for details.

FOURTH OF JULY CELEBRATION
Downtown Riverfront
(904) 630-3690
www.coj.net (search for "Fourth of July Celebration")
The city of Jacksonville celebrates the Fourth in a big way with a four-day festival along the Downtown riverfront and in Metropolitan Park. Festivities include activities, concerts, and events and builds to a big-name concert in Metropolitan Park. The evening ends with a fireworks display over the St. Johns River. Best of all, this event is free, except for the occasional parking fee and the money you spend buying food and drink inside Metropolitan Park (the city won't let you bring your own).

LIBERTY CELEBRATION
Sea Walk Pavilion
6 North Oceanfront Jacksonville Beach
(904) 249-3868
www.jacksonvillebeach.org
If you'd rather celebrate the Fourth of July at the beach, Jacksonville Beach also does things up in a grand way. And there are big crowds (150,000 one year) to prove it. The Liberty Celebration begins early in the day with bands, a burger cook-off, and Frisbee-dog demonstrations at Sea Walk Pavilion, right next to the ocean in Jacksonville Beach. All day long, vendors serve up fresh delights, from funnel cakes dusted with powdered sugar to hot dogs smothered in mustard, ketchup, relish, and onions. More ambitious revelers may decide to pack their own food and set up on the beach for a full day of swimming and eating. By 9:30 p.m. everyone is ready for the traditionally large, booming fireworks display, which can be seen for miles up and down the beach.

AUGUST

JACKSONVILLE HUMANE SOCIETY TOAST TO THE ANIMALS
(904) 725-8766
www.jaxhumane.org
For more than a decade, local animal lovers have supported this foodie event at the Florida Theatre, where they nosh on food from some of Jacksonville's best restaurants and sip hundreds of different wines from local distributors. The wine makes silent auction bidding lively, so much so that in 2009 the event raised over $50,000 "for the care of the animals that call the Jacksonville Humane Society their temporary home." Visit the Web site for dates.

JAGUARS PRESEASON GAMES
Jacksonville Municipal Stadium, 1 Stadium Place
(904) 633-2000, (800) 618-8005
www.jaguars.com
Not so Insider, but popular with football fans who begin to smile more often and step more lively once the pigskins start flying around. After seven months of waiting, fans return to Jacksonville Municipal Stadium to watch the Jaguars toss the ball around in preparation for the coming season. (College football also gets under way in earnest this month.) Check out the Jaguar's Web site for a game schedule.

SEPTEMBER

THE 4TH ANNUAL WEDDING CRASHERS PARTY
(904) 807-7582
www.jacksonvillescene.com
One of Jacksonville's largest and most mad-cap annual fund-raising charity events, the Wedding Crashers Party is a mock wedding and reception that people dress up for and actually pay to crash. Crashers enjoy free drinks all night, as well as free food, Angie's Wedding Cakes, activities, and surprises that seem to up the ante every year. Past "weddings" have been held at locations like the historic St. Andrews church outside the Baseball

Grounds. Your crashers' wristband gets you into a crashers-only after-party at a different location each year. With a motto like, "Invites are for losers. If you can't cry fake it, and dance like you mean it! Life's a Party. Crash it," how could you go wrong? The event is sponsored by Jacksonville Scene. Tickets are $25 in advance; $35 at the door; and the proceeds benefit a different local charity each year. Past beneficiaries have been the Jacksonville Historical Society and Cystic Fibrosis Foundation.

START! HEART WALK
American Heart Association
(904) 739-0197
firstcoastheartwalk.kintera.org
Every year thousands of people participate in this walk, the American Heart Association's premier fund-raising event, which has raised about $800,000 for the American Heart Association. Designed to promote physical activity and heart-healthy living, the walk usually begins at 9 a.m. and covers a three-mile course from Metropolitan Park, through Downtown, around The Jacksonville Landing, and back to Metropolitan Park. Participants often collect donations ahead of time, and walkers who raise $100 or more receive a Heart Walk T-shirt. The American Heart Association also offers a health fair and activities for children. "Walk with friends, family, coworkers or strangers you'll bond with along the way," says the Association. "Any way you choose to do it, your heart will thank you for it!"

UP AND CUMMERS ANNUAL FASHION FORWARD
The Cummer Museum of Art & Gardens
829 Riverside Ave.
(904) 899-6018
www.cummer.org
The Up and Cummers, a Cummer Museum–affiliated group of motivated 24- to 45-year-olds, hosts their annual Fashion Forward fashion show every September. This is the Up and Cummers' biggest event of the year and brings together approximately 500 of Jacksonville's best and brightest who share a love of fashion and the arts.

The Up and Cummers select a different emerging clothing designer to feature each year. Visit the museum's Web site to learn more about the fashion show, Up and Cummer membership, and monthly events.

OCTOBER

THE FLORIDA-GEORGIA GAME
Jacksonville Municipal Stadium,
1 Stadium Place
(904) 630-3690
www.coj.net (search "Florida Georgia Game")
This annual match-up between college football rivals is played on a Saturday, but University of Florida and University of Georgia fans begin arriving the Wednesday before in 40-foot RVs for five days of elaborate tailgating. If you attend the game, take a few minutes to walk through RV City, where friendly rivalry and partying between Gator and Bulldog fans is the name of the game. After all, there's a reason this game was dubbed "the World's Largest Outdoor Cocktail Party."

THE GREATER JACKSONVILLE AGRICULTURAL FAIR
Jacksonville Fairgrounds
510 Fairgrounds Place
(904) 353-0535
www.jacksonvillefair.com
Like all good agricultural fairs, this one offers more activities than the average family could possibly take in on one visit. For 4-H participants it's a livestock show, for cooks it's a chance to win a blue ribbon, and for country music fans it's a chance to hear a different musical act every evening. And children of all ages can scare themselves silly on death-defying rides. The fair usually lasts 11 days, with the best music and largest crowds on the weekends.

JACKSONVILLE PUBLIC LIBRARY'S ANNUAL GREAT JACKSONVILLE BOOK SALE
Jacksonville Fairgrounds
510 Fairgrounds Place
(904) 630-2304
www.fjpl.org

Come to The Jacksonville Fairgrounds in October to rummage through tens of thousands of books from 50 cents to $2 in what is easily one of the greatest, three-day, no-holds-barred book-sale events imaginable. Every year The Friends of the Jacksonville Public Library set up more dusty tomes than you can imagine in the fairgrounds' exhibit halls, giving Jacksonville bookworms a chance to pad their bookshelves with every type of literature from cookbooks to DVDs to children's books to large-print books.

MAGNOLIAFEST (AND SPRINGFEST IN MARCH)
Spirit of the Suwannee Music Park
3076 95th Drive, Live Oak
(904) 249-7990 (administrative offices)
www.magmusic.com
Magnolia Music & Events puts on the best folk music festivals in North Florida, hands-down. Enhanced by the bucolic setting of Spirit of the Suwannee Music Park, MagnoliaFest draws the best in Americana or grassroots music, a rich blend of new and traditional folk, bluegrass, newgrass, roots rock, alternative country, singer/songwriter, rhythm and blues, Cajun, and Celtic music, plus a few indefinable hybrids.

Spirit of the Suwannee Music Park sits about an hour outside of town on 580 wooded acres on the banks of Florida's Suwannee River. Plan to camp, especially if you like to fall asleep to the sounds of jam sessions coming from neighboring campsites. The park has plenty of sites available with complete facilities for both RVs and tent campers.

Along with the camping, the park offers nearly 12 miles of trails for hiking, biking, horseback riding, and nature exploring. Bring along a fishing pole and drop your line from the dock on Rees Lake. Canoe and bike rentals are available at the on-site canoe outpost. If the weather's not too chilly, nearby Suwannee Springs offers great swimming.

If camping's not your thing, the town of Live Oak is close enough and offers enough hotel rooms so that you can overnight close by, but out of the elements.

Visit the Web site to purchase tickets for a single day, the full festival, or any variation in-between. Look to the March section for the listing for the sister festival, SpringFest.

THE PUMPKIN RUN
Evergreen Cemetery
4535 Main St.
(904) 731-3676
The Pumpkin Run, which generally falls close to Halloween, is a 5k and 10k run through Evergreen Cemetery sponsored by 1st Place Sports and benefiting The Jacksonville Historical Society. The course tracks a beautiful circuit through Evergreen Cemetery Downtown and takes runners on trails past centuries-old headstones and under stately oak and magnolia trees. The tree canopy ensures that the course remains about 90 percent shaded. There is also, of course, a post-race party with free food and drink. (Beer is served, but only after the race.) Participants are welcome to take the pumpkins lining the course home with them, but only after all of the 10k finishers have crossed the line.

RED WAGON PARADE
Hemming Plaza—Corner of Laura and Duval Streets
(904) 202-2881 or (904) 202-2250
www.wolfsonchildrens.org (search "Red Wagon Parade")
The annual Red Wagon Parade benefiting Wolfson Children's Hospital is one of those sweet-as-pie children's events that parents love. Teams pony up for sponsorships from $1,000 to $5,000 for the opportunity to decorate wagons in the theme of their favorite children's book. Teams then parade their wagons around town as part of the Jacksonville Children's Commission Family Festival, which also kicks off Mayor Peyton's RALLY! Book Club. All proceeds go to provide care for the children at Wolfson Children's Hospital. Afterward, the wagons remain on display at the Jacksonville Public Library's main Downtown branch. In the spirit of egalitarianism, all participating wagons are invited to represent Wolfson Children's Hospital in the New Year's Eve Winn-Dixie Hometown Gator Bowl Parade telecast on live television.

NOVEMBER

THE DOWNTOWN SIDEWALK CHALK CONTEST
The Jacksonville Landing
www.jaxchalkfest.com

On the second Saturday in November, artists from around the region have four hours to create prize-winning chalk drawings at The Jacksonville Landing. Artists are judged in multiple categories based on age and level of professional expertise. The Landing sponsors live music throughout the day, an awards ceremony party in the afternoon, a fashion show, and a post-event party throughout the evening. At midnight, everyone participates in the ceremonial Splash Party, using gallons of water to wash the artwork away forever. Ah, impermanence!

THE JACKSONVILLE LANDING TREE LIGHTING
www.jacksonvillelanding.com

Traditionally held on the Friday after Thanksgiving, The Jacksonville Landing Tree Lighting kicks off the holiday season. The lighting is a big deal celebration around town and involves a full lineup of choirs and bands, and gives the city yet another reason to shoot off some fireworks.

JACKSONVILLE LIGHT PARADE
St. Johns River, Downtown
(904) 630-3690
www.coj.net (search "Light Parade")

Bring the grandparents, bring the kids, and head to the riverfront on the weekend following Thanksgiving for this gilded boat parade. Local captains decorate their boats in creative Christmas themes with thousands of lights and parade their vessels in front of judges at The Jacksonville Landing. Jacksonville's nautical community hails it as one of the best ways to get into the holiday spirit. And that's not all—the evening ends with a large fireworks display—the biggest of the year with glittering bombs launched from two barges in the river and a cascade of waterfall fireworks falling from two bridges. It's no wonder the Southeast Tourism Society named the Jacksonville Light Parade one of the top 20 events in the Southeast.

JACKSONVILLE SEA AND SKY SPECTACULAR
The Beaches or NAS Jacksonville
(904) 542-3152
www.coj.net (search "Sea and Sky Spectacular")

The Sea and Sky Spectacular may be just a fancy name for an air show, but there are many who believe this over-the-ocean air show has earned the moniker many times over on the basis of its sheer awesomeness. Feel the ground shake as the Blue Angels fly low overhead, imagine the stamina of aerobatic pilots who repeatedly loop the loop and battle g-forces with every bank and roll, and cheer as U.S. Marine amphibious assault units "take" Jacksonville Beach. The event is free to the public and also includes a street festival featuring displays of aircraft and military vehicles, simulators, the Kiddy Hawk Kids Area, and Aviation Alley Autograph Sessions. The Sea and Sky Spectacular also has Fleet Week components with events Downtown and at Naval Station Mayport.

PLANETFEST
Metropolitan Park
(904) 636-0507
www.planetfest10.com

For over a decade, Planetfest music festival has drawn massive 20-something crowds to Metropolitan Park for an all-out musical smack-down where national and local acts like Papa Roach, Chevelle, Jet, Framing Hanley, Skindred, and Halestorm play 45- to 60-minute sets on two stages. The smaller Jack Rabbits Stage is named after the local venue where a Battle of the Bands competition is held to select the local bands that will play at the festival. (Check out the Nightlife section to find out more about Jack Rabbits.) Generally, the top nine acts from the competition are awarded 30- to 45-minute sets at Planetfest. The festival is sponsored by PlanetRadio 107.3, and the tickets are super-cheap (between $15 and $35, depending on how early you get them). Don't forget to stick around for the after-party.

i Watch the Jacksonville Light Parade and fireworks display from the River Deck at the Hyatt Regency Jacksonville Riverfront (225 East Coastline Dr.). Admission to the festivities on the deck is only $5, but bring a new, unwrapped toy for charity and you'll get in free. If you're planning to party, why not stay over? The Hyatt offers enticing Light Parade packages; visit www.jacksonville.hyatt.com for more information.

RIVERKEEPER OYSTER ROAST
At the Garden Club of Jacksonville
1005 Riverside Ave.
www.stjohnsriverkeeper.org
(904) 256-7591
Support the St. Johns Riverkeeper, a nonprofit advocacy group for the St. Johns River that gains its funding through donations and memberships, and also enjoy one of the best parties of the year! The Annual Riverkeeper Oyster Roast, held at the Garden Club of Jacksonville, provides outstanding food, live music, new friends, and, of course, lots of oysters. Tickets are $125 each, or $75 each for those 35 or younger.

VETERANS DAY PARADE
Downtown
(904) 630-3690
www.coj.net (search "Veterans Day Parade")
Veterans Day is an important day in Jacksonville, where the United States Navy is one of the largest employers. Patriotism rules at this Downtown event, which features military members of all ages from junior ROTC cadets to retired veterans. State dignitaries often lead the parade along with the mayor, as thousands of parade-watchers line the streets to cheer for high school marching bands, veterans' posts, military commands, and the Jacksonville Fire and Rescue Department. The parade caps off the Week of Valor, a seven-day tribute to the city's military that begins with the arrival of the Blue Angels, concludes with the Veterans Day Parade, and includes the Sea and Sky Spectacular. The week also provides a great

opportunity to take ship tours aboard Navy and U.S. Coast Guard vessels, as well as attend military movies and a speakers' series.

DECEMBER

ANNUAL TUBA CHRISTMAS CONCERT
The Jacksonville Landing
www.jacksonvillelanding.com
For the last 15 years, the city's underground contingent of about 100 tuba enthusiasts has shown up on a mid-December afternoon to hoot out everyone's favorite holiday classics to a loyal group of listeners. This is such a Jacksonville Insider event that it's a crime to miss it. Really. Trust me.

ART & ANTIQUES SHOW TO BENEFIT WOLFSON CHILDREN'S HOSPITAL
Prime Osborn Convention Center
1000 Water St.
(904) 202-2886
www.artandantiquesshow.com
For more than 25 years, dealers and guest lecturers from all over the world have participated in this three-day art and antiques show that raises money for Wolfson Children's Hospital. Recent speakers include HRH Princess of Kent, who spoke on Louis XIV and the arts of 17th-century France, interior designers Barry Dixon and Jeffrey Bilhuber, and editor of *Flower* magazine Margot Shaw. The show launches new exhibitions each year, ranging from heirloom silver to table settings designed by area hostesses. Charlie Miller is on hand to offer antiques appraisals. Lunch is prepared daily by a local restaurant, and tea and pastries are served in the afternoon. Become a benefactor to attend the Benefactor Preview Reception & Opening Night Party, or come to the Children's Fashion Show on Saturday afternoon.

THE BIKE JAX LUMINARIA RIDE
www.bikejax.org
www.riversideavondale.org
Every holiday season, hundreds of Jacksonville bicycle enthusiasts meet at Riverside Park on a December evening to pedal en masse among

A Christmas Storey

Anyone who grew up in Jacksonville will remember **The Dorcas Drake Christmas Party,** the philanthropic work of a Jacksonville matron who gathered over 50,000 toys a year and gave them out to the city's underprivileged children during an annual holiday party Downtown. After Ms. Drake passed away in the early '90s, the program faltered and stalled but was taken up again in the 1999 by Travis and Margaret Storey and renamed **The Children's Christmas Party.** The story of their personal generosity and selfless devotion to this event is one for the record books.

In December 1998 the Storeys learned that the Drake party was faltering without the leadership of its founder. Margaret had the idea to donate bicycles. They went out, spent $5,500 of their own money, and bought 100.

The next year, when it looked like the Drake party might not happen at all, volunteers called Travis for help, and The Children's Christmas Party was born.

Travis brought heavy-hitters on board with donations, convincing Stein Mart Chairman Jay Stein, Mac Papers President Sutton McGehee, Gate Petroleum President Herb Peyton, and *Times-Union* General Manager Bobby Martin to give $5,000 each. By the party, Storeys had raised $45,000.

Ten years later, the Storeys and their efforts are still going strong.

Thanks to their dedication, every year upwards of 10,000 children, who otherwise might not receive toys for Christmas, are treated to wrapped gifts and visits with Santa. The lines are extraordinary, and hundreds of volunteers are on-hand to hand out the gifts, which come from the Toys for Tots program and from private and corporate monetary donations. In 2008 enough funds were collected to buy 30,000 brand new toys and over 600 bikes and helmets. An additional 50,000 toys, pencils, and coloring books were gifted to the kids. Toys donated by citizens and the Marine Corps Toys for Tots program were also handed out. This is truly one of the city's most beloved holiday traditions and a real Insider treat to participate in.

---

the Riverside/Avondale luminaria. Imagine 300 riders on bicycles wrapped in Christmas lights, waving to friends, and making a spectacular scene. Many pedalers go all out, with elaborate designs and even costumes. All in all, you can't ask for a better way to spend a winter's eve. All are welcome to pedal along.

THE CHILDREN'S CHRISTMAS PARTY
Prime Osborn Convention Center
1000 Water St.
(904) 504-3589
www.ccpoj.org
This annual holiday toy giveaway warms the hearts of every Insider on the block. The event,

run by a superhero band of Jacksonville philanthropists, piggybacks on the legacy of Dorcas Bartram Drake and does her memory proud with toys going out to 10,000 (or more) children a year. (Read the Sidebar in this section to learn more about this time-honored tradition.)

FIRST COAST *NUTCRACKER*
Times-Union Center for the Performing Arts,
Moran Theater
300 West Water St.
(904) 354-5547
www.jaxsymphony.org
There's scarcely a Jacksonville native around who has not either been taken to, or taken their

own young friends to, this annual holiday ballet. The First Coast Nutcracker attracts internationally acclaimed dancers as well as the city's finest dancers of all ages to this full-scale, annual production. Tchaikovsky's beloved melodies, performed live by the Jacksonville Symphony Orchestra under the direction of conductor Michael Butterman, provide the score and the basis for a lifetime of memories.

GOLDEN ISLES CHRISTMAS ON THE RIVER
Amelia River Cruises
www.ameliarivercruises.com
Book a special, holiday, extended trip on the Bald Eagle/Cumberland Sound Ferry vessel. The cruise runs to and from Jekyll Island and includes accommodations at the Jekyll Island Club and additional meals and activities, including a private sunset dinner, Sunday brunch, tour of the Georgia Sea Turtle Center, and a trolley tour of the downtown historic area. The weekend also features bagpipers, a private screening of *Miracle on 34th Street* (with popcorn), and "snow"-covered grounds. The cruise sails from downtown Fernandina Beach.

NEW YEAR'S EVE CELEBRATION
Downtown
(904) 630-3690
www.coj.net (search "New Year's Eve")
Ring in the New Year Downtown with midnight fireworks along the St. Johns River. The Gator Bowl Association adds to the festivities with a 5K Gator Bowl run in the morning and a parade in the afternoon. Sports fans love the Gator Bowl pep rallies at The Jacksonville Landing, and everyone loves the New Year's Eve concerts around town, so be sure and check www.coj.net/events for the performance schedule. Best of all, these citywide festivities are free.

RAP LUMINARIA
Locations throughout Riverside and Avondale
www.riversideavondale.org
Riverside and Avondale neighborhoods go all out for this beloved, time-honored tradition. Taking place at a time when Jacksonville actually feels crisp and wintry, the multi-neighborhood luminaria stroll takes you past the historic districts' modest bungalows and restored mansions where front yards and walks are lined with glowing paper bags. Check the Web site for specific events associated with the current year's luminaria, which in the past have included bike rides and festivals, as well as the traditional lighting of the luminaria lanterns at sundown.

WINN-DIXIE HOMETOWN GATOR BOWL PARADE
Downtown Jacksonville
www.gatorbowl.com/events_parade.html
If you like festive floats and marching bands, then you'll want to make a beeline for the Winn-Dixie Hometown Gator Bowl Parade on New Year's Eve day. The parade, which starts at 3 p.m., follows a loop from the Prime Osborn Convention Center, down Laura Street, to Bay Street, and back to the Prime Osborn Convention Center. *NOTE:* If you don't feel up to jockeying for a decent vantage point, plunk down $10 for a reserved seat along the route.

THE ARTS

The old-school image of Jacksonville as an arts desert with little to offer in the way of contemporary culture and new influences can finally be put to rest. Thanks to an influx of new blood and a kindling of like-minded spirits, the city has turned into an arts-focused entity enlivened by Downtown Art Walks, Arts Markets, annual arts events, experimental theater, and new galleries popping up all over town.

Sure, the city has its own symphony and pops orchestra, but it also has the oldest continually operated community theater in the country. The city has also become a prime stop for traveling Broadway musicals and ballet companies, and has one of the finest performing arts high schools in the country.

The most exciting evolution of all is happening in the visual arts scene. Jacksonville has turned into a hub for up-and-coming visual artists seeking a lower cost of living and year-round good weather. This burgeoning arts scene means that the city has become a great place for novice aficionados to start building their art collections. Many soon-to-be-discovered artists live in the area and, lucky for us, their work remains affordable. And thanks to events like Art After Dark, Art Walk, and the Riverside Arts Market, the city provides loads of opportunities to meet new talent and purchase works directly from the artists. All you need is a good eye and a modest bank account to get started. In addition, we've listed several excellent galleries to help you find what's out there, but be sure to check local listings as new galleries pop up (or, unfortunately, close) all the time.

This chapter is organized in four ways: by venue, concert series, production company and gallery with lots of valuable extra tips and Close-Ups in between. Our goal is that, with just a visit to a Web site or a phone call, you can find out "who's doing what where" all over town.

THE VENUES

5 POINTS THEATRE
1028 Park St.
(904) 359-0047
www.5pointstheatre.com
The 5 Points Theatre has gone through many incarnations over the past few decades (anyone remember Club 5's midnight free-for-alls?), but the theater has remained one of the city's best Insider venues for indie films and the arts. Originally the Riverside Theatre, it was the first theater in Florida built to show "talkies." (Architecture buffs take note: the same architect, Roy Benjamin, also designed the Florida Theatre.) In its current incarnation, the 1927 theater provides an excellent venue in which to see the latest releases or indie films, many of which are free. Order a frosty beer or a glass of wine while you watch; the theater remains one of the only two places in town where you can do so.

ADELE GRAGE CULTURAL CENTER
716 Ocean Blvd., Atlantic Beach
(904) 247-5828
www.ci.atlantic-beach.fl.us (search "Adele Grage Cultural Center")
Touted by local musicians as one of the most lovely venues in town, the Adele Grage Cultural Center serves as a performance center for the city of Atlantic Beach and the home of the Atlantic Beach Experimental Theatre company, which stages performances from September to May.

A Walk to Remember

Learn about Downtown art galleries firsthand on the first Wednesday of every month when Downtown Vision sponsors the **First Wednesday Art Walk,** a free, self-guided, walking tour of Downtown Jacksonville's galleries and museums. Once a month, the historic district of Downtown turns into a living, breathing 15-block art gallery offering a high-energy dose of culture and community. Think live music, street performers, hands-on art projects, and more with cultural venues, restaurants, and businesses all joining in the fun. Get your map stamped at each stop along the way and win a free gift! The event runs from 5 to 8 p.m., with free street parking after 6 p.m. For maps and more information go to www.downtownjacksonville. org/first-wednesday-art-walk or call (904) 634-0303. (See also First Fridays in 5 Points in this chapter.)

For a special treat, show up for Songwriter Nights when the lovely local songbird Lauren Fincham has been known to take the stage.

i Bring a blanket or bring the lawn chairs. The City of Jacksonville Beach sponsors many free concerts in its outdoor band shell at Sea Walk Pavilion. Call the events hotline (904) 247-6100 or visit www .jacksonvillebeach.org for the latest schedule.

CUMMER MUSEUM OF ART AND GARDENS
829 Riverside Ave.
(904) 356-6857
www.cummer.org

Upon her death in 1961, Ninah Mae Holden Cummer bequeathed her home, extraordinary gardens, and collections to establish the Cummer Museum, which has come to symbolize the very definition of Southern elegance in Jacksonville's arts scene. From the massive live oak behind the galleries to the sweeping views of the river, the grounds of the Cummer soothe with their quiet beauty and old-world charm. The museum's collection of Meissen porcelain is one of the three finest in the world, and the collections of European and American art and Japanese woodblocks draw art lovers from all over the Southeast. Perhaps best of all are the two acres of English and Italian gardens, which Mrs. Cummer coaxed out of Florida's sandy soil. Parents love the Cummer for its award-winning children's wing, called Art Connections. (See the Kidstuff chapter for more on Art Connections.) The Cummer is open 10 a.m. to 9 p.m. Tuesday, from 10 a.m. to 4 p.m. Wednesday through Friday, from 10 a.m. to 5 p.m. on Saturday, and Sunday from noon to 5 p.m. The Cummer is closed on Monday and major holidays. A good time to visit the Cummer is on Tuesday after 4 p.m., when museum admission is free.

EUROPEAN STREET LISTENING ROOM
1704 San Marco Blvd.
(904) 399-1740
www.hackingcat.com
One of the best places in town to listen to acts on the small stage. European Street's unassuming stature and living-room atmosphere makes every show feel like its being played just for you and your friends. European Street is primarily a neighborhood café and bar, so the food and beer selections are exceptional. Shows run from 8:30 to 10:30, and the venue only holds 75 people, so get there early. Visit the Web site to check out the upcoming lineup and ticket prices.

FIRST FRIDAYS IN FIVE POINTS
Intersection of Park, Margaret and Lomax Streets
www.5pointsjax.com
Considered both an arts event and a nightlife event, First Fridays in 5 Points bring out Jacksonville

🔍 Close-up

The Nicest Son of a Gun in the Whole Goshdarn City (or something to that effect)

If you're trying to get a play produced, get a tip on the best new restaurant, or find out the best place to hear live music, **Robert Arleigh White** is your guy. Currently the executive director of The Cultural Council of Greater Jacksonville, Bob, as he is known to his friends—and in this city, everyone either is or wants to be his friend—has possibly the longest and most storied past of anyone in the Jacksonville arts scene.

White came to the city in 1978, taking a job as a high school theater, English, and creative writing teacher, making permanent impressions on his students—many of whom have gone on to become accomplished visual artists, actors, writers, and musicians themselves—and influencing a whole generation of future arts activists, many of whom cite White as their sole reason for coming to school every day.

In 1984, while still teaching high school full-time, White become the artistic director of **Theatre Jacksonville,** the city's oldest and most well-respected community theater and served as the producing and/or artistic director for six seasons of "Shakespeare at the Met," a production recognized as being among the best outdoor theater offerings by the State of Florida. By 1990, he had become the theater's full-time chief executive and artistic director. Because of White, the theater was finally financially viable.

But the big break for both White and the city came in 2000 when he agreed to take the helm of the city's Cultural Council where his leadership and arts advocacy on behalf of cultural institutions in Jacksonville is legendary. "The move from the theater to the Cultural Council allowed me to affect cultural change on a much bigger scale. At the same time, I've maintained my artistic partnership with Charlotte Mabrey, principal percussionist with the Jacksonville Symphony Orchestra, which has yielded a large body of original performance pieces. Working as an artist keeps me honest and focused on all the best parts of my work as an arts administrator."

Insiders in droves. This year-round, boozy mash-up of art, music, and food signifies the best of what's happening in the city's grassroots arts scene and provides great cause for optimism. Ignore the fact that the event starts at 5 p.m.; it doesn't really get going until around 7 p.m. or after the sun goes down. Five Points businesses put on the dog with hors d'oeuvres, wine, and arts happenings of all kinds. Be sure to check out The Underbelly (inside Anomaly), Blu salon, and Flat File Gallery at the 5 Points Theatre, all of which use the event to promote art by emerging artists.

FLORIDA THEATRE PERFORMING ARTS CENTER
128 East Forsyth St.
(904) 355-2787
www.floridatheatre.com

The interior of this 1,900-seat theater looks something like a Moorish palace, with touches of Art Deco thrown in for good measure. Sadly, there are only four theaters like this left in the state. The Florida Theatre hosts hundreds of performances every year, from the Hong Kong Ballet to Judy Collins. Local legend says that this is where Elvis Presley played his first indoor concert. The Florida Theatre also serves as the location for Art After Dark (see Annual Events for details). The theater is just a short walk from Downtown hotels and restaurants, especially handy for people coming in from out of town for a show.

FRIDAY MUSICALE AUDITORIUM
645 Oak St.
(904) 355-7584
www.fridaymusicale.com

Over the years he has won awards in all areas of the arts, from two Outstanding Arts Advocate awards, to an Individual Arts Award, a "Making a Difference" Award (for which he was the Jessie Ball DuPont Fund's inaugural recipient), a Rachel B. Davis Humanitarian Award, and *Folio Weekly* Theatre Awards for Best Director, Best Sound Design, Best Plays, and Best Actor. His performances with Charlotte Mabrey sell out year after year.

"Jacksonville has been the perfect place to fashion a career in the arts and in arts administration because I've found that if you have an earnest desire to make something happen here, you pretty much can. Earnest desire is not enough in bigger cities, and it's irrelevant in smaller towns where there aren't the resources to float your dreams," says White.

White is both fun-loving and fiercely devoted to making sure the city's arts funding stays intact, stating, "There really is no challenge facing Jacksonville that art and culture can't, on some level, solve. Art provides comfort and solace. It creates the space that we human beings require to refocus our energy. Jacksonville hungers for the nourishment that art provides."

While he isn't a City Hall wonk, White isn't a stereotypically flighty artist either. He is—as he refers to other artists he loves—the real deal. He walks the walk and talks the talk of the city. His home, an art-filled bungalow in historic Avondale, has no television but is visually rich with paintings, photographs, and sculpture by local artists Tom Schifanella, Sarah Crooks Flaire, Ronnie Land, Nofa Dixon, Oscar Senn, Christian Pierre, Maribel Angel, Bob Broward, and Ted Johnson. White plays guitar, composes music, and attends practically every folk music festival from Jacksonville to North Carolina. In 2008 he directed Barbara Colaciello Williams in *Life on the Diagonal* at TheatreLab in New York City.

You can find him out, almost every night, at some Avondale nightspot, usually Biscotti's, having a raucous late supper with a table full of pals or engaged in a whispery tête-à-tête over drinks with an old friend.

As for the title, The Nicest So-and-So in the Whole Bleepin' City, the real (yet sadly unprintable) version is far more colorful, but nonetheless true.

The Friday Musicale is a true Jacksonville tradition, started in 1890 as a club for local women who enjoyed music and playing instruments. Today the club meets in a beautiful Downtown building with a modern 250-seat auditorium. Members host free concerts every Friday evening from October through May. The auditorium is also a popular place for music teachers to hold recitals. Located in Riverside, the auditorium is a Jacksonville institution that's so Insider that many locals don't even know about it. Visit the Web site to check out the upcoming concert schedule.

i *Arbus,* a free local arts magazine, is a must for the latest on the arts. You can usually find a copy at a coffee shop or bookstore. To learn more, visit www.arbus.com.

JACKSONVILLE VETERANS MEMORIAL ARENA
300 A. Philip Randolph Blvd.
(904) 630-3900
www.jaxevents.com
Located in close proximity to the new baseball park, the historic St. Andrews Church, and Metropolitan Park, the new Jacksonville Veterans Memorial Arena opened in 2003 with a performance by Elton John. Able to hold 16,000 concertgoers, the venue attracts acts from across the country with performances by such diverse acts as Brad Paisley, AC/DC, and the Lipizzaner Stallions.

METROPOLITAN PARK
1410 Gator Bowl Blvd.
(904) 630-0837
www.coj.net (search "Metropolitan Park")

From rap concerts to the symphony's outdoor family concert series, Starry Nights, a lot happens at Metro Park. Located on the St. Johns River, this beautiful outdoor venue can hold up to 10,000 persons. Seating for large concerts basically means spreading out a blanket or bringing a chair, but there is also a canopy that provides limited covered seating. Sadly, the city usually does not allow picnic baskets inside the park for concerts and prefers that you buy from the vendors who sell food and drink at Metro Park events.

i The Cultural Council of Greater Jacksonville is the city's clearinghouse for the arts. The council compiles a great monthly arts calendar, which is available on their Web site at www.culturalcouncil.org.

MUSEUM OF CONTEMPORARY ART (MOCA)
333 North Laura St.
(904) 366-6911
www.mocajacksonville.org
MOCA occupies a renovated space in a 1931 Art Deco building that used to house the Western Union Telegraph Company. The city's new Downtown library rubs elbows with the museum, giving each an added luster of vitality. The collection here includes more than 700 works of art, but shines the brightest in its collections of regional art, photography, and prints. In addition, works by Alexander Calder, Robert Rauschenberg, Frank Stella, and Helen Frankenthaler augment the collections. Be sure to bring the children to the top floor, where an interactive family learning center called ArtExplorium teaches kids all about line and design, photography, and folk art.

On your way out, don't miss Cafe Nola (short for North Laura). This mini-bistro is a great place to eat lunch or sip a pot of tea and enjoy something sweet. The museum is open from 10 a.m. to 4 p.m. Tuesday through Sunday; Thursday it stays open until 8 p.m. Sunday it's open from noon to 4 p.m. and is free for families. The museum is also open (and free) from 5 p.m. to 9 p.m. on the first Wednesday of the month for Art Walk. The museum is closed on Monday. Visit the Web site to confirm the current hours of operation.

Visualize the Music

Every year, the **Jacksonville Jazz Festival** hosts a **Commemorative Poster Contest** for the design that will become the next year's public face of the festival. All artists are welcome to submit JPEG or PDFs of their design by e-mail. The winner receives a cash prize, a complimentary booth at the Art in the Heart juried show, and recognition as the official Jacksonville Jazz Festival poster artist. Visit www.cultural council.org to learn more.

NATHAN H. WILSON CENTER FOR THE ARTS
11901 Beach Blvd.
(904) 646-2222
www.fscj.edu
Located on the South Campus of Florida State College at Jacksonville (FSCJ), the Wilson Center for the Arts is a four-building complex consisting of a 530-seat proscenium theater, a studio theater, an art gallery, a conference center, music studios, visual arts labs, media-arts computer labs, and graphic design technology. One of the city's finest performing and visual arts facilities, the center also serves as a state-of-the-art learning facility for students. Shows of all kinds take place in the Main Stage Theatre, Art Gallery, and Studio Theatre. A two-story, glass lobby leads patrons to the lakeside art gallery, the main theater, and a studio theater designed for smaller audiences. Locals love the center's variety of opera, dance, and multidisciplinary productions integrating visual art, music, theater, and the humanities. The center also offers popular workshops led by nationally recognized performance and visual artists.

THE PRIME F. OSBORN III CONVENTION CENTER
1000 Water St.
(904) 630-4000
www.jaxevents.com
Housed in one of Jacksonville's most historic buildings, The Prime F. Osborn III Convention Center hosts The Jacksonville Home & Patio Show, The Southern Women's Show, Christmas Made in the South, and a variety of other community events. The building alone is worth a visit as it was the city's first multi-line railroad terminal and, for decades, served as the gateway to the state. Converted to a convention center in 1986, the venue retains its historic charm and railroad personality. Listed on the National Register of Historic Places, The Prime Osborn is largest meeting and convention facility in the region.

SAN MARCO THEATRE
1996 San Marco Blvd.
(904) 396-4845
www.sanmarcotheatre.com
Locals love being able to order wine and a pizza at this landmark movie theater where every third seat had been replaced by a bar table and waitstaff roam the aisles taking orders. Built in 1938 by architect Roy Benjamin (who also built the beautiful Florida Theatre), the theater still retains the Art Deco style that locals cherish. Recognized by *USA Today* as one of 10 best classic cinemas in the United States, the San Marco Theatre remains one of two movie theaters in town (the other being the 5 Points Theatre) where you can enjoy dinner, a frosty beer, and a movie simultaneously. Check the Web site for showtimes and upcoming special events.

SEA WALK PAVILION AT JACKSONVILLE BEACH
Events Hotline: (904) 247-6100
www.jacksonvillebeach.org
The Sea Walk Pavilion, an outdoor concert and festival venue at the beach, sponsors events and activities throughout the year including the 4th of July Celebration, Summer Jazz Concert Series, Summer Beach Run, Out of the Darkness Community Walk, and the Moonlight Movies Film Series where you can watch classic movies outdoors under the stars on five consecutive Fridays in mid-summer. Smooth jazz lovers will thrill at the Smooth Sounds of the Hot Summer Nights jazz concert series held on specific Sunday nights throughout the summer. The pavilion is also the site for the Great Atlantic Seafood and Music Festival and the annual Springing the Blues Festival. Visit the Beaches' Web sites for current festival dates.

STAGE AURORA THEATRE COMPANY
Stage Aurora Performance Hall, Gateway Town Center
5188 Norwood Ave.
(904) 765-7372
www.stageaurora.com
Darryl Reuben Hall has received awards and accolades for his dedication to Stage Aurora Theatre Company in Jacksonville's Northside. Since its founding in 1999, the company has presented 14 main stage productions including *Miss Evers' Boys, Crowns, A Raisin in the Sun,* and, most recently, Hall's original play, *Frat House.* Through Stage Aurora's Summer Performing Arts Institute and the 100 Youth Voices Musical Theatre group, Hall has provided artistic opportunities to hundreds of Jacksonville students. Visit the company's Web site for a schedule of upcoming productions.

THEATRE JACKSONVILLE
2032 San Marco Blvd.
(904) 396-4425
www.theatrejax.com
Theatre Jacksonville is not only one of the area's best-attended and most-beloved venues, but is also Florida's longest-running community theater with 90 seasons under its belt as of 2009. The theater relies on community participation in theater arts and pays Jacksonville back by offering summer kids workshops and a compelling variety of productions throughout the year. Many aspiring actors, including former Jacksonville resident and Emmy winner Michael Emerson from television's *Lost,* have graced this stage.

TIMES-UNION CENTER FOR THE PERFORMING ARTS
300 West Water St.
(904) 633-6110
www.jaxevents.com
Located in the city's Downtown across the street from The Jacksonville Landing and several large hotels, this is the city's premier performing arts facility. The Times-Union Center for the Performing Arts has three auditoriums. The first is the 1,700-seat Jacoby Symphony Hall, home to the Jacksonville Symphony Orchestra; the second is the Moran Theatre with a seating capacity of 3,000; and the third is the 600-seat Terry Hall. Traveling productions of Broadway shows, part of the FSCJ Artist Series, are performed here. The Times-Union Center was renovated in the mid-nineties and now has state-of-the-art sound systems and theater production facilities. The glass lobby provides a spectacular view of the St. Johns River.

WAREHOUSE 8B
8B Wambolt St., Downtown
At the time of publication, Warehouse 8B was just a fledgling multipurpose art space with studios, concerts, and some art exhibition. We don't really know what is going to come of it, or if it will even still be around by the time you read this, but the fact that the two founding artists are making use of a long-abandoned warehouse in the Talleyrand district of Downtown bodes really well for the future of the progressive Jacksonville arts scene. Stay tuned.

CONCERT SERIES

THE ARTIST SERIES: BROADWAY IN JACKSONVILLE
Times Union Center for the Performing Arts
(904) 632-3373
www.artistseries.fccj.org
Originally developed as a vehicle for making the arts more accessible to students, The Artist Series has broadened its focus over the past 43 years and become the primary source for national and international professional productions in Jacksonville, bringing Broadway blockbusters like *Wicked*, *The Lion King*, and *The Producers* to the Times Union Center for the Performing Arts and the Nathan H. Wilson Center for the Arts. With over 150 performances available, Jacksonville theatergoers never have to feel out of the show-tunes loop.

BEACHES FINE ARTS SERIES
(904) 270-1771
www.beachesfinearts.org
Dedicated to breaking down the artificial boundaries of race, class, religion, education, age, and economic status, the Beaches Fine Arts Series brings an exciting lineup of music and dance in eight free performances a year to venues around town. The BFAS schedule is a balanced, yet exceptional, mix of jazz, world music, and dance, in traditional and avant-garde forms. Stick around for the reception after the concert to meet the performers.

THE CUMMER CONCERT SERIES
829 Riverside Ave.
(904) 899-6038.
www.cummer.org
Throughout the year, the Cummer Museum showcases a variety of artists in classical forms from classical piano to Croatian quartets. The Tree Cup Cafe, located inside the Cummer, offers brunch before each show. The concerts are free to museum members. Non-members pay $10. Reservations are suggested.

RIVERSIDE FINE ARTS SERIES
1000 Stockton St.
(904) 389-6222
www.riversidefinearts.org
Now in its 16th season, Riverside Fine Arts series' lineup channels "artistic excellence, youthful energy, and a sense of surprise." This iconic concert series brings talent like The Kings Singers, Denver Brass5, The Harlem String Quartet, Esperanza Spalding, the Georgia Guitar Quartet, and the Rastrelli Cello Quartet.

THE PLAYERS

JACKSONVILLE CHILDREN'S CHORUS
225 E. Duval St.
(904) 353-1636
www.jaxchildrenschorus.com
Some 30 voices strong, the Jacksonville Children's Chorus is the official children's chorus for the Jacksonville Symphony Orchestra. It's divided into a girls' choir, a boys' choir, and a concert and chamber choir. Under the direction of Artistic and Executive Director Darren Dailey, the chorus has performed with the Jacksonville Symphony Orchestra at the Times-Union Center for the Performing Arts and at many civic events, as well as area schools, churches, and senior centers. Each singer in this diverse group must audition to be a part of the chorus. Singers, and families, must be dedicated to singing as chorus members log many hours practicing for concerts and traveling all over town to perform.

i If you have the opportunity to see work by any of the following local artists, jump at the chance: Robert Arleigh White (actor), Lee Hunter (musician), Ed Cotton (musician), Arvid Smith (musician), Lauren Fincham (musician), Thomas Hager (photographer), Daryl Bunn (photographer), Allison Watson (painter), Reet London (painter), Jim Draper (painter), Walter Parks (musician), Charlotte Mabry (musician), Jim Smith (multimedia artist), Laura Evans (photographer), Hillary Hogue (painter), Steve Williams (artist).

JACKSONVILLE HARMONY CHORUS/SWEET ADELINES
San Jose Church of Christ (rehearsal space)
233 San Jose Blvd.
(904) 350-1609
www.jaxharmony.com
Jacksonville's premier, all-women's, a capella harmony chorus is a large, fun-loving group of real women, singing real four-part harmony, making real friendships, and having real fun. The chorus, a chapter of Sweet Adelines International, performs

around the city and competes around the region (the chorus came in second place in the 2009 Region 9 Gulf-Atlantic competition). Any woman who is passionate about singing and is interested in joining is welcome to attend a rehearsal and learn more.

JACKSONVILLE SYMPHONY ORCHESTRA
Times-Union Center for the Performing Arts
300 West Water St.
(904) 354-5547
www.jaxsymphony.com
Under the solid artistic leadership of Brazilian conductor Fabio Machetti, the Jacksonville Symphony Orchestra provides top-caliber performances, often with guest appearances by international artists. The symphony, now well into its second half-century, begins playing in mid-October and continues for 32 weeks through late May. The cornerstone of the season is the Masterworks series, which features selected works by legendary composers. Locals also love pops concerts, Friday-matinee coffee concerts, and the family concerts under the stars in Metropolitan Park.

PLAYERS BY THE SEA
106 Sixth St. North, Jacksonville Beach
(904) 249-0289
www.playersbythesea.org
A former laundry has been transformed, believe it or not, into a cozy community theater in Jacksonville Beach. The main stage theater features some of the most popular musicals, dramas, and comedies in town and seats up to 120 people. Theatergoers enjoy being able to order cocktails before the show or during intermission in the lounge, which also features rotating exhibitions of art, photography, and other mediums. Players by the Sea also hosts a busy children's program called Acting Up, which includes a popular summer camp and special theatrical performances by the kids. Season memberships are affordably priced and can save you around $3 to $85 over regular admission prices. Visit the Web site to check out the current lineup.

⊙ Close-up

United We Stand

Some artists create better in a vacuum, some find inspiration from the company of like-minded individuals with whom they can share ideas and evaluate projects. The following arts groups are open to all and invite local artists to find their community.

The **Kalliope Women's Writer's Collective** supports local women writers by holding critiquing workshops, sponsoring public readings of members' works, holding discussions of writing issues, and participating in local writers' festivals. Poets meet the first Monday of the month and are asked to bring 10 copies of an unpublished poem. Prose writers meet the fourth Saturday of the month and are asked to submit original prose pieces before the meetings. Call (904) 646-2081 for locations and information.

The **Theatre Alliance of Greater Jacksonville** hosts "Poor & Hungry Theatre Tavern" at The Players Grille in San Marco on the last Sunday of the month at 4 p.m. Local actors, directors, and playwrights gang up for lively discussion about Jacksonville's theater community, upcoming productions, and auditions. Visit www.theatrealliance.ning.com to learn more.

Darren Dailey of the Jacksonville Children's Chorus organizes a monthly **First Friday Lunch Bunch** for Artists, Actors, Musicians, and Dancers so that local artists can learn about each other's work. Bring your business cards to Clara's at the Cathedral, 613 West Ashley St., from 11 a.m. to 1 p.m. Visit www.culturalcouncil.org to learn more.

The **Jacksonville Consortium of African American Artists** encourages African-American arts and artists to flourish and succeed through monthly workshops and quarterly exhibitions (no artist is excluded on basis of race). Come to the Karpeles Manuscript Library at 6:30 p.m. on the first Tuesday of every month. Membership dues are $25 annually. Call (904) 537-3364 or visit jcaaa.blogspot.com to learn more.

RIVER CITY BAND
841 Prudential Dr., Suite 150
(904) 390-1999
www.rivercityband.com

For over 25 years, The River City Band has played America's music, including jazz and swing to a loyal fan base around the city and country. The band has played with such musical notables as Wynton Marsalis, Dave Brubeck, Doc Severinsen, and Rosemary Clooney, and offers several ensembles that play everything from Dixieland to easy rock. The River City Band plays free concerts all over town including at the new Riverside Arts Market. Visit their Web site or call for a schedule.

THEATRE JACKSONVILLE
2032 San Marco Blvd.
(904) 396-4425
www.theatrejax.com

Since its opening in 1919, Theatre Jacksonville has produced quality community theater, making it one of the longest-running community theaters in the Southeast. And you don't keep 'em coming by producing schlock. This is the grande dame, if you will, of the city's community theaters. Its location in San Marco makes for a delightful evening out. Schedule dinner at Matthew's before the show, then coffee or drinks at a San Marco club, like The Grotto, afterward. (See the Dining and Nightlife sections for more on Matthew's and The Grotto.)

ART GALLERIES

BUTTERFIELD GARAGE ART GALLERY
137 King St., St. Augustine
(904) 825-4577
www.butterfieldgarage.com

Close-up

Calling All Artists!

Sadly, too frequently the aspiring artist's work never sees the light of day because of lack of a venue. Not so in Jacksonville where an amazing number of arts-friendly outposts around town accept submissions directly from artists for display in their art-in-public-places programs. Submit your work to the venues below and get ready to watch your star rise. (This list is not exhaustive, so be sure to visit www.culturalcouncil.org to keep up with the latest opportunities.)

The **5 Points Theatre** chooses one 2D artist per month to exhibit in the theater lobby. In addition to providing the space, the theater will host two receptions during that run of the show (providing there are no major disasters or scheduling conflicts). Interested? Contact the theater's general manager at gm@5pointstheatre.com.

The 30 artists who make up the **Art Center Cooperative** feature an artist in their Downtown gallery at The Carling each month. Artists are required to volunteer at the gallery to participate in the co-op, which seems only fitting. Visit www.blogfromthecenter.blogspot.com to inquire about submitting your work for consideration.

The **Women's Center of Jacksonville** floats four exhibitions per year at the Women's Center of Jacksonville as a part of the Art & Soul program. Visit www.womenscenterofjax.org for an application.

Bethel Gallery inside the Ponte Vedra Presbyterian Church was established in 2001 and now runs eight exhibits per year. Call (904) 280-9075 for more information.

The **FCCJ South Gallery**, Wilson Center for the Arts sponsors 11 exhibitions per year of work by student, faculty, local, regional, and national artists. Submissions are reviewed in the fall but can be submitted at any time. To be considered, mail a letter of intent, resume, and 20 slides or digital images to: South Campus Gallery, Florida Community College of Jacksonville, 11901 Beach Blvd., Jacksonville, FL 32246. Call (904) 646-2023 for more information.

The Haskell Gallery at The Jacksonville International Airport hosts approximately four exhibitions per year. Consideration is given to all artists. The gallery also sponsors Art Kiosks throughout the airport displaying 3D sculpture. Artist applications are available online at www.jiaarts.org.

Players By The Sea showcases visual artists in their theater lobby both in conjunction with new productions and between shows. Call (904) 249-0289 or visit www.playersbythesea.org to learn more.

The St. Augustine Art Association hosts six to eight exhibitions per year, however the ones in the fall and the spring are the only ones open to all members. The association also produces two Arts & Crafts festivals. Check their Web site to find out how to participate; www.staaa.org.

If you're in the market for original art at a price you can actually afford, make the drive to St. Augustine's Butterfield Garage where stoneware and handbags sit next to a wide variety of original paintings. Housed in a former auto showroom and garage, the gallery retains some of the original tenants' flavor juxtaposed against the work of 13 contemporary artists. Well worth the trip!

CULTURAL CENTER AT PONTE VEDRA BEACH
50 Executive Way, Ponte Vedra Beach
(904) 280-0614
www.ccpvb.org
Every neighborhood should have a cultural center like this. It's a place for artists and budding artists of all ages to take art classes and show their

work. Every spring the center hosts an art extrava-ganza, which includes an exhibit honoring pro-fessional artists from Ponte Vedra and beyond. This is a great place to catch free or inexpensive concerts and music classes. The center hosts eight annual exhibitions with opening receptions that are free and open to the public. The center also hosts two fund-raisers: celebrate in the late spring and Arts Alive on the first Saturday of October. Sign up for a class, workshop, or lecture and use your free time to learn to paint, draw, sculpt, dance, play an instrument, or learn a new language. The center is open Monday through Friday 9 a.m. to 5 p.m. and Saturday 1:30 to 4:30 p.m., closed Sunday. Call or visit the Web site for the latest schedule of events.

FLAT FILE GALLERY
1022 Park St.
(904) 349-6666
www.flat-filegallery.com or
www.flatfileprojects.com
Residing in the space that used to be the back alley of the 5 Points Theatre, Flat File Gallery is one of Jacksonville's newest galleries. Owners Chris and Calder Yates traditionally have a new show for each 5 Points First Friday. The shows most often feature less-expensive custom edition photography, with some 2-D mixed media mixed in. Flat File is a gallery, meeting place, and arts advocate bent on providing easy access to "fun, provocative, quality works of art" by emerging artists. Their goal: encouraging the "uncommon collector," those who want to start their own art collection but haven't been able to afford to do so. At Flat File, custom edition photographs start at $20. Open Wednesday through Friday 11 a.m. to 3 p.m. and Saturday 11 a.m. to 5 p.m. Open First Fridays from 6 p.m. to late.

FOGEL FINE ART
3312 Beach Blvd.
(904) 296-1414
www.foglefineart.com
Originally a corporate art provider, Fogel has branched out to provide fine art to some of Jacksonville's most tony clientele. Most of design

staff have a background in art, art history, and/or interior design and are well equipped to help you choose the right addition to your collection.

JANE GRAY GALLERY
643 Edison Ave.
(904) 762-8826
www.janegraygallery.com
Showing the work of noteworthy local contem-porary artists Daryl Bunn, Sarah Crooks Flaire, Thomas Hagar, Joe Segal, and more, Jane Gray Gallery is another standout art space in the city's Downtown. Technically in Riverside, the gallery sits close enough to Downtown that it's a simple hop over to view a fine collection of work by emerging and mid-career artists working in vari-ous media including painting, photography, and works on paper.

i If you're a young professional, you may want to join the Up and Cummers. Members support the Cummer Museum of Art and Gardens and enjoy a host of art-oriented social events to boot. The top event is Fashion Forward, a fash-ion show held every fall featuring the areas hottest boutiques and highlighting the work of an up-and-coming designer from Jacksonville. Go to www.cummer.org for more information.

J. JOHNSON GALLERY
177 Fourth Ave. North Jacksonville Beach
(904) 435-3206
www.jjohnsongallery.com
You can't miss this 15,000-square-foot, Medi-terranean-style gallery across the street from the ocean. Jennifer Johnson made a bold deci-sion when she chose to spend millions building this state-of-the-art facility in Jacksonville Beach, which has long had a fairly seedy reputation. But she and many others believe that reputation is changing. Johnson, herself, is an excellent pho-tographer, and the gallery features a wide variety of photography from nationally and internation-ally known shutterbugs. The paintings and sculp-tures alone, much of it modern, are worth the

trip to the beach. The gallery hosts several major exhibits each year. The gallery is open Tuesday through Friday 10 a.m. to 5 p.m. and Saturday from noon to 5 p.m.

MUSSALLEM ORIENTAL RUGS AND FINE ART
5801 Philips Hwy.
(904) 739-1551
www.mussallem.com

This place is a trip! Mussallem is one of the most enduring and astonishing art galleries in all of Jacksonville and is located inside a rug store. Don't be misled or put off by the scrappy location on Philips Highway, this gallery carries some serious art dating back to the 16th century as well as an impressive collection of glass, including works by Tiffany and Stuben. Schedule a chunk of time to wander around this huge space, which also encompasses the rug collection. Open Monday through Saturday 10 a.m. to 6 p.m.

PARK STREET STUDIOS
2746 Park St.
(904) 747-4769
www.megancosbygallery.com

Park Street Studios is yet another bright star in the new wave of Jacksonville's progressive arts scene. At this new Park Street studio and gallery, a consortium of painters, Megan Cosby, Shannon Estlund, and Jonathan Lux, create art and show throughout the year. Park Street Studios is known for their interactive art openings replete with wine, desserts, and musical guests.

R. ROBERTS GALLERY
3606 St. Johns Ave.
(904) 388-1188
www.rrobertsgallery.com

Art collectors of all budgets will find something here; this gallery carries a wide variety of media, from original paintings to limited-edition serigraphs to blown glass. The gallery features work by Mackenzie Thorpe, Maxim Lipzer, and Dave Hind, with pieces available by both Pablo Picasso and Theodore Seuss Geisel, a.k.a. Dr. Seuss. Open Tuesday and Wednesday 10 a.m.

to 6 p.m., Thursday through Saturday 10 a.m. to 5 p.m., by appointment Sunday and Monday. R. Roberts also exhibits work at bb's and Biscotti's restaurants. (See listings for both in the Restaurants section.)

SOUTHLIGHT GALLERY
100 North Laura St.
(904) 358-1002
www.southlightgallery.com

Showing the work of local faves like Jim Smith, Steve Williams, Hillary Hogue, Jim Draper, and Daryl Bunn, Southlight Gallery is ready to help support the city's rising tide of great contemporary art. The gallery presents work from both established and emerging local artists. The space, which is packed to the gills during monthly Art Walks, is fresh in the sense that each artist manages the sale of his or her own artwork, and the gallery does not extract a commission. Instead, the workings of the gallery are supported by a cadre of volunteers and a system of sharing expenses. The space is given to the artists for free by the building owner; he just asks that they cover the utilities on the 4,000-square-foot space. "I'm just trying to be supportive of downtown," building owner Mike Langton told Roger Bull of the *Florida Times-Union*. "If we can get the art cooking, it'd help bring the vitality we need."

The gallery will move if Langton finds a permanent tenant, but until then, this is a great venture worthy of great support. Check the Web site for updates.

STELLERS GALLERY
1409 Atlantic Blvd.
(904) 396-9492
240 A1A North
(904) 273-6065
115 Bartram Oaks Walk
(904) 230-4700
www.stellersgallery.com

Stellers Gallery has three locations: the larger in San Marco and two rapidly expanding galleries in Ponte Vedra and Julington Creek. All art galleries should be this busy. The galleries' success comes in part because it serves as the exclusive gallery for Jacksonville local-boy wildlife artist, C. Ford Riley. In fact, Riley's brother, Scott, operates the galleries. The gallery also shows work from Jennifer J.L. Jones, Jim Draper, and Steve Williams. In the end, though, if you want a marsh landscape, this is the place to get it. The galleries are generally open Tuesday through Friday 11 a.m. to 6 p.m. and Saturday 10 a.m. to 3 p.m. (except for the Ponte Vedra Beach Gallery, which is also open on Monday). Opening times vary by location, so call ahead or visit after 11 a.m.

THE UNDERBELLY
1021 Park St.
(904) 354-7002
www.jaxunderbelly.com

Insiders discovered The Underbelly hidden behind a bookcase in Anomaly, a clothing store in 5 Points. Insiders love stuff like that. The Underbelly is a new gallery with serious vision bolstered by the fact that owner Shea Slemmer doesn't see any reason why Jacksonville shouldn't be the Southern center of contemporary art. Slemmer stressed to MetroJacksonville.com "the need for the community to support galleries in order to aid Jacksonville in thickening the core of its blossoming art scene." The Underbelly features painting, photography, assemblage, and installation art by local artists on the rise.

WAREHOUSE 8B
8B Wambolt St.

At the time of publication, Warehouse 8B was just a fledgling multipurpose art space with studios, concerts, and some art exhibition. We don't really know what is going to come of it, or if it will still be around by the time you read this, but the fact that the two founding artists are making use of a long-abandoned warehouse in the Talleyrand district of Downtown bodes really well for the future of the progressive Jacksonville arts scene. Could be a performance space. Could be a gallery. Could be both, and more. Stay tuned.

PARKS

When Harriet Beecher Stowe, author of *Uncle Tom's Cabin*, wrote the first Jacksonville travel book, *Palmetto Leaves*, in 1873, she waxed poetic about the area's outdoor charms. She wrote extensively about the St. Johns River, "the great blue sheet of water [that] shimmers and glitters like so much liquid lapis lazuli." She loved the number of wildflowers that grow here, the climate, and the opportunity to spend much of the winter outdoors.

These days some of the best places to enjoy the St. Johns River, the native flowers, and the weather are in Jacksonville's parks. We are rich in them. Jacksonville has about 350 city parks, and if you include all our state and federal parks, the city claims that Jacksonville has the largest urban park system in the country. City officials like to boast that, as of 2005, Jacksonville had 96 acres of parks per 1,000 residents. Still, most Jacksonville residents will tell you that it's not enough; they want even more parks in the years ahead.

What follows is a list of some of the favorite greenspaces in this park-crazy town, especially parks in areas where tourists are likely to (or should) ramble. For even more information on Jacksonville's park system, visit www.coj.net and search "Parks."

BETHESDA PARK

10790 KEY HAVEN BLVD.
(904) 630-2489
www.coj.net (search "Parks")

For what the city calls "barrier-free outdoor recreation" you can't beat Bethesda Park. Off the beaten path for the average tourist, Bethesda's particular charms make it well worth a mention. Like Hanna Park, this is a good place for a reunion or a company picnic. But here your event doesn't need to be subject to the vagaries of weather or charcoal grills. The Bethesda Park Lodge offers a full kitchen and restrooms for groups up to 200. The park also has four fully equipped cabins for overnight stays, each with four bunk beds, a restroom, kitchenette, screened porch, and outdoor grill. The big attraction here is a 20-acre stocked lake, where guests fish and canoe. (A fishing license is required for all anglers ages 16-64.) The 1,400-foot boardwalk over a boggy area near the lake makes for an easy hike for almost everyone.

BOONE PARK

3700 Park St.
(904) 384-8687
www.coj.net

Boone Park and the rest of the Avondale parks are about as old-Jacksonville as it gets. Established in 1926, this delightfully woodsy, mossy, hilly, and rambling Avondale park is full of benches, grills, picnic shelters, playground equipment, and some mighty fine (and well-maintained) clay, public tennis courts.

GUANA RIVER STATE PARK

2690 South Ponte Vedra Blvd., Ponte Vedra Beach
(904) 825-5071
www.dep.state.fl.us (search "Guana River State Park")

When you think of Guana, think of kayaking, fishing from a kayak, and hiking past centuries-old Native American burial mounds. Tackle all this on your own, or take advantage of several tour opportunities, including kayak tours. (See the Attractions and Tours chapter for more information.) Jacksonville businessman Herb Peyton sold these 2,400 acres to the state in the late eighties, saving this portion of Highway A1A from becoming a South Florida concrete jungle.

The park is located halfway between Jacksonville and St. Augustine and offers beach access,

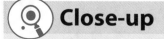 **Close-up**

The Ribault Club

The first time we ever saw the **Ribault Club** it was but a shadow of its former self. The once-venerable 1928 building used to be a hangout for millionaires wintering in South Georgia and North Florida, but a decade ago the building was rotten with termites, and state park employees were desperately seeking funds to save it before the clubhouse was eaten to its core.

Not any more. These days the termites are gone, and the park service has completed a $4 million four-year facelift. Thanks to a mix of state, private, and federal funding, the Ribault Club is back in the business of entertaining guests.

The Ribault Club enjoys one of the best locations in all of Northeast Florida. The big white plantation-style house with Georgian columns sits on the Fort George River in the **Fort George Island Cultural State Park** overlooking Little Talbot Island. Kingsley Plantation is just a short walk away. In the seventies and eighties, the building was headquarters for a country club, and many Jacksonville residents have fond memories of eating dinner there—the men, of course, in coat and tie, the women in smart dresses.

The state purchased the club in 1989 and closed the golf course forever. Nature quickly took back most of the 18 holes, but you can still make out a bit of the old course underneath spreading palmetto bushes. Covered picnic tables have been added along the river under majestic live oak trees, where you can eat a snack and watch the world go by.

Part of the old clubhouse is now a museum dedicated to the history of Fort George Island. Watch the videos to learn about manatees and bobcats, then visit the especially interesting display about the island's Native American shell mounds, which are many years older than Florida itself.

The rest of the club is for hire for weddings, family reunions, or corporate parties. But don't let that stop you from driving out to Fort George with a picnic basket in your backseat. Just follow the signs for Kingsley Plantation. Once you get to Fort George Road, don't turn left for Kingsley. Go along the river and wind your way toward the Ribault Clubhouse. It was, and still is, a relaxing place to visit, walk around, and revisit a more natural Florida.

More information on the Ribault Club can be found at www.theribaultclub.com.

---

great fishing, and significant opportunities to learn about this country's earliest history. There are 17 historic and cultural sites within the park, including the remains of an early Spanish mission from the 1600s—Nativity of our Lady of Tolomato—and a 1800s Minorcan water well that's listed on the National Register of Historic Places. There is no camping at Guana, but the Guana Lake area is such a popular fishing spot—especially for redfish—that the Park Service keeps it open 24 hours a day.

i Camping reservations are accepted at all state parks in Florida up to 11 months in advance. Call (800) 326-3521 or do yourself a favor and book online at www.floridastateparks.org.

HUGUENOT MEMORIAL PARK
10980 Heckscher Dr.
(904) 251-3335
www.coj.net (search "Huguenot Memorial Park")
The geography out here is exciting because the park is basically just a spit of land bordering the St. Johns River that then curves around into the Atlantic Ocean. In fact, much of this city park's 295 acres is prime riverfront and beachfront. Fort George Inlet sits on the inside of this horseshoe and attracts outdoor enthusiasts who love to camp, swim, and fish from primitive riverfront campsites. Campers also appreciate the bathhouse and the park's 24-hour security. This is also

the only park in Duval County that has a section where you can still drive your car on the beach. Consequently, on sunny weekends the beach and inlet areas are packed with cars and guests setting up grills for picnics. But all this beauty comes with words of caution: the inlet is subject to swift tidal changes, and there have been numerous drownings here. Please be careful.

JENNINGS STATE FOREST AND BLACK CREEK
1337 Longhorn Rd., Middleburg
(904) 291-5530
www.fl-dof.com/state_forests/jennings.html
Wild and untamed, Jennings State Forest and Black Creek encompass almost 24,000 acres of true Florida forestland. The area offers a network of trails and waterways for hiking, horseback riding, and canoeing. Prepare for a challenging time if you come during the wet season when the upper reaches of Black Creek get especially rugged with swift water flowing through downed trees and thickets. This is also a place where you are smart to keep an eye peeled for gators. Sound treacherous? Before you run in fright, consider the counterpoint of rare plants such as Bartram's Ixia and St. John's Susan as well as many uncommon herbs that grow in seepage slope communities. Botanists will love the forest's more than 15 different natural biological communities each with unique plants, animals, and physical characteristics that have resulted from the abundance of wildlife residing in the forest. Stay alert for sightings of raccoon, otter, alligator, and wading birds along North Fork Black Creek. Meanwhile, white-tailed deer, wild turkey, hawks, and songbirds make their homes in the uplands. The forest has five entrances, so visit the Web site to find the one that's most accessible to you.

i Jacksonville loves its two oceanfront parks: Kathryn Abby Hanna Park and Huguenot Memorial Park. Huguenot is one of the few parks in Northeast Florida where you can still drive your car on the beach.

KATHRYN ABBY HANNA PARK
500 Wonderwood Dr., Atlantic Beach
(904) 249-4700
www.coj.net (search "Hanna Park")
Hanna Park is a great place to get away from it all without having to get away from the city. Located at the beach, Hanna Park is 450 acres of natural Florida: thick forests, open beachfront, and plenty of saltwater and freshwater fishing. With 293 campsites, this is often the park parents pick to introduce their young children to camping. If the campout turns into a disaster in the middle of the night, it's easy enough to pack up and go home without a long drive. The campsites have water and sewer hookups and electricity, and there's also a small store, bathhouse, and public laundry facility in the park.

Hanna Park offers a playground and summer water park for children, as well as biking and hiking trails. Dogs are allowed here as long as they're kept on a leash. Besides surf-casting in the ocean, there are several freshwater lakes and ponds to fish in. You need a valid Florida fishing license to drop a line here, but the freshwater areas are well stocked with largemouth bass, bluegill, sunshine bass, and catfish, which makes the licensing process worthwhile.

If tent or RV camping isn't your thing, reserve one of the four new rustic cabins. They rent for $34 a night and sleep four. (Bathrooms are still a walk away in the bathhouse.) Best of all, each cabin features a charming screened porch, so you can eat outside without fear of bugs.

There is also a new oceanfront building here called Dolphin Plaza that's a perfect place for a wedding, Eagle Scout ceremony, or small corporate meeting. Dolphin Plaza is air-conditioned, has a refrigerator and outdoor grill, and has ocean views to die for. It seats 125 people banquet-style, or 96 people classroom-style, and rents for about $640 a day. Just be sure to book early—Dolphin Plaza is very popular.

LITTLE TALBOT AND BIG TALBOT ISLAND STATE PARKS
Heckscher Drive
(904) 251-2320
www.dep.state.fl.us/parks

These two state parks epitomize natural beauty. Both the landscape and the drive out to reach them make an impression on naturalists and outdoor neophytes alike. The Talbots are located about 20 miles east of Jacksonville and bear the names of the barrier islands on which they're located. NOTE: Little Talbot, which sits about 5 miles south of Big Talbot, is actually the bigger facility.

The big attraction at both of these parks is the beach, where you can swim and fish. Both islands offer picnic facilities and hiking trails. Just bring along plenty of bug repellant if you hike, or you won't last long on the trails. The scenic Sarabay Center on the south end of Big Talbot Island is perfect for your next family reunion or company meeting. It can accommodate up to 55 people indoors and 200 outdoors.

Some huge beached tree stumps on Big Talbot offer great photo possibilities. Whole trees fell victim to erosion and ended up on the beach; others were put there to stop erosion. The trees have been worn smooth by time and tides and are much photographed.

There is no camping at Big Talbot Island State Park, but Little Talbot offers 40 campsites (no cabins) on Myrtle Creek on the west side of the island. Both parks have boat ramps, and you can rent bicycles and canoes at the ranger station on Little Talbot. The closest convenience store is 5 miles south of Little Talbot.

MEMORIAL PARK
1620 Riverside Ave.

Nestled between Riverside Avenue and the St. Johns River, Memorial Park has been a Riverside staple since 1924. Broad and genteel, the park stands as a point of reference in Riverside and features the bronze sculpture *Life,* created by Charles Adrian Pillars (1870-1937).

NORTHBANK RIVERWALK
201 East Coastline Dr.

SOUTHBANK RIVERWALK
1001 Museum Circle

FRIENDSHIP FOUNTAIN
1015 Museum Circle
(904) 630-2489
www.coj.net (search "Parks")

If you visit no other city parks, try to see these. The Northbank and Southbank Riverwalks and Friendship Fountain skirt the heart of Downtown Jacksonville. The riverwalks, which are basically boardwalks on the north and south banks of the St. Johns River, are great places for uninterrupted walks or runs anytime of the year. The Southbank Riverwalk, in particular, is a favorite exercise spot for Southbank workers who like to get up from their desks and get their hearts pumping on their lunch hours. The Southbank Riverwalk ends (or begins) at Friendship Fountain, a large fountain with arcing streams that are especially picturesque when lit up at night. The Museum of Science and History and the Maritime Museum are located just off the Southbank Riverwalk near Friendship Fountain. Shops and restaurants line both riverwalks, though the Northbank Riverwalk has more to offer in this regard because it includes The Jacksonville Landing.

SOUTH BEACH PARK AND SUNSHINE PLAYGROUND
Corner of South Beach Parkway and Osceola Street, Jacksonville Beach
(772) 589-7828
www.jacksonvillebeach.org (click on "Departments/Parks and Recreation")

This is truly a community park. It's the brainchild of two Beaches moms, who worked for 2 years raising the money, designing the park, and organizing 2,106 volunteers who built it in just five days. Kids love climbing on, crawling through, and swinging on all of the play structures in the playground. Be sure to check out the clever touches built into the structures themselves, such as musical instruments and artistic tiles created by local kids. The park has gone through a recent renovation and now has restroom facilities, jogging trail, basketball courts, tennis courts, and picnic shelters as well as the children's playground, gazebo, two grills, and three volleyball courts. The park is open daily from 7 a.m. to 7 p.m. Admission is free.

ℹ️ Pets are allowed in state campgrounds if you have proof of current vaccinations.

TIMUCUAN ECOLOGICAL AND HISTORIC PRESERVE
12713 Fort Caroline Rd.
(904) 221-5568
www.nps.gov/timu/index.htm
Not many cities can boast a 46,000-acre park within city limits. Thanks to the Timucuan Ecological and Historic Preserve, Jacksonville can!

Seventy-five percent of the preserve is water and marshland, but included within its boundaries are Kingsley Plantation, Fort Caroline National Memorial, the Theodore Roosevelt Area, and the Cedar Point Area.

The preserve is named for the Native Americans who lived here for 4,000 years before the French and then the Spanish arrived.

Since the park is largely water, the best way to get a feel for what it's really like is in a kayak, and tour companies are set up to help you do just that. (See the Attractions and Tours chapter for information on Kayak Amelia.) The preserve is a great place to get up close and personal with alligators, wood storks, great blue herons, and manatees. There are hiking and shore fishing opportunities at the Theodore Roosevelt and Cedar Point Areas (don't forget your fishing license) and camping opportunities on elevated platforms at Cedar Point, but you'll need a boat or kayak to get to them.

Hikes through the Theodore Roosevelt Area of the Timucuan National Wildlife Sanctuary take you through pristine upland woods, coastal hammock, high dunes, and freshwater and saltwater marshes. Bring your binoculars and bird books and make a day of birdwatching. Three miles of trails connect the sanctuary to the Spanish Pond marsh and Fort Caroline, which also has a good trail loop that's riddled with live oaks and Spanish

moss. Insider trivia: the park was donated to the National Park Service by longtime hermit, Willie Brown, who turned down millions from developers to keep the place the way he loved it.

TREATY OAK AT JESSIE BALL DUPONT PARK
1123 Prudential Dr.
(904) 630-2489
www.coj.net (search "Treaty Oak")
Jacksonville's Treaty Oak is the city's most famous tree. Some say it's 800 years old; others say it's merely 200. Some say Seminole Chief Osceola and General Andrew Jackson signed a peace treaty beneath its branches. Others say that's hogwash, that the tree bears no historical significance other than that it was saved from destruction in the early sixties by wealthy matron Jessie Ball duPont. Whatever you believe, this is a majestic tree and a perfect place for stressed-out travelers to unwind. It's located close to such Southbank hotels as the Hilton and Hampton Inn and is a lovely spot for reading or picnicking. If you visit, take home an acorn to plant in your backyard and perpetuate this wonderful tree.

ℹ️ From stargazing to counting bald eagle chicks in their nest, the City of Jacksonville hosts a variety of nature programs called NatureScope. For a calendar of events, go to www.coj.net and click on Department of Parks and Recreation or call (904) 630-4100.

TREE HILL NATURE CENTER
7152 Lone Star Rd.
(904) 724-4646
www.treehill.org
Tree Hill is a city park, urban wilderness, and wildlife preserve located right in the middle of Arlington. The center encompasses 50 acres of hilltops, woods, wetland areas, and a fresh-water stream. Tree Hill is riddled with wildflowers, and is chock-a-block with wildlife-viewing areas. Visit the indoor nature center, where kids can learn about the environment and the critters that live in it through the interactive exhibits, learning laboratory, wildflower gardens, and nature trails.

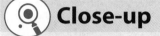

Close-up

Hang Ten, Betty!

Saltwater Cowgirls, Jacksonville Beach's all-girl surf camp, is girl-power central. From June through October for the last 10 years, hundreds of girls ages 7 to 70 have bellied up to the board with the Cowgirls and learned how to stand up, spot barrels, or bail out if need be. Women from all over the country flock to the camp thanks to the magnetism and patience of Cowgirls' well-trained instructors—all of whom are full to the gills with aloha spirit.

Part of the Insider charm of the camp is that all of the lessons are taught by local girls who hold the "girls' club" atmosphere sacred. "Most of our instructors are local yokels and former SWC students who have been on staff nearly the entire existence of camp," say the Cowgirls. And all of the instructors have major water time under their belts; their passports show stamps from beach destinations worldwide. They've faced down far dicier breaks than Jacksonville Beach will ever produce, so you know you're in good hands.

The camp caters to girls ages 7 to 17 during the week. The 18-and-older gals have to wait until the weekend to hit the waves with the Cowgirls. They suggest board shorts instead of bikini bottoms, and hammer home the importance of hydration and fuel; you don't want to feel weak in the face of a breaking wave. And even though it's all about safety first (lifeguards are on duty during camp hours), and the Cowgirls emphasize board control over freestylin', these girls still really know how to make mastering the waves fun.

NOTE: If you're looking for the perfect, nontraditional bachelorette party or girlfriend getaway, give them a call. After all, what could be better than shredding it with your gal pals before saying "I do" at the altar?

Perhaps things are a little rough at home and you're looking for a way to bond with your pre-teen? The Cowgirls run mother-daughter sessions every summer. And the ratios are always 1:3, so you're never far from your own personal Cowgirl who's ready to help you hang ten.

And, yeah, they've been known to teach a guy or two, but only after camp is through. During business hours, chicks rule!

Open Monday through Saturday from 8 a.m. to 4:30 p.m. Closed on Sunday and major holidays.

WILLOWBRANCH PARK
2870 Sydney St.
(904) 630-2489
www.coj.net (search "Parks")
Located in Riverside, along the course of Willowbranch Creek, Willowbranch Park has held a spot in the hearts of Riverside and Avondale locals and their children since its establishment in 1930. Through the 80 years since, it has remained one of the city's most picturesque parks. Locals love to take their children to the adjoining Willowbranch Library, the oldest still-open library in the city, which is housed in a beautiful Mediterranean-revival style building at the corner of Cherry and Park Streets, and then retire to the park to read on one of the benches under the immense live oak trees.

i You can swim for free in any of the 33 pools the City of Jacksonville opens to the public from late May through early September. One of them, The Cecil Aquatics Center, is an indoor pool and is open year-round. The city also sponsors free citywide recreational swim teams for boys and girls ages 5 to 14. Competitions among the teams include a district swim meet and a citywide competition. Call (904) 745-9630 for pool locations and swim team information. Visit www.coj.net and search "public swimming pools."

GOLF

The Northeast Florida climate is well suited for year-round play, and over the past three decades, the environs around Jacksonville have transformed into a golfing mecca. The area is home to over 60 courses, many of which are renowned for their beauty and layout. Perhaps the most famed is the TPC Sawgrass Stadium Course, the annual site of The Players Championship, one of the PGA Tour's most prestigious tournaments. Each spring the world's best professional golfers gather in Ponte Vedra Beach to compete for more than $9.5 million in prize money.

The presence of World Golf Village in northern St. Johns County, home of the World Golf Hall of Fame and the PGA Tour Golf Academy, further cements the region's reputation as a prime duffer's destination. World Gold Village is home to two courses, one open and one wooded: the King & Bear, designed by Arnold Palmer and Jack Nicklaus, and the Slammer & Squire, designed by Bobby Weed with design consultants Sam "The Slammer" Snead and Gene "The Squire" Sarazen.

Jacksonville offers an abundance of course choices, ranging from plush oceanside resorts to popular public courses. In all, the area's 1,400-plus holes of golf offer challenges for players of all skill levels. Visitors can choose from dozens of quality public and semiprivate courses, with price ranges to fit every golfer's budget.

Sure, it gets hot in the summer, making afternoon play brutal, but the relatively mild winters compensate by allowing temperate play throughout the cooler months. Jacksonville's courses are mostly flat terrain with plenty of water and marsh hazards. The abundance of marshes, especially at courses nearer the ocean, provides habitat for all kinds of wildlife, including osprey, egrets, and even the occasional alligator.

All the courses listed below are open year-round unless otherwise noted. All distances are from the men's white tees.

AMELIA ISLAND PLANTATION LINKS COURSE
4700 Amelia Island Parkway, Fernandina Beach
(904) 261-6161
www.aipfl.com
Consistently named a Silver Medal Golf Resort by *Golf Magazine,* Amelia Island Plantation stands as one of the best golf resorts in America. Amelia Island Plantation's 72 holes of championship golf capture the natural elements of the island's terrain while preserving the near-pristine habitat. Situated beneath a canopy of moss-covered oaks, the greens and fairways, which were designed by Pete Dye, Bobby Weed, and Tom Fazio, border

the ocean and coastal marshes and are lined with live oaks, sabal palms, pines, and wax myrtle.

BLUE CYPRESS GOLF CLUB
4012 University Blvd. North
(904) 762-1971
www.bluecypressgolf.net
Blue Cypress is Jacksonville's newest golf course and winner of Jax Hot List's Best Public Golf Course category. Opened in November 2003, the nine-hole, par-36 course bills itself as the closest golf course to Downtown Jacksonville. Situated on part of the former University Country Club course on property now owned by the City of Jacksonville, Blue Cypress is just a 15-minute

drive from the city's business district. The course has a driving range and a snack bar that serves sandwiches, beer, wine, and mixed drinks. Greens fees (with cart) for 18 holes are $27.50 Monday through Thursday and $34 on weekends and holidays. Ask about the discounts for seniors, active military, firefighters, and police officers. The hole of interest: No. 5. It's a par-5, 475 yards. However, the green is 60 yards long and slopes away. The distance from tee to hole isn't tough, but the putting is a bear.

CECIL FIELD GOLF CLUB
13715 Lake Newman St.
(904) 778-5245
www.capstonegolf.net (look under "Golf Course Portfolio")

Cecil Field Golf Club, located on the former Cecil Field Naval Air Station on Jacksonville's Westside, was originally built in 1953 by the Navy Seabees. As part of the wave of base closures several years ago, Cecil Field was handed over to the City of Jacksonville. While most of the facility is being converted into commercial and industrial use, the city has retained the golf course for public use.

A St. Augustine–based golf course management company that now operates the course for the city has brought the par-72, 6,643-yard course up to U.S. Golf Association standards. It's not a bad course, especially for beginners—and you can't beat the cost. Weekday greens fees, including cart, are $24; weekend fees are $30.

Carts are required only before 1 p.m. on weekends and holidays. A snack bar serves food and beer, and a beverage cart cruises the course on Saturday and Sunday. There's also a driving range and practice putting green.

> **i** Looking to play some low-key golf in Ponte Vedra? Try the Palm Valley Golf Club and Practice Range at 1075 Palm Valley Rd., where you can play nine holes with a cart for $12 (only $10 on weekdays). Visit www.palmvalleygolfing.com or call (904) 824-9279 for details and directions.

THE CHAMPIONS CLUB AT JULINGTON CREEK
1111 Durbin Creek Blvd.
(904) 287-4653
www.championsclubgolf.com

The Champions Club is located at the Julington Creek Plantation community in northwest St. Johns County, about 12 miles south of Downtown Jacksonville. The par-72, 6,872-yard course was originally opened in 1988 as a nine-hole course. In 1991 new owners expanded it to a full 18-hole facility with clubhouse, restaurant, and practice driving range.

The semiprivate course was designed by former PGA Tour player and former ABC Sports golf commentator Steve Melnyk. The United States Golf Association used this links-style course in the summer of 2002 for a junior amateur qualifying tournament.

You can reserve a tee time two weeks in advance. Greens fees, including cart, are $30 Monday through Friday and $45 on the weekend. Special group rates are available. Walking the course is not permitted, and required attire includes collared shirts, soft spikes, and no denim. Champions Club has a full bar in the lounge and also offers a 10-week Kids' Clinic every summer.

CIMARRONE COUNTRY CLUB
2800 Cimarrone Blvd. (Route 210)
(904) 287-2000
www.cimarronegolf.com

If you're looking for one of the toughest final holes in Jacksonville, as voted by local golfers, Cimarrone's your course. The 18th hole is 380 yards from the white tees, with the final 80 yards leading up to the green over water. Truth be told, the entire course is tough. Water and marsh come into play on 16 of the 18 holes. (*Golf Digest* magazine has given Cimarrone four stars.)

Designed by David Postelwaite and opened in 1988, the course is par-72 and 6,891 yards. The facility has a full-service restaurant, pro shop, driving range, and putting and chipping practice greens.

EAGLE HARBOR
2217 Eagle Harbor Parkway, Fleming Island
(904) 269-9300
www.eagleharboronline.com
Eagle Harbor Golf Club is nature's answer to challenging golf and gracious lifestyles. This Clyde Johnston–designed course gives the visitor a memorable round. Eagle Harbor was selected by *Golf Digest* as a four-star course. Fees and cart are $49 Monday through Friday and $59 Saturday and Sunday.

i If you're looking for a new set of clubs, consider having a set made for you. It's not as expensive as you might think. A local company, Masterfit Golf, can make them for you in four to five days. Plus, the grip size, the length, and the weight of the clubs will be perfect. A fitting takes about 25 minutes. Visit www.master fitgolfltd.com or call (866) 779-1177.

THE GOLF CLUB AT FLEMING ISLAND
2260 Town Center Blvd., Orange Park
(904) 269-1440
www.flemingislandgolf.com
Opened in September 2000, this semiprivate club features a championship layout designed by Bobby Weed. The par-71 course, offering playing lengths from 4,801 to 6,801 yards, can challenge golfers at every skill level. Fleming Island Golf Club has two PGA golf professionals on staff.

To reach the course, take US 17 south past County Road 220 to Fleming Island in Orange Park. Greens fees are $48 during the week and $58 on the weekend.

GOLF CLUB OF AMELIA AT SUMMER BEACH
4700 Amelia Island Parkway Fernandina Beach
(904) 277-8015
www.summerbeach.com
Designed by PGA Tour veterans Mark McCumber and Gene Littler, this 18-hole course embodies the tranquil beauty of Amelia Island. The meticulously maintained course was the site of the 1998

Liberty Mutual Legends of Golf, a prestigious Senior PGA Tour event that attracted such golfing legends as Lee Trevino, Chi Chi Rodriquez, and Sam Snead. The course winds through majestic palm, pine, and oak trees. A few holes offer views of the Atlantic Ocean.

i Most golfers never see the most exclusive golf club in the city. Pablo Creek Golf Course has only about 200 members, who pay about $100,000 to join. This is where David Duval and Vijay Singh often play to avoid the crowds.

GOLF CLUB OF JACKSONVILLE/BENT CREEK
10440 Tournament Lane
(904) 779-0800
www.golfclubofjacksonville.com
The Golf Club of Jacksonville is maintained to the exacting standards of the PGA Tour. It'd better be. The PGA Tour, which also operates the famed Tournament Players Club at Sawgrass, runs the 18-hole course. But while the TPC is exclusive—and pricey—the Golf Club of Jacksonville is open to the public and charges reasonable fees. *Golfers Digest* gives the club four stars.

Opened in 1989, the par-71, 6,007-yard course was designed by Bobby Weed, who designed the TPC's Valley Course with Pete Dye. The Golf Club's most picturesque hole is the 12th—a par-4 with water running along the left side of the fairway. The course's most challenging hole is the 11th—a par-4 that traverses two marshes. It's been voted one of the most difficult par-4 holes in Jacksonville.

The course is located on Jacksonville's Westside, about 4.5 miles west of I-295 on 103rd Street. Since this is one of the more popular public courses in the Jacksonville area, reservations are a must. Tee times can be secured two weeks in advance. Greens fees are $39 Monday through Friday and $49 on weekends; prices include cart rental. You can practice at a lighted driving range or work on your putting and chipping. The course's PGA pros also give lessons. *NOTE:* Wear a collared shirt, and leave the denim at the hotel.

Close-up

Wanted: A Few Good Men (Women and Children, Too)

When it comes to putting together two of Jacksonville's major sporting events, **The Players Championship** and the **MPS Group Championships** (formerly the Bausch & Lomb Championships), organizers say they could never do it without their volunteers.

The Players Championship uses some 1,500 volunteers every year to quiet the crowds, pick up trash, check tickets, flip burgers, answer phones in the media center, and even drive disabled fans to special seating areas via golf cart.

The MPS Group Championships has a different yet just as critical need for volunteers. Every year organizers of the premier tennis tournament on the First Coast must find some 80 children to work as ball girls and ball boys during tennis matches. These volunteers run after balls during competition and make sure the players are supplied with plenty of cold water and fresh towels. Adult volunteers are also needed at the MPS Group Championships to usher spectators to their seats, drive tournament buses, and answer questions for guests and players.

In both cases volunteers say they do it for the love of the game and often take a week off work or school to attend the event. They return year after year, making both volunteer efforts run like well-oiled machines. In the case of The Players Championship, adults pay $85 a year for the privilege of volunteering. This fee gets volunteers a job during the golf tournament, as well as a badge for the week, and a tournament shirt, hat, and parking pass. Best of all, it lands them a free round of golf on the Stadium Course later in the year, provided they work at least 24 hours in their volunteer position. Most volunteers make sure they do.

HYDE PARK GOLF CLUB
6439 Hyde Grove Ave.
(904) 786-5410
www.hydeparkgolfclub.com
For a faint glimpse of old-time Jacksonville golf, hit the links at Hyde Park. One of Jacksonville's older, more scenic courses, it was designed in 1925 by the legendary Donald Ross. Hyde Park has all of Ross's trademark designs: smaller greens and difficult holes down the back nine. The last four holes at Hyde Park are made tougher with a rolling terrain.

The par-72, 6,153-yard course was on the PGA Tour in the 1940s and 1950s as the Greater Jacksonville Open. Hyde Park's most infamous hole is the 6th, or, as it is fondly called, Hogan's Alley. During one pro tournament, it took golf legend Ben Hogan 11 strokes to complete the par-3 hole.

Playing at Hyde Park today is a pleasant affair. The locals who regularly play the course or gather in the lounge for political chitchat reflect the open Southern hospitality found throughout Northeast Florida. Greens fees are $40 on the weekend and $30 Monday through Friday. You can play nine holes during the week for $18. The pro shop begins taking reservations for weekend play on the preceding Monday.

i To stay up to date on Jacksonville's golf courses and the specifics of each one's yardage, par, and distance from the center of town, visit www.golflink.com and search "Jacksonville, FL Golf Courses."

JACKSONVILLE BEACH GOLF CLUB
605 South Penman Rd. Jacksonville Beach
(904) 247-6184
www.jacksonvillebeachgolfclub.com
Newly redesigned and reopened, Jacksonville Beach Golf Club now offers memberships for $50 to $100 per year. The club, which is owned and operated by the city of Jacksonville Beach, first opened in 1960 and was redesigned in 1987 by

At the MPS Group Championships, ball girls and ball boys get free tennis togs, including shoes, shirt, shorts, and sweatshirt. They also get meals on volunteer days. Ballpersons must be between 12 and 20 years old and able to catch and throw a tennis ball. They also must pass a basic training course held a day before tournament play. As ballpersons, the kids get the best seat in the house and the chance to be up close and personal with the likes of Melanie Oudin and Caroline Wozniacki.

But if a player is having a bad day, this can be a double-edged sword. Players have been known to yell at ballpersons, but the kids are coached beforehand not to take this personally. Older, returning ballpersons land the best matches and work the televised finals.

Officials for Jacksonville's 2005 Super Bowl spent several days huddling at The Players Championship in 2002, studying the tournament's volunteer structure. Super Bowl officials recruited some 7,000 volunteers to work during the week of the game. Benefits for Super Bowl volunteers did not include tickets to the big game, although they did include the opportunity to be a part of all the hoopla.

If you're interested in volunteering for The Players Championship, call (904) 285-7888 for more information. Call early though, because so many volunteers return every year, only a small number of new volunteers are needed.

If you're interested in volunteering for the MPS Group Championships, go to the tournament's Web site at www.mpsgroupchamps.net, where you can download a volunteer application form.

Bob Walker, who, along with Ray Floyd, oversaw the redesign of storied Augusta National.

The 6,181-yard, par-72 course is relatively flat but has a fair amount of water hazards. The 14th hole, for example, is a short par-3, but navigating the water surrounding the hole can be tricky. The course is easy to walk, which is what most late weekday afternoon players do. Surprisingly, summer play can be pleasant, thanks to afternoon sea breezes that often blow in from the Atlantic, located about a quarter mile to the east.

Weather permitting, the course is open year-round except Christmas Day. Greens fees for walkers are $22 to $30 during the week and $28 to $37 on weekends. Fees for 18 holes, including a cart, are $38 to $45 during the week and $36 to $45 on weekends. Annual memberships are available at discounted rates. The course offers a teaching academy called FUNdamental Golf School; call the club to inquire about rates. There's also a lighted driving range and putting green. Inside the clubhouse you'll find the Clubhouse Grill and lounge. Also of note: golf carts

are equipped with GPS systems that give players a precise distance to the hole.

i For help planning your golf outing or golf vacation, try Florida's First Coast of Golf (FFCG), a not-for-profit corporation that markets its Northeast Florida member hotels and golf courses throughout the world. You can choose from 20 hotels and 27 prestigious golf courses. For more information visit www.florida-golf.org.

MILL COVE GOLF CLUB
1700 Monument Rd.
(904) 642-6140
www.millcovegolfcourse.com
Located off Atlantic Boulevard halfway between Downtown Jacksonville and the Beaches, Mill Cove Golf Club is one of the best-looking public golf courses in the city. Designed by Arnold Palmer and opened in 1990, Mill Cove is situated in a heavily wooded area and features gently roll-

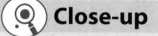

Close-up

World Golf Village

One of the best things about golf on the First Coast, say avid golfers, is walking around the lake at the **World Golf Village** and finding the signatures of Hall of Fame members. Located off I-95 about 45 minutes south of Jacksonville in St. Augustine, WGV hosts the World Golf Hall of Fame and two first-class golf courses: the King & Bear, designed by Arnold Palmer and Jack Nicklaus, and the Slammer & Squire, designed by Bobby Weed with Sam Snead and Gene Sarazen. There's also a state-of-the-art golf school, the PGA Tour Golf Academy, which features a 2,700-square-foot teaching center located at the far end of the Slammer and Squire range. There are two indoor hitting bays at the academy, eight outdoor bays, video instruction, and three full-time instructors.

The World Golf Village opened in 1998 with two resorts, an IMAX theater, and a variety of shops and restaurants within the complex. The most popular restaurant is the Murray brothers' Caddyshack, founded by actor Bill Murray and his four brothers and named for the golf movie Murray starred in as a deranged greenskeeper. World Golf Village is fully accessible online at www.wgv.com, where you can book not only vacations but also tee times.

---

ing hills. Unlike many other Florida golf courses, there are few houses located on the fringe of the course. An adjoining nature preserve provides plenty of wildlife.

The 6th hole of this 6,671-yard, par-71 course is perhaps the most challenging. A par-4, it has trees on either side of the fairway. Your second shot needs to carry over water. If you do lose a ball or two, the picturesque setting provides some compensation.

Greens fees during the week are $35 for 18 holes. Weekend and holiday fees are $45 for 18 holes, cart included. There's a full-service restaurant and bar.

PONTE VEDRA GOLF AND COUNTRY CLUB AT SAWGRASS
254 Alta Mar Dr., Ponte Vedra Beach
(904) 285-0204
www.pontevedragolfandcc.com
Want to play a private course without busting your budget? Try Ponte Vedra Golf and Country Club at Sawgrass, Ponte Vedra Beach's oldest exclusive gated community. Ponte Vedra Golf and Country Club at Sawgrass isn't for beginners, however. It's a par-70, 6,413-yard course that has narrow fairways and lots of water.

The most difficult hole is the 7th—a monster par-5 measuring 537 yards from the white tees. Ball placement, especially off the tee, is tricky. If the trees don't get you, the ponds might. For a semiprivate course, the greens fees, including cart rental, aren't unreasonable: $53 Monday through Friday, $63 on the weekends. The course is open year-round.

Walk-ons are welcome, but nonmembers are advised to get tee times in advance. (You can call up to seven days in advance.) Dress requirements are collared shirts, no denim, and no metal spikes. Ponte Vedra Golf and Country Club at Sawgrass has a full-service lounge that's also open to nonmembers.

QUEEN'S HARBOUR YACHT AND COUNTRY CLUB
1131 Queen's Harbour Blvd.
(904) 220-2118
www.queensharbourcc.com
Queen's Harbour is a semiprivate course, but you can play there if you're staying at one of the area hotels. Just get the front desk or concierge to make arrangements.

Located in the Queen's Harbour gated community along the Intracoastal Waterway, the par-

72, 7,017-yard course has wide-open fairways but plenty of marsh and water hazards. The course's signature hole is the 18th—a par-3 island hole surrounded by water.

The course is open year-round. A snack bar is open to the public. The dining room, however, is reserved for members. A round of 18 holes costs from $45 to $55, depending on the season.

THE TOURNAMENT PLAYERS CLUB
AT SAWGRASS
110 Championship Way, Ponte Vedra Beach
(904) 273-3235
www.tpc.com/sawgrass/index.html

Hardcore golfing enthusiasts visiting the Jacksonville area will want to play the TPC's par-72, 7,215-yard Stadium Course, at least once in their life. The 18-hole course, which was designed by Pete Dye and opened in 1980, is home to The Players Championship every March and features one of the most photographed holes in the United States—the famed 17th island.

Greens fees are seasonal and range from $130 during off-season (summer months) to as high as $375 during peak season. For less money, you can play the TPC's Valley Course, which was designed by Bobby Weed and Pete Dye and opened shortly after the Stadium Course.

i Visit The University of North Florida campus to play or practice on the four-hole Golfplex, a state-of-the-art practice facility and training center with four championship golf holes, a lighted driving range with target greens, a 10,000-square-foot short game area that includes both putting and chipping greens, and a full-service golf pro shop with golf instructors on staff. Better yet, Golfplex is designed so that golfers can practice and play multiple holes within their own available time frame. The facility also offers Coach Schroder's Golf Camp every summer. Of course, the public is always welcome. For more information, visit www.thegolfplex.com or call (904) 620-2050.

If you want to play either The Players Stadium Course or Dye's Valley Course, you can do so by either being a guest of the Sawgrass Golf Resort and Spa, or by booking starting times at TPC Sawgrass within 14 days of your arrival. To do so, call the TPC Sawgrass Golf Reservations Department at (904) 273-3430 or book online at www.tpc.com/sawgrass.

WINDSOR PARKE GOLF CLUB
13823 Sutton Park Dr. North
(904) 223-4653
www.windsorparke.com

Considered by some local golf pros to be Jacksonville's top public course, Windsor Parke received a four-star rating from *Golf Digest* magazine and ranks among the top 100 golf courses in Florida according to *Golf News*. Open since 1990, and considered very beginner friendly, the Arthur Hills–designed course is nestled in the tall Southern pines off Butler Boulevard on the way to Ponte Vedra Beach. The par-72, 6,043-yard course has mostly flat terrain but a fair amount of water hazards as you approach the greens.

The signature 16th hole is a par-3—only 150 yards from the white tees—but the carry to the green is almost entirely over water. The course is open year-round, except Christmas Day. After a round of golf, you can enjoy drinks and appetizers at the 19th hole lounge or dinner at a full-service restaurant.

The club's PGA professional staff offers lessons. The course also has a driving range and putting, chipping, and sand practice areas. Collared shirts and soft spikes are required. Greens fees, including cart rental, are $39 Monday through Friday for Florida residents ($45 for non-residents) and $49 on weekends and holidays for Florida residents ($55 for non-residents). Located off Butler Boulevard, the course is easily accessible from Baymeadows, Southpoint, Downtown, and the Beaches.

BOATING AND WATER SPORTS

At times, it seems that everyone in Jacksonville has some connection to the water. On weekends the roads are dotted with pickup trucks hauling sportfishing boats. You can also tell when there's a good swell hitting the shores by the number of cars zipping along with surfboards strapped to their roofs. During the summer months, a steady procession of both tourists and locals, makes its way to the Beaches for an afternoon of swimming, hanging out, and being seen.

In fact, it's hard to avoid even seeing water. Either the St. Johns River, one of its many creeks, or the Intracoastal Waterway crosses almost every major road.

If you're planning to visit Jacksonville, you owe it to yourself to make full use of our abundant watery resources. Fishing enthusiasts can launch their boats at the well-used public boat ramps around town and head out for a day of fishing in the river or open waters of the Atlantic Ocean. Sailors love to hoist their sails on the wide stretches of the St. Johns River south of Downtown. Pleasure boaters can spend entire days navigating the scenic Intracoastal Waterway. Surfers, Jet Skiers, and kayakers have miles and miles of potential area in which to play.

If someone offers to take you out on a boat, say YES! There's nothing like seeing this city from the water. If you bring your own, don't fret about how you'll get it into the water. The numerous public boat ramps conveniently located throughout Jacksonville make launching a breeze. If you don't bring a boat, rental and charter companies await your call year-round.

For those who prefer to experience nature a little closer to the shoreline, Jacksonville offers some wonderful spots for kayaking, surfing, and swimming.

Jet Skis and other personal watercraft (PWCs) are popular in Jacksonville. You can ride them on the Intracoastal Waterway, the ocean, and the St. Johns River. If you bring your own PWC or rent one while you're here, be sure to inquire about where you can and can't operate them. For example, you can launch PWCs from the beach only at specific places. Once in the water, you must maintain a safe distance from swimmers and surfers.

BOAT AND PWC RENTALS

ATLANTIC WATERSPORTS
2327 Beach Blvd., Jacksonville Beach
(904) 270-0200
www.atlantic-watersports.com
Atlantic Watersports is located on the Intracoastal Waterway at Beach Marine marina in Jacksonville Beach. Atlantic Watersports has Yamaha Waverunners, a 19-foot Bayliner Bowrider Capri, a 24-foot pontoon boat, and 19-foot Cobia fishing boats. All of their vessels rent for the same rates: one hour for $79; two hours for $139; four hours for $229; eight hours for $349. Atlantic Watersports is open from sunrise to sunset, every day, year-round.

DOCK HOLIDAY BOAT RENTALS
3108 Highway 17 South, Orange Park
(904) 215-5363
www.dockholidayboatrentals.com
Dock Holiday specializes in renting Glastron sport boats, 20- to 24-foot pontoon boats, and Hurricane Fun Decks. If you want to be sure that one is available when you need it, make a reservation. Dock Holiday is located at Doctors Lake Marina in Orange Park and is convenient to the St. Johns River. They don't allow any of the rental boats

to go north of the Buckman Bridge on the St. Johns River because of the swift currents that run through Downtown Jacksonville. The boats can be taken as far south on the St. Johns as a renter wants. They do not rent PWCs.

i Be careful traversing the St. Johns River. The currents in the St. Johns—one of the few rivers in the world that runs south to north—can be treacherous. In some spots currents can clock 8 knots.

SAILING

Jacksonville's sailing community maintains a strong presence in the city through yacht clubs, private boat owners, regattas, and schools' sailing programs. Most day sailing is done in the St. Johns River south of Downtown, where the river widens considerably, but the open ocean waters off Jacksonville's beaches provide for excellent offshore sailing. But be warned, making your way to the open ocean by way of the St. Johns River can take hours.

If you have the time, make like the locals and sail north to St. Augustine or south to Fernandina Beach via the ocean or Intracoastal Waterway.

While staying in the Jacksonville area, why not take sailing lessons from one of the three certified sailing schools in the area?

JACKSONVILLE SAILING SCHOOL AT WHITEY'S MARINE
3027 Highway 17, Orange Park
(904) 2690027
www.whitneysmarine.com
The sailing school at Whitey's Marine, located about 30 nautical miles from the ocean on the St. Johns River in Orange Park, teaches "the gospel of sailing" through instructors qualified by the U.S. Coast Guard and certified by the American Sailing Association. Captain Montie Froelich was recognized by the A.S.A. as an Outstanding Instructor in both 2005 and 2006. The Sailing School, certified by the U.S. Sailing Association, offers lessons from basic sailing all the way to offshore coastal sailing. Learn the basics on their 306 Hunter with in-mast

furling, or commit to a week and live aboard Whitey's new 38-foot Hunter yacht.

THE SAILBOAT CLUB AND SAILING SCHOOL
50 34th Ave. South, Jacksonville Beach
(904) 612-3444
www.sailboatclub.com
With an excellent array of courses, unlimited sailing for members, and free seminars, The Sailboat Club and Sailing School offers one of the better ways to learn to hoist a mainsail in the Jacksonville area. An accredited training facility of the American Sailing Association (ASA), The Sailboat Club offers instruction in basic keelboat sailing, coastal cruising, bareboat chartering, coastal navigation, instructor's qualification, and captain's licensing. Members sail from seven year-round locations—five on the St. Johns River South of Jacksonville, one in Jacksonville Beach, and one in Saint Augustine. In association with Schooner Freedom of St. Augustine, members of The Sailboat Club are invited to sail aboard the tall ship *Freedom*, which sails from historic St Augustine.

WINDWARD SAILING SCHOOL
714 Beech St., Fernandina Beach
(904) 261-9125
www.windwardsailing.com
Named Outstanding School of the Year in 2008 by the American Sailing Association, Windward Sailing School retains its position among the top five sailing schools nationwide. Located in Fernandina Beach, about a 40-minute drive from Jacksonville, Windward Sailing School offers basic and advanced sailing instruction and navigational lessons. Windward also operates out of an Ortega River location for those who prefer to stay close to Downtown.

If you're already an experienced sailor, you can rent a boat at Windward or book an overnight sail on their Hunter 28- or 27-foot Beneteau 265. Each boat holds a maximum of six people, including your captain, and your bareboat qualifications must be verified by a Windward Sailing captain. Rental rates range from $250 for four hours to $700 for two days and two nights, with each additional day at $200.

KAYAKING

Jacksonville's waters offer a variety of conditions for both the beginner and advanced kayaker. Enjoy the quietude of paddling through the placid waters of a nature preserve, skim among the dolphins on the Atlantic Ocean, or catch some of the big, rough surf that hits our shores on a consistent basis.

BLACK CREEK OUTFITTERS AND BLACK CREEK GUIDES
10051 Skinner Lake Dr.
(904) 645-7003
www.blackcreekoutfitters.com
Black Creek sells outdoor gear, apparel, footwear, and accessories addressing adventure travel, backpacking, hiking, and kayaking. Take some of their outdoor education classes, which range from stand-up paddleboarding to coastal kayaking, climbing, and basic outdoor skills. Black Creek also offers basic and advanced kayaking instruction and guided kayak trips throughout Northeast Florida. (You must be an American Canoe Association certified paddler to rent a kayak for unguided trips.)

Black Creek is open Monday through Friday 10 a.m. to 8 p.m., Saturday from 10 a.m. to 6 p.m., and Sunday noon to 6 p.m.

KAYAK ADVENTURES
Jacksonville Beach
(904) 249-6200
http://kayakadventuresllc.com
Kayak Adventures' guides will meet you at locations from Guana River State Park to Cumberland Island to the Timucuan Preserve marsh for half-day and full-day trips. They specialize in organizing photography and fly-fishing and light-tackle fishing trips via kayak throughout the region's waterways. All equipment is provided. The cost for the tours ranges from $55 to $100 per person for a half day ($45 and up for children). Be sure to bring a lunch or snacks and water. Three-hour kayak instruction costs $75 per person within a group, or $150 for private instruction. The company accepts all major credit cards except American Express. Reservations are required.

Lead guide and owner, Rachel Austin, is an ACA Level 3 Coastal Kayak Instructor and a Florida Master Naturalist.

KAYAK AMELIA
13030 Heckscher Dr.
(904) 251-0016, (888) 305-2925 (30-KAYAK)
www.kayakamelia.com
Looking for an adventure? Hop in a kayak and see Amelia Island from the water. You'll feel like a Timucuan as you paddle through the marshes and slip silently by wading egrets. The guided trips include paddling instructions for beginners, all the equipment you'll need, and knowledgeable guides to answer your natural history questions. All you need to bring is the sunscreen. Reservations are required, so plan in advance if you don't want to miss out. Rumor has it there are cookies, as if you needed more incentive.

RIPPLE EFFECT KAYAK ECOTOURS
St. Augustine
(904) 347-1565
www.rippleeffectecotours.com
Chris Kelley teaches science from a kayak at this real-deal environmental outfitter. Voted Best Place to Kayak in *Folio Weekly*'s 2007-2009 Best of Jacksonville issues, Ripple Effect runs tours throughout the week to some of the areas most beautiful and ecologically diverse locales in Faver Dykes State Park, Guana River, Anastasia State Park, Marineland, and the Guana Tolomato Matanzas National Estuarine Research Reserve (formerly known as Guana River State Park). Join owner Chris Kelley or guide Joe Woodbury for one of Ripple Effect's Zen Kayak Tours where they teach about topics such as the connection between mindfulness and kayaking. Be sure to check the schedule on Ripple Effect's Web site for upcoming trips like the Guana Astronomy Star Gazing Kayak Tour where paddlers get to gaze at the night sky above the Guana River from one of Ripple Effects' glowing "firefly" kayaks. Check out the Close-up on Ripple Effect and Chris Kelley in the Attractions & Tours chapter to learn more about this gem in the waterways.

SURFING

Although Florida's not known for big surf, the Northeast Florida coastline gets its share of good waves, especially fall through spring. The surf generally goes flat in the hot summer months—that is, until a passing hurricane or tropical storm sends large swells our way.

You can surf anywhere along the Florida coast, but some spots are better than most. Here are the four top spots.

The Jacksonville Beach Pier

Located in the heart of Jacksonville Beach, the "Pier" has long been known for its exceptional break and attractiveness to both long and short boarders. One big drawback: when it's breaking well, the Pier can attract big crowds. Inexperienced surfers would be wise to avoid the throngs and surf on the fringe of the crowds.

To get there from Third Street, turn east on Fourth Avenue where there's decent parking and an outdoor shower for afterward.

i If you rent a Jet Ski or other personal watercraft, be careful. While PWCs represent less than 13 percent of registered vessels in Florida, they account for 32 percent of all accidents and 45.7 percent of all injuries, according to the Florida Fish and Wildlife Conservation Commission's Division of Law Enforcement. If you are involved in an accident while riding a PWC, you have an 80.1 percent chance of suffering an injury requiring more than first aid. Also, be aware that a person must be over the age of 14 to operate a PWC in Florida.

The Poles

The Poles is unquestionably the best surf break in the Jacksonville area, if not along the entire east coast of Florida, so it can get crowded on big-wave days. It's located just south of the mouth of the St. Johns River, adjacent to Naval Station Mayport.

Unless you have a military pass to get onto the base, access to The Poles is through Jacksonville's Hanna Park. The Poles got its name from the pilings sticking out of the beach dividing the naval base from the park.

Admission to Hanna Park is $1 per person. Ask the attendant at the gate for directions to The Poles.

The North Jetties

The beach between Fort George Inlet and the mouth of the St. Johns River, known locally as the North Jetties, also offers ideal surfing waves. The long, gradually sloping beach at Huguenot creates surf that almost always breaks.

Access is through Huguenot Park, which is located off Heckscher Drive east of Fort George Island. Admission to the park is $1 per person from 8 to 10 a.m. and $3 per car with up to six persons from 10 a.m. to close with $1 per each additional person. The park is open from 8 a.m. to 8 p.m. in the summer, but the park closes at 6 p.m. in the winter. Call before visiting the park. Capacity, tide, and wildlife conditions periodically require temporary closures of the park's beach access.

Anastasia State Park

Another dependable spot for waves is St. Augustine's Anastasia Park, which sits just south of the inlet. Surf is usually a little bigger here than in the Jax Beach area and often breaks better. Anastasia can be good on any swell direction but can be absolutely epic on an Atlantic storm swell. Anastasia is often ignored by the Jax-based surfers, but it shouldn't be. In general, if you are unsure about where to go, head to Anastasia for some good times.

From St. Augustine head east across the Bridge of Lions and look for the Anastasia State Park signs on the left side of the road. Park admission is $4 for a single-occupant vehicle, $8 per vehicle with two to eight passengers. Showers and restrooms provided. Too tired to drive home? You can camp overnight for $28. For more information check out www.floridastateparks.org.

Surf Shops

AQUA EAST SURF SHOP
696 Atlantic Beach, Neptune Beach
(904) 246-2550
(904) 828-4848 (surf report)
www.aquaeast.com
Located on Atlantic Boulevard in Neptune Beach, Aqua East is the largest of the surf shops at the Beaches and stocks a good selection of clothing and boards.

AUSTIN'S SURF SHOP
615 South Third St., Jacksonville Beach
(904) 249-9848
austinsurfshop.biz
Want to see what an old-fashioned surf shop looks like? Drop in on Austin's in Jacksonville Beach. The selection isn't extensive, but you'll get personalized attention from Jimmy Austin himself.

FORT GEORGE ISLAND SURF SHOP
10030 Heckscher Dr., Fort George
(904) 251-3483
(904) 251-9283 (WAVE) surf report
www.ftgeorgeislandsurfshop.com
Fort George Island Surf Shop is located on Heckscher Drive, on the way to the North Jetties, in the 43,000-acre Timucuan Nature Preserve at the north mouth of the St. Johns River. The shop sells boards and gear and rents surfboards and kayaks. The owner, Jim, is a veritable font of local knowledge.

SUNRISE SURF SHOP
834 Beach Blvd., Jacksonville Beach
(904) 241-0822
(904) 241-0933 (surf report)
www.sunrisesurfshop.com
Also known for their surf camps and lessons, this shop carries a good selection of new and used boards and apparel. Sunrise has also been known to rent surfboards and body boards; call directly to make sure they are still doing so.

Surf Camps and Lessons

SALTWATER COWGIRLS CAMP
7th Avenue South, Jacksonville Beach
(904) 242-9380
www.saltwatercowgirls.org
This popular surf camp held in the summer in Jacksonville Beach is for Betties only. The camp offers beach and water instruction with a strong focus on water and board safety. The camp keeps an amiable 3-to-1 student-instructor ratio. Costs vary according to age and other variables, so call to check the current rates. (See the Close-up on Saltwater Cowgirls in the Parks chapter.) Boards—both soft and hard—are provided.

SUPER SURF CAMP (SUNRISE SURF SHOP)
16th Avenue South, Jacksonville Beach
(904) 241-0822
(904) 241-0933 (surf report)
www.sunrisesurfshop.com or
www.jacksonvillebeach.org
Offered by Sunrise Surf Shop and the City of Jacksonville Beach from June through August, the camp is geared to wanna-be surfers age seven and up. Each beginner's session runs for one week, from 8:30 to 11:30 a.m. Campers learn water safety, first aid, and how to surf. Soft boards are provided. For more information or to reserve a spot, call Sunrise Surf Shop.

Surf Contests

The Wavemasters' annual surf contest in Jacksonville Beach is the largest amateur surfing contest in Florida. About two decades ago the Wavemasters decided to hold a contest in hopes of attracting a bevy of bikini-clad girls and, in the process, raise a little money for local charities. Today that contest has evolved into Florida's largest and most prestigious open amateur surfing contest. This annual contest attracts more than 300 competitors from all over the Southeast and draws thousands of enthusiastic spectators.

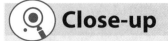 **Close-up**

Manatees

The challenge: is it possible to write a story about manatees without calling them "gentle giants"? Overused past the point of cliché when describing manatees, the term, albeit appropriate, has lost its meaning. Still, these docile creatures, these sea cows, deserve their moment in the sun. So, here goes.

Manatees, or sea cows, are aquatic herbivores that live primarily in Florida's warm freshwater, including the St. Johns River. Scientists believe that these slow-moving mammals live for 60 years or more—if they don't get slashed to death by the propeller of a fast-moving powerboat, that is. The average adult manatee is 10 to 12 feet long and weighs 1,500 to 1,800 pounds. Scientists figure that a 1,000-pound manatee must eat 100 to 150 pounds of food a day. That's a lot of plants. Sometimes they get help from the folks who live along the St. Johns River, who've been known to spot a manatee by their dock and run inside for a head of lettuce for the endangered creature to munch on.

Although their eyes are small, scientists believe that these gent . . . (oops) sea cows can see pretty well. They communicate with one another by making sounds underwater. To the human eye, most manatees look alike. The only sure way scientists have to tell them apart—if they haven't been tagged—is by the propeller scars on their backs. Sadly, practically every manatee has at least one, older manatees often have more.

Jacksonville isn't the best place in Florida to see a manatee. Crystal River or Homosassa Springs north of Tampa would probably get that designation. But lucky visitors and Jacksonville residents sometimes happen upon a floating gray mass in the **St. Johns River,** usually when walking on the Southbank Riverwalk just east of the Charthouse.

For decades manatees have flocked to this part of the St. Johns River in January or February when the air temperature hits freezing. That's because the Southside Generating Plant around the bend used to discharge water that was about 10 degrees warmer than the rest of the St. Johns. Those 10 degrees made a big difference to a freezing manatee.

But in October 2001 the Jacksonville Electric Authority, which owns the Southside Generating plant, closed the plant down. JEA is selling the prime riverfront property and building a bigger power plant elsewhere. But if you're a manatee, old habits die hard. The sea cows still swim to this area in cold months, searching for warmer waters. When they don't find them, they often must be rescued by scientists from SeaWorld in Orlando, who have a contract with the state to take in wayward manatees, nurse them back to health if necessary, and then release them back into the wild, usually around Crystal River or Homosassa Springs.

By most counts, there are about 1,000 manatees left in Florida, however the U.S. Geological Survey estimates that manatee populations in the Upper St. Johns River region have been growing annually at 6.2 percent.

Still, a debate is raging in the state legislature between boaters and manatee lovers over how best to protect these gentle giants (oh, what the heck!) from death by collision with motorboats. The state stringently enforces manatee speed zones, which slow boaters to a virtual crawl. Violators must appear in court, where a judge will set the fine and possibly include jail time. Some in the boating community feel there are too many regulations relating to manatees, while the environmental community feels there are nowhere near enough protections in place to preserve the dwindling numbers of manatees in Florida. Boaters want to remove manatees from the endangered species list after their numbers climb to a certain level. The **Save the Manatee Club** (www.savethemanatee.org) is fighting passage of any legislation that would put such a process in place.

WINDSURFING

The best place for windsurfing in the Jacksonville area is The Pond, located at the southern end of Ft. George Inlet and accessible through Huguenot Park, which has its own designated windsurfing area. The Pond is tidal but has no strong currents, and gets exceptional northeast winds, perfect for beginners and advanced windsurfers alike. Be careful at mid- to low-tide, which is when sandbars—the primary hazard at this spot—emerge.

From Huguenot Park you can gain access to the St. Johns River and its gorge-like conditions. Sailable only on a counter opposing wind and tide (east or west wind), the river is very dangerous and, unquestionably, an experts-only site.

Ocean sailing from the beach area is also an option. Look for epic conditions on days when the wind comes in from the southeast (best for advanced to intermediate windsurfers). On days when the wind blows in from the northwest or southwest, conditions are best for advanced windsurfers only.

Sailing the beach at Huguenot on a northeast wind is not recommended. There is a large sea jetty, and if you break down, you'll be eating jetty rock.

From I-95 take Heckscher Drive east to Fort George Island. About 2 miles west of the Mayport ferry dock, turn right into Huguenot Park. Look for the sailing area on the south bank of the inlet.

Huguenot Park admission is $1 per person from 8 to 10 a.m. After 10 a.m. admission is $3 per car with up to six persons and $1 for each additional person over that.

i **Every fall Jacksonville Beach is the site of an extraordinary parade: the return of the right whales, which visit the area to calve in Florida's warm coastal waters. The endangered right whale is 45 to 55 feet long and can weigh up to 70 tons. Hunted to near extinction before coming under governmental protection in the 1930s, there are only about 300 right whales in existence today.**

KITEBOARDING

Kiteboarding, also known as kitesurfing, is gaining popularity in Jacksonville, especially at the Beaches. It offers the speed of waterskiing, the tricks of wakeboarding, and the carving turns of surfing.

A kiteboarder rides a lightweight board with foot straps while holding an aluminum bar that controls the kite. Jeff Weiss, a kiteboarding instructor, says that Jacksonville's beaches are ideal for kiteboarding. "All you need is a 10-knot wind and you're loving life," he says.

Before you run out and try it, however, lessons are highly recommended. For more information, visit KGB Kiteboarding at www.kgbkiteboarding.com or call (904) 434-8987.

SCUBA DIVING

With offshore depths from 40 to 120 feet, natural, limestone reef ledges, and a long history of artificial reef building, Jacksonville offers the diver looking for an abundance of marine life and seascapes great SCUBA opportunities. Visibility can range from 20 to 120 feet, depending on the season (summer is best). Start with the list below to find information on dive instructors, retail dive shops, and charters.

ATLANTIC PRO DIVE
1886 South Third St., Jacksonville Beach
(904) 270-1747
www.atlanticprodivers.com
The shop offers classes, offshore charters, retail equipment, rentals, and service. Open Monday through Saturday, 10 a.m. to 6 p.m.

DIVERS SUPPLY
9701 Beach Blvd.
(904) 646-3828
www.divers-supply.com
Divers Supply sells and rents equipment, tanks, and accessories; offers certification lessons and basic open-water instruction; and schedules dive trips from May through September to freshwater springs in central Florida. Ocean trips to artificial reefs are available during summer. Open Monday

through Saturday 10 a.m. to 7 p.m. and Sunday noon to 5 p.m.

OFFSHORE DIVE CHARTERS
Joe Carlucci Boat Ramp (pick-up location)
8414 Heritage River Rd.
(904) 463-3236
www.offshoredivecharters.com
Captain Dan Lindley offers one-day, overnight, and two-day dive trips up to 40 miles offshore in water depths of up to 130 feet on *The Diamond Diver*, his 46-foot Newton. Rates do not include dive gear or tanks. If gear is needed, please contact the local dive shops.

i The Jacksonville Marine Association conducts two boat shows annually: Boat-A-Rama in February and the Jacksonville Fall Boat Show in August. Both shows are held in the Prime Osborn Convention Center. JMA is also a great resource for everything from boat charters to yacht sales. Contact them at (904) 724-3003.

ADDITIONAL ONLINE RESOURCES FOR SURF AND WEATHER CONDITIONS

Surf reports
www.fluidgroove.net
www.surfline.com
www.magicseaweed.com
www.swellinfo.com

Live surf camera
www.jaxsurfcam.com

Conditions in St. Augustine Beach
Surf Station's Web site:
www.surf-station.com

Tides
www.saltwatertides.com

Marine forecast
www.wunderground.com

MARINAS

The Intracoastal Waterway running through Jacksonville is busy every fall and spring as sailboats and motorboats make their way up and down the Atlantic coast.

Whether you are merely passing through area waters, arriving for an extended stay, or trailering a boat behind your car, a handful of marinas in the Jacksonville area are equipped to handle almost any need.

AMITY ANCHORAGE MARINA
1106 Friendship Dr., Switzerland
(904) 287-0931
If you find yourself sailing or motoring on the St. Johns River way south of Downtown and want to spend a night or two in a quiet marina enveloped by the sounds and sights of old Florida, Amity's your anchorage. Just make sure you call ahead. The marina has only 48 slips, most of which are usually occupied by locals.

Best described by its owner as a "quiet marina in the country," Amity Anchorage is a no-frills operation. There's water and power for your boat and a bathroom and a shower for you. And you can buy a bag of ice. That's about it. But you can't beat the scenery and the price: 50 cents per foot per night. The marina office is open Wednesday through Friday from 3:30 to 9 p.m. and on Saturday and Sunday from noon to 9 p.m.

i Want to charter a pontoon, runabout, or houseboat? Call the folks at Doctors Lake Marina in Orange Park at (904) 264-0505 or visit http://doctorslakemarina .tripod.com.

BEACH MARINE
2315 Beach Blvd.
(904) 249-8200
www.jaxbeachmarine.com
So maybe quietude isn't your thing. Beach Marine, located on the Intracoastal Waterway at Beach Boulevard in Jacksonville Beach, offers all the noisy fun you'd expect to find in a big marina: big boats coming and going, some real live-aboard characters, and nearby restaurants and nightclubs.

The marina itself has 170 wet slips. The dock house sells gas and diesel and offers pump-out services. Transient boaters have access to a weight room, sauna, Laundromat, and mail service. The cost for transient docking is $1.85 per foot per day, but you can rent wet slips by the week, month, or year as well for as little as $10 per linear foot per month. Each slip has a 30- and 50-amp hookup, with 100 amps available on request. The marine has restrooms with showers, and can set up long-term tenants with a temporary phone hookup.

MORNINGSTAR MARINAS
4852 North Ocean St., Mayport
(904) 758-1092
www.morningstarmarinas.com
Currently managed by the Morningstar Marinas group, this marina is located in the working fishing village of Mayport. The marina sits just 2.5 miles from the open ocean, making it Jacksonville's closest marina to the Atlantic. The marina has just 15 slips for transient and overnighters, but its dock can handle vessels measuring up to 150 feet. The marina also has 200 dry-storage slips for smaller boats.

Diesel and gas are available, and there's a live bait shop. A full-service marine shop can do all repairs, including engine rebuilds. The deli sells sandwiches, snacks, beer, and ice. The per-day cost is $1.95 per foot. Services are available Monday through Thursday 8 a.m. to 6 p.m. and Saturday and Sunday 6 a.m. to 6 p.m.

PALM COVE MARINA
14603 Beach Blvd.
(904) 223-4757
www.palmcovemarina.com
Located on the western shore of the Intracoastal Waterway at the Beach Boulevard drawbridge (about 9 miles from the ocean), Palm Cove Marina is one of the last full-service marinas on Jacksonville's Intracoastal Waterway. The marina is just a short cab ride over the Intracoastal from the Beaches, where plenty of nightlife and good restaurants await.

Palm Cove offers docking, dry storage for 420 boats, and 200 wet slips, a few of which can accommodate vessels up to 100 feet in length. Boaters can expect a full range of marine services, including repairs, fuel, pump-out station, toilets, and a travel lift to pull boats out of the water. There's also a full complement of newer amenities for the sailor: a lounge, bathrooms, and showers. The cost for transient vessels is $1.75 per foot per night.

The marina's store sells tackle, bait, beer, and ice. The marina does not rent boats. During your stay, be sure to make a reservation at the excellent Marker 32 restaurant, located on the marina's grounds. Marina services are available Monday through Thursday from 7 a.m. to 7 p.m. and Friday through Sunday 6 a.m. to 9 p.m.

PUBLIC BOAT RAMPS

If you trailer your boat to Jacksonville, you can launch it at 25 public boat ramps, free of charge. Following is a list of some of the more popular boat-launching sites maintained year-round by the City of Jacksonville. Visit www.coj.net (search "Boat Ramps") for a comprehensive list of all of the city's public boat ramps.

St. Johns Marina (901 Museum Circle) is located on the Southbank of the St. Johns River in the heart of Downtown between the Main Street and Acosta Bridges.

Bert Maxwell (500 Maxwell Rd.) is located on the Northside just off I-95.

Mayport (4870 Ocean St., Mayport) is located near Highway A1A, next to Morningstar Marinas. The Mayport public boat ramp offers the best access to the Atlantic Ocean. There's ample parking for your vehicle and trailer, but it can get especially crowded on the weekends and holidays.

Intracoastal Waterway (2510 2nd Ave. North at Beach Boulevard) is located in the same basin as Beach Marine marina. This is a great spot for launching your boat for quick runs up and down the Intracoastal Waterway. Parking is limited.

Wayne B. Stevens (4555 Ortega Farms Blvd.) is located on the Ortega River with quick access to the St. Johns River south of Downtown.

Arlington (intersection of Arlington Road and River Bluff Road North) is located off Arlington Road at the St. Johns River.

Hood Landing (Hood Landing Drive at Julington Creek) is located in the extreme southern end of the county. Julington Creek flows into the St. Johns River.

Sisters Creek Marina (8300 Heckscher Dr.) is located in the northwest quadrant of the intersection of the Intracoastal Waterway and the St. Johns River. The City of Jacksonville acquired the site in 1999 and spent several million dollars building new docks and a boat ramp. Sister's Creek is also home to the annual Greater Jacksonville Kingfish Tournament, held in July. This is often confused with the nearby Sisters Creek Joe Carlucci Marina and Boat Ramp. Both are fine places to put in.

SPECTATOR SPORTS

Jacksonville's miles of ocean and river shorelines and relatively mild year-round climate provide a great playground for everything from golf and tennis to fishing and surfing. But the city also offers a variety of exciting professional and amateur spectator sports for even the most discerning fan.

Want to take in an NFL game in one of the league's most modern stadiums? Check out the Jacksonville Jaguars schedule at Jacksonville Municipal Stadium. Jonesing to watch match-ups between the country's top professional women tennis players? The MPS Group Championships comes to Sawgrass Country Club every April. Craving an up-close view of the world's best golfers tackling one of the most photographed holes in professional golf? Then The Players Championship in Ponte Vedra Beach is for you. For minor-league baseball, you can't beat a sunny afternoon with The Jacksonville Suns at the city's new, classically designed ballpark.

If you prefer college sports, there's the annual Gator Bowl and the always-entertaining Florida-Georgia game, an annual event that pits the Florida Gators and the Georgia Bulldogs against each other in a long-sustained rivalry. Three area colleges—University of North Florida, Jacksonville University, and Edward Waters College—also offer plenty of sports action during the school year.

JACKSONVILLE DIXIE BLUES

Most people don't know it, but Jacksonville has a very successful women's tackle football team. Forget touch football, these gals deliver crushing blows and game-stopping interceptions. Part of the Women's Football Alliance since 2001, the Dixie Blues won the Atlantic Coast Conference their first year of play and advanced to the first annual World Bowl in San Diego. In 2002, the Blues again went to the World Bowl where they decimated the Indianapolis Vipers and were crowned the 2002-2003 National Champions.

Over the next couple seasons, the Dixie Blues joined the Independent Women's Football League (IWFL) and are now in their fifth season with the league.

The Dixie Blues went undefeated in 2006 and went on to become the Superior Bowl Champions in 2006 and again in 2007.

The Dixie Blues sat out 2008, but took to the field again in 2009 as a part of the Women's Football Alliance and have been named, by the league, as possible contenders for the 2009 national title. Visit the Dixie Blues Web site to keep up with the Blues at www.jaxdixieblues .com.

JACKSONVILLE JAGUARS

Football sits at the top of the sports heap in Jacksonville. And, in recent years anyway, the king in Jacksonville has been the Jaguars. After years of trying to win an NFL team, Jacksonville scored big in 1995, when the league awarded the city one of two new franchises.

Since entering the league the Jaguars have become one of the most successful expansion franchises in the history of the National Football League. The Jaguars have been to the play-offs four times and played in the AFC Championship game twice. The Jaguars won 49 games in their first five seasons, including an NFL-best record of 14–2 in 1999.

The Jaguars play in Jacksonville Municipal Stadium, located near Downtown on the banks

The Long Road to an NFL Franchise

For years Jacksonville's quest for a National Football League team seemed hopeless. The city's overeagerness for a pro team was often used by NFL owners as a bargaining chip to extract better deals in other cities, while the misses only fed Jacksonville's inferiority complex.

But community leaders and fans never gave up the dream. In 1989 yet another partnership was formed to lasso an NFL team. The group, **Touchdown Jacksonville**, included several prominent Jacksonville businessmen as well as former Governor Jeb Bush, and Hamilton Jordan, former President Jimmy Carter's chief of staff.

A year later, chances improved when the NFL announced it would expand the league by two teams for the 1993 season. The City of Jacksonville quickly cranked up its acquisition efforts. The city council unanimously voted to spend $60 million to renovate the Gator Bowl should the city be awarded an expansion football team. Jacksonville was one of 11 cities to apply for one of the two expansion teams, and reporters quickly traveled to each of those other cities to size up our chances in comparison.

To beef up its ownership team, Touchdown Jacksonville added several more partners, including Nine West shoe store magnate J. Wayne Weaver. By late 1991 the group, which had selected "**Jaguars**" as the team name, presented its bid to Commissioner Tagliabue and other NFL officials in New York.

An ongoing labor dispute with players, however, delayed the NFL's selection of the expansion cities until 1993, with play beginning in 1995. Jacksonville's hopes were dashed yet again when city hall balked at spending more money to make further stadium improvements needed to meet NFL specifications.

Eventually the city and Touchdown Jacksonville reached a new lease agreement. But then Weaver, who had became the managing partner, said he'd pursue bidding for the team only if 9,000 club seats were sold in a 10-day period. Unbelievably, the city exceeded the daunting challenge, selling 10,112 club seats. On November 30, 1993, Jacksonville was awarded a franchise team, making it one of the smallest NFL cities in the league.

of the St. Johns River. Formerly called the Gator Bowl, the stadium was completely rebuilt to accommodate a professional team. With 73,000 seats, Jacksonville Municipal Stadium is one of the biggest NFL stadiums in one of the smallest cities. While those facts often give team owners heartburn when they're trying to fill the stands, it generally means good news for visitors. There are usually spare seats at Jaguars games, unlike at many other NFL venues. And it gets better: In preparation for the Super Bowl in February 2005, the city and the Jaguars spent millions of dollars to upgrade the stadium and add more corporate skyboxes.

Jacksonville Municipal Stadium is easily accessible by special game-day public buses. There's also ample parking around and near the stadium. You can get ticket and game-day information from the Jaguars' Web site, www.jaguars.com, and follow them on Twitter and Facebook.

ℹ Want a good deal on Jacksonville Jaguars tickets? You can usually buy tickets at the stadium on the day of a game. If you wait until just after the game has started, you might get a better deal on tickets. *NOTE:* Under Florida law it used to be illegal for scalpers to sell tickets to a sporting event for more than $1 over their face value. Not anymore. In 2006, the State Senate passed a bill making ticket scalping legal. The law now allows a person to resell tickets for as much as they want—or can get—over the face value. The lesson here: buy your tickets early and through legitimate channels, unless you like handing over your entire vacation fund outside the stadium on game day.

JACKSONVILLE ROLLER GIRLS ROLLER DERBY

We are so not kidding when we tell you that this is one of the most fun ways in town to spend a Saturday night. The Jacksonville Roller Girls bring on the pain with a full season of matchups filled with flying elbows and wheel-spinning stunts. Die-hard derby girls with names like Ivanna C.U. Bleed, Kat von SkratchErEyezOut, and Jiffy Feet match up to stunning effect. If football leaves you cold, a night of roller derby is guaranteed to get your pulse pounding. For real fun, visit the Web site, www.jacksonvillerollergirls.com, and watch their helmet-cam videos.

The Roller Girls face-off at Jax Ice Sports Plex, 3605 Philips Hwy., and Mandarin Skate Station, 3461 Kori Rd. Visit their Web site for this season's schedule.

JACKSONVILLE SUNS

If you're visiting Jacksonville in the spring or early summer and you enjoy the intimacy minor-league baseball offers, you'll want to catch a Suns game. With about 70 home games each season, you'll certainly have plenty of opportunities.

The Suns are a Class AA Southern League farm team that plays at a 10,000-seat cupcake of a stadium called The Baseball Grounds of Jacksonville.

To make sure you get the best seats available, purchase tickets on the Internet at www .jacksonvillesuns.com. All Internet orders must be placed at least four hours prior to game time. You can also order by phone at (904) 358-2846 or just walk up and buy game-day tickets at the box office. (Phone orders placed less than one week prior to the game will be left in your name at the will-call window.)

Regular season ticket prices start at $6.50 for seats in the bleachers or on the grassy berm in left field. Reserve seating from $9.50 will get you a seat in right field. Behind home plate, seats go for the incredibly affordable price of $12.50. And tickets in a special box right behind the dugout run only $21.50 each. Seniors age 62 and over and military personnel with an ID get a discount, as do children. Play your cards right and you may even catch the famous mascot, a concert, or fireworks. Talk about getting some bang out of your buck!

THE PLAYERS CHAMPIONSHIP

One of professional golf's biggest tournaments, The Players Championship, comes to the TPC at Sawgrass in Ponte Vedra Beach every May. The Players Championship attracts top players, including local players David Duval and Vijay Singh, with its $9.5 million purse, one of the richest on the PGA tour.

The TPC is best known for its 17th island hole, and each year it is the most popular among spectators. The signature hole is a short-length par-3 with a wide green that narrows to the right side. The right side of the green is protected by a small well-maintained bunker, which sometimes will be a relief to players who come up short of the green. Club selection on this hole is critically important; with the tricky winds of spring, the Championship could be won or lost here. A larger spectator mound has been created behind the green.

Grounds tickets currently cost $45 per day or $145 for the week, but are set to increase soon. Check the Web site, www.pgatour.com, for up-to-date pricing. You can also purchase tickets and take a virtual tour of the TPC Stadium course on the Web site. The Tournament Players Club at Sawgrass is located in Ponte Vedra Beach west of Highway A1A, south of J. Turner Butler Boulevard.

i The First Coast Soccer Association hosts a big tournament every September called the First Coast Labor Day Shoot Out. Boys and girls travel here from all over the Southeast to play in the tournament, which attracts college coaches seeking new talent. Learn more about it at www.first coastsoccer.com.

THE MPS GROUP CHAMPIONSHIPS

The MPS Group Championships at Sawgrass Country Club in April at Sawgrass in Ponte Vedra Beach draw many of the world's top women tennis players for nine days of singles and doubles. The tournament has undergone a number of name changes since it began in April 1980, but one thing hasn't changed: it has consistently attracted such top names as Oudin, Graf, Hingis, Evert, Navratilova, Seles, Sabatini, and the Williams sisters. The Racquet Club at Sawgrass Country Club has been ranked among the nation's 50 Best by *Tennis* magazine and as a five-star tennis destination by World Tennis.

For tickets and more details, including details on how to become a volunteer or a ballperson, call (800) 486-8366 or visit the tournament's Web site at www.mpsgroupchamps.net.

COLLEGE FOOTBALL

The Konica Minolta Gator Bowl is played every New Year's Day at Jacksonville Municipal Sta-

dium. Started in 1944, the Gator Bowl always pits a top team from the Atlantic Coast Conference against either a top team from the Big East conference or Notre Dame. For information and tickets, visit the Web site at www.gatorbowl.com or call the Gator Bowl Association at (904) 798-1700.

The Florida-Georgia football game is played every September at Jacksonville Municipal Stadium. The football rivalry is fierce, and the pre- and postgame partying is legendary. The Florida-Georgia matchup is often (only partially in jest) referred to as the world's biggest cocktail party.

JU DOLPHINS

For a small liberal arts college, Jacksonville University fields some surprisingly competitive teams in cross-country, tennis, rowing, and football, but especially in basketball. The JU Dolphins gained national fame in the early 1970s when 7-foot center Artis Gilmore led the team to the NCAA finals. While JU has yet to replicate that early splendor, the Dolphins still consistently produce competitive teams.

JU, which competes in the Atlantic Sun Conference, also offers spectators exciting baseball, football, and soccer games. For more information and schedules of all JU games, visit the team's Web site at www.judolphins.com. You can get more information about the Atlantic Sun Conference at www.atlanticsun.org.

EDWARD WATERS COLLEGE

The school may be small, but the football team is mighty. EWC, one of the oldest black colleges in the country, fields one tough football team (the team has produced seven All-Americans since 2001) and a scrappy basketball team, too. Both teams play a full schedule of games, mostly against other small colleges. For a schedule of Tiger games, visit the school's Web site at www .ewc.edu/athletics. By the way, Jacksonville's much-loved former sheriff, Nat Glover, is a graduate of EWC and an alumnus of its football team.

i Why be a sports spectator? Join the Jacksonville Track Club for fun, fitness, and fellowship. The club hosts a variety of runs all year long, including training runs to get you in shape for the 5-mile Summer Beach Run, The Guana River 50k Trail Run, The Gate River Run, or The Last Gasp cross-country race in December. The Track Club also sponsors morning and afternoon drop-in workouts on The Bolles School's state-of-the-art track. The workouts are open to all JTC members. Not a member yet? A $20 annual fee gives you access to a host of member benefits, including the workouts. (Wednesday morning workouts go from 5:30 to 7 a.m. Afternoons sessions go from 5:30 to 7 p.m.) For additional information go to www.jtcrunning .com.

THE MUG RACE

The annual Mug Race, purported to be the world's longest river race, is a 38.5-nautical-mile sail-racing classic that runs from Palatka to Jacksonville on the St. Johns and is sponsored by the Rudder Club of Jacksonville. To make the race open to sailboats of all sizes, there are two courses. The South course, which starts in Palatka, is for boats with masts under 44 feet. The North course, starting just south of the Buckman Bridge (Downtown), is for boats with masts 44 feet and taller. The race uses a pursuit start in which each boat is assigned a start time based on their rating, thus giving slower boats an earlier start. More than 100 trophies are awarded based on categories including: first all-female crew to finish, first dingy monohull to finish, and last boat to finish. For more information, visit www.rudder club.com/mug.html or call the Rudder Club at (904) 264-4094.

FISHING

After golf, fishing is the largest sports industry in Florida. According to the Florida Fish and Wildlife Conservation Commission, the state hosts over 3,000,000 anglers per year, making Florida the No. 1 fishing destination in the United States. In Jacksonville, it's easy to see why.

With quick access to the Atlantic Ocean, miles and miles of sandy beaches, a deep-channel river, and thousands of acres of tidal marshes, the Jacksonville area offers anglers a variety of fishing habitats. There's something for everyone. You can sit at anchor in the mouth of the St. Johns River and pursue the elusive flounder, paddle a kayak around shallow salt marshes searching for tailing redfish, or head offshore for kingfish. There's also excellent freshwater bass fishing on the St. Johns River south of Jacksonville.

For the best fishing in the Jacksonville area, you'll need a boat. If you bring your own, there are ample public boat ramps scattered throughout the area for quick access to either the Intracoastal Waterway or the ocean. If you don't have your own, you can rent a boat or hire one of the dozens of fishing charters available in the area.

Jacksonville also is home to a number of well-known fishing contests, most notably the AT&T Greater Jacksonville Kingfish Tournament, billed as the largest kingfishing tournament in the United States.

Before you begin fishing, though, make sure you've got the proper licenses.

---

i It is unlawful to harvest, possess, land, purchase, sell, or exchange the following species of fish: Nassau grouper, jewfish, sawfish, basking shark, whale shark, spotted eagle ray, sturgeon, white shark, sand shark, big eye sand tiger shark, and manta ray.

FISHING LICENSES

Florida law requires that you obtain a fishing license if you attempt to catch fish for noncommercial use. Nonresidents are required to obtain a saltwater fishing license when saltwater fishing from either a boat or land. Anglers under the age of 16 are exempt from the law. Residents are allowed to fish from land or a bridge without a license but must have a license when fishing from a boat, unless they are under the age of 16. Freshwater and saltwater fishing licenses are required for both Florida residents and nonresidents. Florida residents can purchase freshwater or saltwater licenses in annual, five-year, or lifetime increments for $17, $79, or $301.50, respectively. Annual nonresident licenses run $47.

Regular licenses are available at the Duval County Tax Collectors offices (904) 630-1916, www.taxjax.com, and most bait shops. For more information call the Florida Fish and Wildlife Conservation Commission regional office in Lake City at (850) 488-4676 or in Jacksonville Beach at (904) 270-2500. The Division of Law Enforcement can provide a complete listing of Florida's regulations of protected species and restrictions on size and number of fish you can keep. Visit the commission's Web site at www.myfwc.com to learn more.

JACKSONVILLE-AREA FISH

You've got your fishing license in hand, and you've determined where you want to angle. Let's take a look at the many species of fish that inhabit Jacksonville's local waters.

Redfish

Reds are a great fish to catch and eat, making them one of the more popular targets for area anglers. You can land redfish in inland waters or in the ocean, off the beach.

If you're fishing the Intracoastal Waterway and its marshes, the reds feed around oyster mounds and on the flats. In shallow waters, the tail fins of reds will poke out of the water.

The best inland fishing opportunities for redfish are on lower tides in the middle of the day or afternoon. The sun warms the dark mudflats, and the reds are more active. March through December offer the best results for catching redfish.

In recent years, fly-fishing for redfish has become popular with flies resembling shrimp or fiddler crabs, available at most fly-fishing shops, attracting the most attention.

i Local anglers say winter is the best time to fish for redfish in Northeast Florida because the reds are clustered in schools.

King Mackerel

If you're interested in catching king mackerel, or kingfish, you've come to the right place. Kingfish can be caught off Jacksonville's fishing piers, from the surf, and from as far as 80 miles offshore in the Gulf Stream. The king mackerel is a slender, streamlined fish, slightly flattened from side to side with a tapered head and an iridescent bluish green back. The kingfish, which can fold its two dorsal fins back in to a groove to enhance its speed, feeds on any available food but favors jacks, sea trout, sardinelike fishes, ribbonfish, herring, shrimp, and squid.

The most popular method for catching kingfish is to slow-troll live menhaden shad, also known as pogies, either on a downrigger or free-lined.

King mackerel are a highly sought after gamefish. A challenging catch, they put up a spectacular fight by leaping and skyrocketing out of the water. Most kingfish hooked off Jacksonville weigh about 20 pounds. The Florida record is 90 pounds, so come prepared for a fight.

The best season for kings in North Florida is the summer. Kings begin migrating from southern waters in the spring. As the kingfish move north during the summer months, kingfish tournaments pop up along the coast. The annual AT&T Greater Jacksonville Kingfish Tournament & Festival is held every July.

Kingfish are tasty, as long as they aren't too heavy. Locals love to grill the steaks and fillets, but be warned: kingfish more than 15 pounds have a heavy oil content, which makes for a strong "fishy" flavor. You can smoke larger fish with appetizing results.

Bluefish

When the bluefish run along the coast during fall and spring, catching them from the beach is a snap—they'll eat almost anything.

The name bluefish is something of a misnomer, as this species is most commonly a seagreen color above, which fades to a silvery shade on its lower sides and belly.

Bluefish eat a variety of small-bodied animals such as shrimp, small lobsters, crabs, larval fish, and mollusks. Adult bluefish are opportunistic feeders, commonly focusing on schooling species such as menhaden, squid, and sand eels. For bait, most locals use dead shrimp.

Bluefish anglers fish from a boat or the shore along nearly every harbor entrance, town dock, beach, and jetty. Wire leaders are a must. Bluefish are equipped with sharp teeth that can snap through monofilament lines.

i Like to fly fish from a canoe or kayak? Then head to the Pellicer Flats west of the Intracoastal Waterway between Marineland and Palm Coast. Anglers call this spot "redfish heaven."

Jack Crevalle

Known as the bulldog of inshore waters, the jack crevalle run between 3 and 10 pounds. When these fighters begin feeding off the top, get ready. They strike like a mad fish and will test any tackle that you own. The best time to fish for jack crevalle is April through November.

The new 1,300-foot concrete pier in Jacksonville Beach at 503 1st St. North (at 5th Avenue) is a great place to drop your line. There's also a bait shop right on the pier as well as restrooms and a concession stand. Admission to the pier is $4; no fishing license is required, and you can drop up to three lines per fisherman. Spectators need only pay $1 and children under six can come along for free. To learn more, visit www.jacksonvillebeach.org.

Ladyfish

Often referred to as the "poor man's tarpon," ladyfish perform aerial acrobats when hooked. Like tarpon, they can come out of the water several times before being landed.

Ladyfish range from about 2 pounds to 5 pounds. The best months for ladyfish action are April through August.

Tarpon

If you're in search of real tarpon, Jacksonville's waters aren't your best bet. Southwest Florida, for example, offers better inshore tarpon fishing. That's not to say the area is devoid of tarpon. Anglers going after reds or trout in inshore waters accidentally hook tarpon from time to time. Lucky folks. Tarpon hooked in Jacksonville's inshore waters can weigh anywhere from 25 to 200 pounds. Overall, however, they are very difficult to hook.

Trout

Trout are plentiful in the mouth of the St. Johns River and in the inland creeks off the river and Intracoastal Waterway. Local anglers use dead and live shrimp and artificial lures. Like redfish, trout has become a favorite among the growing ranks of local saltwater fly fishers. The best times of year for trout are from mid-March through mid-December.

Other local species include dolphin, pompano, flounder, and cobia.

WHERE TO FISH

There are basically four different areas to fish in the Jacksonville area, each offering its own distinct fish and fishing nuances: the freshwater rivers mostly to the west of Jacksonville; the Intracoastal Waterway and tidal marshes that stretch north and south along the backside of the Beaches; the Beaches where surf casting rules; and the ocean where deepwater fishing in the open waters of the Atlantic provides a thrill of a lifetime.

Anglers love the Florida Sportsman Fishing & Boat Show every fall at the Prime Osborn Convention Center at 1000 Water St. A dozen top fishing pros offer advice on subjects from catching monster blue marlin to sight-casting for redfish. Seminar speakers share their knowledge from the bow of a flats boat floating in a 10,000-gallon pond and an offshore boat fully tricked out for deepwater angling. Admission for adults is $8; children 12 and under attend for free with a parent.

SURF FISHING

Surf fishing in Northeast Florida, indeed throughout Florida, has greatly improved since the state banned the use of large commercial nets near the shore in the late 1990s. Locals report that surf-casting has been yielding some of the best results in decades.

Locals love ocean fishing because you never know what might end up on the other end of your line from whiting, redfish, and Spanish mackerel to bluefish, trout, pompano, and, everybody's favorites, stingrays and catfish.

Whiting holds strong as the most sought-after species in the Jacksonville surf. But come fall, the blues run along the beaches in thick schools, and redfish make an appearance from time to time. And with the disappearance of the commercial nets, your chances of hooking a colorful—and very tasty—pompano have greatly improved.

For the best results, fish on the incoming tide. That's when small, bait fish get carried closer to shore, with larger fish following in hungry pursuit. Local anglers prefer dead or live shrimp or cut-up mullet as bait.

OFFSHORE FISHING

On the floor of the Atlantic Ocean, 9 miles off Jacksonville's shore, sits debris from Jacksonville's old Gator Bowl. The old cement chunks have created a wonderful, artificial-reef environment for fish, and thus a great place to cast a line.

Since there are no natural formations off the coast of Jacksonville, man-made reefs such as sunken vessels and the Gator Bowl debris, make for excellent fish concentrations and great catching.

Most offshore fishing is done by trolling, drawing your line behind a slow-moving boat, which is the best way to attract the interest of one of the mighty kings. But, if you're just in it for the fun, try setting your sights on cobia. They are reported to be more fun to catch and make for great eating.

Amberjack, barracuda, cobia, grouper, mackerel, permit, snapper, and shark tend to congregate around wrecks. Bluefish, barracuda, bonito, dolphin, mackerel, mako, marlin, sailfish, tuna, and wahoo are best caught offshore.

FISHING CHARTERS

Hook up with one of these local charter-fishing outfits for a thrilling day on the high seas.

CAPTAIN JIM'S FUN FISHING CHARTERS
17184 Dorado Circle
(904) 757-7550
www.hammondfishing.com
Captain Jim Hammond covers the St. Johns River, backwater creeks off the Intracoastal Waterway, and the jetties. He specializes in helping anglers catch red bass, speckled trout, jack crevalle, bluefish, flounder, sheepshead, shark, tarpon, and black drum. His 65-foot party boat can hold up to 40 anglers.

KING NEPTUNE DEEP SEA FISHING
4378 Ocean St., Mayport Village
(904) 220-6363
www.kingneptunefishing.com
Captain Scott Reynolds has been taking large groups deep-sea fishing for more than 25 years.

His new, custom-built, 70-foot, deep-sea fishing boat, the *Majesty*, can hold up to 40 anglers and travels at speeds up to 25 knots. Reynolds, who has recently upgraded his gear to include the latest high-speed reels and 7-foot custom Ugly Stick rods, departs from Monty's Marina in Mayport, takes you 15 to 30 miles offshore, and supplies you with a rod, reel, bait, and fishing license. The *Majesty* has a large, comfortable cabin and a snack bar, or you can bring your own munchies along with you. Non-fishers can come along for the ride for only $30. Charter prices vary, but are consistently reasonable. Reservations required.

MAYPORT PRINCESS DEEP SEA FISHING
4378 Ocean St., Mayport Village
(904) 241-4111
www.mayportprincessfishing.com
Captain George Strate has some 30 years' experience taking large groups of anglers deep-sea fishing. Captain Strate knows these waters like the back of his hand, including hundreds of the best fishing spots for the current water and weather conditions. He will supply you with a rod, reel, bait, and fishing license. The *Mayport Princess*, however, does not have a galley, so if you want anything to eat or drink while out on the water, bring a cooler. The *Mayport Princess* sails daily, year-round. Prices vary, and reservations are required.

FISHING GUIDES

THE SALTY FEATHER
2683 St. John's Bluff Rd.
(904) 645-8998
www.saltyfeather.com
The Salty Feather, a full-service fly-fishing center that's been in business since 1994, offers a full array of flies, rods, reels, lines, leaders, fly-tying tools, accessories, gadgets, clothing, books, videos, gift items, and much more. Salty Feather also offers guides for whole- or half-day fly-fishing trips as well as fly-fishing classes year-round. The guides specialize in fishing the hot spots from St. Augustine to Cumberland Island.

DAY TRIPS

ST. AUGUSTINE

Ironically, when Harriet Beecher Stowe first visited St. Augustine in 1872, she didn't get there by going "seaward." She traveled south on a riverboat on the St. Johns River from Jacksonville to a settlement called Tekoi, which no longer exists, then headed east by rail. "The railroad across to St. Augustine is made of wooden rails; and the cars are drawn by horses," she wrote. Needless to say, it took hours to get there.

Today it only takes about 45 minutes to get to St. Augustine from Jacksonville, and chances are you'll find it as quaint as Stowe did.

Tourism is a billion-dollar industry in St. Johns County with much of those dollars spent in St. Augustine, the oldest permanently occupied European settlement in America. And tourism doesn't show any signs of slowing down. According to the St. Augustine & St. Johns County Chamber of Commerce, some 3.5 million tourists visit the county every year.

St. Augustine is good for families, and its old-world charm is great for couples who enjoy hiding away in historic B&Bs, dining by candlelight at restaurants of note, and taking moonlit walks along the Matanzas Bay sea wall.

NOTE: Parking is a problem in St. Augustine, so once you find a parking space, keep your car there as long as possible. Everything you need is within walking distance anyway.

Getting There

You can still get to St. Augustine from Jacksonville by water, but go by way of the Intracoastal Waterway or the Atlantic Ocean, not the St. Johns River. Once there, try docking your boat at the St. Augustine Municipal Marina, located in the heart of town. For more information on the marina, visit www.staugustinemarina.com.

Most people drive the 38 miles to St. Augustine, choosing one of three main highways to get there. The most obvious is I-95 south to exit 318. Turn left at the exit, heading east on SR 16, until you hit US 1. Turn right onto US 1 heading south, then turn left onto King Street. Follow King Street into the heart of town.

Highway A1A is the scenic route to St. Augustine because it runs parallel to the ocean. Take A1A south through Ponte Vedra. Continue south for nearly 40 minutes until you hit Vilano Beach. Turn right at the Vilano traffic light, and head west over the Vilano Bridge. Turn left at the first traffic light, at the intersection of A1A and San Marco, and follow San Marco into the heart of town.

The third highway from Jacksonville to St. Augustine is US 1 (or Philips Highway). Take US 1 south for about 40 minutes until you get to the intersection with King Street. Turn left on King Street, and follow it into the heart of town.

A Short History

We have the Spanish to thank for St. Augustine. They arrived in 1565 led by Pedro Menendez de Aviles and started a small settlement named St. Augustine some 55 years before the Pilgrims landed at Plymouth Rock.

The Spanish managed to keep St. Augustine and "La Florida" under their thumb for nearly 200 years, despite repeated attacks by the British. By 1695 they'd finished construction of a fort, the Castillo de San Marcos, to shelter themselves from those attacks. But the efforts of the British and U.S.-backed patriots, who attacked La Florida from strongholds in Georgia, finally took their toll. La Florida became a U.S. territory in 1821 and a state in 1845.

Enter railroad baron Henry Flagler, who arrived in the 1880s with a big checkbook and even bigger dreams of turning St. Augustine into the American Riviera. He built several grand hotels before losing interest in St. Augustine and moving south to Palm Beach. Those grand hotels are much beloved by residents and tourists today.

In the 1920s St. Augustine became a popular artists' colony. This creative influence brought a bohemian spirit that never entirely left the city. Countless artists still call St. Augustine home and continue to draw inspiration from the city.

i On the first Friday of every month, St. Augustine art galleries host a citywide Art Walk. From 5 to 9 p.m. galleries throughout the city invite you to stroll between them and enjoy wine, cheese, live music, and art. The festivities often continue throughout the weekend, making the first weekend of any month a great time for art lovers to visit.

Where to Stay

BAYFRONT WESTCOTT HOUSE
146 Avenida Menendez
(904) 825-4602 or (800) 513-9814
www.westcotthouse.com
Built in the 1880s for Dr. John Westcott, this Victorian house has two beautiful porches overlooking Matanzas Bay. Sleep late and enjoy your breakfast on the second-floor porch. Each of the 16 rooms is brimming with antiques as well as such modern amenities as a king- or queen-size bed, private bath, cable television, wireless Internet, and telephone.

CASA MONICA HOTEL
95 Cordova St.
(904) 827-1888, (800) 648-1888
www.casamonica.com
This 138-room hotel is super-luxe. Franklin Smith, a Boston architect who founded the YMCA, designed it in 1888. The hotel closed during the Depression and remained closed for some 30 years until the county bought the building in

1968 and turned it into a courthouse. By 1997 St. Johns County had built a new, modern courthouse, and hotelier Richard Kessler bought the Casa Monica for $1.2 million. He gutted the sixties courthouse interior and created a premier, AAA four-diamond hotel in the heart of St. Augustine. This is where the king and queen of Spain ate lunch during their visit in 2001. (Their tight schedule did not permit an overnight stay.) The decor is Moorish Revival, and amenities include an outdoor pool, a whirlpool spa, an exercise room, the four-star 95 Cordova restaurant, and a rooftop garden and pavilion that resemble a sultan's tent. Best of all, walk outside the hotel's front door and you're in the thick of things, directly across the street from the heart of old St. Augustine.

COASTAL REALTY
3942 A1A South
(800) 587-2287
coastalrealtyfl.com
Try something new—stay in a fully furnished condo in St. Augustine Beach. It's not as costly as you'd expect, plus with a full kitchen you can cook some of your meals if you so desire. Many of the condos are within walking distance of the ocean and include amenities like tennis courts and pools. Lots of local real estate companies specialize in both long- and short-term rentals; Coastal Realty is just one of them. For more rental companies, check out www.staugustine.com, the award-winning Web site for the local newspaper, the *St. Augustine Record*.

i Every third Thursday from 5 to 9 p.m. Beaches residents turn out at Beaches Town Center for the North Beaches Art Walk when 25 shops and restaurants display artisans' wares and host arts demonstrations. The streets fill with live music, children's activities, prizes and street performers. For more information, visit www.nbaw.org.

Attractions

CASTILLO DE SAN MARCOS
www.nps.gov (Search "Castillo de San Marcos")

The Castillo de San Marcos, now operated by the National Park Service, is a must-see. The star-shaped fortress is made from coquina blocks extracted from a quarry in what is now Anastasia State Park. Built by the Spanish, the fort was finished in 1695. Once Florida became a state, the Castillo was renamed Fort Marion, and it was there that Seminole Chief Osceola was held prisoner for a time before escaping. Take a picnic lunch and spread out a blanket on the 20 acres surrounding this fort, the only extant 17th-century fort in North America.

LIGHTNER MUSEUM
75 King St.
(904) 824-2874
www.lightnermuseum.org

The Lightner is full of beautiful and interesting objects from the early 19th century, from antiques to mechanical musical instruments to costumes to toys. There's also a stained-glass room featuring the work of Louis Comfort Tiffany. The three-story museum building is itself a work of art. The former Hotel Alcazar was built in 1887 by Henry Flagler and designed by the same architects who designed the New York Public Library. The collection now housed within its walls belonged to Chicago publisher Otto Lightner, who purchased the Alcazar in 1946. (He's also buried there.) The Alcazar's former indoor swimming pool and casino now house the Cafe Alcazar, a great (and unique) place for lunch.

RIPPLE EFFECT KAYAK ECOTOURS
St. Augustine
(904) 347-1565
www.rippleeffectecotours.com

Chris Kelley teaches science from a kayak at this real-deal environmental outfitter. Voted Best Place to Kayak in Folio Weekly's 2007-2009 Best of Jacksonville issues, Ripple Effect runs tours throughout the week to some of the areas most beautiful and ecologically diverse locales in Faver Dykes State Park, Guana River, Anastasia State Park, Marineland, and the Guana Tolomato Matanzas National Estuarine Research Reserve (formerly known as Guana River State Park). Join owner Chris Kelley or guide Joe Woodbury for one of Ripple Effect's Zen Kayak Tours where they teach about topics such as the connection between mindfulness and kayaking. Be sure to check the schedule on Ripple Effect's Web site for upcoming trips like the Guana Astronomy Star Gazing Kayak Tour where paddlers get to gaze at the night sky above the Guana River from one of Ripple Effects' glowing "firefly" kayaks. Check out the Close-up on Ripple Effect and Chris Kelley in the Attractions & Tours chapter to learn more about this gem in the waterways.

ST. AUGUSTINE ALLIGATOR FARM ZOOLOGICAL PARK
999 Anastasia Blvd.
(904) 824-3337
www.alligatorfarm.com

Who says you can't get friendly with a crocodile? Here's your chance to get, if not friendly, at least up close and personal with its cousin, the alligator. There are more than a thousand alligators here, and some are absolutely huge (probably because they've been enjoying three square meals a day in captivity for a while). The running joke in St. Augustine is that if a hurricane comes ashore and knocks down the fences surrounding the alligator farm, watch out. Make sure you take in one of the entertaining programs by staff naturalists, who are full of fun facts about these prehistoric reptiles, as well as the farm's extensive collection of birds, snakes, and other scaly critters. (See the Kidstuff chapter for more on the Alligator Farm.)

ST. AUGUSTINE LIGHTHOUSE AND MUSEUM
81 Lighthouse Ave.
(904) 829-0745
www.staugustinelighthouse.com

You can't miss it. The black-and-white-striped St. Augustine Lighthouse is one of only about three dozen lighthouses still standing in Florida—and one of only six that are open to the public statewide. Climb the 219 stairs to the lantern room and enjoy great views of the Atlantic Ocean, Intracoastal Waterway, and St. Augustine. A museum in the restored lightkeeper's house chronicles the history of this faithful lighthouse and the role it played in Florida's maritime history. There's also a dynamite gift shop with all sorts of nautical goodies for sale.

ST. GEORGE STREET AND THE SPANISH QUARTER VILLAGE
Old Town Historic District
(904) 825-6830

When you leave the Castillo de San Marcos, walk southwest down quaint St. George Street, the oldest shopping street in St. Augustine. Stop at the Spanish Quarter Village at 29 St. George St. to see the living history museum, a tiny version of Colonial Williamsburg. Here you can get a feel for a Spanish colonialist's life in the early 1800s: a blacksmith makes wrought-iron pot handles, a señora feeds her goats and tends her garden, and a carpenter hammers furniture. This is a favorite destination for school field trips, so consider visiting during non-school hours.

Where to Eat

95 CORDOVA
Casa Monica Hotel
95 Cordova St.
(904) 810-6810
www.95cordova.com

This is St. Augustine's premier restaurant, located in the city's premier hotel, the Casa Monica. The restaurant prides itself on combining fresh, local ingredients in new, masterful ways, which means guests get to enjoy specialties like shrimp and goat cheese grits, cashew crusted salmon siracha, and artichoke bisque. Locals love the First Wednesday Fashion Shows and famously delicious Sunday brunch.

A1A ALEWORKS
1 King St.
(904) 829-2977
www.a1aaleworks.com

Sure there's food here, but most people come to A1A Aleworks for the selection of handcrafted lagers and ales on tap. Try the award-winning A. Strange Stout and Bridge of Lions Brown Ale. Or better yet, go for the six-beer sampler and taste them all. The restaurant has a great second-floor veranda that's excellent for an afternoon burger and beer, and makes a perfect, birds-eye-view perch for people watching.

CONCH HOUSE RESTAURANT AND LOUNGE
57 Comares Ave.
(904) 829-8646
www.conch-house.com

If the Conch House were located in Key West, you'd expect to see Jimmy Buffet lighting up at the bar. Considered one of the area's best-kept secrets, this casual, fun, tropical hangout with tiki huts and a large wooden deck overlooking the scenic Salt Run has been drawing locals for decades. Dine indoors while still enjoying the waterfront view and Caribbean cuisine. Think seafood, steaks, salads, and island-style cuisine. For a unique experience, try out the Seminole Raw Bar and eat on the Everglades Dining Patio with its live alligator exhibit. The lounge offers a very popular two-for-one happy hour during the week. The Conch House also operates a 200-slip marina just off the Intracoastal Waterway, only 1,000 feet from the St. Augustine Inlet.

i Like to sail? Take a day trip on the *Schooner Freedom,* a replica of a 19th-century blockade-runner that used to frequent the waters around St. Augustine. *Freedom,* which is a classic tall ship, is available for both day and evening cruises. The *Freedom* is based at the public marina in downtown St. Augustine. Call (904) 810-1010 or visit www.schoonerfreedom.com for reservations.

GYPSY CAB COMPANY
828 Anastasia Blvd.
(904) 824-8244
www.gypsycab.com

Gypsy Cab Company has been a fixture in St. Augustine for decades. Thanks to its menu items forged from Italian, German, Cajun, Mediterranean, classical European, Southern, Oriental, and Floribbean influences, Gypsy Cab Company has always been a popular lunch and dinner spot, known for its soups and fish dishes. The restaurant is located just blocks from the St. Augustine Alligator Farm and the St. Augustine Lighthouse.

i **Enjoy wine? Then you may want to tour the San Sebastian Winery in St. Augustine. The actual vineyards are miles away in Central Florida, but at the winery, located in one of Henry Flagler's historic railway buildings, you can learn how San Sebastian's wine is made, sample different vintages, and purchase a few bottles for your private collection. Make time to hang out at The Cellar Upstairs, San Sebastian's rooftop jazz and blues bar. San Sebastian is located at 157 King St. Visit www.sansebastian winery.com to learn more.**

MANATEE CAFE
525 Highway 16
(904) 826-0210
www.manateecafe.com

If you like healthful food prepared with filtered water and organic ingredients, don't miss this restaurant. The location's not so pretty, and it's open only for breakfast and lunch, but the owners do a powerful job of making both of those meals memorable. Order eggs in a pita with a fresh salad and homemade dressing, a breakfast burrito, Cajun-style chicken, or a homemade pizza, to name a few specialties. For dessert try a piece of homemade Key lime pie or a homemade cookie of the day.

OPUS 39
39 Cordova St.
(904) 824-0402
www.opus39.com

When it comes to fine dining in the nation's oldest city, Opus 39 continually satisfies. At the table, guests have three choices: a la carte ordering, the chef's five-course Menu Spontane, or a seven-course tasting menu. The a la carte menu contains delightful choices such as cast iron–seared kurobuta pork loin with celeriac purée, Brussels sprouts, and apple sauce; or seared sea

bass cheeks with cannelini bean ragout, arugula, and smoked bacon sauce. The choices change constantly, depending on the freshest ingredients available. The wine room is fun, too, and is full of selections from small Napa, Sonoma, and Russian River wineries. Creativity abounds here, from the open kitchen to the local art displayed on the walls. Even wine sales are a mark of the owners' creativity. That's because a city ordinance prohibits sales of alcoholic beverages within 100 feet of a church. Since a Methodist church sits directly across the street from the restaurant, the owners get around the law by inviting all guests into a "wine boutique" in back of the restaurant, 101 feet from the church. Guests enjoy a wine tasting and a chance to buy the wine their waiter will later bring to the table.

O'STEEN'S RESTAURANT
205 Anastasia Blvd.
(904) 829-6974

There are those who say that the fried shrimp at this restaurant are the best in Northeast Florida. Ditto the Minorcan clam chowder, which is beloved by many as a local delicacy. The Minorcans, by the way, came to St. Augustine as indentured servants, and their descendants still form a small core of the city's population. Their tomato-based clam chowder certainly lives on, and you can taste the history in every bite. Plan to arrive at O'Steen's as early as possible; there's always a wait, and the restaurant doesn't take reservations. Stick it out—you won't be disappointed. Closed Sunday and Monday.

SALTWATER COWBOYS
299 Dondanville Rd.
(904) 471-2332
www.saltwatercowboys.com

Drive south of town to this restaurant perched over a salt marsh. The food is backwater-heaven, and the restaurant, which is reminiscent of a turn-of-the-century fish camp, houses a mash-up of willow furniture and rusted tin ceilings. Eat on the outdoor deck if you can, an especially picturesque option come sunset. The menu includes oysters, crawfish, and pit barbeque, which somehow make sense against the backdrop of old wooden floors and snakeskins hanging on the walls. Better yet, try the Florida Cracker Combo of frogs' legs, cooter, and alligator tail. Now that's country!

Take a Tour
ANASTASIA STATE PARK
1340A Highway A1A South
(904) 461-2033
www.floridastateparks.org/anastasia
This is one of Florida's most popular state parks. Much of it used to be a coquina quarry for the Spanish during colonial times when huge blocks of coquina were cut from the earth and hauled by slaves over to St. Augustine to build structures such as the Castillo de San Marcos. Park naturalists give guided tours of the Spanish quarries and the park's salt marsh. Call about a month in advance to book a quarry walk. You can also take a self-guided tour through the oak hammock. While you're there, have lunch at Island Joe's camp store, rental shop, and grill, voted the second best lunch restaurant by the people of St. Augustine via the *St. Augustine Record*.

FLAGLER'S LEGACY TOURS
Flagler College
Tours depart from the lobby at 74 King St.
(904) 829-6481
legacy.flagler.edu/Tours-sp8.html
This is your chance to see the inside of Henry Flagler's once-famous Hotel Ponce de Leon, now Flagler College (named a National Historic Landmark in 2006). Beautiful woodwork from the 1880s remains, as do the original Tiffany windows and ornate murals. There's also a small museum featuring paintings and artifacts from when the building was a grand hotel. Your college-student tour guide will give you an Insider's perspective on Henry Flagler. Tours depart at 10 a.m. and 2 p.m. April 30 through September 1. Purchase tickets 15 minutes before the tour or at Flagler's Legacy located at 59 St. George St.; $7 for adults, $1 for children under the age of 12, $5 for St. Augustine residents with ID.

GHOST TOURS OF ST. AUGUSTINE
2 St. George St.
(888) 461-1009
www.ghosttoursofstaugustine.com
A city as old as St. Augustine is bound to have its share of ghosts. Ghost Tours of St. Augustine will introduce you to them by way of a 90-minute walking tour that begins nightly at 8 p.m. Many companies give these ghostly tours, and it's hard to say which one is best since much of the experience depends on the theatric ability of your tour guide (Ghost Tours of St. Augustine employs 20 excellent, professional storytellers). If you have little ones in tow, the company offers family-oriented ghost tours designed not to scare the wits out of your children. The group was voted #1 Guided Tour in Florida by the readers of *Florida Living* magazine and has been featured on the Discovery and Travel Channels.

RIPLEY'S SIGHTSEEING TRAINS
(800) 226-6545
www.redtrains.com

OLD TOWN TROLLEY TOURS
(800) 868-7482
www.trolleytours.com/st-augustine
These two trolley-train companies provide a great way to see the St. Augustine sights, especially in the heat of summer. Tour guides/drivers amuse guests with interesting St. Augustine stories while ferrying them through narrow streets and lanes. You can get off and on when you please, and one ticket is good for three consecutive days. Buying a ticket at either one of these companies is a solid vacation investment.

i Up for an adventure? Try parasailing. Three people can fly side by side at the same time. And fly you will, up to 1,400 feet into the blue. Call Smile High Parasail at (904) 819-0980 to book your trip.

MARINELAND
9600 Ocean Shore Blvd.
(904) 471-1111, (877) 933-3402
www.marineland.net

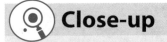

Close-up

Bridge of Lions

For more than 20 years now, St. Augustine residents have been arguing over how best to re-bridge the gap over the **Matanzas River,** a gap currently spanned by the rapidly aging beauty, the **Bridge of Lions.**

The Bridge of Lions, which opened in 1927, is a much-photographed, much-loved St. Augustine landmark—but it's also outdated. The reason this matters in a city filled with operational antiquities is because the bridge plays a vital role as a transportation link between downtown St. Augustine and the northern part of Anastasia Island. Yet the bridge is suffering from structural problems and no longer meets safety requirements.

In 1998 bridge-lovers banded together and formed a group called **Save Our Bridge.** Members scored a major coup when they got the Bridge of Lions listed on the National Register of Historic Places. They feel that there's no better gateway into or out of the nation's oldest city than the stately drawbridge with its four tile-roofed towers, antique light poles, and proud Italian-marble lions standing guard. The original bridge, they say, is especially picturesque when decked out in Christmas lights or adorned with American flags waving from every light post. A larger, more modern span, they argue, would forever alter the landscape and only serve to dump more traffic into the already crowded, narrow streets of downtown St. Augustine.

The opposition is not moved. Many opponents live on Anastasia Island and have to use the bridge every day to reach the mainland. They know all too well how frustrating it can be when the Bridge of Lions closes abruptly because the ancient drawbridge gets stuck in the "up" position. These are the people who must wait in long lines of traffic for the bridge to reopen, only to find themselves late to work, late to class, and in a foul temper. Opponents argue that there's nothing historic about the Bridge of Lions. As far as they're concerned, the fact that it's listed on the National Register of Historic Places only means someone did a good job filling out a lot of paperwork. They want the state to build a new, higher, fixed-span bridge over the Matanzas River.

In 1999 state transportation officials all but ended this debate when they announced plans to "rehabilitate" the Bridge of Lions. Three years later, when construction plans were finalized, St. Augustine residents finally learned just what "rehabilitate" means: as little as 5 to 10 percent of the original 1927 bridge would actually be saved and restored. The rest would be new construction made to look just as the bridge looked when it opened in 1927. This has given new life to the opposition, which argues that the state is basically building a new bridge and should therefore make it as modern as possible.

In February 2005, the state forged ahead with plans to rehabilitate the bridge, at a cost of $76 million, with financing coming from Bridge Replacement Funds, which included both federal and state funding. To begin, a temporary bridge was built just north of the existing bridge. In mid-2006 crews began disassembling the old bridge, careful to retain the structures that qualified it for the National Historic Register in the first place. Piece by piece the bridge was rehabilitated and restored to its 1920s glory, with details such as period streetlights and a hand railing reminiscent of the original one set in place in 1927.

The City of St. Augustine took great pains to restore the lion statues standing guard at the mouth of the bridge, removing them before construction, cleaning them, and storing them far from harm's way.

Once the bridge is complete, the city will return the lions to their rightful posts. At the time of publication, the bridge was scheduled to reopen, to great fanfare, in 2010. Check the Bridge of Lions Rehabilitation Web site, www.fdotbridgeoflions.com, to find out the exact dates and make a point to be one of the first to drive across this gloriously restored span.

When it opened in 1938, Marineland was the world's first oceanarium. The owners built it primarily as an underwater movie studio, and classics like *Tarzan of the Apes* and parts of *Creature from the Black Lagoon* were filmed here. But the oceanarium's real mission began when the public started to visit. Tourists loved the place and flocked there for a chance to see marine life up close. In its heyday in the fifties and sixties, up to half a million people visited Marineland every year, making it the biggest tourist attraction in Florida at the time.

But slowly things started to change. I-95 opened, making it faster and easier for tourists to bypass Marineland and drive farther south to the newly opened SeaWorld and Disney World. Tourist dollars drained away, and by the eighties the resort was struggling to keep its head above water. The park's owners filed for bankruptcy in 1998, and part of the resort was eventually acquired by the Trust for Public Lands and an Atlanta developer. In 2000 the foundation that owned the oceanarium filed for bankruptcy and was purchased by the same Atlanta developer who had bought part of the resort 1998.

Marineland then returned to basics and tapped into the one resource that made it so famous in the first place: the oceanarium. Guests were allowed to SCUBA or snorkel in the oceanarium for the first time. They were also allowed to swim with the park's dolphins.

Today Marineland is back on top, offering an intimate family experience that larger theme parks just can't touch.

Getting There

Marineland is located about an hour south of Jacksonville. The easiest way to get there from Jacksonville is to drive south on I-95 until you reach exit 305/SR 206. Turn left, heading east on 206, until you reach Highway A1A. Turn right on A1A and head south for 7 miles. Marineland will be on your left. The park is open every day from 8:30 a.m. to 4:30 p.m. except Thanksgiving and Christmas.

What to Do

For starters, children will love the dolphin show, which includes a chance to pet and hold out a fish to feed a dolphin. Kids also love the sea lion show and the park's nine African penguins. Are your kids curious about what the marine life does once the sun goes down? Then sign them up for Twilight Adventure, an evening exploration into the nocturnal habits of sea creatures.

The more adventurous will want to SCUBA or snorkel in Marineland's 1.3 million-gallon reef oceanarium. The oceanarium is home to more than 500 marine creatures, including a 100-pound black drum, two stingrays, and three rare sea turtles. The oceanarium is 18 feet deep and is continuously fed by seawater from the Atlantic. Wave to your family and friends as they watch your underwater adventure from the park's observation window, which is a great photo spot.

Finally, don't miss the chance to swim with the dolphins. It's one thing to sit in the stands and watch them perform aerial tricks, quite another to be in the water rubbing their backs. Marineland's Dolphin Conservation Center offers up-close-and-personal swim-with-the-dolphin encounters in their Quest program, as well as a deep-water swimming experience called the Immersion. One especially interesting new program, the Enhanced Immersion and Training Adventure, teaches guests how to apply positive reinforcement training techniques used with the center's dolphins to training your four-legged pets at home. The truly ambitious will love Marineland's Trainer for a Day program where everyday Joes get the chance to try their hands at one of the coolest jobs in the world.

Recently, Marineland partnered with Ripple Effect Ecotours (look for their profile in the Attractions & Tours chapter) and the University of Florida's Whitney Lab to offer kayak tours through the Guana Tolomato Matanzas Natural Estuarine Research Reserve. These remarkably informative tours are $50 per person and include admission into the Marineland Dolphin Conservation Center, a guided tour, and photos taken by your naturalist guide.

General admission to Marineland is $8 for those 13 and above, $3.50 for children, $6.75 for those over 60.

AMELIA ISLAND

Getting There

Some say the best thing about Amelia Island, 32 miles northeast of Jacksonville, is getting there. Getting there means driving the Buccaneer Trail (SR 105/A1A), one of the most scenic two-lane highways in the South. Roll down the windows and wend your way along miles of pristine marshes, thick oak hammocks, and tiny marinas. You'll see snowy egrets and, if you're lucky, a great blue heron. You'll also cross a number of bridges, where locals line up with rod and reel to fish some of Florida's finest waters. For nature lovers, this is as good as it gets in Northeast Florida.

To get to the Buccaneer Trail from Downtown, take I-95 north to the Heckscher Drive/SR105E, exit (358-A). Turn right, heading east onto Heckscher Drive (the Buccaneer Trail), and follow it for about 30 miles until you reach Fernandina Beach.

Once you get to Fernandina, the main town on Amelia Island, stroll along Centre Street and enjoy the shops and restaurants. Amelia Island calls itself the birthplace of the modern shrimping industry, so be sure to check out the shrimp boats on the dock, and enjoy some boiled, fried, or grilled shrimp or another local delicacy, a grouper sandwich.

Amelia Island was named among *Condé Nast's* Top 10 North American Islands from 2007 through 2009.

A Short History

Frenchman Jean Ribault is the first European credited with landing on Amelia Island. When he arrived in May 1562, he named the island "Isle de Mai." But the French didn't hold on to the island for long. In 1565 Pedro Menendez, headquartered in St. Augustine, wiped out the French, claimed the island for Spain, and renamed it Santa Maria. Spain held on to it (and to Florida) for

nearly 200 years, at which point the English took over. The English named the island Amelia Island after King George II's daughter.

In 1783 Britain gave Amelia Island, and all of Florida, back to Spain, and from 1783 to 1821 Florida was a mighty unstable place in which to live. Amelia Island is proof of that. This tiny island changed hands at least three times as Spain tried to hang on to it. U.S.-backed Patriots took over for a short time, as did a Scotsman named Sir Gregor MacGregor and even Mexican rebels (i.e., pirates).

Pirates/smugglers had their heyday here in 1807, when President Thomas Jefferson signed the Embargo Act, stopping all foreign imports, especially from Britain and France. Pirates, working from the natural deepwater port of Fernandina, found a lucrative trade breaking that embargo.

Life calmed down considerably when Spain ceded Florida to the United States in 1821. Forty years later, in 1861, the Confederate States of America took control, but only for a year.

Local historians have nicknamed Amelia Island the Isle of Eight Flags because of the eight flags that flew here: Spanish, French, English, Patriot, Green Cross of Florida (Gregor MacGregor), Mexican Pirate, Confederate, and, finally, U.S. Pirate, who by the way are said to have buried a still-unfound treasure on Amelia "beneath an oak that is pierced by a hanging chain." If you find it, let us know.

Where to Stay

If you're staying the night on this 13-mile barrier island, two world-class resorts—Amelia Island Plantation and The Ritz-Carlton, Amelia Island—offer stellar accommodations. There are also a dozen or so B&Bs. Our list is by no means conclusive, but it will help you start planning your stay. (Check the Accommodations chapter for more lodging options.)

AMELIA ISLAND WILLIAMS HOUSE
103 South Ninth St.
(904) 277-2328, (800) 414-9258
www.williamshouse.com

To many people the Williams House is everything a B&B should be: a historic home from the 1850s, beautifully decorated from top to bottom and filled with antiques. The inn has won all sorts of awards, including designation as a Historic Landmark Site, the highest honor awarded by the Florida Department of State, because the owners keep it in such great shape. Book a room around the Christmas holidays when the proprietor turns the inn into something out of a Dickens novel. There's a lot of history here. For instance, Jefferson Davis, president of the Confederacy, is said to have stayed at the Williams House. Around the same time, the house was also a stop on the Underground Railroad.

ELIZABETH POINTE LODGE
98 South Fletcher Ave.
(904) 277-4851, (800) 772-3359
www.elizabethpointelodge.com
If you think you're in Cape Cod, we forgive you. This oceanfront inn looks more New England than Florida, which only adds to its appeal. The Nantucket shingle-style Elizabeth Pointe Lodge, voted the #2 hotel in the United States in the 2008 *Condé Nast Traveler* Reader's Choice Awards, has 25 rooms, each with a private bath and decorated in old-Florida or maritime themes. A beautiful porch, complete with one long row of white wood rocking chairs, overlooks the ocean. The breakfast here always features fresh fruit, pastries, and something hot—plus you can gaze at the ocean while you eat. The owners are so good at what they do that they run seminars to teach aspiring innkeepers the ins-and-outs of running an inn.

FLORIDA HOUSE INN
20 and 22 South Third St.
(800) 258-3301
www.floridahouse.com
Built in 1857, this is the oldest operating hotel in Florida. The inn once had 25 rooms and no indoor plumbing, but today each of the 22 rooms has a private bath, some complete with claw-foot tubs. In deference to the inn's past, some of the rooms still have working fireplaces, and you can

still rock on the inn's wide porches or lounge in the shady backyard—a cool, quiet oasis anytime of day. The Florida House also operates a popular restaurant in the dining room, which serves delicious home-style Southern cooking. Check out the little bar, reminiscent of an English pub, downstairs. Pets are welcome in the inn. Tip: Add some zip to your trip by renting scooters to tour Fernandina Beach.

GREYFIELD INN
Cumberland Island
(904) 261-6408, (866) 401-8581
www.greyfieldinn.com
Greyfield is located on Cumberland Island, Georgia, the barrier island just north of Amelia, across the Cumberland Sound. A private ferry, the *Miss Lucy*, docks at the Fernandina Beach Harbour Marina and is one of only a few ways to reach the island. Cumberland Island is part national seashore and part private resort, and is where John Kennedy Jr. and Carolyn Bissette married. The Kennedys held their reception at the Greyfield Inn, an old, white house built in 1900 for Thomas Carnegie's daughter. Carnegie's granddaughter, Gogo Fuller, a jewelry artist, now operates the inn. Staying here is a special experience, a chance to live like old money in a bygone era. The meals are top-drawer, as are the accommodations, plus Greyfield offers Cumberland Island as its playground. Book your reservations early. People make plans months in advance for a chance to stay here. With reservations, you can also visit the Greyfield Inn just for dinner or for a day visit.

i Looking to rent a condo on Amelia Island? There are a number of realty companies to serve your needs, and the Amelia Island Chamber of Commerce will help you find them. Go to www.islandchamber.com for information.

Attractions
AMELIA ISLAND LIGHTHOUSE
Lighthouse Circle
www.lighthousefriends.com

Built in 1838, this is the oldest lighthouse still standing in Florida. The structure is currently closed to the public, but you can drive up and see this little gem. It's smaller than the St. Augustine lighthouse because it was meant to guide ships in the Fernandina River and Cumberland Sound, not in the ocean. The lighthouse has weathered hurricanes (and a move from Georgia) and is now located in a residential neighborhood on Egan's Creek.

The City of Fernandina Beach offers tours of the lighthouse every first and third Wednesday of the month for $5 per adult and $3 for children under 12 years old. Lighthouse management requires a minimum of 10 people and a maximum of 25 for each tour. To take the tour, board the bus leaving from the Atlantic Recreation Center (2500 Atlantic Ave.) promptly at 10 a.m. on the day of the tour. Please note that the tour does not allow access to the top of the lighthouse. In addition to the tours, the lighthouse is open to the public on Saturday from 11 a.m. to 2 p.m. To learn more about the tours, visit www.ameliaisland.com.

AMELIA ISLAND MUSEUM OF HISTORY
233 South Third St.
(904) 261-7378
www.ameliamuseum.org

Located in the old Nassau County Jail, the Museum of History is the best place to hear about the backstory on Amelia Island from the Timucuans to modern day. Knowledgeable guides will fill you in on all the facts during both museum tours and walking tours of the historic district during which guests get a peek inside several churches and historic homes.

The Amelia Island Museum of History is the first spoken-history museum in the state and continues its story-telling tradition through a variety of tours. On tour in particular, the Fernandina Beach Pub Crawl, takes you through four popular, notorious, and historic pubs. Your ticket gets you a drink at each establishment and an earful of colorful stories. Tours run on Thursday evenings at 5:30 p.m. and are $25 per person (must be 21). Tours depart from the historic train depot in downtown Fernandina Beach. Call (904) 261-7378 ext. 105 for reservations.

Not so interested in the city's boozy past? Then sign up for a Headstones Ghost Walking Tour and experience Amelia Island's ghost stories first-hand as your creep through dark streets with a master storyteller. One-hour tours begin at 6 p.m. every Friday and meet in the cemetery behind St. Peters Episcopal Church (801 Atlantic Ave.). Purchase tickets in advance at the museum. Tickets are $10 for adults, $5 for students.

CENTRE STREET HISTORIC DISTRICT
Fernandina Beach

Centre Street, the main shopping street in Fernandina Beach, runs through a 50-block area of downtown that's listed on the National Register of Historic Places. As you stroll along Centre Street, notice the circa-1870s, red brick buildings that once housed Fernandina's general stores and businesses. Walk the side streets off Centre Street to get an eyeful of the city's wealth of Victorian architecture.

Once lousy with pirates, Fernandina became downright respectable once it cleared its streets of those eye-patch-wearing rapscallions. The town saw such a turnaround that, by the 1800s, vacationing Northern tourists were flocking to the island by steamship.

As you stroll along North Sixth and South Seventh Streets, make note of the gingerbread adorning the mansions and cottages. Be sure to walk inside the Florida House Inn on South Third Street, the oldest surviving tourist hotel in Florida, and the white clapboard First Missionary Baptist Church on South Ninth, the oldest African-American church in the state.

Unfortunately, Fernandina's early heyday was short-lived. Once Henry Flagler arrived in St. Augustine in the 1880s, he decided to build a railroad south from St. Augustine to Key West, leaving Fernandina Beach off line. But historians say that decision may have actually saved many of the Victorian buildings in Fernandina, which otherwise could have been razed in the name of progress.

FORT CLINCH STATE PARK
2601 Atlantic Ave.
(904) 277-7274
www.floridastateparks.org/fortclinch
Fort Clinch is located on the northern tip of Amelia Island, with the Atlantic Ocean to its east and a coastal hardwood hammock to the west. It's the only state park on Amelia Island that offers camping. The federal government built the fort in 1847; 14 years later, at the start of the Civil War, Confederate troops took control of it. But they didn't stay long. In 1862, one year after they arrived, General Robert E. Lee ordered his soldiers to withdraw because he needed them elsewhere. After the Civil War, Fort Clinch didn't see much action until 1898, when it was called to duty for several months during the Spanish-American War. Today re-enactors don costumes on the first weekend of every month and live like 1864 garrison soldiers—maintaining the fort, cooking their own meals, and taking turns on sentry duty. There are also Confederate garrison reenactments on selected weekends in March, April, and October. (Dates may vary, so check the Web site or call ahead.) Besides the fort itself, Fort Clinch State Park is rich with nature trails, a fishing pier, and beachfront. The beach here, by the way, is a favorite place to find sharks' teeth.

Activities

KAYAK AMELIA
13030 Heckscher Dr.
(904) 251-0016, (888) 305-2925 (30-KAYAK)
www.KayakAmelia.com
Looking for an adventure? Hop in a kayak and see Amelia Island from the water. You'll feel like a Timucuan Indian as you paddle through the marshes and slip silently by wading egrets. The guided trips include paddling instructions for beginners, all the equipment you'll need, and knowledgeable guides ready to answer your natural history questions. All you need to bring is the sunscreen. Kayak Amelia has also just started offering Bike Eco-tours of the uplands hammock of Talbot Islands State Parks. Riders take to the gently rolling trails on comfy Trek bikes, listen for

native songbirds, and keep an eye out for gopher tortoises and the ubiquitous local armadillos. Reservations are required, so plan in advance if you don't want to miss out. Rumor has it there are cookies, as if you needed more incentive.

i Amelia Island is famous for its bird-watching. Spring and summer bring the most colorful visitors, including painted buntings, summer tanagers, and, the local favorite, roseate spoonbills.

KELLY SEAHORSE RANCH
7500 First Coast Hwy.
(904) 491-5166
www.kellyranchinc.com
Saddle up! These guided group rides are slow and safe enough for beginners. You'll see a bounty of island creatures on your trip, especially as you wind your way through the coastal hammock. These trips are for adults only (the minimum age is 13 and they do not make exceptions), and there are other weight, height, and physical restrictions so read through the Web site fully before booking. The ranch is open from 8 a.m. to 5 p.m. daily (except Mondays) throughout the year, including Christmas Day and New Year's Day. Reservations are a must.

WINDWARD SAILING SCHOOL
714 Beech St.
(904) 261-9125
www.windwardsailing.com
Fernandina is a great place to learn to sail. A mild climate and steady winds make it possible to sail year-round, plus the natural deepwater port means that beginners never have to lose sight of land. A retired naval commander runs the school, which is certified by the American Sailing Association. Windward offers classes for all levels of experience and interest including Introduction to Sailing, Basic Keelboat, Basic Coastal Cruising, Bareboat Chartering, Coastal Navigation, Advanced Coastal Cruising, Celestial Navigation, ASA Instructor Qualification Clinic, Small Marine Diesel Engine Maintenance, and Marine Weather. The American Sailing Association awarded Windward Sailing Outstanding School of the Year for 2008.

Where to Eat

BEECH STREET GRILL
801 Beech St.
(904) 277-3662
www.beechstreetgrill.com

In the mood for porcini-dusted, oven-roasted Atlantic salmon over three-mushroom risotto with black-truffle butter? How about the house signature lump crab cake with house remoulade? Meals like these have made this award-winning restaurant famous. Don't bother trying to get in without a reservation, though.

FLORIDA HOUSE INN & FRISKY MERMAID BAR & GRILLE
22 South Third St.
(800) 258-3301 or (904) 261-3300
www.floridahouseinn.com

The Florida House Inn has both a sporadically open restaurant and a bar and grill, and it's important to keep them separate. If you can catch the restaurant when it's open, you'll get to experience real Southern cooking served board-inghouse-style with all the fried chicken, mashed potatoes, and biscuits you can eat. Wash it all down with sweet tea, a true southern tradition. The restaurant is popular with locals, especially firefighters, so you know it's good. The inn's bar and grill, The Frisky Mermaid, is not so sought-after for food, but people love the weekly Song-writers' Night every Wednesday when local and regional songwriters compete for cash prizes by composing songs based on weekly themes.

JOE'S SECOND STREET BISTRO
14 South Second St.
(904) 321-2558
www.joesbistro.com

This cozy little restaurant is located in the heart of the historic district in a restored house that dates back to Theodore Roosevelt's presidency. The menu is filled with popular, well-prepared dishes like grilled New York strip steak with three sauces. The bistro also serves linguine with shrimp and scallops in a white-wine sauce, and grouper filet grilled in cornhusk with roasted jalapeno-lime-cilantro butter. Eat inside by the fireplace or outside in a charming courtyard next to the fountain; whichever you choose, you're bound to leave the table sated.

LE CLOS
20 South Second St.
(904) 261-8100
www.leclos.com

Combine delicious French Provençal food with a romantic 1906 cottage bathed in candlelight and you have the makings of a memorable night on the town. Chef/owner Katherine Ewing received degrees in pastry and cuisine from Le Cordon Bleu and L'Ecole de Gastronomie Francaise Ritz-Escoffier in Paris and trained at the Ritz Hotel in Paris, and it shows. She does amazing things with seafood. Reservations are a must because this cottage is . . . shall we say . . . intimate.

SALT AT THE RITZ-CARLTON
4750 Amelia Island Parkway
(904) 277-1028
www.ritzcarlton.com (search "Salt")

Salt is the place to go for fine dining on Amelia Island. Whet your appetite on a Hawaiian blue prawn cocktail or salt-cured fois gras before moving on to Colorado rack of lamb or Painted Hills beef and Maine lobster. Make the evening one to remember by indulging in Salt's private dining experience where small groups can arrange to eat in the kitchen (with special reservations) and watch as the chef creates memory-making meals. (See the Accommodations chapter for more on A Seat in the Kitchen.) One of only four AAA five-diamond restaurants in Florida, Salt is located on the ocean at The Ritz-Carlton, Amelia Island Resort.

OKEFENOKEE NATIONAL WILDLIFE REFUGE

VISITOR CENTER
(912) 496-3331
www.fws.gov/okefenokee

Why travel halfway around the world to immerse yourself in exotic locales when you can drive 45 minutes northwest of Jacksonville to the 400,000-acre Okefenokee Wildlife Refuge? Located on the Florida-Georgia border, this stark, watery landscape looks like the land where time began. All that's missing are the dinosaurs, which are actually here in a sense in their alligator descendants. The Okefenokee is the largest swamp in North America and was saved for posterity in 1937 by President Franklin Roosevelt, who declared it a wildlife refuge. The swamp was once a major hunting ground for the Creek and Seminole Indians, who named it "land of trembling earth" because of how the small trees and bushes tremble when you stomp on the swamp's peat-bog islands.

Getting There

There are three entrances to the swamp, which is roughly 40 miles long and 20 miles wide. The east entrance, near Folkston, Georgia, is the easiest to reach from Jacksonville. Take I-95 north from Downtown to I-295. Take I-295 heading west, and get off at the US 1 exit. Turn right onto US 1, and head north through Callahan and Hilliard until you reach Folkston. In Folkston, go left at the second light onto Main Street. Then turn left at the second light onto SR 121 South (also known as the Okefenokee Parkway). Head south for 7 miles to the east entrance marked by the big wooden Okefenokee Wildlife Refuge sign on the right.

What to Do

There are three major things to do in the Okefenokee Swamp: boat, view wildlife, and camp. For starters, stop at the visitor center at the east entrance for free brochures and information to help you enjoy your visit. Then drive the 9-mile loop road at the east entrance to get an idea of what the park is all about. Chances are very good that you'll see an alligator or two on this drive. You'll also pass the camping and picnic areas.

Bring your own boat and tour the swamp, rent one at the entrance of the park, or sign up for a guided half-day, full-day, or overnight boat trip

with Okefenokee Adventures. For a real adventure, camp overnight in the swamp on one of seven designated overnight platforms that sleep up to 20. Just don't roll off! Alligators are plentiful around these platforms because, unfortunately, they've learned that they're good places to find food. There's also a campground on terra firma operated by the U.S. Fish and Wildlife Service, which you can return to after your half-day or full-day boat tour. To make camping reservations call (912) 496-3331.

The swamp water looks like iced tea because it's full of tannin, a compound derived from decaying tree bark. In its deepest spot, the water in the swamp is only about 9 feet, and in the summer it can be even shallower. Ninety percent of the water in the Okefenokee comes from rainfall, and when there's a drought the swamp dries up. Forest fires become a big problem, and paddle trails become unnavigable.

As you boat in the swamp, keep an eye out for the Suwannee Canal, dug by the forest industry in the late 1800s in an attempt to drain the swamp. Walk around Billy's Island, former home of Seminole Billy Bowlegs, and take pictures of the bald cypress trees. Learn what life was like in the swamp before the Civil War at the Chesser Island Homestead, a historic swamp family home built in 1927 by Tom Chesser, a descendent of the area's original 1950s homesteader, W. T. Chesser.

But it's the wildlife that most people come to the Okefenokee to see. The swamp is home to Florida black bears, bobcats, otters, raccoons, opossums, and alligators. It's also a well-known haven for birds, with frequent visits from such rare species as ospreys, bald eagles, red-cockaded woodpeckers, and great blue herons. The refuge is home to 50 species of fish and more than 600 species of plants.

Kayaks, canoes, and motorboats can be rented in the park near the east entrance through Okefenokee Adventures; call (866) 843-7926 or visit www.okefenokeeadventures.com for more information.

ICHETUCKNEE SPRINGS STATE PARK

12087 S.W. US 27, Fort White
(386) 497-4690
www.floridastateparks.org/ichetucknee springs

Floating in an inner tube down the Ichetucknee River makes for one of the best day trips around, plus it's a unique North Florida experience—best shared with friends and family on a hot July day, when just walking across a parking lot to your car makes you swelter. The name is Native American, and it's rumored to mean "pond of the beaver." We've never seen any beavers while tubing down the Ichetucknee, but they're probably around somewhere. The water in this crystal-clear, aquifer-fed river is 73 degrees year-round, a little icy on your bum, but a numb bum is worth all of the natural beauty and good, clean fun that tubing down this river brings.

The concept is simple: rent a big inner tube on-site or nearby, jump in the water, drape your limbs over the sides of your tube, and let the river do the work. The slow current will carry you down river, giving you plenty of time to enjoy the scenery, which includes lots of cypress trees, cliffs, swamps, and even a famous blue hole. Bring a mask and snorkel, or just lay back in your inner tube and enjoy the view of the treetops.

If you plan to travel down the Ichetucknee any time of year besides summer, we recommend that you do it in a canoe or while wearing a wetsuit. We also recommend that you start early. To protect the river, park officials limit the number of people who can tube each day. Only 2,250 people are allowed to tube the river from the midpoint, and only 750 people are allowed to tube the entire length of the river on a daily basis. Be nice to the river while you are in it. Don't leave behind any trash, and don't destroy the vegetation. If a lot of damage occurs, park officials will further limit the number of people who can tube down the river.

Getting There

From Jacksonville, take I-10 west to the US 90 exit. Follow US 90 to Lake City and SR 41. Follow SR 41 south to SR 47 south. Follow the signs, which will lead you straight to the park. It takes about 90 minutes to get to the Ichetucknee from Jacksonville.

There are two park entrances, a north entrance and a south entrance. Most people use the south entrance in the summer. Park your car and carry your tube to the tram, an open-air bus that takes you through the woods to the midpoint launch area where you can jump into the water and begin your float. The trip from the midpoint area to the end point, where you must get out, takes about 90 minutes. Another tram will take you from this area back to your car in the main parking lot.

If you want to tube the entire river, you need to arrive early because only the first 750 people are allowed to do so. Floating the entire river takes about three and a half hours, and the setup is a bit complicated. You need to have a driver drop you and your tubes off at the north entrance. Then the driver must take the car to the main parking lot at the south entrance. A shuttle van will return the driver to the north entrance to rejoin his or her party. At the end of your full-river float, a tram will take you back to your car in the south parking lot. The park charges $5 per person to float from the north entrance; children under age five are free, or $6 per group of two to eight people tubing from the south entrance during off season (Labor Day through Memorial Day). One more planning note: the latest you can start your float from the north entrance is four hours before sunset. There is no tram service from Memorial Day through Labor Day, and during those times tubing is only accessible via the south entrance.

Tube Rental

Nothing is rented inside the park. You have to stop and rent your tubes and/or snorkel gear from vendors outside the park entrance or bring it all from home. But don't worry; vendors are not hard to find. Just look for the roadside shops with hundreds of huge black and yellow inner tubes and rubber rafts. Some vendors are cheaper than others, but not by much. The vendors will even tie the tubes to the roof of your car, and you don't have to drive the tubes back at the end of the day. The vendors come to the park and collect them.

i It seems that every time we go tubing on the Ichetucknee, we see some poor soul who's dropped his or her car keys in the water while floating down the river. Needless to say, this is a huge drag. Keep your car keys on a lanyard around your neck or pinned inside your bathing suit.

Where to Stay

The easiest way to overnight near the springs is to camp. There aren't any hotels nearby, just farm country. Ichetucknee Springs is a day park only, so there are no camping facilities within its boundaries. The closest state campground is 12 miles away at Oleno State Park. Oleno has lots of camping options, but you can also rent one of the park's 17 cabins for $25 to $150 per night from September through April. From May through August, all 17 cabins must be rented together as a group, but the cost for the whole group is only $300 plus tax, which is actually quite a value. This cost also includes the use of the dining hall and recreation hall. Visit www .floridastateparks.org/oleno or call (386) 497-4690 for information and reservations.

Where to Eat

The park runs a large concession stand inside the south entrance, but the lines are usually long and the food is nothing to write home about. Do yourself a favor: pack a picnic lunch and eat at one of the many picnic tables inside the park. There are also grills—just remember to bring the charcoal. Large groups may want to reserve a covered picnic pavilion.

RELOCATION

N ow it's time to change hats. With this chapter, I'll take off my tour guide hat and don my Chamber of Commerce hat. Consider this chapter, and all the ones to follow, part of an Insiders' relocation guide with helpful information to make your move to Jacksonville that much easier.

Really, who wouldn't love Jacksonville? The skies are blue, the light is crisp and clear, and in January, when winter winds are causing misery elsewhere, there's no place I'd rather be.

Because of the great weather (if you can stand the summer humidity) we Floridians tend to be more fit than our cousins to the north. While other folks in other cities are busy being couch potatoes, Jacksonville residents are outside running and biking and burning up calories thanks, in part, to the fact that Jacksonville has the largest urban park system in the United States.

Let's not underestimate the importance of being able to find gainful employment. You'll be happy to know that it's fairly easy to find a job that you'll actually like in this city. Other people must realize this, too; according to *Inc.* magazine and *Expansion Management* magazine, Jacksonville is one of the hottest cities in America for both business and quality of life. And you'll be bringing more of your paycheck home thanks to the absence of state income taxes.

But many newcomers to the city are overwhelmed by the size of the city and the number of choices in neighborhoods. Each neighborhood offers its own attractions and personality, making choosing a challenge. The neighborhoods have also changed significantly in the past decade. Downtown has become much more multi-use and hip, is now considered the hub of the city's arts scene, and offers exciting urban housing options for couples and young professionals.

So, to save other people the frustration that comes from having to choose among so many options (and the gas it takes to drive all over the city looking for your ideal neighborhood), I'll start the relocation section of this book with an overview of neighborhoods and the types of folks who tend to gravitate to each.

i The State of Florida offers a homestead exemption to Florida residents who own and occupy a home by January 1 of any given year. The exemption is $25,000 (and could be up to $50,000) off the assessed value of your home. In most counties, you must renew this exemption annually.

THE URBAN CORE (a.k.a. Downtown): Attracts turnkey hipsters, City Hall up-and-comers, and DINKS (dual-income no kids)

For a long time, Jacksonville's urban core was largely composed of low-income communities and Downtown office buildings. But that's all changed. Today, the urban core is a hotbed of real estate activity, especially with the erection of several new riverfront high-rises. Hipsters love the new luxury riverfront buildings like The Peninsula, The Strand, and Berkman Plaza. This high-rise riverfront housing with an urban edge has completely changed the tenor of the Northbank and Southbank. Think 24-hour concierge service, yacht slips, heated indoor and outdoor swimming pools, golf simulators, and spas with saunas and steam rooms.

The condos sell for from $200,000 to the millions, but the amenities combined with the nighttime views of Downtown are worth every penny.

Across the river, in Downtown-proper, many formerly vacant buildings are seeing new life as lofts, and older buildings, like the ones along Bay and Forsyth Streets, are considered "the" place to live by many cosmopolitan 20- and 30-somethings.

It's still a little hard to have brunch or buy a latte in the urban core come the weekend, when all the Monday-through-Friday businesses have closed, but city leaders hope that as more people move to Downtown, more shops and restaurants will open to take care of those needs.

SPRINGFIELD: Attracts urban pioneers, community organizers, and HGTV junkies

Historic Springfield is the largest residential historic district in Florida, with wide tree-lined streets and architecturally distinguished houses. You have to be an urban pioneer to live here, but the gumption pays off. Springfield used to be Jacksonville's premier neighborhood, but over the years it fell into deep disrepair. Many once-beautiful Victorians were either condemned or became rooming houses or crack houses. Today preservationists like those at SPAR (Springfield Preservation and Revitalization Council) are helping to revive Springfield house-by-house. Located just north of the Downtown business district, Springfield is the sort of place where you can buy a tumbledown Victorian for about $60,000, sometimes even with city aid. Renovation costs are significant because in many cases the entire house needs to be rebuilt, but often the folks buying these houses are handy and do a lot of the work themselves. The neighborhood attracts a mix of artists, educators, developers, and people who not only work in the mayor's office but also care deeply about the revitalization of this precious historic district.

i Want to work for the City of Jacksonville? Check out the job listings on the city's Web site, www.coj.net.

RIVERSIDE and AVONDALE: Attracts preservationists, artists, and traditionalists

Even for the residents of these historic neighborhoods, it is hard to tell where Riverside ends and Avondale begins. The district is bordered on the west by Highway 17 and on the east by the St. Johns River. The bulk of it lies between I-10 to the north and the Ortega River to the south. Riverside and Avondale are both well-established neighborhoods with historic homes and majestic oak trees draped in Spanish moss.

Riverside offers a short commute to Downtown, and the houses range from Arts and Crafts bungalows and 1920s fourplexes to magnificent estates on the river. Riverside is also a medical hub, with the St. Vincent's Medical Complex and numerous medical offices near the hospital. Publix, a large Florida-based grocery store chain, recently opened a grocery store in the heart of Riverside, so many residents can now walk to the market (and the adjoining Starbucks). Numerous shopping areas in the district, like 5 Points, feature some of the city's best restaurants, independent clothing stores, and art galleries.

In Avondale, a little farther west, homebuyers are restoring stately brick homes to their original grandeur. Like Riverside, Avondale has its own collection of small shopping districts and quaint streets. Both neighborhoods enjoy a small-town charm in the shadow of a big city, with numerous public parks, tennis courts, and softball and soccer fields.

ORTEGA: Attracts old money…and new money that's trying to pass for old money

Ortega used to be synonymous with conservative folks with cash to spare. The neighborhood sits on a peninsula in the St. Johns River, with the St. Johns to the east and another smaller waterway, the Ortega River, to the north and west. The Florida Yacht Club and Timuquana Country Club form the social hub of this community, which also happens to be where many of Jacksonville's current movers and shakers grew up. Many attended private schools like Bolles and Episcopal and attended the same churches. *Worth* magazine once ranked Ortega 46th among the nation's top-50 wealthiest neighborhoods. Homes run from average ranch-style homes to stately water-front estates. If you approach Ortega from the north, you will drive across a narrow two-lane drawbridge, a gorgeous relic from the 1920s, to get over the Ortega River.

SAN MARCO: Attracts young families, cool singles, and dog owners

San Marco is one of Jacksonville's prettiest neighborhoods. Some of the homes here sit on the river, but most are snuggled into great tree-lined streets. For those of you familiar with the Washington, D.C., area, San Marco reminds a lot of people of Chevy Chase, Maryland. The houses are nicely sized, often brick—and can be expensive. San Marco enjoys a convenient location to Downtown; it's only about a five-minute commute. San Marco Square, a popular shopping district, sits in the center of the neighborhood and has shops, restaurants, nightclubs, and a single-title movie theater. Talk of a small supermarket has been in the wind for a few years, but no one's holding his or her breath.

OLD SAN JOSE, LAKEWOOD, MIRAMAR, and MANDARIN: Attracts everyday people, newlyweds, and young families looking for a little more space

Old San Jose, Miramar, San Jose, Epping Forest, Beauclerc, and Mandarin occupy a 10-mile stretch along the river to the south of San Marco and are popular for their older, brick homes and proximity to the river.

San Jose Boulevard, one of the city's main arteries, runs parallel to the river, and homes in the neighborhoods on the river side of San Jose Boulevard fetch far higher prices than those on the inland side where the homes are older, more modest, and generally single-story ranch-style houses.

Old San Jose, Miramar, and Lakewood consist of small one-story brick homes and larger, more-stately properties closer to the river. Of the three, Old San Jose is the most popular, then Miramar, with Lakewood coming third.

Next in line is San Jose, where The Bolles School, the city's premier private school (former Governor Jeb Bush's son was a student here) presides over the St. Johns River. The campus was formerly of one of Florida's turn-of-the-century grand hotels and is a Jacksonville architectural treasure.

To the south Mandarin is one of the oldest residential communities in Jacksonville, with thousands of people moving into its quiet, shady neighborhoods every year. Mandarin was largely farmland until the late 1960s, when developers discovered the area. Now there are far more cars than there ever were cows in Mandarin. To its west, Mandarin is bordered by the St. Johns River. To its south lies St. Johns County with the neighborhoods of Julington Creek and Fruit Cove.

Mandarin has strong schools, churches, and synagogues, as well as many strip malls and shopping centers. The area is rich in history; it is here that Harriet Beecher Stowe once owned an orange grove. Thanks to the efforts of the Mandarin Historical Society, much of the area's history is remembered in the Mandarin Store and Post Office, an old country store that was once the heart of the area. Mandarin is located about 30 minutes from Downtown in rush-hour traffic.

SOUTHSIDE: Attracts newcomers who want bigger houses for less money, no matter how close together

Centrally located, the Southside is bordered by Arlington to the north and east, St. Johns County to the south, and San Marco and I-95 to the west. The Southside is a hub of new construction with new residential communities popping up all the time. This is where the University of North Florida is located, as well as Tinseltown, a popular movie theater and restaurant district. Southpoint, an area of office parks and hotels, Mayo Clinic, the Avenues Shopping Mall, and the most-excellent new St. Johns Town Center shopping area all fall within this region.

Southside has a wide range of housing opportunities, including the most apartment complexes in the city. Southside also offers gated communities such as Deerwood and a multitude of new development along Southside Boulevard. Southside residents enjoy easy access to the

Beaches (about 20 minutes away) via J. Turner Butler Boulevard and easy access to I-95. You can be in the heart of Downtown in about 20 minutes, depending on the time of day.

This is not the area for people who are interested that old-Jacksonville charm. Southside can be fairly sterile and tends to attract newcomers to the city or people interested in new building versus old architecture.

ARLINGTON: Attracts multigenerational Jacksonville natives, Spanish-moss lovers, NRA members

If you want to live on the river but don't have gobs of money, Arlington is a good place to look. In the past, you could buy a 1950s cinder-block home with a killer view, but that window is closing rapidly. Still, a lot of waterfront property in Arlington, which is surrounded by the St. Johns River to the west and north and the Intracoastal Waterway to the east, remains as it was in the 1950s. Fort Caroline National Park, site of the oldest European settlement in America, is nestled in the heart of Arlington. Jacksonville University is also located here, as is Jones College. The small-but-busy Craig Airport serves corporate jets and private planes, and Tree Hill Nature Preserve is a local-favorite suburban park.

Arlington was one of the first suburban neighborhoods in Jacksonville, so it has long played a role in the city's housing history. It enjoys a central location 10 minutes from Downtown and 20 minutes from the Beaches. And since Arlington is generally an older neighborhood, it's full of stately oaks that provide welcome shade during Jacksonville's long, hot summer.

Although there is an abundance of older cinder-block ranch homes in Arlington, there are also many newly developed communities in East Arlington around Fort Caroline and Monument Roads. Neighborhoods like Hidden Hills (yes, there are actually hills!), with homes built in the late eighties and early nineties, are surrounded by good schools and are convenient to shopping centers.

WEST BEACHES: Attracts people who want it to have their beach and city, too

West Beaches, located 10 to 15 minutes west of the Beaches, is one of the fastest-growing areas of Jacksonville. This is where you can buy a brand-new three-bedroom, two-bath home with a two-car garage in the $200,000 to $300,000 range (depending, of course, on the strength of the housing market).

If you want trees, West Beaches is generally not the place to look. Developers have been known to clear-cut many of these neighborhoods to construct rows of new homes without any of those pesky trees in their way. The West Beaches development of Queen's Harbour is an exception to this no-tree trend. Queen's Harbour offers beautiful upscale homes with plenty of trees on man-made canals. Homeowners can park their boat out back and, through a series of locks, motor their way from their backyard to the Intracoastal.

West Beaches homes are generally new and conveniently located to Downtown, Southside, and the Beaches. They are also convenient to many new shopping centers, which are cropping up in their wake. West Beaches has recently added several new schools to accommodate the growth in the neighborhoods. In normal conditions, it takes about 20 minutes to drive into Downtown from here, but expect a longer commute in heavy rush-hour traffic.

i Got a question about city services? Call (904) 630-CITY. As the city likes to say: "One call does it all."

THE BEACHES: Attracts early-morning runners, surfers, people who pride themselves on taking it easy

Living at Atlantic Beach, Neptune Beach, Jacksonville Beach, Ponte Vedra, or Sawgrass is like living in a small town near a big city. You can work in the big city (Jacksonville) and enjoy all the opportunities it has to offer, then come home to your small town, where it's not unusual to walk or ride your bike to shops and restaurants. Plus the greatest park of all, the Atlantic Ocean, is right at the end of the street.

The Beaches, as Jacksonville's beach communities are collectively known, are made up of Atlantic Beach, Neptune Beach, Jacksonville Beach, and Ponte Vedra. Ponte Vedra is actually outside the Jacksonville city limits in St. Johns County, but because it is such a bedroom community, Jacksonville all but claims it as its own. Even though Atlantic, Neptune, and Jacksonville Beaches are technically within Jacksonville's city limits, they are still cities unto themselves, each with a separate police force and their own elected city officials. Beaches residents pay taxes to the City of Jacksonville, and Jacksonville, in turn, gives a portion of that money back to the beach communities. Children who live at the Beaches and go to public school attend Duval County schools.

It's a different story for Ponte Vedra residents, who are governed by the St. Johns County Commission, which meets in St. Augustine. Taxes are fractionally less in St. Johns County, and schoolchildren in Ponte Vedra attend St. Johns County schools. Still, because of geography, Ponte Vedra residents are often closer to parts of Jacksonville than they are to St. Augustine and many choose to (and can afford to) send their children to the top-tier private schools in Jacksonville-proper.

Sawgrass is the name of a large subdivision in Ponte Vedra Beach. It's confusing sometimes, because some people think that Sawgrass is actually a city on a map. It's not. (The Stadium Course at Sawgrass in Ponte Vedra Beach is where The Players Championship, a large golf tournament, is played every year.)

The Beaches provide a lot of entertainment in the spring and summer when festivals, fairs, and outdoor concerts crop up almost every weekend.

Beach living offers an abundance of lifestyle choices from high-end gated communities like Marsh Landing in Ponte Vedra where homes can reach into the millions, to more modest neighborhoods like Neptune Beach where you can pick up an older ranch house in the $300,000 range. Perhaps a wood-shingled beach cottage that looks like something straight out of a Maine village is more your style; look to Atlantic Beach where you can find a number of these "cottages"

for $500,000 and up. As a rule, the closer to the ocean or even the Intracoastal, the higher the price of the house.

The Beaches is also home to one of the city's two naval bases, Naval Station Mayport, and attracts military bachelors and families. The base is located adjacent to the fishing village of Mayport, where working shrimp boats line the docks. The St. Johns River Ferry, popularly called the Mayport Ferry, will take you and your car across the river to scenic Heckscher Drive, also called the Buccaneer Trail. The Buccaneer Trail takes you to Amelia Island (see the Day Trips chapter).

i If you are a Duval County resident, you can vote in Jacksonville. To register to vote, go to a Department of Motor Vehicles office, a public library, or to the Supervisor of Elections Office. Visit www.duvalelections.com or call (904) 630-1410 for more information.

AMELIA ISLAND and FERNANDINA BEACH: Attracts tan retirees in tennis whites and people who've had enough of the city

Head north of Jacksonville along I-95 and you'll hit Nassau County, home to Amelia Island—a place known around the world for its beautiful golf and tennis resorts and wide, sandy beaches. Amelia is a popular destination for wealthy out-of-towners who want to own a second home, be it a house or condominium, in Florida. Consequently, there are a number of upscale residential communities on Amelia Island. Fernandina Beach is the largest town on Amelia Island; its downtown is listed on the National Register of Historic Places because of its many well-preserved Victorian homes. Fernandina Beach is full of inns and B&Bs, restaurants, and recreational activities, including Fort Clinch State Park. Fernandina also plays host to an annual shrimp festival that attracts thousands of visitors. Life got a lot easier for many Amelia Island residents with the opening of a Publix grocery store (and their delightfully addictive fried chicken) conveniently located near the popular year-round resort community of Amelia Island Plantation.

Close-up

Habitat for Humanity

Champagne corks popped in 1989 as workers at the new Jacksonville branch of **Habitat for Humanity** celebrated their first year in operation. HabiJax, as it is called here, built three homes that year, a modest yet glorious beginning for a group that since has helped more than 1,630 low-income Jacksonville families have homes of their own.

Using donations and volunteer labor, HabiJax builds homes at below-market cost. Then it sells those homes with interest-free mortgages to low-income homebuyers, who generally have been unable to buy a home of their own. Homebuyers, who often are single mothers with full-time jobs, must put down $500 and log 300 hours of sweat equity in building their own home. It's a formula that has paid off for HabiJax, which has a long waiting list of local residents who dream of owning a HabiJax house.

HabiJax attributes much of its success to strong partnerships with local groups like the **Northeast Florida Builders Association.** The two paired in 2000 to build Fairway Oaks, an entire subdivision of 101 homes built in just 17 days. It was a feat never before accomplished by a Habitat for Humanity group in the United States, and former president Jimmy Carter, a driving force behind Habitat for Humanity, spent a day framing a house to help ensure that it would happen. Corporations donated money to buy materials and provided an army of volunteers to help build. Local restaurants donated food to feed everyone, and the builders supplied trained carpenters and other tradespeople with the expertise to quickly frame a house. Before it was transformed into Fairway Oaks, the neighborhood was called Golfbrook Terrace and was well known to police as one of the most dangerous housing projects in the city. Today the sound of children playing tag on the sidewalk has replaced the sound of gunfire.

The partnership with the Northeast Florida Builders Association has worked so well for Habi-Jax that the two joined forces again and again over the years, building hundreds more homes together, sometimes up to 40 homes in a month. HabiJax would like to do more big projects, but the big parcels of land needed for such projects are not easy to come by. The majority of HabiJax homes have been built one by one in Jacksonville's urban core, where the city has knocked down dilapidated, abandoned crack houses and given the land to HabiJax to build new homes. The group's signature one-story, three-bedroom house with a living room, dining area, and front porch dots many a street in the city's urban core.

HabiJax has received commendations from the U.S. Department of Housing and Urban Development as a model for other communities to follow, was named Habitat for Humanity's affiliate of the year, and opened HabiJax ReStore, a home improvement retail outlet at 5800 Beach Blvd. that sells new and refurbished building materials, appliances, furniture, lighting, and accessories to the public at 50 to 60 percent off their normal retail prices. The proceeds provide an important additional source of additional funding for HabiJax.

Besides building homes for those who need them, HabiJax serves another important purpose. It creates a sense of community—not just in Jacksonville but also beyond. For instance, low- and middle-income volunteers rub elbows with the city's elite at building sites, laying tile, and painting walls. College students spend their spring breaks building HabiJax homes. Churches sponsor homes, with church members raising the money, organizing the build, and supplying the labor. Individual families sponsor entire homes in the name of a deceased loved one. There are even retirees who travel the country by RV to build homes. Almost everyone who volunteers to work on a HabiJax home is touched by the experience almost as much as the family who will eventually live in it. Visit **www.habijax.org** to learn more about how you can help.

WESTSIDE: Attracts ruralists, hunting enthusiasts, and people who have no interest in being categorized

Much of the Westside, an amorphous area on the west side of the city, is largely rural. But growth is heading west in the form of huge residential neighborhoods, strip malls, and office parks. The former Cecil Field Naval Air Station, closed by the federal government in 1993, is located on the Westside. The navy gave Cecil Field's 17,224 acres to the City of Jacksonville, and the complex now houses one of the Florida State College at Jacksonville campuses. Another portion of the old base has become the Cecil Commerce Center.

The Westside is a large community starting just north of I-10 and stretching south to Clay County. It's bordered on the east by I-295 and continues west to Baker County and east to Riverside. Other neighborhoods on this side of town include Ortega Forest, Ortega Hills, Lakeshore, Cedar Hills, Murray Hill, and Normandy. Argyle Forest and Chimney Lakes are two large Westside neighborhoods bordering Clay County. They each offer affordable single-family homes, schools, bike paths, shopping centers, and restaurants.

NORTHSIDE: Attracts lovers of privacy, the great outdoors, and a good land deal

North Jacksonville runs roughly from 20th Street north to the Nassau County line and from I-295 on the west almost to the Atlantic Ocean. It's a vast area that includes pretty marshes, new housing developments, and attractions like the Jacksonville Zoo and Gardens. The eastern portion of this area also includes two of Jacksonville's most popular playgrounds: Huguenot Memorial Park and Little Talbot Island State Park.

Like the West Beaches area of Jacksonville, North Jacksonville is a growing corner of our city. Communities like Oceanway, New Bern, and San Mateo are growing as housing developments and strip malls find their way to North Jacksonville. The ever-expanding Jacksonville International Airport is located here, as is the new River City Marketplace and two growing business parks: the International Tradeport and Imeson International Industrial Park. North Jacksonville is about a 15-minute drive to Downtown and includes remote communities like Black Hammock Island, an unspoiled pocket of old Florida marshland that was once known only to local fishermen. That's changing as new homes find their way to Black Hammock Island, which, as the name suggests, boasts some beautiful waterfront.

ORANGE PARK: Attracts Naval families and those seeking a less-expensive cost of living

South of Ortega, outside the Jacksonville city limits, lies the city of Orange Park. At first glance, Orange Park appears to be nothing more than suburban sprawl, but get off the main highways and into some neighborhoods, and you will see lovely tree-lined streets full of homes that are generally less expensive than those in Jacksonville. Orange Park is located in Clay County, which includes many other popular municipalities, such as Green Cove Springs, Keystone Heights, Penney Farms, and Middleburg.

Many people live in Orange Park and commute some 30 minutes to work in Jacksonville. Many an Orange Park neighborhood is also filled with families whose father and/or mother works at NAS Jacksonville, just to the north. The St. Johns River borders the east side of Orange Park, and there are some lovely riverfront homes over that way.

i **New Florida residents must apply for Florida tags and car titles within 10 days after they begin working, apply for a homestead tax exemption, or enroll their children in school. Proof of Florida insurance is also required before the tags can be issued.**

EDUCATION

COLLEGES AND UNIVERSITIES

If you're interested in attending a four-year college in the Jacksonville area, you have state universities, private universities, and small liberal arts colleges, including a historic African-American school, to choose from. Several of the schools, like the recently revamped Florida State College at Jacksonville (formerly Florida Community College at Jacksonville) are upping the ante for Jacksonville's adult students.

EDWARD WATERS COLLEGE
1658 Kings Rd.
(904) 470-8000 or (888) 898-3191
www.ewc.edu
Edward Waters College is a historically African-American, four-year, private college. Founded in 1866 by the African Methodist Episcopal Church, the school is located on the city's Northside.

With about 800 students, the school offers bachelor's degrees in communications, music, psychology, criminal justice, biology, elementary education, mathematics, and business administration. Annual tuition is about $9,200, excluding room and board.

The College was highlighted in *The Florida Leader* magazine in "The Best of Florida Schools 2004" for the Biggest Growth for Private Colleges. The Music and Fine Arts Department was also listed as having the "Best Music for Private Colleges," which highlighted the world renowned EWC Choir and the Triple Threat Marching Band. The Purple Thunder Dance Squad, the group of plus-sized ladies who perform with the band, was highlighted in The Best of Florida Schools 2005 as the "Best Non-Traditional Dance Squad."

In recent years Edward Waters has struggled with accreditation, enrollment, and finances. But the school has continued to receive donations from individuals and major corporations, including a $1 million personal donation from CSX's Chief Executive Michael Ward. EWC also has received nearly $700,000 in grants from the U.S. Department of Housing and Urban Development, aimed at revitalizing area homes and businesses.

FLAGLER COLLEGE
74 King St., St. Augustine
(904) 829-6481
www.flagler.edu
Founded in 1968, Flagler College is a four-year, private, nondenominational college located in historic downtown St. Augustine. The college occupies the former Hotel Ponce de Leon, built in 1888 by the late oil magnate and Florida developer Henry M. Flagler. Eight of the college's structures are designated as historic buildings; some are adorned with murals by American painters Martin Johnson Heade and George W. Maynard.

With about 2,650 students, the college offers a 21-to-1 student-teacher ratio. Flagler features 20 major courses of study and 26 minors leading to baccalaureate degrees. The most popular majors are business administration, sports management, graphic design, communication, and political science.

Flagler is accredited by the Commission of Colleges of the Southern Association of Colleges and Schools. Sixty percent of the students come from Florida, with the remainder hailing from 44 other states and 20 foreign countries. Tuition is about $13,300 (excluding room and board).

FLORIDA STATE COLLEGE AT JACKSONVILLE
101 West State St.
(904) 633-8100
www.fscj.edu

Close-up

What's In a Name?

On August 1, 2009, a long-standing and well-loved Jacksonville institution leapt into the next phase of its evolution when Florida Community College at Jacksonville became **Florida State College at Jacksonville.** The new Florida State College now has five campuses in the Jacksonville area, and seven additional centers hosting classes and programs for students. (In 2008, the College enrolled more than 80,000 students.)

Name changes are not new to the school. In 1986, what had always been Florida Junior College renamed itself Florida Community College at Jacksonville (FCCJ). However, the new name is causing a stir among some, especially FSU grads who feel that the name bears too close a resemblance to Florida Sate University in Tallahassee.

But the change is about more than just a name. The school has raised the stakes by adding four-year degrees in information technology management and public safety management, with a planned seventh bachelor's degree program, in early childhood education, to its already strong four-year programs in fire science management, nursing, computer systems networking, and supervision and management.

A core aspect of the school's mission has always been affordability for all. Tracy Pierce, FSCJ's vice-president of Economic Development and Student Success, told *The Jacksonville Observer*, "Traditional students with above average financial resources have no problem getting a four-year education in this city. Our economic opportunity lies in helping working adults and a broader cross-section of traditional students gain access to higher education. Our four-year degrees are practitioner-oriented and address regional employment needs. We believe passionately that high-quality learning should be available to our friends and neighbors with minimal student debt."

Florida State College at Jacksonville opened its doors in 1966 as Florida Junior College; in the 1980s the school expanded to become Florida Community College at Jacksonville, and in August 2009, the institution changed again, this time becoming Florida State College at Jacksonville.

Today, the recently re-branded FSCJ serves more than 80,000 students enrolled in degree-seeking or continuing education courses with a median age of 27 in college credit programs and 39 in continuing education programs. The university also offers a strong and well-subscribed-to stable of online courses.

Based on enrollment figures, the most popular degrees are the associate of arts degrees, followed by the associate degrees in nursing and computer information sciences. In-state tuition is $85.16 per credit hour. Most classes are three to four credits, so Florida residents can expect to

pay about $256-$341 per class. Twelve credits, which is considered a full load for a semester, will run you $1,022 (excluding room and board).

FSCJ has five campuses and seven training centers throughout Northeast Florida and serves as a feeder school to Florida's four-year universities. In Florida, students who receive an associate in arts degree from FSCJ are guaranteed admission into one of the 11 state universities.

FSCJ offers seven B.S. programs, 53 A.S. degree programs, and 53 vocational and technical certificate programs. Over the years the community college has worked closely with Jacksonville businesses to design training programs to meet the city's workforce needs. The Donald Zell Urban Resource Center at the Downtown campus provides customized workforce training in all facets of business. Consequently, FSCJ offers strong programs in business, health care, computer sciences, and culinary arts and hospitality.

FSCJ's campuses and centers are conveniently located all over the city. Besides the Downtown campus, FSCJ has three primary satellite locations: the Kent Campus, located on Roosevelt Boulevard on the Westside; the North Campus, located 8 miles north of Downtown; and the South Campus, located on Beach Boulevard about 8 miles west of the Atlantic Ocean. FSCJ also operates an Open Campus, which is a global, online college for students worldwide.

In 2002 FSCJ expanded its job-training capabilities when it opened the $25 million Advanced Technology Center adjacent to its Downtown campus. The tech center offers training programs in four key areas: information technology, biotechnology, advanced manufacturing, and transportation technology. These are the emerging sectors targeted by Jacksonville economic development officials.

JACKSONVILLE UNIVERSITY
2800 University Blvd. North
(904) 256-8000
www.jacksonville.edu
Founded in 1934 by local businessmen, Jacksonville University has maintained strong ties to the business community. In 2000 the school completed one of the largest capital campaigns in city history by raising $60 million. The campaign got a major boost with a single $20 million contribution from the Davis family, founders and principal owners of the Jacksonville-based Winn-Dixie supermarket chain.

JU is located on a picturesque campus on the St. Johns River in the Arlington section of the city. With 3,007 students, it boasts a low, 14-to-1 student-faculty ratio. Annual tuition is about $12,650 (excluding room and board).

JU offers undergraduate and adult degree programs as well as graduate programs. JU is best known for its nursing school, school of education, biology and marine science programs, and its school of fine arts. JU offers master's degrees in teaching and business administration and professional programs in engineering, dentistry, law, and medicine. The university also offers a well-regarded executive MBA program that many area businesspeople have completed. There's also an Accelerated Degree Program designed for working adults that is popular with Jacksonville professionals for its evening and weekend class times.

The school fields 17 Division-1 athletic teams, with nearly 400 students competing in a sport. Locals love the school's Dolphins basketball and baseball teams. Its football program is the only non-scholarship football program in the state.

i Catch a concert by the UNF Jazz Department. The jazz bands there are ranked some of the best in the nation.

UNIVERSITY OF NORTH FLORIDA
4567 St. Johns Bluff Rd. South
(904) 620-1000
www.unf.edu
Recognized as one of the country's best values in public colleges in 2009 by *The Princeton Review*, the University of North Florida is one of Florida's fastest-growing four-year universities. The school, founded in 1972, doesn't offer nearly the number of degrees and programs as Florida's bigger, better-known institutions—University of Florida in Gainesville and Florida State University in Tallahassee—but UNF is adding programs and expanding its facilities yearly. The university's Distinguished Voices Lecture Series has attracted cultural icons like Desmond Tutu, commentator George Will, and broadcaster Dan Rather. The UNF Jazz Program is considered one of the top jazz programs in the country and offers excellent concerts in the Lazzara Fine Arts Center.

UNF is going green in a big way with all new campus construction conforming to LEED standards. Under those auspices, the school opened a new Student Union in 2009, and in 2006, the school unveiled the new 63,000-square-foot Social Sciences building, the first LEED-registered facility in Jacksonville and the first green building on campus.

The 1,300-acre campus, located off Butler Boulevard in Jacksonville's bustling Southside, services more than 15,500 students with extensive undergraduate and graduate degree programs spread among five colleges: arts and sciences; business administration; computing, engineering and construction; education and human services; and the Brooks College of Health. The school boasts a 22:1 student-faculty ratio.

The most popular majors at UNF are business management, education, and health professions. Like most of Florida's other public colleges and universities, UNF's in-state tuition is (relative to other states) modest. Annual tuition and fees for Florida residents in 2009/2010 were $139.78 per credit hour. Rooms can add between $1,835 and $2,325 per semester depending on the level of housing you choose. There are about 2,400 students living on campus.

i Former two-term mayor John Delaney, who spearheaded the Better Jacksonville Plan, is now the president of the University of North Florida.

SPECIAL SCHOOLS AND PROGRAMS

FLORIDA COASTAL SCHOOL OF LAW
8787 Baypine Rd.
(904) 680-7700
www.fcsl.edu

The Florida Coastal School of Law, Jacksonville's only law school, opened in 1996 with 140 students. Today the school has around 1,300 students, many of whom attend part-time. Annual tuition and fees total $16,331 (excluding room and board).

FLORIDA TECHNICAL COLLEGE OF JACKSONVILLE
8711 Lone Star Rd.
(904) 724-2229
www.flatech.edu

Founded in 1984, Florida Technical is a private two-year college that offers students technical training and degrees in computer programming and computer-aided drafting and design. The school also offers diplomas in network administration and C++/JAVA programming.

JONES COLLEGE
5353 Arlington Expressway and
1195 Edgewood Ave. South
(904) 371-1112
www.jones.edu

Jones College is a four-year private college that offers Bachelor of Science and Associate of Science degrees with majors in computer accounting, information systems, marketing, management, medical assistant, and other business-related fields. The school has about 600 full- and part-time students.

UNIVERSITY OF PHOENIX
4500 Salisbury Rd.
(904) 636-6645
www.phoenix.edu

University of Phoenix, a private school, offers bachelor's degrees in arts and sciences, business and management, criminal justice, education, human services, nursing, psychology, and technology. Master's and doctoral programs are available in several of these disciplines. Phoenix also offers many courses and programs online. Tuition varies by campus and program, but comes in around $395 per credit hour.

WEBSTER UNIVERSITY
10407 Centurion Parkway North
(904) 268-3037
www.webster.edu/jack

Webster University's Jacksonville campus opened in 1993. The university offers both Master of Arts and Master of Business Administration programs in various fields of business, management, education, liberal arts, and fine arts. Full-time tuition is $21,056 per year (excluding room and board).

PUBLIC SCHOOLS

DUVAL COUNTY PUBLIC SCHOOLS
1701 Prudential Dr.
(904) 390-2000
www.duvalschools.org

The Duval County Public School system consists of 103 elementary schools, three K-8 schools, 26 middle schools, 19 high schools, one 6-12 school,

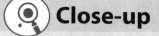

Close-up

Magnet Schools

Many of Duval County's best and brightest high school students attend **Stanton College Preparatory School,** an all-honors public magnet school named the best public high school in the nation in 2000 by *Newsweek* magazine. Paxon School for Advanced Studies, another all-honors public magnet school, earned the seventh spot on that same list. Both schools provide a rigorous academic program of advanced academic courses, and students are clamoring to get in. About 1,500 high school students attend Stanton (www.stantoncollegeprep.org), and there's a waiting list about that long for others who want admission. In fact, Paxon started its academic magnet program in 1999 in response to the demand for more seats at Stanton.

Both schools offer the **International Baccalaureate program**—a two-year comprehensive liberal arts education for academically talented and highly motivated students. Stanton's IB program is one of the largest and most successful in the world. In 1999 the IB class was ranked first in the nation out of 257 high schools and second in North America out of 370 high schools for the number of IB diplomas awarded (104). The IB program puts nearly impossible demands on students, who always seem to rise to the challenge. For instance, there's no kicking back for seniors in the IB program. They must take IB English literature, calculus, or IB math studies, as well as foreign language V, IB science, IB contemporary history, an elective, and an IB class on research and critical thinking. And if that's not enough, all students are also encouraged to participate in after-school activities like sports, band, or the debate team.

If Stanton College Prep is the quintessential Duval County high school for left-brain thinkers, then **Douglas Anderson School of the Arts (DASOTA)** is its right-brain counterpart. Students with an exceptional talent for creative writing, dance, theater arts, visual arts, instrumental music, or vocal music can audition for a spot at DASOTA. Entry into Douglas Anderson is just as competitive as at Stanton and Paxon, and the waiting list is just as long for students who don't get in on the first round. At DASOTA (www.da-arts.org) talented students explore the arts in depth. They travel and perform in an award-winning jazz band, dance in recitals and musicals, produce an annual literary anthology, and display their artwork all over town. Students can take honors and advanced-placement courses and take a minimum of two classes each day in the arts. They can take more arts classes each day in the upper grade levels once their graduation requirements are met.

Duval County's **magnet school program** began after a 1972 court order mandating that the county desegregate its schools. After several tries the county finally arrived at the magnet school idea and opened Stanton, its first magnet school, in 1981. Many magnets, including Stanton, are located in economically disadvantaged neighborhoods. Still, students from all over the city flock to these schools because of the programs offered.

three alternative schools, three exceptional student centers, and eight charter schools.

i For information regarding Duval County's stellar magnet school program—schools focusing on specific interests, needs, and talents—visit www.magnetprograms.com.

Bright spots in Duval County's academic magnet programs include Stanton College Preparatory School, which has ranked in *Newsweek* magazine's top five schools in the United States every year since 2000; and Paxon School for Advanced Studies, which was ranked eighth in the nation by *Newsweek* in 2008.

The county's high school arts magnet, Douglas Anderson School of the Arts, made *Newsweek's* list in 2000 and again from 2002-2008, and was named a Florida Department of Education A+ school every year from 2001-2008. Douglas Anderson's Jazz Ensemble won first place in the Essentially Ellington High School Jazz Band Competition and Festival in New York. (See the Close-up in this chapter for more information about these exceptional public high schools.)

> **i** All public school students in Florida must pass the FCAT, Florida Comprehensive Assessment Test, to advance to the next grade level. Students in grades 3 through 10 take the FCAT reading and math tests. Students in grades 4, 8, and 10 take the FCAT writing test. Students in grades 5, 8, and 10 take the FCAT science test.

Jacksonville's public schools offer special programs to students who are physically or mentally handicapped, sensory impaired, and emotionally disabled, as well as to those who are gifted. Currently more than 24,000 exceptional students are served in 18 programs.

PRIVATE SCHOOLS

Jacksonville has a number of excellent private schools, ranging from pre-K through high school. The growth in private school enrollment over the years is partly a response to concerns about the public system and partly the result of an increase in well-to-do Jacksonville residents who are looking to provide their kids with a leg up. For younger students there's a wide choice of church-affiliated and Montessori schools. The Diocese of St. Augustine operates a number of parish schools, which usually have long waiting lists. Many begin with some sort of preschool program and continue through eighth grade.

The following is a list of some of Jacksonville's top primary and secondary private schools.

Primary

JACKSONVILLE COUNTRY DAY SCHOOL
10063 Baymeadows Rd.
(904) 641-4166
http://new.jcds.com

The first accredited independent elementary school in Jacksonville, JCDS began as a family endeavor in 1960 by a group of parents seeking an independent, non-denominational environment. JCDS is fully accredited and serves pre-kindergarten through sixth grade students.

RIVERSIDE PRESBYTERIAN DAY SCHOOL
830 Oak St.
(904) 353-5511
www.rpds.com

RPDS was founded in 1948 as a mission of Riverside Presbyterian Church. The school now serves over 500 students. The campus has five buildings, an athletic field, and three playgrounds. Located in the historic Riverside community, the school is fully accredited and accepts students in pre-kindergarten through sixth grade.

SAN JOSE EPISCOPAL DAY SCHOOL
7423 San Jose Blvd.
(904) 733-1811
www.sanjoseepiscopal.com

Located in the historic buildings that were once the headquarters for the 1920's San Jose Estates Development company, which was responsible for much of the city's Spanish-style architecture (including The Bolles School, which sits across the street), San Jose Episcopal Day School is fully accredited and serves students from pre-kindergarten through sixth grade with traditional Christian values and a solid education.

Primary and Secondary

ARLINGTON COUNTRY DAY SCHOOL
5725 Fort Caroline Rd.
(904) 762-0123
www.acdsonline.com

Founded in 1954 as an elementary school, Arlington Country Day School added a high school in 1995. The school is known for its small classes, from preschool through grade 12. In 2003, 37 of the school's 52 graduates earned either academic or athletic scholarships to colleges or universities. Despite its small student population, ACDS has a powerhouse of a basketball program. The school's varsity team has been ranked among the top high school teams in the country.

BISHOP KENNY HIGH SCHOOL
1055 Kingman Ave.
(904) 398-7545
www.bishopkenny.org

Located on a sprawling campus across the St. Johns River from Metropolitan Park, Bishop Kenny was founded in 1952 and remains one of Jacksonville's more respected private schools. A four-year Catholic preparatory school with 1,600 students, Bishop Kenney instills strong Catholic ethics alongside a rigorous academic program. More than half the school's 84 faculty members have master's degrees.

THE BOLLES SCHOOL
7400 San Jose Blvd.
(904) 733-9292
www.bolles.org

Located on a stunning riverfront campus in Jacksonville's San Jose area, The Bolles School is considered by many to be the city's premier private preparatory school. The school was founded in 1933 as an all-boys military school in one of the era's grand hotels on the banks of the St. Johns River. In 1961 the school dropped its military status, and 10 years later, in 1971, Bolles began admitting girls.

Today Bolles serves more than 1,800 K-12 students on four campuses. Bolles' upper-school campus is located on San Jose Boulevard. The middle school Bartram Campus is located nearby. Bolles also operates a lower-school campus in Ponte Vedra Beach and another lower school program on the Whitehurst Campus adjoining the San Jose campus. Bolles is the only high school boarding program in North Florida and draws students from 25 countries and 17 states.

In addition to its stellar academic reputation, Bolles has some of the state's top athletic programs, including a swimming program whose participants have swum in every Summer Olympics since 1972. (Forty-four Bolles students and alumni have competed on behalf of 24 different countries; 10 of these swimmers have won a total of 13 medals.) As of 2009, the school's swim teams have won 13 national championships. Bolles' football team, coached by the iconic Corky Rogers, has won nine state championships. The riverfront location enables the school to support an excellent crew program, which is housed in the school's new state-of-the-art boathouse.

EPISCOPAL HIGH SCHOOL
4455 Atlantic Blvd.
(904) 396-5751
www.episcopalhigh.org

Episcopal High School, Jacksonville's other top private prep school, is located on a scenic 56-acre riverfront campus and serves grades 6-12. Episcopal's curriculum focuses on critical thinking and problem solving. Even though it serves 900 students, the school is known for its small class sizes and supportive environment. Episcopal offers 21 AP and 19 Honors classes. In 2009, 84 percent of Episcopal students who took Advanced Placement exams passed with a score of 3 or higher; 91 students earned a perfect score. The school has excellent athletic facilities, including a heated pool.

ST. JOHNS COUNTRY DAY SCHOOL
3100 Doctors Lake Dr.
(904) 264-9572
www.sjcds.net

St. Johns Country Day School is a private, independent, coeducational, non-denominational college preparatory school set beneath a lush canopy of live oak trees on a 26-acre campus. The school serves 760 students from pre-kindergarten through 12th grade with a traditional liberal arts curriculum.

CHILD CARE

Taking care of kids is big business in Jacksonville. With more than 400 licensed child care centers in this city, Jacksonville offers plenty of choices, which can make the task of finding the provider that's right for you seem daunting. Fear not. Jacksonville offers something unique to help demystify your search. It's called the Jacksonville Children's Commission, which (among other things) operates a citywide child care resource and referral program. This service will help you find child care that's right for you and your family.

We've included a few of the larger centers in this chapter to get you going. But parents still need to do their homework—visit a number of potential caregivers and check up on them with the Licensing Unit of the State of Florida's Department of Children and Families at www.state.fl.us/cf_web or (904) 723-2064. The Licensing Unit will tell you whether the child care provider you are checking out has been cited by the state or if there are any client complaints against them.

There's nothing more agonizing for parents than putting their children in day care. Taking advantage of the city's resources, however, can make some of those child care choices easier.

RESOURCES

JACKSONVILLE CHILDREN'S COMMISSION CHILD CARE RESOURCE AND REFERRAL PROGRAM
1095 A. Philip Randolph Blvd.
(904) 630-3647
www.jaxchildrenscommission.org

CHILD CARE PROVIDERS

CHAPPELL CHILD DEVELOPMENT CENTERS (NINE LOCATIONS)
8400 Baycenter Rd.
(904) 739-1279
www.chappell-schools.com

i The YMCA of Florida's First Coast offers great after-school care and summer programs for children at all of its locations. Visit www.firstcoastymca.org or call (904) 296-3220 for information.

MAGELLAN ACADEMIES
10550 Deerwood Park
(904) 646-9596
www.magellanacademies.com

i Looking for something to keep the young ones stimulated over holiday or summer breaks? Check out the mini-camps at the Museum of Science and History at 1025 Museum Circle. Visit www.themosh.org or call (904) 396-6674 for details.

UNF CHILD DEVELOPMENT RESEARCH CENTER
University of North Florida
1 UNF Dr., Building 49
(904) 620-2372
www.unf.edu/dept/cdrc

YMCA RIVERSIDE CENTER
221 Riverside Ave.
(904) 355-1436
www.firstcoastymca.org/yates

HEALTH CARE AND WELLNESS

Rest assured. If you or your loved ones fall ill while visiting Jacksonville, you will get some of the best health care available. The city is blessed with some internationally renowned health care facilities, such as Mayo Clinic, Wolfson Children's Hospital, and Nemours Children's Clinic, a medical and surgical specialty clinic.

There's been plenty of movement and change among Jacksonville's hospitals in recent years. The state-of-the-art Baptist South (off I-95 at exit 335) opened in 2005 and has nearly doubled in size since then with additional new maternity facilities and a state-of-the-art, 14-bed, Level II, Newborn Intensive Care Unit (NICU) that allows Baptist South to partner with the neonatal intensive care program at Wolfson Children's Hospital.

HOSPITALS

BAPTIST MEDICAL CENTER/BAPTIST HEALTH

Baptist Medical Center is one of the largest health care providers in Jacksonville. Under the umbrella of Baptist Health, the Baptist Medical Center functions as a collection of medical facilities rather than one single hospital.

BAPTIST MEDICAL CENTER DOWNTOWN
800 Prudential Dr.
(904) 202-2000
www.e-baptisthealth.com
The Baptist Medical Center Downtown is a 545-bed facility conveniently located on Jacksonville's Southbank. Baptist Downtown offers a full range of medical and surgical specialties, including adult and children's emergency centers, cardiovascular care, comprehensive cancer services including a breast cancer institute, and a full complement of women's and children's services. Baptist Downtown also offers joint replacement, bloodless medicine and surgery, hyperbaric oxygen therapy, and a sleep center. The Downtown center was named among *U.S. News & World Report*'s Best Hospitals 2009-10 and among the top 50 in the country for neurology and neurosurgery. The hospital also features advanced clinical technologies, including the robot-assisted da Vinci Surgical System, and the Novalis Tx and Gamma Knife stereotactic radiosurgery systems. In addition, Baptist Downtown is home to a Certified Primary Stroke Center and Accredited Chest Pain Center with PCI.

If you are driving south on I-95 through Jacksonville, you can see the hospital to the left after you cross the St. Johns River.

BAPTIST MEDICAL CENTER BEACHES
1350 13th Ave. South, Jacksonville Beach
(904) 627-2900
www.e-baptisthealth.com
Baptist Medical Center Beaches has 146 private rooms, including 16 maternity suites, six state-of-the-art operating suites, outpatient surgery, diagnostic testing, a sleep disorders center, and a new endoscopy suite. The Beaches branch also has the only 24-hour emergency service east of the Intracoastal Waterway.

BAPTIST MEDICAL CENTER NASSAU
1250 South 18th St., Fernandina Beach
(904) 321-3500
www.e-baptisthealth.com
To the north of Jacksonville in Fernandina Beach, Baptist operates a 54-bed acute-care center that serves Nassau County and Southeast Georgia residents. Services include an emergency department, a critical care unit, a small maternity unit,

and three surgical suites. The center also recently opened the Betty and David Berkman Building for Patient Care, which includes an advanced intensive care unit and 48 private suites.

BAPTIST MEDICAL CENTER SOUTH
I-95 Exit 335
14550 Old St. Augustine Rd.
(904) 271-6000
www.e-baptisthealth.com
In 2005, Baptist Health completed construction on Baptist Medical Center South to serve southern Duval and northern St. Johns Counties. As of 2009, Baptist South opened a new eight-story patient care tower, which added 76 new patient beds, including a state-of-the-art, 14-bed, Level II, Newborn Intensive Care Unit (NICU) in partnership with the neonatal intensive care program at Wolfson Children's Hospital. The new patient tower adds 10 new maternity suites—bringing the total to 22—48 acute care beds, four more intensive care beds, and a new inpatient pharmacy. Baptist South now has 196 beds, more than double its size when it opened in 2005 with 92 beds. Baptist South is considered "the" place to deliver your baby in Jacksonville.

i In addition to four full-service hospitals and Wolfson Children's Hospital, Baptist also operates 17 primary care health centers located throughout neighborhoods in Duval, Nassau, and St. Johns Counties.

BROOKS REHABILITATION HOSPITAL
3599 University Blvd. South
(904) 858-7600
www.brookshealth.org
Brooks Rehabilitation Hospital is a 143-bed, not-for-profit, acute physical rehab hospital that specializes in treating patients with brain injury, strokes, spinal cord injury, and comprehensive orthopedic problems. It is the eighth-largest rehabilitation hospital in the country and has 25 outpatient centers around town. Brooks is located at the corner of Beach and University Boulevards, next door to Memorial Hospital.

MAYO CLINIC
4500 San Pablo Rd.
(904) 953-2000
www.mayo.org
The renowned Mayo Clinic in Rochester, Minnesota, opened its first satellite facility in Jacksonville in 1986 on land donated by the late J. E. Davis, Jacksonville's legendary businessman and one of the founders of the Winn-Dixie supermarket chain. Like its counterparts in Minnesota and Arizona, Mayo in Jacksonville is a multi-specialty outpatient clinic, and is known for its team approach, where specialists from many different areas consult for the benefit of the patient. Consequently, Mayo refers to its staff physicians as "consultants." As a result of all of this, *U.S. News & World Report* has named Mayo one of America's Best Hospitals for 20 years in a row.

In 2008, Mayo began offering inpatient care in a new 214-bed facility with 16 operating rooms, transplant and epilepsy units, and advanced cardiac and neurosurgery facilities.

Mayo Clinic offers a range of special services including an executive health assessment for CEOs that combines a resort package of golf, tennis, or spa with a comprehensive series of physical exams.

Mayo operates three primary care centers, in Jacksonville, Jacksonville Beach, and St. Augustine. The Jacksonville clinic operates a nicotine dependence center and a sleep disorders center.

If you want to be treated at the Mayo Clinic in Jacksonville, you can make your own appointment. The clinic also welcomes physician referrals. Patients who need hospitalization are admitted to Mayo Clinic's hospital, established in 2008 and located on the clinic campus.

MEMORIAL MEDICAL CENTER
3625 University Blvd.
(904) 399-6111
www.memorialhospitaljax.com
Opened in 1969, Memorial is now one of Jacksonville's largest full-service community hospitals, with 353 beds. Memorial recently completed a $34 million, 72-private-room, tower expansion to meet the growing number of patients com-

ing through its doors. Among the additions, the hospital increased its emergency room bays from 20 to 33, added a third cardiac catheterization lab, and expanded the number of outpatient surgery rooms from six to eight. Memorial also added a state-of-the-art CyberKnife Cancer Center and Neuroscience Center. In 2007, the Southside Cancer Center began offering oncology services, and the Memorial Spine Clinic opened to treat acute and chronic spinal pain, injury, and malformations. Memorial has received a Bariatric Center of Excellence designation along with a five-star rating for Clinical Excellence.

NEMOURS CHILDREN'S CLINIC
807 Children's Way
(904) 697-3600
www.nemours.org
Located beside the Baptist Medical Center complex and connected to Wolfson Children's Hospital, Nemours Children's Clinic has more than 60 pediatric specialists on staff. The specialist physicians at Nemours treat more than 38,000 children each year. Nemours is not a hospital and has no overnight facilities; children requiring hospitalization are admitted to the adjacent Wolfson Children's Hospital at Baptist Medical Center.

Nemours is funded by a trust set up by the late Alfred I. duPont, one of Jacksonville's most generous benefactors. DuPont's desire to alleviate suffering lives on at Nemours, where children with severe medical conditions get treatment regardless of their family's ability to pay. Nemours also provides health education to all through www.KidsHealth.org.

SHANDS JACKSONVILLE
655 West Eight St.
(904) 244-0411
www.jax.shands.org
Shands Jacksonville, affiliated with the University of Florida Health Science Center, is one of Jacksonville's two teaching hospitals (the other being Mayo Clinic). Shands, a Level-1 trauma center, treats many Medicare patients and people with little or no health insurance. Shands dedicates about half of its patient hours to serving these

demographics; however, state budget crises have led to decreased funding, a move that many fear may be the death knell of the hospital.

Shands Jacksonville's hope has been to keep an academic medical center in Jacksonville's growing metropolitan area. But, financially speaking, the merged hospitals have had a difficult time. Still, the city, State of Florida, and Shands Gainesville all express a willingness to keep Shands Jacksonville operating because of the vital role it plays in serving the area's health care needs. Shands has the only dedicated stroke center of its kind, which has reversed the effects of strokes in many patients.

i Jacksonville Area Sexual Minority Youth Network, Inc. (JASMYN) provides a safe and accepting space for Jacksonville's LGBTQQ (lesbian, gay, bisexual, transgendered, queer, and questioning) youth and provides programs and assistance in the form of support groups, peer educators, OUTLOUD panels, a drop-in center, and more. JASMYN offers Jacksonville's youth valuable information on safer sex, partner negotiation, healthy relationships, piercing, tattoos, HIV, and abstinence. Events, such as the fall Coming-Out Day breakfasts, are fun and well-attended. Youth Information Line: (904) 389-0089; Web site: www.jasmyn.org.

ST. LUKE'S HOSPITAL
4201 Belfort Rd.
(904) 296-3700
www.stlukesjax.com or www.jaxhealth.com
St. Luke's Hospital is a 289-bed, not-for-profit, nondenominational hospital conveniently located near the intersection of I-95 and Butler Boulevard. It offers general acute-care services and specializes in medical and surgical procedures.

St. Luke's has been providing health care to Jacksonville residents since 1873, when it opened as Florida's first private hospital. The hospital has come a long way from its original two rooms and four beds. In 2008, St. Vincent's HealthCare took over operations of St. Luke's Hospital, making additional resources available to the residents of Jacksonville's Southside.

ST. VINCENT'S MEDICAL CENTER
1800 Barrs St.
(904) 308-7300
www.jaxhealth.com
St. Vincent's Medical Center is located on the west bank of the St. Johns River in the Riverside section of Jacksonville. The 528-bed hospital is a full-service tertiary care center and was ranked in the top 5 percent of hospitals nationwide in 2009 by HealthGrades.

St. Vincent's is a faith-based, nonprofit health system serving the health care needs of North Florida and South Georgia. The center was founded by the Daughters of Charity in 1916 to provide health services to the sick and the poor. Now St. Vincent's is a member of Ascension Health, the largest Catholic health system in the United States and the successor organization to Daughters of Charity National Health.

WOLFSON CHILDREN'S HOSPITAL
800 Prudential Dr.
(904) 202-8000
www.wolfsonchildrens.org
Named among the top three children's hospitals in Florida in 2007 by *Child* magazine, Wolfson Children's Hospital is also a part of the Baptist Hospital network. A 178-bed regional referral hospital for children that is adjacent to the main Southbank hospital, Wolfson Children's Hospital is the only children's hospital serving Northeast Florida and Southeast Georgia. Besides providing a full range of pediatric medical care, Wolfson also has a 48-bed Neonatal Intensive Care Unit for critically ill newborns.

The hospital is in the middle of adding 70 new pediatric inpatient beds on three new floors of dedicated pediatric space along with more family and education areas. If you visit Wolfson, be sure to check out the unique 660-foot-long Kids' Walk—a suspended covered walkway over I-95 that connects Wolfson Children's Hospital to Nemours Children's Clinic.

Orange Park
ORANGE PARK MEDICAL CENTER
2001 Kingsley Ave.
(904) 276-8500
www.opmedical.com
Located in suburban Clay County, Orange Park Medical Center is a 230-bed hospital offering a full range of services, from emergency care and wellness to psychiatric and diagnostic services. Doctors at The Women's Center delivered over 2,000 babies in 2009. The center also offers inReach, an electromagnetic system for early detection of lung cancer. The hospital recently opened an $8 million addition to house its expanded women's health and pediatric services.

St. Augustine
FLAGLER HOSPITAL
400 Health Park Blvd.
(904) 819-5155
www.flaglerhospital.org
Named after famed Florida industrialist Henry Flagler, this sprawling facility comprises 440,000 square feet of medical space on a 75-acre health park conveniently located on US 1. In 2009/2010, Flagler Hospital's Maternity Care Center earned the only HealthGrades five-star rating in Jacksonville, and was named among America's Best Hospitals in 2007 by *U.S. News & World Report*.

Flagler Hospital is a full-service medical complex offering a cancer center, heart center, imaging center, spine center, women's health center, and bariatric surgery center. In addition, Flagler offers emergency care and pediatrics. The complex was recently expanded to include an eight-story patient tower; larger birth, pediatrics, and intensive care units; a new oncology center; and an expanded heart and lung center.

MENTAL HEALTH SERVICES

Mental health facilities are included in many of Jacksonville's hospitals. In this listing you'll find some of the facilities that provide more comprehensive and specialized care.

Executive Physicals

Life changes when you become a CEO. You fly first class, you sign checks for millions of dollars, and you no longer have the time (or inclination) to sit in a waiting room reading back issues of *Sports Illustrated* while you wait to see a doctor.

Enter the **Executive Health Program at Mayo Clinic** in Jacksonville, a one- or two-day checkup tailored to meet the demands of busy corporate executives. The program began over 10 years ago and has become so popular that it's now copied by clinics throughout the state.

Here's how it works: on the day of your appointment, you arrive at the clinic where employees who will shepherd you through the process greet you at the front door. There are no forms to fill out or questionnaires to answer. All that pesky paperwork was completed back at the office and sent in ahead of time. Shortly after you arrive at Mayo Clinic, you change your clothes and a battery of testing begins: blood tests, urine samples, X-rays, glaucoma tests, prostate cancer screenings, mammograms, resting electrocardiograms, colonoscopies—you name it. This is your chance to get tested without a wait and, best of all, to find out the test results before you leave the clinic. This is also your chance to meet with some of the best doctors in the country to discuss your health and wellbeing. And if the doctors suspect a problem, you will see a specialist during this same visit.

Mayo can accommodate up to 20 physicals in a day. Bear in mind that you need not be an actual executive to take part in the program, just someone who has the means and the inclination to probe deeply into their overall wellness. And if the whole thing stresses you out, Mayo is happy to arrange a golf outing for you following your exams.

The package affords you the best medical screenings money can buy, and it comes with an executive price tag: $2,000 to $5,000, or more, depending on the tests. Many executives, or their companies, pay for the program out of pocket because this sort of checkup is not usually covered by health insurance. But more and more companies are picking up the tab because a healthy executive is a good investment. Convenience is also a good investment for busy corporate executives, who know all too well that time, as they say, is money. Visit www.mayoclinic.org/executive-health to learn more.

HOPE HAVEN CHILDREN'S CLINIC AND FAMILY CENTER
4600 Beach Boulevard
(904) 346–5100
www.hope-haven.org

Hope Haven, a not-for-profit facility, provides a range of psychological testing and therapy for children. Hope Haven first opened in the late 1800s to provide medical care for children suffering from tuberculosis. By the 1930s the facility had expanded its care to include children afflicted by polio. In the 1980s the board decided to shift Hope Haven's focus to meet the needs that families face when raising children in contemporary society. The center recently completed a 15,594-square-foot addition to help better serve 5,000-plus families each year.

MENTAL HEALTH CENTER OF JACKSONVILLE
3333 West 20th St.
(904) 695-9145
www.coj.net (search "Mental Health")
The Mental Health Center has been operating in Jacksonville since the mid-1960s, providing emergency evaluation and crisis stabilization, medication management, and 24-hour emergency services. The Mental Health Center and the Mental Health Resource Center are affiliated.

MENTAL HEALTH RESOURCE CENTER
11820 Beach Blvd.
(904) 642-9100
www.coj.net (search "Mental Health")
Like its sister facility, the Mental Health Center, the Mental Health Resource Center offers crisis stabilization services as well as inpatient and outpatient case management services. The Mental Health Resource Center also has a children's unit for treating children under age 18, and operates programs for the homeless.

RIVER POINT BEHAVIORAL HEALTH
6300 Beach Blvd.
(904) 724-9202
www.riverpointbehavioral.com
River Point Behavioral Health offers some of the most comprehensive mental health services in the city. This mental health hospital has a full range of inpatient, residential, partial hospitalization, and intensive outpatient programs for children, adolescents, families, adults, and seniors. Known for its multidisciplinary team approach, River Point's program is designed to provide the highest level of direct patient care possible and includes physical, social, spiritual, medical, and psychotherapeutic treatment. River Point also offers structured programs for adults who are chemically dependent.

i Looking for a holistic physician or dentist in Jacksonville? We recommend you pick up a free copy of *Natural Awakenings* magazine at the library. The ads inside will steer you in the right direction. Better yet, visit www.najax.com to read the full magazine online.

HOSPICE CARE

COMMUNITY HOSPICE OF NORTHEAST FLORIDA

EARL B. HADLOW CENTER FOR CARING
4266 Sunbeam Rd.
(904) 268-5200
www.communityhospice.com
Community Hospice of Northeast Florida, operating with a staff of 750 and nearly 950 volunteers, maintains four inpatient facilities throughout Jacksonville. Not enough can ever be said about hospice workers and the organizations that support them. They manage pain, counsel family, and, I can attest from two separate experiences, make the transition of a loved one easier and more dignified than ever imagined. Community Hospice offers care in a variety of settings: at home, in a long-term-care facility, in an assisted-living facility, in a hospital, or at the Earl B. Hadlow Center for Caring, a residential facility set on 12 acres in Mandarin.

ALTERNATIVE CARE

Alternative treatments such as chiropractic, acupuncture, aromatherapy, homeopathy, massage, and biofeedback have been gaining wider public followings in the United States in recent years. You'll find plenty of providers of alternative care in Jacksonville. Here are just a few of them:

ACUPUNCTURE AND HOLISTIC HEALTH CENTER
Dr. Michael Kowalski, AP, Dr Ac
4237 Salisbury Rd., #107
(904) 296-9545
www.treatrootcause.com

CENTER FOR NATURAL HEALING
Beth Hopkins-Acampora, AP
1525 San Marco Blvd.
(904) 396-3896

LEE ACUPUNCTURE & HERB CLINIC
Dr. Weon Seob Lee, AP, OMD, LAc, PhD
6817 Southpoint Parkway, #2202
(904) 296-7272
www.acupunctureofjax.com

SANDY EVANS, AP, NCCAOM
Acupuncture Physician Board Certified
Herbalist
4150 & 4154 Herschel St.
(904) 680-7344
www.yogaanandastudio.com

AIDS AND HIV SERVICES

DUVAL COUNTY HEALTH DEPARTMENT
BOULEVARD COMPREHENSIVE CARE
CENTER
1833 Boulevard, Suite 500
(904) 253-1040
www.dchd.net

LUTHERAN SOCIAL SERVICES
4615 Phillips Hwy.
(904) 448-5995
www.lssjax.org

NORTHEAST FLORIDA AIDS NETWORK
2715 Oak St.
(904) 356-1612
www.nfanjax.org

SENIOR LIVING

With a median age of 36, Jacksonville doesn't have a huge senior citizen population like some South Florida cities do. Still, many people across the country are discovering what we locals learned a long time ago: Jacksonville is a great place to retire. The weather is warm, outdoor recreation is plentiful, housing is affordable, and the number of resources and opportunities for seniors grows every day. In short, Jacksonville helps seniors maintain active, independent lifestyles for as long as they are physically able.

One of the best things about retiring here is that the city of Jacksonville really appreciates its seniors, especially for their volunteer contributions.

In the late 1980s Jacksonville established a Special Events for Senior Citizens program that hosts events such as The Forever Fit 50 & Beyond Jacksonville Senior Games, MOB advisory meetings (Mayor's Older Buddies), the Mayor's Holiday Festival for Senior Citizens, the Jacksonville Senior Games, the Mayor's Walk for Senior Wellness, and the Mayor's Fish-a-Thon, to name only a few.

After talking with a number of senior citizens, we came up with a top-10 Insiders' list of why it pays to be a senior in the River City. By no means is this list exhaustive, but it does contain some of the city's star programs.

TOP 10 REASONS FOR SENIORS TO LIVE IN JACKSONVILLE

1. Senior discounts. From a round of golf to a round of food, Jacksonville seniors have it made when it comes to discounts. Check below for some of our favorite discounts.

2. Learning never ends. Jacksonville University and UNF both host stellar continuing education programs. So do the city's museums, hospitals, and libraries.

3. City programs. City Hall takes care of Jacksonville's seniors with programs and events, from the mayor's annual Christmas party to an annual volunteers' luncheon.

4. Senior centers. The City of Jacksonville operates 19 senior centers throughout the city where seniors can socialize, play games, and get a hot midday meal for just pennies. Several locations even have weekly dances with live bands. Transportation is available Monday through Friday through the Senior Services Transportation Coordinator at (904) 630-0801.

5. Volunteer opportunities. City Hall will match volunteers over age 55 with their ideal volunteer opportunity.

6. Travel and wellness clubs. Local hospitals and tour companies take regular seniors-only bus trips to nearby points of interest.

7. Health care. From physicians who make house calls to the Mayo Clinic, Jacksonville offers a full range of health care options for seniors.

8. Retirement communities. Jacksonville's retirement communities, both upscale and moderate, offer a full range of services for the elderly, from independent living to assisted living to skilled nursing.

9. Senior publications. Jacksonville offers a variety of free publications for seniors that are chock-full of information and articles.

10. The beach. No top-10 list of anything in Jacksonville is complete without a listing for the beach, our greatest natural resource.

Senior Discounts

CONCERTS AT JACKSONVILLE UNIVERSITY
2800 University Blvd. North
(904) 256-7345
www.ju.edu (search "Concerts")
Students from the College of Fine Arts at Jacksonville University offer concerts throughout the school year, usually in the school's intimate Terry Concert Hall. Ticket prices are low, and the quality of performances is high. Single tickets are about $7, and groups are eligible for discounts. Some concerts are even free. Seniors say that these concerts make them feel young again as they relive their college days with a return to campus life.

CUMMER MUSEUM OF ART AND GARDENS
829 Riverside Ave.
(904) 356-6857
www.cummer.org
Every Tuesday from 4 to 9 p.m., the Cummer offers free admission. The Cummer also hosts special Seated Gallery Talks & Tea especially for seniors. These seated gallery talks are popular with seniors, especially those who can't stand for long periods of time. The events cost $6 but include admission to the museum and gardens and free refreshments. Call the Cummer for a calendar of events, and while you're at it, ask about becoming a volunteer docent. The Cummer is fully wheelchair accessible, even the gardens, and the museum has wheelchairs available at the front desk.

ℹ️ The State of Florida is looking for volunteers of all ages to become "Ambassadors for Aging." To learn more about this grassroots program that helps increase awareness of the contributions of elder Floridians, contact the Department of Elder Affairs in Tallahassee at (850) 414-2000 or visit http://elderaffairs.state.fl.us.

JACKSONVILLE ZOO AND GARDENS
370 Zoo Parkway
(904) 757-4463
www.jacksonvillezoo.org

Seniors age 65 and over receive discounted admission ($10) and are privy to special behind-the-scenes zoo tours designed just for them with an advance reservation. The zoo also has a number of senior volunteer opportunities from docents to assistant animal keepers. Want to get even more involved? The zoo always needs volunteers for special events, community outreach, and more. Wheelchairs are available for rent on-site. Call (904) 757-4463, ext. 176, for information on volunteering.

Toot Your Own Horn

The Recycles Orchestra invites age 55+ musicians to dust off their musical instruments and join them in performing for Jacksonville retirement communities, churches, schools, and civic organizations. The Recycles Orchestra is always looking for new volunteer talent. No audition required. Call (904) 543-0234 to learn more.

THEATRE JACKSONVILLE
2032 San Marco Blvd.
(904) 396-4425
www.theatrejax.com
Jacksonville's official community theater has been serving up quality productions since 1919. Every season includes a diverse mix of musicals and dramas. Seniors enjoy discounted season subscription packages as well as a $5 discount off ticket prices for Thursday and Sunday performances.

ℹ️ The Sunshine Pass is available for free to seniors 60+ living in Duval County and can be used for free rides on JTA buses and reduced fares (10 cents) on the Skyway. The pass can also be used as a library card. Passes are available at all Jacksonville Senior Centers. Call (904) 630-0995.

WINDSOR PARKE GOLF CLUB
13823 Sutton Park Dr. North
(904) 223-4653
www.windsorparke.com

Challenge is the name of the game at Windsor Parke Golf Club, which is conveniently located on Jacksonville's Southside between Downtown and the Beaches. From June through January, seniors only pay $32 to play a round of golf. (From February to May the senior discount is still available, but only on Tuesday.) Call ahead and reserve a tee time.

i The Tree Cup Café at The Cummer Museum of Art and Gardens provides an excellent rest stop among the museum's collections.

Continuing Education Programs

ART FOR ART'S SAKE
Jacksonville University
2800 University Blvd. North
(904) 256-7759
http://arts.ju.edu/art/AFAS/AFAS.htm

Jacksonville University offers noncredit courses in ceramics, glass art, photography, and painting through their Art for Art's Sake program. Learn to throw pots on a wheel, master Photoshop, or try your hand at painting portraits. The program welcomes all ages and experience levels. Other noncredit classes are offered by the Continuing Education Department and include everything from foreign languages to golf to computers. Seniors love it!

EXPLORITAS (FORMERLY ELDERHOSTEL)
(800) 454-5768
www.exploritas.org

From Amelia Island to Cumberland Island to St. Augustine and the Okefenokee Swamp, Northeast Florida offers a variety of Exploritas travel opportunities for seniors. Known for decades as Elderhostel, Exploritas is headquartered in Boston and offers educational and travel experiences for seniors worldwide. To request a catalog of upcoming courses, call the number above or visit

their Web site. Duval County Public Libraries carry current Exploritas catalogs; ask for them at the information desk.

COMMUNITY EDUCATION PROGRAMS
Duval County Schools
(904) 858-6080
www.duvalschools.org (Community)

Select Duval County schools offer very affordable continuing education classes in the evenings. Sign up to learn a foreign language or learn about computers. The courses do fill up quickly, so register early. Seniors over age 60 receive a $5 discount off the registration price of some courses.

JEWISH COMMUNITY ALLIANCE (JCA)
8505 San Jose Blvd.
(904) 730-2100
www.jcajax.org

A favorite social, educational, and cultural destination for seniors of all denominations in Jacksonville, the JCA is a membership organization with myriad social and exercise programs throughout the day. Seniors love the JCA's top-of-the-line facilities (including indoor and outdoor pools) and their welcoming attitude. Members also receive discounts on program fees, and seniors enjoy low membership rates, so it's worthwhile to join. In addition, the JCA runs weekly senior programs such as Culture Mavens outings, Upper Crust Club brunches, and Sing Sing Sing! oldies sing-alongs.

City Programs

COMMUNITY AND SENIOR CENTER SERVICES PROGRAM
8200 Kona Ave.
(904) 726-5161
www.coj.net (search "Seniors")

The City of Jacksonville operates 19 well-loved senior centers all over town. Seniors show up to meet other retirees, play cards and bingo, exercise, eat a hot meal, or take a computer class. Every center offers additional classes like painting, knitting, line dancing—you name it. Many

Four-part Fun

Ever secretly dreamed of joining a barbershop quartet? Now's your chance! Jacksonville's **Big Orange Barbersho**p Chorus is continually looking for new male singers of all skill levels (and all ages). The only requirements are a little singing ability and a love of four-part harmony. Meetings are held in the San Jose Church of Christ Fellowship Center. Call (904) 355-SING or visit www.bigorangechorus.com and start harmonizing.

of the centers hold monthly—in some cases weekly—dances for seniors. The list of activities, which also includes day trips, is long; call the senior center nearest you and ask for a calendar of events. Or access a calendar at the Web site listed above.

ARLINGTON SENIOR CENTER
1078 Rogero Rd.
(904) 723-6142

BENNIE FURLONG BEACHES SENIOR CENTER
281 19th Ave. South
(904) 241-3791

CLANZEL T. BROWN COMMUNITY CENTER
4415 Moncrief Rd.
(904) 764-8752

C. T. JOSEPH SENIOR CENTER
6943 Buffalo Ave.
(904) 768-4762

HAMMOND COMMUNITY CENTER
3312 West 12th St.
(904) 786-8554

JIM FORTUNA SENIOR CENTER
11751 McCormick Rd.
(904) 996-0211

J. S. JOHNSON COMMUNITY CENTER
1112 Jackson St.
(904) 630-0948

LANE WILEY SENIOR CENTER
6710 Wiley Rd.
(904) 783-6589

L. D. CLEMONS COMMUNITY CENTER
55 Jackson Ave.
(904) 693-4918

LINCOLN VILLA COMMUNITY CENTER
7866 New Kings Rd.
(904) 765-2654

LONGBRANCH SENIOR CENTER
4110 Franklin St.
(904) 630-0893

LOUIS DINAH SENIOR CENTER
1805 Flag St.
(904) 630-0728

MANDARIN SENIOR CENTER
3848 Hartley Rd.
(904) 262-7309

MARY L. SINGLETON SENIOR CENTER
150 East First St.
(904) 630-0995

MAXVILLE SENIOR CENTER
10865 Pennsylvania Ave.
(904) 289-7157

MONCRIEF SENIOR CENTER
5713 Teeler Ave.
(904) 764-0330

OCEANWAY SENIOR CENTER
12215 Sago Ave. West
(904) 696-4331

RIVERVIEW SENIOR CENTER
9620 Water St.
(904) 765-7511

WALLACE SMALL SENIOR CENTER
1083 Line St.
(904) 630-0697

FOSTER GRANDPARENT PROGRAM
150 East First St.
(904) 630-5450
www.coj.net (search "Foster Grandparent")
This is one of the city's best volunteer programs. Seniors are assigned to programs like Head Start, the Youth Detention Center, or the Police Athletic League, where they befriend, mentor, and tutor at-risk children and children with special needs. Seniors are asked to spend up to 20 hours a week working with children. In return, seniors get a small tax-free stipend for their work, transportation reimbursement, special training, a lunch allowance, an annual physical exam, and the knowledge that they can change the life of a young person.

INDEPENDENT LIVING PROGRAM
1093 West Sixth St.
(904) 630-0966
www.coj.net (search "Independent Living")
The city's Independent Living Program provides respite care for caregivers, giving them a chance to get out of the house for a break while a volunteer takes care of their homebound loved one. It's also a good place to call if an elder needs help finding medical care, food stamps, or transportation. This program serves low-income residents, and its goal is to keep these residents living independently for as long as possible. If elders need assistance with household chores or grocery shopping, the Independent Living Program can help. Caseworkers will assess the situation and send in the volunteers to help, if the elder qualifies.

MAYOR'S SPECIAL EVENTS FOR SENIOR CITIZENS
117 West Duval St.
(904) 630-3690
www.coj.net

The City of Jacksonville honors its seniors with a variety of programs and activities promoting recreation and outreach. The mayor's office hosts more than a dozen of these events, which are open to the public and are extremely popular. There are Senior Games in the fall; Fun With the Suns baseball outings in the spring; safety and security seminars presented by the Jacksonville Sheriff's Office; a Senior Expo every spring; and the popular Senior Prom every summer at the Prime Osborne Convention Center. The city provides transportation to all these events from senior centers and senior residences all over Jacksonville.

i Don't miss out on all the fun! Pick up a copy of the *Jacksonville Senior Services Directory,* an annual publication of services, goods, and activities for senior citizens and their families in the greater Jacksonville area. The directory is available at all senior centers and public libraries as well as City Hall.

RETIRED & SENIOR VOLUNTEER PROGRAMS (RSVP)
150 East First St.
(904) 630-0998
www.coj.net (search "RSVP")
Do you have two hours a week to donate to the Jacksonville Public Libraries or five hours a week to cook at the local homeless shelter? Whatever your available time and whatever your interest, RSVP, one of the largest volunteer efforts in the country, will help you find the volunteer opportunity that's right for you. You could become an RSVP Tale Teller and read to pre-kindergarten and kindergarten children from disadvantaged families, or a SWAT (Senior Workers Available Today) member who takes short-term assignments doing everything from staffing health fairs to assisting with special events. Maybe you'd enjoy making knitted, crocheted, or sewn items for children—from home. No matter what your interest, RSVP will connect you with a rewarding and fun way to reach out.

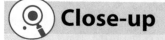

Close-up

King of the Colada

Ninety-year-old **Ricardo Gracia** loves to recall the past—particularly 1954, the year he invented the piña colada.

Wait a minute, that drink had an inventor? Wasn't there always a piña colada? Besides, how do you know Gracia, who still works as a sommelier at Cafe on the Green at the Sawgrass Marriott Resort, really came up with the idea? Well, here's his story. You decide.

First, some background. In 1950 Elizabeth Taylor married playboy Nicky Hilton, heir to the Hilton Hotel chain, touching off a Hilton/Hollywood heyday that would last for years. Although Taylor and Hilton divorced within months of their marriage, Hilton International Hotels became a popular playground for Hollywood stars.

Enter Ricardo Gracia, a dapper 36-year-old bar manager at the first Hilton International Hotel, the **Castellana**, in Madrid. He loved his job, and tending bar was in his blood. He'd been born above his grandfather's bar and restaurant in Barcelona in 1914, where he used to play among the bottles, mixing concoctions, when he was just a toddler.

In 1954 the Castellana was "party central," and each guest, upon arriving at the hotel, was greeted with a complimentary **Coco Loco**—a rum drink mixed with coconut milk and cream of coconut and served in half a coconut. An integral part of these drinks were the coconut cutters, who'd scramble up tall coconut trees each day to cut down the necessary number of coconuts needed for arriving guests, then slice open the hard-shelled seed.

One day management fired the coconut cutters after a labor dispute, and bar manager Ricardo Gracia found himself with a huge problem: how to make and serve the hundreds of Coco Loco welcome drinks the hotel had become famous for without the coconuts. Not only did he need the coconut milk, but a simple glass seemed so unworthy of the Hilton panache. Gracia turned to the pineapple. He told his team of bartenders to substitute pineapple juice for the coconut milk and serve the drink in half a hollowed-out pineapple. That worked for a while, until Gracia and his bartenders began experimenting with all the leftover fruit. Within weeks Gracia was blending a new concoction of crushed pineapple, pineapple juice, cream of coconut, and

Travel and Wellness Clubs

CLUB 55+
St. Vincent's Medical Center
(904) 308-7357
www.jaxhealth.com/Club55
Club 55+ is a wellness club offered by St. Vincent's Medical Center. Membership entitles you to unlimited free parking at St. Vincent's, guest meal trays for hospitalized members, the quarterly newsletter, and all or part of the cost of health fairs, holiday parties, and other activities. Members can also get help filling out their insurance forms or getting papers notarized for free. Members pay a one-time fee to join and a small annual fee.

i Need transportation to one of the city's senior centers? Call (904) 630-0801 to arrange a pickup.

DESTINATIONS UNLIMITED TOURS
3060 Leon Rd., Suite 202
(904) 722-8100
www.destinationsunlimitedtours.com
Destinations Unlimited runs bus trips up and down the Eastern Seaboard, as well as right here in Florida. Seniors attend a monthly meeting and hear talks about upcoming points of call. Even if they don't take the bus trip, seniors enjoy getting out for the meeting and hearing about the trips. The company operates a 24-hour travel hotline (904-399-2770), which lists a long calendar of

rum. He threw in some crushed ice because another bartender, Monchito, was using it with great success in a drink of his own that he called a pineapple freeze.

Such was the piña colada's humble beginnings, a start so lacking in fanfare that it's hard not to believe Gracia's story is true. There was no copyright, no money, and no fanfare. The piña colada just sort of evolved at the hands of Ricardo Gracia and his team of bartenders.

In short order, the drink took off, and Gracia brought in 26 blenders so that his bartenders could keep up with demand—up to 1,000 piña coladas a day. Somewhere along the line, Gracia decided that his new drink needed a name. Piña, which means "pineapple" in Spanish, seemed logical; someone suggested colada, which means "strained" in Spanish, and thus the drink was christened.

Gracia worked for Hilton Hotels for 36 years, at more than half a dozen properties worldwide. Everywhere he worked, he introduced the piña colada, and it was always a sensation. He served it to movie stars, millionaires, famous singers, and renowned artists. He often had his picture taken with the luminaries, and he still carries those photographs with him today in a well-worn scrapbook. There's Ricardo with Ava Gardner, Errol Flynn, Vic Damon. And wait, look at that picture of Marilyn Monroe wrapped in a black lace teddy. "I served her a piña colada in San Juan," said Gracia. "Joe DiMaggio joined her down there. I asked him for a photograph of Marilyn, and he gave me this."

Looking back, Gracia says he's made millions of piña coladas, not millions of dollars from inventing the drink. He'll still mix one for you at Cafe on the Green. It comes in a tall glass with a piece of fresh pineapple, a strawberry, a straw, and a little paper umbrella. Not exactly like the old days, but the drink holds its own. Take one sip and you'll know that a master prepared it: the texture is perfect, creamy not frozen, with no big chunks of ice or pineapple.

Gracia tried retirement for three months after he and his wife moved to St. Augustine in 1987, but he longed to be serving drinks again and took a job at the Sawgrass Marriott just as it was opening. He's been with them ever since as a sommelier; this former bon vivant may have invented the piña colada, but he no longer drinks them. These days his favorite drink is a quiet glass of Bordeaux. It's more suited, he says, to his memories.

upcoming trips as well as the latest on the travel club meetings. Bonus: These tours include all your attraction admissions and most meals with no hidden charges.

EXPLORITAS (FORMERLY ELDERHOSTEL)
(800) 454-5768
www.exploritas.org
From Amelia Island to Cumberland Island to St. Augustine and the Okefenokee Swamp, Northeast Florida offers a variety of Exploritas travel opportunities for seniors. Known for decades as Elderhostel, Exploritas is headquartered in Boston and offers educational and travel experiences for seniors worldwide. To request a catalog of upcoming courses, call the number above or visit the Web site for the same information. All libraries carry current Exploritas catalogs; ask for them at the information desk.

Senior Publications

SENIOR SERVICES DIRECTORY
7563 Philips Hwy., Building 100
Suite 208
(904) 630-7392
www.heritagepublishinginc.com
This directory is chock-full of phone numbers and information for seniors. Pick one up at one of the city's senior centers, any public library, at the Senior Expo, or contact the publisher for a free copy.

SENIORS HOUSING GUIDE
9838 Old Baymeadows Rd.
(904) 997-0899
www.nefloridaseniorsguide.com
This little glossy, about the size of a *Reader's Digest*, is worth its weight in gold. It's an advertising vehicle for practically every senior housing community in Duval, Nassau, St. Johns, Flagler, Baker, and Clay Counties, from posh independent living to nursing care facilities. Best of all, it's free; you can pick one up at your local library or access the directory on their Web site.

Active Seniors' Retirement Communities

FLEET LANDING
One Fleet Landing Blvd. Atlantic Beach
(866) 215-1647
www.fleetlanding.com
Located in popular Atlantic Beach, Fleet Landing is just a walk away from Jacksonville's wide sandy beaches and the Atlantic Ocean. In fact, it's not uncommon to see residents enjoying a brisk walk to the beach through a lovely tree-lined Atlantic Beach neighborhood. Fleet Landing started as a continuing-care community for navy retirees but has since expanded to include everyone. It's located next door to Naval Station Mayport.

The quiet, gated community offers 320 living units, including independent cottages, patio homes, and apartments. Residents gather for meals and socials at the Lakeside Dining Doom. Health care services are available at the on-site health center, and there's a fully equipped physical therapy department on campus. Fleet Landing also offers an assisted-living residence called Leeward Manor. There's also a skilled nursing wing and a memory-impaired unit for Alzheimer's patients.

i The City of Jacksonville hosts the 50 & Beyond Forever Fit Senior Games every year to encourage and celebrate fitness in anyone over age 50. Call (904) 630-3690 to find out how you can volunteer or, better yet, participate!

CYPRESS VILLAGE
4600 Middleton Park Circle East
(904) 223-4978
www.brookdaleliving.com/cypress-village.aspx
Cypress Village's 120-acre campus is centrally located on Jacksonville's Southside, right next door to the Mayo Clinic Jacksonville. A shuttle bus regularly takes Cypress Village residents to the clinic, so they never have to worry about how they'll get to their doctors' appointments. Cypress Village residents pride themselves on their active lifestyles, whether they're swimming laps in the indoor pool or creating a masterpiece in the woodworking shop. An 18-hole golf course, Windsor Parke, borders the facility and is a favorite golfing locale for residents who enjoy Windsor Parke's senior discount. Residents can live in a house, which they own, or a high-rise apartment. Cypress Village also offers assisted living or skilled nursing care for residents who need help recovering from an illness or operation before returning to their homes. Cypress Village has partnered with the Mayo Clinic to provide residents with a state-of-the-art Alzheimer's facility, which has a research association with Mayo Jacksonville so that patients benefit from the latest in medical care.

SWEETWATER
8557 Little Swift Circle
(904) 519-7071
www.pulte.com/delwebb
Life for active seniors is definitely sweet at Sweetwater, one of Jacksonville's newer and more posh communities for seniors who are ready to dispense with the old family home but still want to enjoy the good life. The complex, which offers condos and carriage homes from 1,400-2,100 square feet, has a state-of-the-art fitness center, multiple pools, a business center, hot tubs, billiards, a library, crafts rooms, team sports, community trails, and a staff whose job it is to help you get the most out of the activities, classes, and trips. Sweetwater is for people who want to live well around others who feel the same.

WESTMINSTER WOODS ON JULINGTON CREEK
25 SR 13
(904) 287-7300
www.westminsterretirement.com

Affiliated with the Presbyterian Church, this 75-acre, tree-filled campus is located on the banks of Julington Creek. Westminster Woods was the first continuing-care retirement community in Jacksonville when it opened over 40 years ago, and it's still going strong. This facility offers 350 living units ranging from villa homes and garden apartments to assisted living, skilled nursing, and Alzheimer's care. There's also a health care and physical therapy facility located right on campus.

The dining room sits on Julington Creek, and residents enjoy sitting near the picture windows and watching their neighbors fish or shrimp from the dock. (One resident even docks his own boat out back.) Westminster Woods likes to say that it's the most affordable continuing-care retirement community in Jacksonville. It's certainly one of the prettiest.

MILITARY

A sk many World War II–era folks what they know about Jacksonville, and chances are a fair number of them will say they served time here in the navy or knew someone who did.

For many of them, Jacksonville conjures up images of aircraft carriers, destroyers, helicopters, fighter jets, and families running across the tarmac to welcome a parent home from a long deployment.

The Jacksonville region is home to three navy bases: Naval Air Station Jacksonville (NAS Jax), Naval Station Mayport (NAVSTA Mayport), and Naval Submarine Base Kings Bay.

NAS Jax is home to numerous helicopter and fixed-wing aircraft squadrons and is where navy aircraft and ground support equipment from all over the world are repaired. The station employs 19,500 people. At the Naval Air Depot, around 3,800 civilian employees (many retired navy) fix it all—from a flat tire on a Seahawk helicopter to a complicated electronic circuit board on an F-16 fighter jet.

NAVSTA Mayport is homeport for 22 ships, as well as a large helicopter engine repair facility.

About an hour up the road, near St. Marys, Georgia, is the Naval Submarine Base Kings Bay. Kings Bay, as the locals call it, is homeport for two large submarine squadrons and six Trident ballistic missile submarines.

Another military location in the heart of Jacksonville doesn't usually get much attention. It's the U.S. Marine Corps Blount Island Command, which maintains 13 pre-positioned ships—supply ships that are always loaded with ground-defense systems and ready to deploy at a moment's notice. Pre-positioned ships carry enough supplies and equipment in their holds to allow troops to engage in several weeks of warfare anywhere in the world.

The Coast Guard also plays a vital and growing role in Jacksonville and is responsible for everything from port security to making sure that shrimpers use turtle exclusion devices on their nets. Its most visible base is located in Mayport.

According to the navy, the economic impact on Northeast Florida and Southeast Georgia from these four bases combined is $6.45 billion. There are more than 227,000 people associated with these bases, from active-duty personnel to reservists, retirees, civilian workers, and their respective families. Put another way, 20 out of every 100 people you will meet in Northeast Florida and Southeast Georgia will have some connection to the U.S. Navy or the U.S. Marines.

Finally, the navy is proud to offer this fact: more than 20,000 navy personnel and marines donate hundreds of thousands of volunteer service hours to the Jacksonville community every year. These volunteers do it all, from building HabiJax houses to speaking to scout groups to mentoring at-risk kids.

(Most of the amenities described in the following listings are available exclusively for active and retired military personnel and their families. We have noted when they are available to civilians as well.)

NAVAL AIR STATION JACKSONVILLE

6801 Roosevelt Blvd.
(904) 542-2345
www.cnic.navy.mil/jacksonville/index.htm
In 1939 Jacksonville residents voted in favor of a $1 million bond issue to purchase 3,896 acres of land for Naval Air Station Jacksonville, making it the only military installation in the nation established by a direct gift of the people. The first pilot landed at NAS Jax on September 7, 1940, before the runway was even finished. In short order, three runways were built here, along with a small aircraft repair facility that would one day become the very big Naval Air Depot, Jacksonville (NADEP). Today NADEP is the largest tenant command at NAS Jax and the largest industrial employer in Northeast Florida. All kinds of navy aircraft and support equipment from around the world are repaired at NADEP. In addition, numerous helicopter and fixed-wing aircraft squadrons are based at NAS Jax. The base is also home to Patrol Squadron Thirty (VP-30), which is the navy's largest aviation squadron and the only "Orion" Fleet Replacement Squadron, which prepares and trains U.S. and foreign pilots and aircrew and maintenance personnel for further operational assignments.

NAS Jacksonville is the birthplace of the Blue Angels, the navy's precision flying team. The Blue Angels are now based in Pensacola but return to Jacksonville almost every year to perform in the annual Sea and Sky Spectacular. (Check out the Annual Events chapter for more on this popular air show.)

i Every year hundreds of military folks participate in the Captain Chuck Cornett 10K Run and 5K Walk at NAS Jax. The start of the race is signaled by cannon fire from the base weapons department.

MULBERRY MARINA AT NAVAL AIR STATION JACKSONVILLE

Bldg. 1072, Ranger Road
(904) 542-3260
www.cnic.navy.mil/jacksonville/index.htm

There's a lot happening at this on-base marina, located on the banks of the St. Johns River. You can rent almost any type of pleasure boat, from kayaks and canoes to sailboats, bass boats, and Boston Whalers. For navy personnel who own a boat, the marina offers slips, moorings, and dry storage on a daily, monthly, or yearly basis. This is a great place to take a sailing or safe-boating class or enter a bass-fishing contest. The Ship's Store sells bait and fishing tackle as well as ice, drinks, sandwiches, and that all-important Florida fishing license. If you're caught angling on the water without one, you could be fined. *NOTE:* You have to pass a safe-boating quiz before you can rent a boat at the marina.

NAVAL AIR STATION JACKSONVILLE GOLF CLUB

(904) 542-3249
www.cnic.navy.mil/jacksonville/index.htm
The Naval Air Station Jacksonville has two golf courses on base offering 27 holes of championship golf--a par-72, 18-hole course and a par-35, 9-hole course. Take a group or private lesson at the Naval Air Station Jacksonville Golf Club. Several golf tournaments take place at this club, including the annual Southeast Military Invitational Golf Tournament in May and the Navy Birthday Golf Tournament in October. The golf course is open to the public Monday through Sunday from 7 a.m. to sunset.

RV PARK AT NAVAL AIR STATION JACKSONVILLE

(904) 542-5898
www.cnic.navy.mil/jacksonville/index.htm
NAS Jax operates a small but lovely RV park overlooking the St. Johns River. The on-base park has 28 full sites (sewer, water, and electric), nine partial sites (water, electric), and seven primitive sites. Make your reservations early, because this RV park fills up fast. The RV park is provided as a recreation facility for active duty, retired military, their dependents, reserve military personnel, Department of Defense civilian employees, and retirees from Naval Air Station Jacksonville.

JAX AIR NEWS
(904) 542-3531
www.JaxAirNews.com
This free, award-winning weekly publication is devoted solely to all goings-on at NAS Jacksonville. It's the best way to keep up with the activities at this large base. The publication also provides a good way to keep up to date with changes in the U.S. Navy.

NAVAL STATION MAYPORT

MAYPORT ROAD
(904) 270-5011
www.cnic.navy.mil/Mayport/index.htm
Most people understand that Naval Station Mayport is a busy seaport, but they don't realize that it's a busy air facility as well. Twenty-two ships are homeported here. The airfield can accommodate any aircraft owned by the Department of Defense, and there are more than 100,000 helicopter and fixed-wing flights from here every year. The airfield is also a popular place with thousands of military personnel, who hop aboard military flights as passengers. In addition to ships' crews and their squadrons, Naval Station Mayport hosts a large maintenance facility that repairs Seahawk helicopter engines.

The current Naval Station Mayport grew slowly from its beginnings in 1939. It was used during World War II then deactivated until 1948. Once reactivated, the base grew steadily, often expanding to accommodate bigger ships and planes. The harbor was dredged deeper, more acreage was added to the base, and runways were extended. Today Naval Station Mayport covers 3,409 acres.

i The USO Center at 2560 Mayport Rd. is open to all military personnel and their families. It offers activities, hospitality, or just a place to go. The center is open from 9 a.m. to 9 p.m. Monday through Friday and from 9 a.m. to 2 p.m. on Saturday. Call (904) 246-3481 for more information.

MAYPORT GOLF CLUB
(904) 270-5380
www.cnic.navy.mil/Mayport/index.htm
Located on the grounds of Naval Station Mayport, this golf club features an 18-hole, par-72 course. Thanks to a recent multimillion-dollar renovation, the course is in its best shape in years. Towering oak and palm trees line the fairways, which sit between the Atlantic Ocean and the Intracoastal Waterway. The course is open from 7 a.m. to 7 p.m. except in the winter, when it closes at 6 p.m. After a round of golf, check out Bogey's, Naval Station Mayport's version of The 19th hole. Bogey's throws a premier happy hour Wednesday and Friday from 4 to 6 p.m.

i The tiny U.S. Coast Guard base at Mayport boasts a great little commissary/post exchange that's open to all military personnel and retirees.

THE NAVY LODGE AT NAVAL STATION MAYPORT
1980 Baltimore St., Mayport
(904) 247-3964
www.navy-nex.com (click on "Navy Lodge")
This Navy Lodge is a wonderful (and still somewhat secret) 52-room, oceanfront hotel located on the base. If you are active duty, a reservist, a retiree, or a Department of Defense employee on orders, you can make reservations to stay at the Navy Lodge. If you are a civilian sponsored by an active-duty member, a reservist, or a retiree, you can stay there, too. Make reservations early, because even though the hotel is something of a secret, enough people know about it to fill the place up almost every night. Request a room on the second or third floor for a view of the ocean. The first floor has a lovely view of the sand dunes. Best of all, you can get a room here for around $61 to $72 a night.

MAYPORT MIRROR
(904) 270-7817
www.mayportmirror.com
Like its counterpart at NAS Jacksonville, the *Mayport Mirror* covers all the news that's fit to print at

Naval Station Mayport. It also has the latest navy news, making this weekly a must-read for navy personnel and their families as well as reservists and retirees.

NAVAL SUBMARINE BASE KINGS BAY

Kings Bay Road, Saint Marys, GA
(912) 573-2000
www.cnic.navy.mil/KingsBay
With 16,000 acres and 9,000 active duty, reserve, and civilian personnel at work here, this is a huge base. It's located in Camden County, Georgia, which, thanks to the U.S. Navy, is one of the fastest-growing counties in the state.

In 1980 Kings Bay was named the homeport for the Atlantic Fleet of Trident ballistic submarines. This sparked a massive, nine-year, $1.3 billion construction program. Crew-training facilities had to be built, as did nuclear-weapons-handling and storage facilities, submarine maintenance and repair facilities, and facilities for all the personnel who would be living and working on base.

The first Trident nuclear submarine, the USS *Tennessee*, arrived in 1989. There are currently six submarines assigned to the base. In the end, construction of Kings Bay was the largest peacetime construction program ever undertaken by the U.S. Navy.

Kings Bay is one of the navy's prettiest bases. In 2007, The Department of Defense named Kings Bay the top naval installation in the Department of Defense. Four thousand of its 16,000 acres are protected wetlands, making the base home to wood storks, alligators, and all sorts of swamp critters. In fact, Naval Submarine Base Kings Bay is home to 229 species of birds, 68 mammals, 67 reptiles (5 poisonous snakes), and 37 amphibians.

NAVY LODGE AT NAVAL SUBMARINE BASE KINGS BAY

1290 U.S. Jackson Road, Kings Bay, GA
(912) 882-6868
www.navy-nex.com (click on "Navy Lodge")

With 26 rooms, this modern motel is smaller than the Navy Lodge at Naval Station Mayport. It also does not enjoy an oceanfront location, but in terms of price (around $50 a night) and convenience (located right on base), it's hard to beat. The rooms fill up fast, so be sure to make reservations early. The Navy Lodge is open to all active-duty personnel as well as reserves and retirees. Civilians who are sponsored by active-duty personnel, reserves, or retirees can stay here as well.

U.S. MARINE CORPS BLOUNT ISLAND COMMAND

There are no tourist opportunities at this command, but we mention it so that you know what goes on here. Located next to Jacksonville's Blount Island port terminal, the 725 marines and civilians who work at this military command maintain 13 pre-positioning ships. These supply ships stand always ready to sail to hot spots anywhere in the world. They are loaded with war machinery and humanitarian-aid and troop-support supplies. Several of the ships stay in Jacksonville; the rest are docked elsewhere but are sent here for routine maintenance. If the president of the United States needs to send troops into battle at a moment's notice, these ships will quickly meet them at the nearest port, carrying up to a month's worth of supplies.

U.S. COAST GUARD SECTOR JACKSONVILLE

4200 Ocean St., Atlantic Beach
(904) 564-7500
www.uscg.mil
Sector Jacksonville was established in 2005 from the reorganization and consolidation of Group Mayport and Base Mayport. Located on 6 acres of land along the St. Johns River in Mayport and adjacent Naval Station Mayport (you'll pass this base if you ever drive out Mayport Road to catch the ferry), the Marine Safety Office staffs four ships, or cutters, that it uses to help rescue stranded boaters.

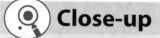 **Close-up**

Firebase Florida

It's all here: the command and control bunker, the machine gun emplacements, even the sandbags—6,000 of them.

Welcome to **Firebase Florida at Camp Blanding,** a composite firebase typical of the kind used in Vietnam between 1965 and 1973. The firebases were small, isolated enclaves in the middle of nowhere, safe havens from the enemy for platoons or even a battalion. They were also used as jump-off points for further operations or for forward observations of the North Vietnamese.

The Vietnam Veterans of North Florida spent 10 years planning and building Firebase Florida after the Museum Society at Camp Blanding asked them to build a memorial symbolic of the Vietnam experience. The veterans decided that a firebase would be perfect, but only after much deliberation. "We were isolated out there in a sense, and the only thing you owned was the perimeter of the firebase," said Sergeant Bill Wilder, a former marine and a Vietnam veteran. "That was really the only secure place; you never really were secure outside the wire."

Firebase Florida is part of **Memorial Park at Camp Blanding,** about an hour south of Jacksonville. It's located in a large field formerly used for training purposes back when Camp Blanding was a busy training facility for the U.S. Army. There's also space in the park for monuments and displays honoring the men and women who served in Korea and Desert Storm. Desert Storm veterans have donated tanks and other transportation equipment. Korean War veterans in Florida have yet to leave their mark.

At the heart of Camp Blanding is a museum dedicated to the World War II experience. Nine infantry divisions trained at the camp between 1940 and 1943. In 1943 soldiers heading out to fight in both Europe and the Pacific also began to train here. **The Camp Blanding Museum** is dedicated to the men who headed off to war from Camp Blanding, some never to return again.

The museum houses all sorts of World War II–era weapons from the United States, Germany, and Japan. There's also a small replica of a World War II barracks, complete with a pot stove, bunk beds, and those infamous green army blankets that were never soft and cuddly but always mighty durable and warm. Mannequins dressed in a variety of officer and enlisted man uniforms tell a silent tale about what life was like at Camp Blanding for the thousands of men who trained here during World War II.

There is no charge to visit the Camp Blanding Museum or Firebase Florida, across the street from the museum in Memorial Park. Both are open almost every day from noon to 4 p.m.

Back at Firebase Florida, crowds of schoolchildren gather. The firebase has become a popular field trip destination, and it's not uncommon to see students or scouts playing with a 105 Howitzer set up inside the sandbag perimeter, a typical cannon from a firebase in Vietnam.

The veterans who built Firebase Florida are proud of the living memorial they've created. It was dedicated on Memorial Day 2000 to the men and women who died in Vietnam and also to those who survived. Organizers hope that veterans who've had a hard time talking about their experiences in Vietnam will visit the firebase and find it therapeutic. Most of all, organizers believe, Firebase Florida will help keep alive the fact that American servicemen and women fought proudly in Vietnam for freedom and their country.

Since it is now part of the Department of Homeland Security, the U.S. Coast Guard is also responsible for protecting the Port of Jacksonville from terrorist attacks. This means that foreign ships must now give several days advance notice of their arrival so the coast guard can board the ship at sea for inspection. Also, no boats are allowed near cruise ships entering or leaving our port. If a private boater violates that protection zone, he or she will have to answer to the coast guard.

Another unit of Coast Guard Sector Jacksonville is called HITRON Jacksonville. This unit is actually based far from the water on the western side of Jacksonville at Cecil Field. Its members help protect the Port of Jacksonville against drug trafficking.

Finally, Coast Guard Sector Jacksonville operates a factory of sorts at the Mayport base responsible for maintaining and reconstructing the large, colorful navigational buoys that help keep boaters on course. Some of the buoys also measure water temperature and wind speed and provide other nautical information to the coast guard.

MILITARY MUSEUMS

CAMP BLANDING HISTORICAL MUSEUM AND MEMORIAL PARK
5629 SR 16 West, Building #3040
(904) 682-3196
www.campblanding-museum.org
This museum, open to the public, houses a collection of weapons as well as a replica of a World War II army barracks. There are also lots of photo exhibits, medals, and uniforms. The museum is open Tuesday through Sunday from noon to 4 p.m. and admission is free. Closed Mondays and major holidays. (See the Close-up above for more information.)

ST. MARYS SUBMARINE MUSEUM
102 St. Marys St. West
St. Marys, Georgia
(912) 882-2782
www.stmaryssubmuseum.com

This museum, open to the pubic, is dedicated to World War II submarines and to all members of the "Silent Service," past and present. Located in St. Marys, Georgia, near Naval Submarine Base Kings Bay, the Submarine Museum is only a 45-minute drive north of Jacksonville. By far, the biggest draw here is the museum's operational "Type 8" periscope, which rises up through the museum's roof for a great view of the quaint fishing village of St. Marys. Museum officials say it is the only periscope in the southeast open to the public for general viewing—unless, of course, you're lucky enough to climb aboard a submarine. There is also an old sonar system console on display as well as the ballast control panel and a ship's atmosphere control panel. All these panels are from the USS *James K. Polk,* one of the 41 original Trident submarines, which was decommissioned in 1999. Also of particular interest at the museum are drawings from several 1940s-era submarine training manuals. Crewmembers had to memorize the drawings of various submarine systems and pass a test to be qualified to work aboard a sub.

The museum is also very proud of its research library, which contains information on hundreds of submarines worldwide, including foreign subs. There's also a movie about life aboard a submarine and computer-interactive kiosks with sub information from the present all the way back to the USS *Holland,* the first submarine recognized by the U.S. Navy. Be sure to stop in at the museum gift shop before you leave, where you can buy a boat patch for just about every submarine from World War II to the present. The museum is open Tuesday through Saturday from 10 a.m. to 4 p.m. and Sunday 1 to 5 p.m. The museum is closed on Monday. Admission is $4 for persons ages 19 to 62, $3 for active-duty and retired military and anyone ages 63 to 99, and $2 for children ages 6 to 18. Call in advance for a group tour.

MEDIA

Staying informed in Jacksonville isn't difficult. There's a ready (and often free) supply of mainstream, alternative print, and electronic media to help you piece together what's going down on any day of the week. Whether you're interested in arts, entertainment, local politics, sports, or the business climate, chances are you'll find what you need in Jacksonville's mix of newspapers, radio stations, TV stations, and Web sites.

DAILY NEWSPAPERS

FINANCIAL NEWS & DAILY RECORD
10 North Newman St.
(904) 356-2466
www.jaxdailyrecord.com

The *Financial News & Daily Record* reports on Jacksonville's business and legal communities. Published since 1912, the *Daily Record* is where you'll find all the city's legal notices.

In recent years the paper has expanded its coverage to include more profiles and feature articles dealing with the business, legal, and real estate industries in Jacksonville.

The *Daily Record* is published Monday through Friday. You can buy a copy at most bookshops and newsstands. Many non-legal types read it faithfully for the daily gossip or Heard on the Street column that appears on the front left side of the paper. Sometimes the gossip is even correct!

FLORIDA TIMES-UNION
One Riverside Ave.
(904) 359-4111
www.jacksonville.com

Founded in 1883, the *Florida Times-Union* is Jacksonville's only major daily newspaper. If you're a newspaper reader, the *Times-Union*, locally known simply as the *TU*, is your best source for all-around news items in the Jacksonville area.

With a daily circulation about 152,000 and Sunday circulation about 212,000, the *Times-Union* is the seventh-largest daily newspaper in Florida. The *Times-Union* is owned by Augusta,

Georgia–based Morris Communications Corp. (In the spirit of full disclosure, Morris Communications Corp. also owns Globe Pequot Press, publisher of the Insiders' Guide series.)

The *Times-Union* covers local politics, business, entertainment, and sports and is a frequent winner of state journalism awards, which, given Florida's strong newspaper industry, is an impressive accomplishment. The *Times-Union's* Web site, www.jacksonville.com, has received numerous national awards for an online news site since it was first launched in 1998.

After the city won a National Football League team, the *Times-Union* beefed up its sports department to provide the type of in-depth coverage required for a major professional sports franchise. The daily also provides comprehensive pro and amateur golf coverage. If you plan to do any fishing during your stay in the Jacksonville area, check out the *Times-Union* outdoor section.

For weekend events and entertainment, look to the paper's Friday edition for comprehensive lists of live entertainment, movie reviews, and other happenings.

For more detailed coverage of Jacksonville's communities, the *Times-Union* publishes 20 different supplements and neighborhood papers covering all of Jacksonville's neighborhoods, military bases, and adjacent counties.

ST. AUGUSTINE RECORD
One News Place, St. Augustine
(904) 829-6562
www.staugustine.com

The *St. Augustine Record* has been chronicling the news in the Ancient City and St. Johns County for more than a century. The *Record* is owned by Morris Communications Corp., just like its sister publication the *Florida Times-Union*. Daily circulation is around 18,000.

The *Record* recently left its longtime home in downtown St. Augustine for an ultramodern facility so that it could better cover fast-growing St. Johns County. The Record also hosts a popular, award-winning Web site, which features stories from the daily newspaper as well as general travel information about St. Augustine.

WEEKLIES AND BI-WEEKLIES

BEACHES LEADER/PONTE VEDRA LEADER
1114 Beach Blvd., Jacksonville Beach
(904) 249-9033
www.beachesleader.com
If you're interested in what's happening at Jacksonville's beach communities, you'll want to pick up a copy of the *Beaches Leader* and the *Ponte Vedra Leader*. Published since 1963, the *Beaches Leader* and its sister publication, *Ponte Vedra Leader*, focus on the communities of Atlantic, Neptune, Jacksonville, and Ponte Vedra Beaches.

The newspapers cover local politics, crime, sports, and entertainment. The *Beaches Leader* also carries good fishing reports from local fishing captains. For those hunting for Beaches real estate, the *Beaches Leader* runs classified ads of homes for sale and for rent. It's also a good place to find area garage sales on the weekends.

The *Beaches Leader* and *Ponte Vedra Leader* are published every Wednesday and Friday; you can buy them at newsstands, at drug and grocery stores, and through home subscriptions, which run $30 per year. The publications are also available for free online.

FLORIDA STAR
P.O. Box 40629
(904) 766-8834
www.thefloridastar.com

Jacksonville's largest black publication, the *Florida Star* has been published since 1951. The *Florida Star* is a statewide weekly newspaper covering all the news that is relevant to Jacksonville's black community—business, human interest, and entertainment as well as politics and education. The *Florida Star* is sold at 200 locations, including Publix and Winn-Dixie grocery stores and Walgreens Drug stores, mostly in the predominantly African-American sections of the city.

FOLIO WEEKLY
9456 Philips Hwy.
(904) 260-9770
www.folioweekly.com
Folio Weekly, which bills itself as Northeast Florida's news and opinion magazine, is the area's spunky alternative paper and, as such, often runs stories and opinions you won't find in the mainstream media. The tabloid-size paper also features movie, arts, and music reviews.

Folio Weekly's comprehensive entertainment listings, movie reviews, and book reviews are indispensable, regardless of whether you live here or are just passing through. *Folio Weekly* also runs the most extensive personals listings of any publication in the area.

Every week, close to 139,000 readers read *Folio Weekly*, copies of which are dropped off on Tuesday at restaurants and stores from Fernandina Beach to St. Augustine. Grab a free copy at public libraries, bookstores, coffee shops, and at many restaurants.

JACKSONVILLE BUSINESS JOURNAL
1200 Riverplace Blvd.
(904) 396-3502
www.jacksonville.bizjournals.com
The *Jacksonville Business Journal* provides weekly news and commentary on the area's businesses and industries. Regular columns cover health care, marketing, real estate, and technology. Editors contribute daily business reports to local television and radio stations. The *Business Journal* also publishes an annual *Book of Lists,* a comprehensive compilation of the city's major companies and firms.

🔍 Close-up

Ron Littlepage, Jacksonville's Populist Voice

You could say that **Ron Littlepage**, opinion columnist for the *Florida Times-Union*, has the best journalism job in Jacksonville. Littlepage himself chuckles at the notion. "It's close," he admits. "But I think the outdoors writer has the best job because he gets paid to go hunting and fishing all the time."

Such are the priorities of Littlepage, who really would prefer to be fishing for flounder than fishing for an exclusive that will shake up City Hall. Still, Littlepage manages to write about the environment a lot anyway, which means he's not usually stuck behind a computer all day. He's often out gathering information for a column, be it from a boat on the St. Johns River or monitoring the antics at a school board meeting.

Littlepage's column is a staple for many local readers, who thumb through the newspaper each day to the back page of the Metro section to see what he's writing about. His column usually appears every Tuesday, Thursday, Friday, and Sunday, but it's often driven by subject matter. If he has nothing to write about on one of those days, readers may have to wait until he does. For fans, it's worth the wait. They like how he champions the underdog, disagrees with the status quo, and frequently criticizes City Hall. City leaders from the mayor down have found themselves the target of his keyboard, and it usually makes for a rotten day when one of their policies is the subject of a Littlepage column. Constituents start calling; so do other reporters—and soon enough that public official finds him or herself on the defensive.

Oddly enough, Littlepage sometimes finds himself on the defensive, especially when angry readers call to disagree with what he's written about. "I get branded a liberal a lot," he says. "Of course in this conservative area, it doesn't take much to be branded a liberal." At times like this, Littlepage makes it clear that his opinions are his own and do not represent the opinions of the newspaper. "That's what the editorial page is for," he says, and frequently, on any given issue, a Littlepage column and a *Times-Union* editorial are light-years apart.

PONTE VEDRA RECORDER
100 Executive Way, Ponte Vedra Beach
(904) 285-8831
www.pontevedrarecorder.com

As its names suggests, the *Ponte Vedra Recorder* covers the upscale community of Ponte Vedra Beach. As chronicler of Ponte Vedra's social scene, the weekly newspaper is generally full of feature stories and photos of the latest soirees.

The *Ponte Vedra Recorder* is published every Friday. You can buy a copy at newsstands and supermarkets or subscribe to receive the magazine in the mail. The parent company also publishes *Clay Today* and *The First Coast Register*.

MAGAZINES

ARBUS
1816 Landon Ave.
(904) 346-1920
www.arbus.com

This is Northeast Florida's arts and business magazine. But don't be fooled; it's not a business magazine like the *Jacksonville Business Journal*. This magazine covers the business of art and boasts a readership of 100,000, which makes sense in a city where the arts are finally taking a front seat. The magazine always features a cover story on a prominent local or regional artist and runs stories about the latest exhibitions at area

Littlepage has been writing his column since 1989. Before that he was the newspaper's assistant managing editor, a job he loved—and hated. He begged his bosses for a change. He was sick of the endless meetings and the budgets and wanted to return to the reason he got into journalism in the first place: to help be a catalyst for change. Littlepage says that he most enjoys writing about Jacksonville's natural resources, from the St. Johns River to the Timucuan Preserve. "We have so much to offer here," he says.

When Littlepage and his wife, Mary, entertain out-of-town guests, they try to provide a sampling of some of Jacksonville's natural areas. "I take them out in a kayak into our marshes and creeks," he says. He also likes to take guests fishing and hiking. His favorite fishing spots are top secret, but they're generally in the marshes off Sister's Creek north of Heckscher Drive. A favorite hiking spot is in Clay County near Green Cove Springs in an area called Bayard Point, near the Shands Bridge.

Littlepage hails from deep in the heart of Texas. He talks with a twang and has created an alter-ego character called Jimmy Ray Bob (married to Sissy Lou), who occasionally makes it into his columns. Jimmy Ray is forever eating boiled peanuts and expounding on the Florida political scene from gubernatorial to local mayoral races. Consequently, Jimmy Ray appears a lot during the political season when Littlepage uses him as a "change of pace."

True to his roots, Littlepage believes that Jacksonville is just getting too big, and he's sad to see it happening. He's not much of a big-city person and prefers to think of Jacksonville as a town of neighborhoods, each with its own distinct flavor, from the fish camps up on the Northside to the fancy homes in San Marco. "It's a good mix," Littlepage says.

Littlepage is modest about the power of his pen. He only hopes his strongly opinionated columns on local issues increase people's awareness, gets them more involved and talking about issues. "If they're not reacting to it in some way," Littlepage says, "then I've probably chosen the wrong subject."

You can read Littlepage's columns before you get to town online at **www.jacksonville.com.**

art museums. *Arbus* also covers music and offers a comprehensive calendar of upcoming art and entertainment events. It's published every other month and is given away at area newsstands, in coffee shops, sandwich shops, and some restaurants.

JACKSONVILLE MAGAZINE
1261 King St.
(904) 389-3622
www.jacksonvillemag.com
Published since 1983, *Jacksonville Magazine* is the area's oldest city magazine. Regular editorial features include personality profiles, restaurant spotlights, travel, local history, and current events. *Jacksonville Magazine*'s regular columns cover personal finance, health, real estate, fashion, and a newsmaker Q&A. Each issue offers a two-month calendar of events and a dining guide listing more than 100 area restaurants. *Jacksonville Magazine* is published monthly and is distributed to 22,000 readers. It can be purchased at newsstands, supermarkets, and bookstores, or by subscription, and is available to online readers with bonus sections such as a cultural arts calendar. The parent company also publishes *Jacksonville Bride, 904* magazine, *HOME,* and *Taste,* as well as a coffee-table book called *Beautiful Homes of Jacksonville*. The magazine also offers a number of e-newsletters that make for fun online reading.

WATER'S EDGE
One Riverside Ave.
(904) 359–4583
http://watersedge.travidia.com

Water's Edge, one of the *Times Union*'s monthly magazines, is an oversize glossy featuring articles on homes, interior design, gardening, restaurant reviews, and profiles of interesting personalities and their homes in the coastal South. It's available at bookstores, select Publix and Winn-Dixie supermarkets, the lobby of the *Florida Times-Union* building at One Riverside Ave., or by subscription. The parent company also produces *Water's Edge Weddings.*

Special-Interest Publications

EU JACKSONVILLE (ENTERTAINING U)
P.O. Box 11959
(904) 730-3003
www.eujacksonville.com

This weekly entertainment newspaper prints features as well as reviews of upcoming movies, theater, dining, music, and nightlife in the Jacksonville area. *EU Jacksonville* is distributed free every week. It's available at public libraries, convenience stores, and drug stores. *EU* is also a great place to find discount coupons for upcoming events and free passes to movie screenings.

FIRST COAST PARENT
P.O. Box 701, Ponte Vedra Beach
(904) 294-5686
www.firstcoastparent.com

The *First Coast Parent* is a monthly news magazine distributed for free throughout the area. It features monthly columns on parenting and health. Each issue also includes a calendar of events for parents and children. *First Coast Parent* is available at many public libraries, convenience stores, and bookstores.

H MAGAZINE
One Riverside Ave.
(904) 359-4058
www.hforhealth.com

Published monthly by the *Florida Times-Union, H Magazine* is all about your health. The magazine offers regular columns like Ask the Experts and Focus on Fitness, as well as monthly features on organ donation and surviving breast cancer. Many doctors, surgeons, and medical specialists advertise in this free glossy, so if you're looking for a physician, this is a good place to start. *H Magazine* is distributed in the first Sunday paper of the month. The publication can also be found for free in news boxes around the city as well as at your favorite public library.

NATURAL AWAKENINGS MAGAZINE – NORTHEAST FLORIDA
P.O. Box 551675
(904) 551-4796
www.najax.com

From Chinese medicine to discovering the ancient healing traditions of the Shamans, this free monthly magazine covers it all. *Natural Awakenings* provides information on how to improve the quality of your life physically, mentally, emotionally, and spiritually. Pick up a copy of *Natural Awakenings* at your local library. The Web site also offers an easy-to-use Natural Living Directory.

WOMEN'S DIGEST
12620-3 Beach Blvd.
(904) 350-0807
www.womensdigest.net

This free monthly tabloid addressing women's issues is available at the library and in various news boxes around the city.

TELEVISION

As in most other growing cities, Jacksonville's television news coverage is very competitive, especially after the Federal Communications Commission allowed media companies to own more than one television station in any given market. Now Clear Channel Communications and Gannett Broadcasting each own two television stations in Jacksonville. Regardless of the changes, experts say local television news in Jacksonville continues to outperform its market size.

WCWJ TV-17
9117 Hogan Rd.
(904) 641-1700
www.yourjax.com
CW-17 is the city's CW affiliate. The CW doesn't run any locally produced news programs, but it does air a selection of popular syndicated programs as well as popular new programming such as *The Vampire Diaries* and *Supernatural*. Channel 17 is owned by Nexstar Broadcasting Group, Inc., a communications company based in Irving, Texas.

WJCT TV-7
100 Festival Park Ave.
(904) 353-7770
www.wjct.org
WJCT is Jacksonville's Public Broadcasting Station. This is where you'll find *Antiques Roadshow, Austin City Limits, The NewsHour with Jim Lehrer,* and *Sesame Street*.

WJEB TV-59
3101 Emerson Expressway
(904) 399-8413
www.wjeb.org
WJEB is a noncommercial educational affiliate of the Trinity Broadcasting Network, the world's largest Christian television network. WJEB has provided Jacksonville and its surrounding areas with Christian and educational programming since 1991.

WJXT TV-4
4 Broadcast Place
(904) 399-4000
www.news4jax.com
WJXT has been a news leader among Jacksonville TV stations for decades. Its news team—consisting of local favorites Mary Baer, George Winterling, Sam Kouvaris, and Tom Wills—has been together longer than any of the other anchor teams in the city and has developed a strong following.

i Check out *First Coast Connect,* a show about issues, trends, and newsmakers, every morning, Monday through Friday 9 a.m. on public radio's WJCT 89.9 FM. Host Melissa Ross helps local listeners stay on top of local current events.

WTEV CBS-47/WAWS FOX 30
11700 Central Parkway
(904) 642-3030
www.actionnewsjax.com
WTEV is the city's new CBS affiliate and a sister station to WAWS. WTEV airs CBS programming as well as a host of local news shows that are produced by the same news team that does the local FOX news.

WTLV NBC 12/WJXX ABC 25
1070 East Adams St.
(904) 354-1212
www.firstcoastnews.com
Local stations WTLV (NBC) and WJXX (ABC) merged their news operations in 2000 to bring viewers one local news team called First Coast News. The same anchors and reporters are seen on both stations in newscasts. Gannett owns both stations and carries the different network programming that belongs to each affiliate; just the local news teams are the same. The merger of the two stations was a bold television experiment, but it has worked out well for both stations. Today WTLV is the station to watch (and beat for local nightly news.

RADIO

With some progressive exceptions, you're likely to be able to locate any style of music you like on Jacksonville's airways. From WJXT favorites like *Morning Edition* and *Wait Wait...Don't Tell Me* to WPLA's Foo Fighters and Nickelback, Jacksonville's airwaves offer something guaranteed to entertain you 24 hours a day.

🔍 Close-up

The Little Station That Could

Want to get a glimpse of a piece of Insider Jacksonville that inspires both devotion and bewilderment? Turn your dial to **92.5**, a.k.a. **The Bargain Channel**, a.k.a. **WJXR,** and listen as the silver-tongued-everyman DJs offer swap-meet-style deals on do-you-really-need-it items like bobble-head Santas and diamond pinky rings. Callers, greeted by the familiar twang of "dubbya-jay-ex-arr," jam the lines throughout the day to pick up deals on everything from applesauce to vacation packages.

On most days, the show plays out like performance art, with the hosts pinballing off each other like sideshow hawkers. One minute they're listening as a caller regales them with tales of their satisfaction with a former purchase. The next, they're patching through to the warehouse, trying to find out if they have any more of those two-for-one cases of Chick-O-Sticks in the back.

Remarkably, the long-term hosts, whom callers identify with as dear friends, know many of the frequent buyers by voice alone, writing down their buyer's number before they even have a chance to offer it. Hosts **Mr. Doug** and **Miss Kathy** address everyone as "dear" or "darlin'" or "my friend." It's all very genteel and civilized, while also being 100-percent redneck, in a way that I think rednecks are darn proud to call their own.

After listening for months, my friend Chris called in one day to take advantage of a landscaping deal that was too good to pass up. "I didn't realize how fast it all happens," he told me afterward. "I just dialed and suddenly there I was, on the air. You've go to call!"

The bottom line is that people either love it or they really, really hate it. It's a guilty pleasure, but mention it at a party and wait to see how many people admit to listening.

As for me, I only listen when the whiskey-voiced Mr. Doug or the preternaturally twangy Miss Kathy are at the mic. It's hypnotic—a slice of the city that I never really come in contact with but can listen to with fascination in the relative privacy of my car.

Adult Contemporary
WSOS 94.1 FM
WEJZ 96.1 FM

Alternative
WPLA 107.3 FM

Children
WBWL 600 AM

Classical/NPR
WJCT 89.9 FM

Easy Listening
WKTZ 90.9 FM

Country
WQIK 99.1 FM
WGNE 99.9 FM

Talk
WOKV 106.5 FM
WOKV 690 AM

Oldies
WKQL 96.9 FM

Religious
WNCM 88.1 FM
WJFR 88.7 FM
WECC 89.3 FM
WNLE 91.7 FM
WIOJ 1010 AM
WROS 1050 AM
WCGL 1360 AM
WZAZ 1400 AM
WYMM 1530 AM

Rock/Classic Hits
WFYV 104.5 FM

Shopping
WJXR 92.1 FM (see the Close-up in this chapter)

Smooth Jazz
WJSJ 105.3 FM
WSJF 105.5 FM

Sports
WFXJ 930 AM
WZNZ 1460 AM
WAOC 1420 AM
WVOJ 1570 AM

Standards
WJAX 1220 AM

Top 40
WAPE 95.1 FM
WFKS 97.9 FM

Urban
WBHQ 92.7 FM
WHJX 105.7 FM
WEWC 1160 AM

i In case a hurricane hits Jacksonville, have plenty of batteries ready for your portable radio. There's a good chance local television stations will be knocked off the air for several days, depending on the severity of the storm. Better yet, purchase a crank radio so that you don't have to rely on batteries at all—just good old elbow grease.

INDEX